THE HANDBOOK OF JOINT VENTURING

The Handbook of Joint Venturing

John D. Carter, Esq.
Chief Council
Bechtel Corporation

Robert F. Cushman, Esq.
Partner
Pepper, Hamilton & Scheetz

C. Scott Hartz, Partner
Price Waterhouse

DOW JONES-IRWIN
Homewood, Illinois 60430

This publication is designed to provide accurate and
authoritative information in regard to the subject matter
covered. It is sold with the understanding that the
publisher is not engaged in rendering legal, accounting, or
other professional service. If legal advice or other expert
assistance is required, the services of a competent
professional person should be sought.

*From a Declaration of Principles jointly adopted by a Committee
of the American Bar Association and a Committee of Publishers.*

Project editor: Jane Lightell
Production manager: Ann Cassady
Compositor: Carlisle Communications, Ltd.
Typeface: 11/13 Times Roman
Printer: The Maple–Vail Book Manufacturing Group

LIBRARY OF CONGRESS
Library of Congress Cataloging-in-Publication Data

The Handbook of joint venturing / edited by John D. Carter, Robert F.
  Cushman, C. Scott Hartz.
    p.   cm.
  Includes bibliographies and index.
DJI Edition: ISBN 0-87094-704-4

Price Waterhouse Edition: ISBN 1-55623-222-5
    1. Joint ventures—Handbooks, manuals, etc.   I. Carter, John D.,
1946– . II. Cushman, Robert Frank, 1931– . III. Hartz, C.
Scott.
HD62.47.H355 1988
658'.044—dc19   88–13430
                                                CIP

Printed in the United States of America
1 2 3 4 5 6 7 8 9 0 MP 5 4 3 2 1 0 9 8

PREFACE

The use of a joint venture as a convenient and flexible vehicle to achieve
varied objectives in diverse contexts, both in the United States and internationally, is becoming increasingly common.

The conscientious businessman and his advising professional who
need to understand the structure and dynamics of the relationships between
the parties to the venture; the form and scope of the relationship; the
rights, duties, and contribution factors; the tax and anti-trust issues; and
dispute resolution ramifications have hungered for information and answers to these issues in one single source. This need could only be met
through a collaboration of well-qualified specialists.

The accountants, lawyers, and businessmen who have been selected
to author these chapters and address these issues were chosen with two
criteria in mind: first, they had to be outstanding authorities within their
field and second, they had to be able to write in understandable, nontechnical language.

We believe that we have chosen wisely and well. Through the generous efforts and skills of the distinguished authors, we have in this guide
developed a reference work that without cooperative effort could have
never existed. The compiling of this book represents the work, advice,
and encouragement of many. We are indebted to each of the authors.
Their reward is filling the void.

John D. Carter
San Francisco, California

Robert F. Cushman
Philadelphia, Pennsylvania

C. Scott Hartz
Philadelphia, Pennsylvania

v

Gilbert Alvarez is a financial analyst with Banco Cafetero International Corp. in Miami. He manages the bank's
daily funds position, as well as its financial hedging
program. He has a background in export-import financing and foreign exchange transactions. A graduate of
Claremont McKenna College, Mr. Alvarez is fluent in
French and Spanish.

Reinhard Augustin, Wirtschaftspruefer (CPA), is the
National Director of German Business Development in
the United States for Price Waterhouse. He has over
twenty years of professional experience in Germany and
in the United States, during which time he had the opportunity to deliver a broad range of professional services
to a variety of large and small, mainly international clients.
Since 1985 Mr. Augustin resides permanently in the
United States.

Richard J. Behrens is a partner in Price Waterhouse
and full-time Chairman of the firm's Real Estate Industry
Services Group. In addition, Mr. Behrens also has had
extensive consulting experience on acquisitions, divest-
itures, and has provided assistance on large-scale systems
development. He serves on the AICPA Real Estate Ac-
counting Committee, the Tax Committee of the Real
Estate Securities and Syndication Institute, the Audit
Committee of the Urban Land Institute, the National
Realty Committee, and the Financial and Accounting
Standards Committee of the National Association of Real
Estate Companies. Currently, he is a co-editor of The

Real Estate Syndicator, a monthly report published by the New York Law Journal.
Mr. Behrens received his B.S. in accounting and economics from Villanova University and has attended the Stanford University Summer Executive Program.

Elana Ben-Haim is a consultant with the Strategic Management Services practice at Coopers & Lybrand in Washington, D.C. where she assists in strategic business planning for international organizations. Elana has worked with Dr. Richard Cooper in developing a framework for analyzing various motivations and managerial structures of international joint ventures across a wide array of industries. Prior to joining Coopers & Lybrand, Elana completed her graduate studies at the University of Michigan in Modern Near Eastern and North African Studies, with a Specialization in International Business.

David M. Bridges, a partner in Thelen, Marrin, Johnson & Bridges, has been Manager of the Houston office of the firm since its opening in 1981. Mr. Bridges practices in the areas of domestic and international construction and finance, as well as general commercial and corporate law since joining the firm in 1962. He is a member of the International and American Bar Associations, the State Bars of Texas and California, and a graduate of Boalt Hall School of Law, University of California.

I would also like to gratefully acknowledge the assistance of the following individuals:

Eric T. Laity, a counsel in the Houston office; practice areas include international business and taxation.

Jimmy E. Miller, Beverly J. Kimmitt, and Christopher A. Jiongo, resident associates in the Houston office; practice areas include general business, business and commercial litigation.

James R. Bridges, a 1964 graduate of U.C. Berkeley's Boalt Hall School of Law, is a partner in the San Francisco office of Thelen, Marrin, Johnson & Bridges. He practices extensively in the international business and tax fields. Mr. Bridges has represented numerous clients with respect to joint venturing in the Middle East as well as elsewhere in the world.

Willard W. Brittain, Jr. is a partner in the management consulting services department of Price Waterhouse. He has extensive experience in analyzing the financial feasibility of major business developments. His particular area of expertise is in the telecommunications and utilities industries. He is a graduate of Yale University and the Harvard Graduate School of Business Administration. He is an active member of a number of community and municipal advisory boards.

John E. Buelt, a senior audit partner with Price Waterhouse and Chairman of the Healthcare Industry Services Group, is responsible for directing the firm's healthcare practice. His thirty-three years of professional experience span the full range of financial accounting, auditing, and management consulting services in healthcare. Jack has served as a project team member and advisor to the President's Management Improvement Council, a subcommittee on health care financing of the Health Care Financing Administration. He has also served on the American Institute of Certified Public Accountants Task Force on Nonprofit Organizations, the subcommittee of health care, and on the Financial Accounting Standards Board Task Force on the Effect of Rate Regulation on Accounting for Regulated Enterprises. He is a member of an advisory board for a large St. Louis hospital and has served previously on the finance committee and strategic planning committee of another large metropolitan hospital.

William Elliott Butler, B.A., M.A., J.D., Ph.D., LL.D. Professor of Comparative Law in the University of London; Director, Centre for the Study of Socialist Legal Systems, University College London; member of the D.C. Bar; and author of the standard work, *Soviet Law* (1983).

John D. Carter is general counsel and a senior vice president of Bechtel Group, Inc. The San Francisco-based Bechtel organization has provided professional engineering and construction services in some 100 nations on all seven continents. The operating companies of Bechtel Group, Inc. are: Bechtel Power Corporation, Bechtel Inc., Bechtel Limited, Bechtel Civil, Inc., Bechtel National, Inc., and Becon Construction Company, Inc.

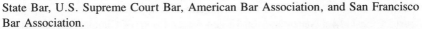

Carter joined Bechtel Power Corporation's legal department in 1982 as chief counsel for the litigation, labor, and legislation group, managing all major claims and litigation. In 1986 he was named assistant general counsel, and in July 1987 was appointed executive assistant to Alden Yates, president, Bechtel Group, Inc.

Prior to joining Bechtel, Carter was a partner with the San Francisco law firm of Thelen, Marrin, Johnson & Bridges, Bechtel's outside counsel.

Carter received a bachelor's degree in history from Stanford University and a Doctor of Laws degree from Harvard Law School. He is a member of the California State Bar, U.S. Supreme Court Bar, American Bar Association, and San Francisco Bar Association.

He has been admitted to practice before the U.S. Court of Appeals (9th Circuit), U.S. Court of Claims, U.S. District Courts (Northern California, Oregon), and U.S. Tax Court.

Dr. Richard V.L. Cooper is a partner in the Washington, D.C. office of Coopers & Lybrand, where he is responsible for the Firm's international trade consulting practice. He has extensive hands-on experience in helping both U.S. companies expand overseas and foreign companies do business in the U.S. During the past five years, he has focused particularly on joint ventures in Japan and China. Dr. Cooper received his B.A. and M.A. degrees, both in economics, from the University of California at Los Angeles and his Ph.D. in economics from the University of Chicago.

D. Kerry Crenshaw is a partner in the Detroit law firm of Clark, Klein & Beaumont, where he practices corporate and securities law. Mr. Crenshaw received his undergraduate degree from The Citadel and his law degree from Duke University. He is also a graduate of the Advanced Management Program at Harvard Business School. Mr. Crenshaw has over 15 years of experience with foreign and domestic joint ventures in the manufacturing, mining, construction and service industries, and is a frequent lecturer and author of numerous articles and publications on business topics.

Robert F. Cushman is a partner in the national law firm of Pepper, Hamilton & Scheetz and is a recognized specialist and lecturer on all phases of real estate and construction law. He serves as legal counsel to numerous trade associations, including the American Construction Owners Association, as well as many major construction, development, and bonding companies. Mr. Cushman is the co-editor of *A Guide to the Foreign Investor* and of *High Tech Real Estate,* both published by Dow Jones-Irwin, as well as many other handbooks and guides in the insurance, real estate, and construction fields.

Mr. Cushman, who is a member of the Bar of the Commonwealth of Pennsylvania and who is admitted to practice before the Supreme Court of the United States and the United States Court of Claims, has served as executive vice president and general counsel to the Construction Industry Foundation, as well as regional chairman of the Public Contract Law Section of the American Bar Association.

James A. Dobkin received his B.Ch.E in nuclear chemical engineering from Polytechnic University in 1961, and his Juris Doctor degree in 1964 from New York University School of Law, where he was Managing Editor of the Law Review. In 1968, he received a Master of Laws degree from Georgetown University Law Center. Following his legal studies, Mr. Dobkin served four years in the Office of the General Counsel of Army Materiel Command, the major procuring agency of the U.S. Army. He joined the Washington, D.C. law firm of Arnold & Porter in 1968 and became Partner in 1973. He was an advisor to the President's Commission on

Government Procurement in 1972 and 1973 and he has published widely on various aspects of the law relating to the transfer and licensing of patents and technology, government procurement and international joint ventures, among numerous other subjects. He is a co-author of *International Joint Ventures,* (Federal Publications, Inc., 1986); editor and co-author of *International Technology Joint Ventures in the Countries of the Pacific Rim* (Butterworth Legal Publishers, 1988); and author of *Contracting with the United States Government* (Longman Group, 1986).

Mr. Dobkin's areas of special expertise include the purchase and protection of intellectual property; the creation and preservation of technology joint ventures, both international and domestic; and all aspects of government procurement. He is also an adjunct professor at the Georgetown University School of Law where he teaches a course in international joint ventures.

Robert H. Garb is a Principal Counsel with the Legal Department of the Bechtel Group of Companies. Mr. Garb joined Bechtel in July 1969 and has been primarily involved in Bechtel's international operations including serving in field assignments in Australia and Papua New Guinea. Prior to his present assignment in heading the legal section located in Gaithersburg, Maryland, Mr. Garb was Chairman of his Legal Department's Committee on Joint Associations. His experience includes the formation of numerous joint ventures and joint companies. He received his Bachelor's and Law Degree from the University of Michigan.

John R. Griffiths, a California native, received both his B.A. and his L.L.B. from Stanford University, and has been a practicing attorney since 1961. He has been trial counsel in a number of suits involving disputes between joint venturers and disputes between joint venture entities and third parties. A Senior Partner in the firm of Crist, Griffiths, Schulz & Biorn, Mr. Griffiths has, in the past several years, extended his practice to include service as a Special Master in both state and federal courts. In this role, Mr. Griffiths has assisted in the resolution and settlement of many multi-party law suits in the areas of construction and high technology.

Scott Hartz is a partner with Price Waterhouse and a senior member of the firm's management consulting practice. He is located in the Philadelphia office where he directs the firm's Southeastern Regional management consulting activities. Mr. Hartz specializes in designing and implementing financial reporting and management control systems for major domestic and multinational organizations. He has also assisted a number of large organizations in long-term financial systems planning projects.

In the joint venture arena, he has assisted one of the largest joint venture organizations in the United States through the transition to majority control by one of the original partners. He has also assisted in the development of worldwide consolidation systems and in the financial reporting problems associated with a U.S.-based entity reporting to a non-U.S. parent company.

Mr. Hartz holds a B.S. degree from Lehigh University and an M.B.A. from the Wharton School at the University of Pennsylvania. He is a Certified Public Accountant and speaks frequently on management and control system issues.

Christopher A. Jiongo received his B.A. from the University of Texas and his J.D. from Southern Methodist University. He is an associate with the Houston office of Thelen, Marrin, Johnson & Bridges and practices primarily in the areas of corporate, construction, and taxation.

David F. Kleeman is a partner in the Philadelphia office of Price Waterhouse and is responsible for the international tax group in that office. He received his B.S. degree from the Wharton School of the University of Pennsylvania and a J.D. from Harvard Law School. As a specialist in international taxation, Mr. Kleeman is a frequent speaker on subjects related to the taxation of international business. He is a Director of the International Business Forum and a member of the International Fiscal Association.

Richard S. Kopf is a General Counsel of Bechtel Investments, Inc., San Francisco, California. Attorney for Southern Pacific Transportation Company from 1969 to 1986, with most recent position of Senior General Attorney. Assistant General Counsel of Santa Fe Southern Pacific Corporation in 1986. Joined Bechtel in September, 1986.

Member of California State Bar, ABA, Association of Transportation Practitioners, and Federal Communications Bar Association.

James S. Lawlor, Esquire is an associate in the Philadelphia office of the national law firm of Pepper, Hamilton & Scheetz. He came to Pepper, Hamilton & Scheetz after graduating with honors from Villanova University School of Law in May of 1987. While at Villanova, Mr. Lawlor was on the editorial board of the Villanova Law Review. At Pepper, Hamilton & Scheetz, he works primarily in the firm's commercial practice department.

Cary Levinson is a partner in the Commercial Practice Group in the Philadelphia Office of Pepper, Hamilton & Scheetz. Mr. Levinson specializes in mergers and acquisitions with an emphasis on international transactions.

Thomas S. Nowinski is also a partner in the firm of Clark, Klein & Beaumont, and practices in the areas of corporate law and taxation. Mr. Nowinski received both his Bachelor of Science in Engineering degree and his Juris Doctor degree from the University of Michigan. His practice includes the planning and implementation of a broad variety of business acquisitions, combinations, and dispositions. He is a member of the bars of the States of Michigan and Florida.

Jack S. Older is a partner in the New York office of Rogers & Wells. His practice is devoted principally to bank regulatory matters, commercial financing transactions and equipment leasing transactions. He has been involved in assisting banks and other providers of financial services in the planning and development of new products and services.

Prior to joining Rogers & Wells, he was General Counsel of the Bowery Savings Bank, from 1972 to 1981. From 1970 to 1972, he was Tax Counsel at Atlantic Richfield Corporation, and prior to that served as Associate General Counsel of the National Association of Mutual Savings Banks and as an attorney in the Office of Chief Counsel of the Internal Revenue Service.

Mr. Older received his B.S. in Economics from The Wharton School of the University of Pennsylvania (1955) and his LL.B. from the University of Pennsylvania Law School (1958). He is admitted to practice in the State of New York and is a member of the American Bar Association and the New York State Bar Association.

He is the author of a monograph on Individual Retirement Accounts published by the American Law Institute of the American Bar Association. He has also published the following articles: "Conversion of Thrift Institutions," **Review of Securities Regulation,** June 1, 1983; "Capital Standards: Regulators Wield a Big New Stick," **Legal Times,** April 30, 1984; "Issuers of MBS [Mortgage Backed Securities] Enhanced by Reforms," **New York Law Journal,** December 10, 1984. Most recently, he prepared an extensive outline on the Taxation of Real Estate Mortgage Investment Conduits (REMICs) for the 1987 ABA Investment Limited Partnership Program.

Irving Rappaport has served since 1984 as Associate General Counsel for Intellectual Property and Licensing for Apple Computer, Inc. He is responsible for Apple's worldwide patent, trademark, copyright and trade secret matters, including related licensing and litigation. Previously, he held the positions of Associate General Counsel for Bally Manufacturing and Chief Patent Counsel of Data General Corporation. He is admitted to the Bars of Illinois, Minnesota, Massachusetts and Missouri and the U.S. Patent and Trademark Office. Through appointment by Secretary of Commerce, William Verity, and U.S. Trade Representative, Clayton Yeutter, he serves on the

U.S. Government's Industry Functional Advisory Committee on Intellectual Property for Trade Policy Matters. He holds a J.D. from George Washington University, an M.B.A. from Boston University and a B.S.E.E. from Washington University in St. Louis.

Barry P. Robbins is a partner in the National office of Price Waterhouse in New York. He consults on a wide range of accounting matters and helps formulate his firm's position on issues under consideration by the Financial Accounting Standards Board. He has also served in the Philadelphia and Washington, D.C. offices of Price Waterhouse. Mr. Robbins holds a B.S. in Economics and an M.S. in Accounting from the Wharton School of the University of Pennsylvania.

Robert Teskey is a partner with the Edmonton, Alberta, law firm of Field & Field, where he has practiced since his admission to the Alberta bar in 1971. His undergraduate and law degrees are from the University of Alberta. Bob practices in the areas of corporate, commercial and real estate law. A large part of his practice is devoted to corporate and real estate joint ventures. He has been a sessional lecturer at the Faculty of Law at the University of Alberta and has presented papers on a regular basis to various professional groups.

Patricia J. Van Horn obtained her B.A. from the University of Colorado in 1967 and her J.D. from the same university in 1970. From 1971–1974, she was on the legal staff of the North Carolina Civil Liberties Union. Ms. Van Horn has been affiliated with the Palo Alto, California, firm of Crist, Griffiths, Schulz & Biorn since 1974 and has been a partner in that firm since 1980. She is the co-author of the article "Job Security for Public Employees" which appeared in the Washington & Lee Law Review in 1974.

Merrick C. Walton is a graduate of Southern Methodist
University and the Southern Methodist University School
of Law in Dallas, Texas. He has practiced law in Dallas
and Houston in law firms and a corporate legal department. In 1985, he resigned as associate general counsel
of Browning-Ferris Industries, Inc., to return to private
practice and became a partner in the firm of Hoover, Bax
& Shearer in Houston, where his practice consists primarily of litigation. He is also a Fellow of the Texas and
Houston Bar foundations, a member of the Commercial
Arbitration Panel of the American Arbitration Association, a member of the State Bar of Texas District 4F

Grievance Committee, and a member of the Board of Directors of St. Luke's Epis-
copal Hospital in Houston. Mr. Walton has represented generators, transporters and
disposers of hazardous waste in Superfund matters and other environmental and toxic
tort litigation, and has also been extensively involved in negotiation and drafting of
contractual documents relating to the transportation and disposal of solid and hazardous wastes. He is the author of a chapter on the waste disposal industry in a soon-
to-be-published Dow Jones handbook on joint venturing, and is a frequent speaker
on the business of hazardous waste disposal.

David Wightman is a solicitor of the Supreme Court of
Judicature, England and Senior Partner of the City of
London Law Firm, Turner Kenneth Brown. He has been
in practice for more than 25 years. Apart from being a
member of the Law Society of England and Wales, he
is also an active member of the International Bar Association, Business Law Section, and Section on Energy
and Natural Resources Law. Mr. Wightman is also Ed-
itor-in-Chief of the International Construction Law Review, published by Lloyd's of London Press.

John R. Wille is a manager in Price Waterhouse and
Partners, the international financial advisory affiliate of
Price Waterhouse. His former positions include: Financial Consultant, Management Financial Consulting Services Department, Price Waterhouse; Head of Planning
and Analysis Department, International Division, AM
International; and Financial Manager, Comptroller's Division, American National Bank and Trust Company of
Chicago.

Mr. Wille has a B.A.—Economics from Northwestern University, and an MBA—Finance from the University of Chicago.

Thomas T. Yamakawa, a CPA, is a partner and National Director of Japanese Business Services in Price Waterhouse. In his 25 years with the firm in New York and Tokyo, he served clients of various nationalities including American and Japanese, and joint ventures among such clients. Tom is a native of Japan with his education, career and professional qualifications spanning Japan and the United States. He graduated from Brigham Young University in 1953.

CONTENTS

PART 1

JOINT VENTURING IN THE UNITED STATES

C. Scott Hartz
Price Waterhouse

The joint venture is an increasingly common form of business organization both within the United States and elsewhere around the world. It is a vehicle that even many of the largest and most sophisticated organizations find useful in launching new businesses, acquiring new technologies, or entering new markets.

The first section of this book deals with strategies that may lead an organization into a joint-venturing arrangement and with the "mechanics" of creating and structuring a joint venture, including legal, tax, accounting, and other matters. This section also deals with joint venturing as it is emerging in various industries within the domestic economy. Later sections deals with offshore joint ventures and joint ventures with foreign entities entering the U.S. market.

The primary rationale for a joint venture is to marry the strengths of two often very different organizations. In the process, the two "parents" create a new entity which is free from the bureaucratic shackles of both parent organizations. The new entity is free-standing and frequently tightly focused on a specific market, product, R&D area, or technology. In a well-structured venture, such key items as capital contributions, legal structure (corporation or partnership), accounting policies, dividend policies, role of the parents in key decisions, etc., are well defined and understood by both parties at the time of formation.

In contrast with most other new business formations, the joint-venture approach facilitates a very rapid start-up situation. The contributions of its "parents" endow the new organization with potentially significant amounts of capital, personnel resources, patents or licenses, and/or production facilities. However, because of the potential speed of assembly in creating and launching the organization, there is, perhaps, a greater need for planning and attention to such structural issues as legal form, capital structure, tax strategy, dividend policy, etc., that in many organizations would emerge over a period of years. For that reason, this book has been assembled to identify the issues and strategies that other organizations have utilized as they enter the world of joint venturing.

CHAPTER 1

JOINT-VENTURING STRATEGIES

John R. Wille
Senior Manager
Price Waterhouse

INTRODUCTION

While takeovers and mergers seem to dominate the news, joint ventures receive relatively short shrift within academic circles and in the financial press. Despite their comparative anonymity, many joint ventures are flourishing in the global marketplace, for they offer an effective competitive alternative in many product areas and geographic environments. Like tools in the workshop of corporate strategy, they work well in certain specific applications but are inappropriate for many others.

This chapter will explore the various motivations for forming a joint venture, from the standpoint of competitive positioning and manufacturing/production effectiveness as well as from a risk-management perspective. In it we will also place the joint-venture concept within the spectrum of corporate development initiatives; contrasting joint ventures with other forms of collaboration such as cooperative agreements, acquisitions and mergers, and licensing and franchising agreements. In addition, we will analyze the question of corporate compatibility; that is, whether two organizations with differing corporate cultures and business approaches can find common ground upon which they may collectively exploit their respective competitive advantages.

Finally, we will examine in detail one of the more notable joint-venture initiatives undertaken in previous years in order to illustrate the importance of the strategic concepts previously discussed. This case study involves Himont, which began its existence in 1983 as a joint venture between Hercules and Montedison to exploit new technologies in polypropylene manufacture and has since proven to be an unqualified success.

In summary, this chapter will attempt to show that, although they are not a business panacea, joint ventures have value as a strategic option for corporations far exceeding their level of visibility and notoriety. However, when improperly conceived and executed, joint ventures can be as contentious, damaging, and wasteful of corporate assets as any prolonged takeover fight.

WHY JOINT VENTURES?

The primary impetus for joint ventures is to accumulate market power via the aggregation of resources as well as through collective action. Ideally a joint venture between partners with complementary capabilities will result in a combined power base stronger than the mere sum of the parts.

The joint-venture concept probably had its origins as a form of political cooperation when early nation-states formed strategic alliances, as a means of countering external threats to their sovereignty that exceeded their individual resources and capabilities. A more recent example is the NATO Alliance, which in fact operates under a joint-command structure. In commerce, the earliest joint ventures were in trading and in the exploitation of natural resources, much like the collaborative efforts that are common in the mining and petroleum industries today.

Broadly speaking, a joint venture can be defined for our purposes as a new business entity formed by two or more independent business entities, sometimes referred to as ''parents.'' A business entity can be defined as an individual, a partnership, or a corporation. Joint ventures are generally formed when one parent seeks another in order to provide needed resources or capabilities, to exploit potential synergies, or to share risks. Joint ventures can be established for a finite time span to accomplish specific objectives, or they can be established as ongoing businesses with no future dissolution envisioned. The contributions of each parent usually consist of capital as well as physical assets, technology, patents, personnel, or other tangible and intangible assets. For practical purposes we have included minority investments under the joint-venture umbrella because many involve some degree of technical collaboration. However, a joint effort in which one partner contributes only capital in exchange for an equity interest in the venture generally falls outside of the joint-venture definition.

MOTIVATIONS FOR JOINT-VENTURE FORMATION

The reasons for forming a joint venture are quite numerous and extend into all areas of business strategy. These strategic motivations can be broadly divided into three major categories:

- Resource-driven joint ventures.
- Market-driven joint ventures.
- Risk-driven joint ventures.

Exhibit 1 outlines these three basic divisions and lists the specific motives included within each category. One will find when researching joint ventures that, as in a marriage, rarely does one motive predominate; each partner in a successful and lasting venture typically has several very strong incentives for entering into and maintaining a given relationship. Each application of the joint-venture concept has its benefits and drawbacks, as we will see below.

Resource-driven Joint Ventures

The joint-venture approach provides an effective means of addressing the specific needs involved when companies (1) require a specialized resource or capability in order to compete effectively or (2) produce an unrelated product in their manufacturing processes which they do not have the capability of distributing.

Obtaining or Retaining a Strategic Resource
Many joint ventures are formed because one parent lacks one or more of the essential ingredients needed to exploit a given market opportunity in a timely or profitable manner. Sometimes the market opportunity is internal, wherein one or both of the parents have a need for the product manufactured by the venture. The desire to integrate vertically is a com-

EXHIBIT 1–1
Joint Venturing Strategies

  I. Resource-driven joint-venture strategies
    A. Obtaining or retaining a strategic resource
       1. Financing
       2. Raw materials or physical plant
       3. Technology or patent
       4. Managerial talent
       5. Market or company intelligence
    B. Profitably utilize byproducts
 II. Market-driven joint venture strategies
    A. Broadening product distribution
       1. Broadening product lines
       2. Increasing volume to achieve scale economies
       3. Efficiently utilizing large minimum-efficient-scale plants
    B. Overcoming market barriers to entry
       1. High start-up costs
       2. Legal and tariff barriers
       3. Market and cultural knowledge
    C. Restructuring mature or declining product lines
    D. Diversifying into new product markets
    E. Raising barriers to the entry of new competitors
    F. Providing a vehicle for international mergers
III. Risk-driven joint-venture strategies
    A. Sharing R&D costs and risk
    B. Sharing productive investment costs and risk

---

mon impetus for joint-venture formation. However, more often the market for the venture's output is external. The following resources are typically sought from joint-venture partners.

Financing. Frequently one parent has the technology and distribution capabilities to exploit a given market opportunity; they merely need the financial wherewithal to carry out their plans. In this instance a joint venture will provide the financing partner with a means of channeling his investment into a specific activity, as opposed to a direct equity or debt position in the technical partner which could be used in any sector of the overall business. Conversely, the technical partner has the ability to limit the financing partner's interest and influence solely to the activities of the joint venture, rather than the entire scope of the technical partner's business.

Raw Materials or Physical Plant.   A firm may form a joint venture to ensure access to a specific physical resource, such as raw materials or manufacturing capacity, which the other parent can provide. This approach can be superior to a long-term supply contract for the parent seeking the resource because, if the venture is structured properly, the resource-providing parent will have increased incentives to:

- Provide the raw material on an exclusive or otherwise favorable basis.
- Price the raw materials at or below market rates to ensure the competitiveness of the joint venture.
- Commit to providing the resource over a longer or indefinite time span.

The scarcer the resource, the greater the potential benefit for the resource-seeking partner offered by the joint-venture approach. In addition, when the resource involved is a manufacturing capability, other more nonquantifiable benefits such as increased quality and responsiveness can be realized. With his equity stake in the business the resource-providing parent has a greater financial interest in good performance than he would under an ordinary supply contract.

The resource-providing parent may also find the joint-venture approach attractive because it gives him greater visibility and control over the resource contributed than he would have under a simple contractual arrangement. This can be a particularly valuable feature when the resource is readily identifiable with the provider through a brand name or trademark and when the provider wants to control the availability or market price of the resource. For example, joint ventures in film distribution, such as CBS/Fox, were designed to tightly control the distribution of movies through the videocassette sales and rental markets so as to maximize total movie revenues. Also many hotel companies, such as Hilton, have used joint ventures instead of licenses or franchises to ensure day-to-day control over the quality of the services delivered under their name.

Technology or Patent.   One of the most common instances of joint-venture activity today involves collaborative ventures between smaller firms which have developed a new technology or patent and a larger firm with the manufacturing and distribution capabilities necessary to properly exploit the technical advance. Many large firms, such as N. V. Philips, will take minority positions in small technology-based companies in order to ensure future access to the fruits of the firm's creative efforts. This is a particularly advantageous approach for those mature companies where creativity has been stifled by bureaucracy or whose R&D capabilities have atrophied over time.

Managerial Talent.   In some joint ventures, one partner may have the physical capabilities to manufacture and market a given product but lacks management expertise in certain key areas associated with that specific business. A joint venture with a partner possessing the necessary management capabilities affords that firm an opportunity to quickly progress up the learning curve and more quickly attain a competitive status. This is frequently the case with joint ventures between multinational corporations (MNC's) and local partners in developing countries. Although the local partner controls the basic factors of production, it cannot compete effectively in the world markets without the modern management techniques which the MNC can provide.

Companies faced with the loss of key personnel have utilized the joint-venture approach to retain this critical expertise. In these instances ownership of the venture is split between the parent company and key employee(s), who might otherwise start up their own operation or jump to a better-paying competitor. This is particularly useful in an environment of continual product enhancement, where continuity of personnel and management is critical in maintaining the desired growth rates.

Market or Company Intelligence.   The joint-venture approach is useful for introducing a firm to new markets or potential merger partners. The information-seeking firm can gain an insider's perspective of an otherwise unfamiliar market or firm through interaction with its partner. This is more common in business cultures such as Japan, where strategic horizons are truly longer term and strategic decisions are made very deliberately based on extensive knowledge and research. However, Western firms are also known to use small joint ventures as a means of "testing the waters," to evaluate the partner more carefully before cooperative efforts of a more substantial nature are undertaken.

Profitably Utilize Byproducts

Frequently a production process will yield significant quantities of marketable by-products unrelated to the primary goods being manufactured. If the manufacturer does not have the distribution capabilities to effectively market these by-products, a joint venture with a qualified distributor may be an appropriate alternative. Depending on the structure of the venture, this approach can be used to minimize the firm's exposure to market risks associated with the by-products (e.g. price fluctuations, competition, etc.). Cost sharing, which is discussed later, can be a parallel motive in this instance.

Market-driven Joint Ventures

Although a firm may have the capability of producing a given product or service, a joint venture can afford it certain market advantages which it would not otherwise enjoy. Also, horizontal and vertical integration are objectives that are frequently accomplished through joint-venture combinations. Overall, there are many ways in which collaborative ventures are beneficial in increasing market access or in repositioning the parents in the marketplace.

Broadening Product Distribution
Joint ventures offer the opportunity to leverage upon the partners' respective distribution capabilities, particularly when they operate in disparate geographic markets but serve similar product markets. This attribute can be used to accomplish several specific strategic marketing objectives, such as those illustrated below.

Broadening Product Lines. When two potential partners are close but not direct competitors, a distribution joint venture affords them the opportunity to both maximize the utilization of their marketing and sales investment and to broaden their customer appeal by offering a wider range of products. This is particularly valuable when one or both of the partners has a large distribution infrastructure in place but because of limited product lines or maturing products cannot effectively utilize this asset. A good example is the case of SmithKline Beckman, which rose to prominence by pioneering the ulcer drug, Tagamet, and a cardiovascular drug, Dyazide. Now that these products have matured and no other products with such considerable market potential are available to maintain the revenue stream, SmithKline must fill the gap with a greater number of drugs which enjoy smaller potential markets. To supplement their own R&D efforts, SmithKline has formed joint ventures and sought licenses from other pharmaceutical firms. In this way they can gain access to new products which can be marketed through their existing distribution network.

Increasing Volume to Achieve Scale Economies.   In markets where the products are viewed as commodities, with the consequent focus on price competitiveness, joint ventures offer a means of realizing greater economies of scale. This can be accomplished through wider product distribution, consolidation of overheads, and increased manufacturing efficiencies. This approach is particularly useful when both parents wish to maintain a presence in the market or utilize the product in their own downstream manufacturing operations.

Efficiently Utilizing Large Minimum-Efficient-Scale Plants.   In some instances cost and technical factors mandate that a threshold volume level of a given product be produced before the unit costs and prices reach an acceptable level for customers. A joint venture can be employed to ensure that adequate distribution capabilities are available for the large volume of product manufactured. For example, several oil companies teamed up to build and operate the Alaska Pipeline, which would not have been cost-efficient handling the throughput of only one producer. Risk sharing, which is discussed below, is frequently a corollary motive in these cases.

Overcoming Market Barriers to Entry

The desire to gain access to a difficult or closed market has been a major catalyst for joint ventures, particularly cross-border business alliances. Many such markets appear at first glance to be economically unattractive to foreign entrants due to perceived barriers to entry, such as the following.

High Start-up Costs.   Due to salary and real estate prices above those in the home market start-up costs may be high. For a company whose products have a limited market appeal because of their specialized nature, the costs of establishing a new distribution network may be prohibitively high. This is a particular problem for companies seeking to penetrate the Japanese market, where real estate prices have escalated dramatically as a result of the influx of foreign financial services firms.

Legal and Tariff Barriers.   These barriers are designed to protect existing local firms or foster the growth of more domestic producers. In many developing countries, joint ventures with local firms are the only legal means of establishing a presence in the domestic market. These ventures are generally up to 51 percent owned by the foreign MNC and are mandated to encourage the development of indigenous management and technical resources.

Market and Cultural Knowledge.   These are intangible factors which can heavily influence the success or failure of an overseas venture. If a foreign firm does not have an understanding of the local business culture, it will be difficult to transact business effectively and will make it difficult for the entity to establish its credibility and viability in the market. Furthermore, if the firm does not fully appreciate the unique characteristics and requirements of the local market, it may incorrectly position the product or otherwise communicate the wrong message to its target customers.

Joint ventures with similar firms in the local market offer several benefits to outside firms seeking access, including:

- The opportunity to utilize the local partner's distribution capabilities to market both firms' products, thereby increasing the overall efficiency of the distribution system by leveraging upon the existing asset base. In many cases, this increased throughput can be effected with little or no increase in fixed-asset investment.

- The opportunity to avoid actual and threatened tariff barriers by establishing a local manufacturing presence in conjunction with a local partner. Many Japanese companies are forming joint ventures with U.S. firms in an effort to ensure continued access to the U.S. market should Congress enact restrictive trade legislation or should the dollar continue to fall in value relative to the yen. The GM-Toyota venture in California is a prime example of this tactic.

- The opportunity to gain exclusive or otherwise favorable access to a closed market through association with a local firm. The domestic partners' participation will not only satisfy statutory requirements, but may provide some protection against future efforts by the government to expropriate or restrict the activities of foreign ventures. For example, because of China's continual lack of foreign exchange, many companies have established joint ventures with Chinese firms in order to ensure continued access to the domestic market. As long as the venture can earn enough hard currency through exports to cover dividend payments to the foreign parent, the balance of the revenues can be invoiced in Chinese renminbi. Most of the venture's expenses can also be incurred in the local currency.

- Insights from the local partner on domestic business practices and cultural habits which can materially influence the success of the venture in identifying and penetrating the appropriate target markets. Also, an association with a known local partner can ameliorate any xenophobic reactions local customers may normally evidence towards foreign vendors. In addition, the local partner can contribute contacts and business relationships which it would take the foreign partner a significant amount of time to develop on its own. In certain industries, particularly pharmaceuticals, knowledge of and experience in dealing with the local regulatory authorities is an absolute prerequisite for doing business in an effective manner. Such market and cultural expertise can be acquired by the adroit hiring of local nationals; however, the institutional identity of a local partner is sometimes as important an asset as the knowledge and expertise which individual employees can contribute.

If the foreign firm prefers to establish its own name in the local market, a joint venture of a finite duration may be set up as a precursor to an independent entity. The foreign partner will still have access to the necessary resources to initially penetrate the market while leaving its future options unfettered.

Restructuring Mature or Declining Product Lines

One of the more innovative uses of joint ventures is to enhance the competitive position of firms in a mature or declining industry. For companies faced with the prospect of competing for a share in a shrinking market, a joint venture provides a vehicle for rationalizing the overall manufacturing investment while strengthening the consolidated venture's position in the remaining market. If the product lines involved are cash generators, this approach can prolong the profitable life of the fixed investment.

Alternatively, one or both partners may view the venture as a means of enhancing the value of their investment in order to fetch a more attractive purchase price later on. The joint-venture entity, if properly restructured, will presumably be more valuable to a potential purchaser than its two smaller and less competitive predecessors. Our case study of Himont provides a vivid illustration of the effective implementation of this strategy.

Diversifying into New Product Markets

If the technical skills and capabilities which a particular firm has developed in one industry are applicable to other products or services, a joint venture with a firm presently serving the target market can be an effective means to capitalize on this expertise. By joining with a partner who provides complementary product and market knowledge, a firm can minimize the risks involved in packaging and marketing an otherwise new product. Sony utilized this strategem in forming joint ventures with Prudential Insurance, Wilson Sporting Goods, and Pepsico. Vertical integration can also be accomplished through this strategy, as evidenced by Knight-Ridder's joint venture with Media General to produce newsprint.

Joint ventures are also a particularly useful approach when developing a new delivery system for an existing product. For example, in 1980 Automated Data Processing (ADP) and Townsend-Greenspan & Co. teamed up to form Econalyst. This firm provided Townsend-Greenspan reports, forecasts, and economic data, previously distributed by mail, to clients via on-line computer access. At the same time, CBS and Twentieth-Century Fox Video formed CBS/Fox to exploit the newly burgeoning videocassette movie market, which has grown rapidly as an alternative to movie theatres.

Raising Barriers to the Entry of New Competitors

The joint-venture approach can be utilized in many situations to forestall or preempt competition by raising the costs of entry. This can be accomplished through several measures, including the following:

- Teaming up with the primary provider of a key resource, thus ensuring exclusive or preferential access.
- Using the combined technological, manufacturing and distribution capabilities of the partners to build volume quickly, thus lowering unit costs and exposing potential competitors to substantial start-up costs and risks.

Providing a Vehicle for International Mergers

As the pace of forming international mergers and acquisitions has accelerated, concerns about foreign ownership of domestic industry leaders have resulted in a rise in economic nationalism within developed as well as developing countries. One of the most notable instances occurred when the Hong Kong and Shanghai Bank was rebuffed by the Bank of England in its attempt to acquire the Royal Bank of Scotland. Although issues such as Hong Kong's lack of a central bank (as a lender of last resort) were advanced as a pretext for rejecting the merger, it is commonly known that the issue of economic sovereignty was paramount.

In order to alleviate such nationalistic concerns, firms contemplating major cross-border mergers and acquisitions have utilized the joint-venture concept as a means of realizing the benefits of a merger while maintaining the national identities of the parent firms. The most recent example of this phenomenon is the Asea-Brown Boveri merger, where the majority of the two firms' assets have been transferred to a joint venture. This entity has emerged as one of the largest electrical contractors in the world. However, Asea retained its identity as a Swedish holding company while Brown Boveri continues to be domiciled in Switzerland. Both play a significant role in the management of the joint venture.

Aside from the political benefits, the use of a joint venture in lieu of a merger offers the opportunity to minimize the tax effects of cross-border remittances, such as dividends, upon the parent and its shareholders.

Risk-driven Joint Ventures

One of the most common motives underlying the formation of joint ventures is the spreading of costs and risks. The two most prevalent examples are R&D joint ventures and production joint ventures, which involve a substantial initial investment for which the ultimate return is not well assured. In both cases the joint-venture concept is used to lay off risks onto other participants, so that the failure of the venture does not threaten the solvency of the individual investors. Also, the corporate joint venture affords the parents the benefit of limited liability, although for moral and public image reasons the partners may not wish to utilize this option should the venture fail.

Sharing R&D Costs and Risks
Joint ventures are frequently established among competitors in order to defray the costs of basic or applied research. This approach is particularly cost-effective in situations where the expected products will be difficult to protect from imitators through patents.

Countless R&D joint ventures are springing up among high technology firms wishing to pool their expertise in pursuit of technological innovations and new products. One of the most visible joint undertakings occurred in 1983 with the formation of Microelectronics and Computer Technology

Corp., (MMC), which was formed by 15 firms to develop advanced computer, software, and semiconductor technology. Many collaborative efforts in product research and development do not use the joint-venture structure; the participants merely coordinate their research and share in the results. However, this is not as effective an approach when a substantial investment in facilities, equipment, and prototypes is required.

Sharing Productive Investment Costs and Risks

Joint ventures are commonplace in the extractive industries, where the costs of setting up a mining or drilling operation in remote areas can run into hundreds of millions of dollars. Because the resource to be extracted, be it petroleum or minerals, is not easily visible or quantifiable, the forecasted return on investment is subject to considerable variance. Also there are a wide variety of exogenous factors which can affect the long-run profitability of the venture, including the risks of foreign exchange fluctuations, expropriation, technological change, and shifts in overall supply-and-demand conditions over time.

Partnerships between smaller investors and mining or drilling companies have provided a significant resource for funding and risk spreading in these industries. Prior to the 1986 tax reform, the financial partners benefited from the interest deductions and depreciation/depletion allowances, which the technical partners frequently could not fully utilize themselves.

In the development of new energy or mineral sources, joint ventures have also played a major role. The first commercial-scale coal gasification plant in the United States was a joint venture between several natural gas suppliers, who shared the costs and output as well as the market and technological risks. The plant commenced shipments in 1983 and was commercially viable until the steep drop in energy prices in the mid-1980s, whereupon the venture foundered and was taken over by the Department of Energy.

DRAWBACKS OF THE JOINT-VENTURE APPROACH

As we have illustrated above, the potential applications of the joint-venture approach run to all areas of corporate strategy. However, despite the versatility of the concept, many otherwise sound collaborative plans fall prey to the one major drawback of joint ventures; the problem of sharing control. Effective joint-venture management involves balancing two competing needs: (1) providing incentives for the partners to devote the necessary resources to the entity, while (2) persuading them to give up a measure of control over these same resources. Because partners do not typically share the same motivations for entering into a joint venture, their interests and requirements frequently come into conflict.

For example, in the early 1980s a prominent U.S. computer manufacturer formed a joint venture with a major Japanese firm to sell the latter's computers in the U.S. market. The U.S. partner wished to invigorate its moribund distribution system with new products, while the foreign partner desired a cost-efficient means of market entry. However, the U.S. partner was not able to provide adequate distribution of the product and the Japanese firm was slow in adapting its products to U.S. market requirements. Each firm's excessive reliance on the other to pull the venture along was the principal cause of its eventual failure. The Japanese firm finally bought out its partner and continued the operation independently.

Corporate machismo has also played a major role in the demise of many joint ventures. When Ford and Fiat announced plans for an automobile-manufacturing joint venture in 1985, the ensuing negotiations soon collapsed because each corporation was too concerned with its own image to be seen subordinating itself to the other partner in the management of the joint enterprise.

In addition, the "not invented here" syndrome frequently afflicts parent-company management, inhibiting meaningful cooperation and technology migration between the venture and its parents.

Walking the tightrope between the two interest groups is a difficult, sometimes impossible task. Therefore, one of the most important factors to consider when contemplating a joint venture, as we will discuss later, is whether the partners can work together effectively.

ALTERNATIVES TO JOINT VENTURES

Now that we have addressed the various reasons for forming a joint venture, we will examine the benefits and drawbacks of the joint-venture approach vis-à-vis the other methods of interfirm collaboration, including:

- Mergers and Acquisitions.
- Franchise/Licensing Agreements.
- Cooperative Agreements.
- Supplier Agreements.

Each alternative is discussed in greater detail below.

Mergers and Acquisitions

The joint-venture concept provides an attractive alternative to a traditional merger or acquisition in those instances where the ownership and management of the firms involved wish to maintain their independence. Also, as noted earlier, national sensitivities to acquisitions by foreign firms can be addressed through a joint-venture structure. A particular advantage of the joint-venture approach is the ability to focus the alliance on those areas in which cooperation is appropriate and beneficial, leaving the other business lines unaffected.

From a managerial perspective, the outright purchase of a firm which can provide necessary resources and capabilities is the simplest form of collaboration, since there is little question as to who is in control. Mergers and joint ventures are generally more difficult to operate because of their inherent potential for political conflicts.

A joint venture generally poses fewer financial risks than an acquisition, for the following reasons:

- The purchase price of a publicly traded company can be higher if significant speculative trading accompanies the tender offer. In a joint venture, assets are contributed at fair market value and are not subject to the same speculative premiums. Thus, the venture does not face the same hurdles in generating an acceptable return on investment.
- Joint ventures are generally carried on financial statements as equity investments; their financial affairs are, therefore, more insulated from those of the parent firms. Joint ventures are also better positioned to take advantage of the shield of corporate limited liability, should the need arise.

From a personnel standpoint, the joint-venture (and merger) approaches can be more effective in retaining key personnel; employees of both parents presumably will feel they have the political leverage to maintain their status. One of the greatest areas of risk in an acquisition, particularly in the high-tech and service industries, is the loss of critical personnel due to the fear of being replaced by favored employees from the acquiring firm.

Finally, from an antitrust perspective, the U.S. government has indicated in the past that joint ventures may be easier to justify in terms of efficiency than outright combinations, particularly among R&D-intensive firms.

Franchising/Licensing Agreements

Franchising or licensing agreements essentially involve granting the right to a particular resource (e.g. patent, brand name, etc.) sometimes in conjunction with other services (e.g. advertising, product development), in exchange for a fixed or performance-based fee (e.g. percentage of revenues). Therefore, the franchising/licensing alternative is a most effective approach when a number of independent entities require a common resource from another entity in order to conduct business effectively.

From the perspective of the franchisor or licensor this arrangement is superior to the joint-venture approach for the following reasons:

- Downside risk is minimized because the firm is not liable for operating losses. In some cases, the firm can actually exert a greater measure of control over the franchise/licensee, for his costs of contract termination are mainly opportunity losses.
- The firm's relationship with the various franchisees or licensees is easier to manage since they are simply a series of bilateral alliances, instead of a multilateral organization with its attendant political complexities.
- There is also a greater pressure on the franchisee/licensee to perform, because he shoulders the business risk.

On the other hand, joint ventures offer a greater opportunity to exploit synergies between the involved firms. In addition, the resource-providing firm is not entirely dependent on the business abilities of the franchisees/licensees, and, therefore, does not face the same potential opportunity loss if they should underachieve.

Some firms will enter into cross-licensing or joint-distribution agreements to broaden the market coverage of their respective products. This tactic is often utilized to forestall the entry of a foreign firm into its partner's domestic market; the enticement being the opportunity to gain licensing revenues from the new market without the risks of a substantial marketing investment.

Cooperative Agreements

This is a less involved form of collaboration because the partners do not legally commit equity or resources, although some moral or contractual commitments may be made. These agreements can cover a broad range of collaborative activities, but are most commonly used in the areas of R&D and industry marketing. The advantage of this approach lies with the low-risk nature of the relationship; it generally is not costly to sever such an agreement. However, there is also less incentive to collaborate effectively or to devote the necessary resources to ensure the success of the cooperative effort.

Supplier Agreements

This is the least interactive form of collaboration, which simply involved a firm committing to provide a product to a distributor under agreed-upon terms. This again is a low-risk/low-synergy approach which limits the involvement of the supplier (e.g. no equity investment) but does not permit him to control the downstream applications of the product. The supplier thus has to rely heavily on the distributor to effectively promote and sell the product to the final customers.

SELECTING THE APPROPRIATE
JOINT-VENTURE PARTNER

Clearly, the success of a joint venture is extremely dependent upon the ability of the parents to cooperate effectively; therefore, the partner-selection process is the most sensitive and critical step in the joint-venture-formulation process. Before actually approaching potential partners, management should first clearly and unambiguously define its own objectives and requirements, which can then be communicated to the candidate firms. If both firms understand each others' needs and avoid the pursuit of hidden agendas, the prospects of achieving an open and cooperative relationship will be greatly enhanced.

Once the selection process has begun, the evaluation of potential partners should focus on the three basic attributes discussed below:

1. *Do they possess the resources and capabilities we seek?* This, of course, is the threshold issue, and, therefore, should not be assessed at a superficial level. A detailed analysis of the capabilities of the potential partner should address the following questions:

- What is their position in the industry? Are they the largest provider?
- How exclusive is their access to the desired resources? What is the extent of their capabilities?

- What is their financial condition and what are their future prospects?
- What other provider relationships do they have? Might these other agreements pose a conflict of interest?
- Do they have a contractual or legal problems affecting the resource in question? Could these problems affect future resource availability?
- Do they have a ''key man'' problem, that is, could the departure of one or more specific people impair their ability to deliver the desired resource or capability?

2. *Is their approach to the business compatible with our own?* The issue of corporate personas, as noted earlier, is particularly important because incompatibility is the most common reason why joint ventures break down. Several relevant questions must be analyzed in evaluating this issue, including:

- What is their approach to business ethics, e.g. will they play fast and loose with laws and regulations in order to make the next sale?
- Do we have an existing relationship with the potential partner? How has it progressed?
- What is the nature of their corporate culture; do they take an arrogant attitude towards other firms?
- What is their attitude towards risk? Are they conservative and risk-averse or willing to take chances?
- What is the nature of their decision-making process; does management react quickly to events or are most major decisions referred to a committee for detailed evaluation?
- How are they organized relative to us? Would we have to deal with several units within their firm?
- Is the size of our business significant in relation to theirs? Would the joint venture be a large scale initiative in their eyes?
- How do the two management teams get along?

3. *Do they have adequate motivation and commitment to the success of the venture?* One major potential error in contemplating a joint venture is assuming that because the venture is in your interest it is also in your partner's. One must look carefully at the proposed venture from the partner's perspective in order to fully understand the risks and consequently the incentives needed to ensure his effective performance. Issues to consider should include:

- What strategic benefits would they hope to realize through the joint venture? How do those interests interact with your own aspirations?
- Are they willing to share control over their contributed assets; for example, will they give over the rights to a key technology or merely license it to the venture?
- What is the extent of the financial commitment they are willing to make? Will they make further equity infusions should the joint venture require interim financing?
- How does this venture fit into the partner's overall strategy? Is this venture critical to the partner's main business or merely a peripheral investment?
- What would the effects of joint-venture failure be on the partner?
- How badly does the partner need this venture? Are they hungry for this business?

The interplay between the three basic factors listed above should also be evaluated, for it is infrequent that a potential partner scores highly on all three. For example, a potential partner who is the industry leader may not be as committed to joint venturing by virtue of its already dominant position. However, a smaller firm which possesses the requisite capabilities may display a greater desire to make the venture work. When dealing with very large companies as partners, there is also the risk that the joint venture may lose visibility as the firm's attention is diverted to other matters. Taking the time to carefully scrutinize potential partners is an investment whose value cannot be overstated. As in any area of business, a strategy is only as good as its execution.

We will next look at a detailed example of a successful joint venture in order to better appreciate the complex interplay of motivations involved in the venture-development process.

HIMONT: A CASE STUDY

If one measures the success of a joint venture by the current market value of the entity, then surely Himont must rank among the high achievers. The company is no longer a joint venture since the U.S. partner, Hercules, recently sold its share to the Italian partner, Montedison, for a reported after-tax gain of $600 million. However, the Himont case is illustrative of the considerable benefits of a well-conceived joint venture.

Himont today is the largest producer of the chemical polypropylene and is a major manufacturer and distributor of polypropylene-based products worldwide. This 50–50 joint venture resulted from the merging of the polypropylene businesses of Hercules and Montedison in November 1983 (later a 20 percent stake was sold to the public). The strategic motivations underlying this venture center on the marketing and distribution clout of Hercules and the technical expertise of its Italian counterpart. Specifically, in 1981 Montedison developed a more efficient process for mass polymerization, interestingly enough through another R&D joint venture with Mitsui Petrochemical Industries Ltd. This innovation, known commercially as the SPHERIPOL process, utilized new high-yield catalysts which reduced the amount of physical capital, raw material, and energy required to manufacture polypropylene, a very price-competitive commodity chemical. The new process also reduced the overall amount of pollution and unwanted residuals involved. Montedison contributed the rights and the technology to this joint venture as well as its current polypropylene production and marketing organizations.

Hercules, for its part, put up its considerable production capabilities (13 percent of world capacity versus 7 percent for Montedison), which fortunately could be cheaply converted to the new process. To balance the deal Hercules also received an equity share in a lucrative pharmaceutical company owned by Montedison and a cash payment.

This venture illustrates the many factors that enter into the joint-venture equation; in this case three primary motivational forces were involved:

1. Polypropylene products represent a commodity chemical business which is characterized by cutthroat competition and razor-thin margins. Before the joint venture both parents were dissatisfied with the financial performance of their polypropylene operations; in 1982 Hercules reportedly lost $9 million overall on plastic sales while Montedison had suffered a string of losing years. Thus, both partners had an incentive to combine their businesses in order to maximize scale economies and to rationalize their operations.

2. Hercules' polypropylene operations were not profitable, as noted earlier, so the introduction of cost-saving technology by a competitor would have placed them at an extreme disadvantage in the market. Therefore, being able to co-opt the competition through a joint venture would enable Hercules to realize the full value of its productive capacity by becoming a shareholder in the industry's new low-cost producer.

3. Montedison had a significant market presence in Europe, including a 30 percent share of the Italian market, but virtually no U.S. sales. Although Hercules produced and sold polypropylene abroad, it was not considered a major player overseas. Therefore, the venture provided access to new markets for both parents, making Himont a truly international competitor of significant proportions. Both parents hoped that this new market access would provide a means through which their high value-added products could also be sold overseas.

The venture proved to be very successful, with after-tax profit margins averaging over 8 percent and a return on equity of over 20 percent before their 1987 equity issue.

Part of Hercules' long-range strategy has been to reduce its presence in commodity chemicals. In other instances this would mean either (1) the gradual phase-out of physical plant and the reduction of the workforce as the product lost market share, or (2) the sale of the underperforming business entity, presumably at a lower earnings multiple. However, by capitalizing on Montedison's technical advances, Hercules was able to reinvigorate its polypropylene investment and divest itself of its interest at a very handsome profit. Thus the joint venture ultimately proved, for Hercules, to be an effective means of disinvestment from a mature industry.

CONCLUSION

With the increasing integration of world markets and the relentless increase in competitive pressures, the need for joint ventures as a means of corporate survival is mounting. As Peter Drucker observed:

> "The joint venture is the most flexible instrument for making fits out of misfits. It will become increasingly important. It is at the same time the most demanding and difficult of all tools of diversification, and the least understood."[1]

The strategic applications of joint ventures are indeed manifold; however, the success of such collaborative ventures is highly dependent

---

[1]Peter F. Drucker, *Management: Tasks, Responsibilities and Practices* (New York: Harper and Row, 1974), p. 720.

on the ability of the partners to build and maintain a mutually beneficial relationship. This can only be accomplished through the clear enunciation of both common and individual objectives and a coordinated strategy designed to exploit the collective strengths of the partners in meeting their respective aims.

CHAPTER 2

LEGAL CONSIDERATIONS OF JOINT VENTURES

Cary Levinson
James S. Lawlor
Pepper Hamilton, & Scheetz

INTRODUCTION

Planning a joint venture from a legal standpoint requires recognition at the outset that, despite the game attempts of a few scholars and jurists, no legally substantive distinction has been made between the joint venture and the business form which it takes. That is, no body of case or statutory law recognizes the joint venture as a form of business organization to which an insular set of rules apply. Rather, despite articulable arguments to the contrary, the joint venture will be evaluated for purposes of liabilities, fiduciary duties, and the like according to the standards of the legal pigeonhole into which it most nearly fits—be that corporation, partnership, or some hybrid form.

Structuring a joint venture, therefore, involves the same legal process as does structuring any business; anticipation of the legal issues and planning for them. Anticipation of the legal issues requires recognition of potential external legal liabilities, including antitrust law and liabilities to outside parties, as well as the internal legal issues incidental to relationships among the joint venturers. While the synergies of the venture will be of little consequence in predicting the external legal liabilities, planning for those liabilities often requires acute attention to the structure and dynamics of the relationship of the parties involved. In this section we will examine the types of issues which may be anticipated at the formation stage, and suggest that they are better planned for at the outset, than after they actually arise.

DISCUSSION

Scope of the Venture

When two or more independent business organizations agree to form an alliance for some specific purpose, they create duties and rights among themselves and also between the alliance and the third parties with which it deals. These rights and duties are distinct from those of the individual business components acting in their individual capacities. The venturers must be careful, therefore, to adequately define the scope and purposes of the venture. The venturers themselves should have a clear understanding of what activities are those of the venture and what activities they may pursue in their individual capacities. The parties should also have a clear understanding of which assets they will own jointly. Most importantly, these understandings should be documented at the outset so that not only the venturers, but a third party—perhaps a court—required to examine the issue at some later date, will clearly understand the scope of the venture.

The importance of a clear definition of scope can be shown by a simple illustration. Take for example, the type of joint venture discussed in the strategies chapter in which a research firm with strong technology teams up with an industrial enterprise which has manufacturing capabilities. Assume the research firm has the technology to develop light bulbs for use in the poultry industry, which would use ultraviolet rays to disinfect chickens and eggs in their coops. The manufacturer has the ability to make the bulbs. They form an alliance to share their resources. Does the manufacturing firm have a right to participate when the research firm develops an application of the same technology for use in vegetable hothouses? What if the technology is one day applied in the medical profession and a large market develops for hospital lights? Will these products be within the scope of the venture, or is the research firm free to find other manufacturers for these applications? In a more drastic case, what if the technological member of the venture develops technology that will compete with or render obsolete the product manufactured by the venture? Should further developments of the technology be considered opportunities for the venture, or only for the individual venturer?

The issue of the scope of the venture will also arise in the context involving rights other than those of the venturers themselves. For instance, in a manufacturing-distribution venture, what will happen if the distributor, in delivering products of the venture, as well as goods it distributes in its individual capacity, causes injury to an outside party? The injured party will be interested in the issue of whether the injury was caused within the scope of the venture, thus permitting actions against the venture as well as its parents.

While the law provides answers in some cases, setting rights as between the venturers themselves and between the venture and the third parties with which it deals, difficult issues may be avoided by a clear definition of the scope of the venture at the outset. The parties may choose to place specific limitations on the product involved, the duration of the venture, the product market which it will serve, the geographic market, or even a specific customer the venture will serve (*e.g.,* U.S. Government). Of course, the parties may be equally clear regarding the scope of their venture by providing that it covers all markets, all new products, and so forth. Defining the scope is not likely to be a simple task, and each particular venture has its own facts to which the parties must be sensitive. At the formative stages, however, the venturers have to anticipate the future growth of the venture and their individual businesses. They should discuss and decide the extent to which their operations will be allied, and the extent to which they will retain their rights as separate business organizations.

Capitalization

At the handshake stage, the joint venturers will probably have an understanding of what each will contribute to the venture at the outset. The new venture may be capitalized with any combination of cash, equipment, real property, management skills, patents, and so forth. Beyond the initial contribution determination, the venturers have to consider the consequences of their capital contributions, and what they will do in the future when additional capital is required.

The primary consequence of the initial contribution is that it provides the basis for apportionment of participation interests in the venture. This is a relatively simple mathematical matter when both parties contribute cash. When assets other than cash are contributed, the venturers must reach an agreement regarding the value of those assets. Valuation, of course, will involve negotiation. The contributing venturers should bear in mind that the valuation will impact the amount of control the contributing party is able to exercise over the venture and the extent to which it may share in profits and proceeds. Additionally, the value of its contribution may impact its own internal accounting and bookkeeping. These considerations may have an impact on the nature of the venturers' contribution. For instance, a venturer who owns a patent may decide to contribute the patent to the venture, rather than merely license the venture to use the patent, in order to obtain a higher valuation of his contribution and thus attain a greater right to the control and proceeds of the venture.

Another issue incidental to the initial capitalization decision is its impact on future capital requirements. If the parties are to maintain the proportions of interest they own at the outset, they will have to meet future capital requirements on a proportionate basis. Each party should consider at the outset whether it will be able to satisfy the obligation to fund future growth in proportion to its original interest. The determination is a tricky one even when both parties are contributing cash, but in some cases it will be clear that one party will not be able to shoulder its proportionate share of any future capitalization burden.

Take for instance, the typical "brains-and-money" venture. One party has a patent and the other party has the financial ability to fund the start-up of a production facility. They agree that the value of the patent is equal to the amount they anticipate will be needed for the facility. They agree to make their respective contributions and form a venture in which each will have a 50 percent interest. It turns out that the facility costs 10 percent more than anticipated and the patent party is still cashless. What are the consequences if the money party pays the additional funds? There are three possibilities: the parties could agree that half the additional money is a loan from the money party to the patent party which will be repaid in some agreed-upon fashion (likely from profits); they could agree that the patent be revalued to equal the actual amount of cash paid for the facility; or they could decide that the money partner now has a greater interest in the venture than the other. If the determination is made at this stage of the game, the money partner is likely to have the power to force the third result.

The parties are able to plan for this eventuality at the outset, when they have more equal bargaining power. Each party should assess what it will need or want in a future capitalization requirement. The party with greater resources should consider the likelihood that it will be the only party able to provide cash to the venture when it hits hard times. The party with fewer resources should consider the risk of losing control to the other party as that party funds the growth of a profitable venture. With the consequences of future capital needs in mind, the parties may develop a plan which accommodates both their interests.

Setting aside for moment the issue of how the parties will agree that additional capital is necessary (See the Dispute Resolution section of this chapter), the parties may agree that when such a determination is made it will have specific consequences. A typical arrangement will provide that each party initially has the right to contribute its proportionate share of the additional requirement. Beyond that, the parties may agree that each party will have the right to contribute that portion of the other party's share as that party may be unable or unwilling to contribute. With a structure such as that, the parties should also determine whether the consequence of one party's larger contribution will be a loan to the other party, or a dilution of the other party's interest. Other typical provisions could limit the amount parties would be required to contribute, either over a specified period of time or in the aggregate; specify that additional amounts be borrowed; or delineate circumstances in which additional capital may be raised by adding a new venturer.

Given the fact that when additional capital will be needed, the venture will either be struggling, or have an opportunity for growth, it makes sense to facilitate the capitalization process at the outset. It would be an injustice to allow a staggering venture to fall, or a growth opportunity to pass, because infighting among venturers hampered their ability to raise the capital necessary to bolster the venture or seize the opportunity.

Formation

As noted in the introduction, a joint venture is not recognized as a separate form of business organization to which an insular set of laws apply. Rather, each venture is analyzed according to the laws pertaining to the form which that venture takes. Thus, at the outset the joint venturers have to select the form of business enterprise. As discussed below, different forms of business have different consequences in terms of taxability, liability to other parties, control of the business, and duties between the co-venturers. Venturers should examine these consequences, select a form of business which is most suitable to their needs, and proceed according to the rules for that form.

An appropriate starting point is a partnership, because courts treat joint ventures according to partnership laws unless the joint venture has specifically taken a different form. Rights and duties of partners are prescribed by state partnership acts as well as common-law rules. Partners usually are given rights in the partnership property, rights in the partnership interest, and rights to participate in management of the business. The right to partnership property means, among other things that, if the joint venture is a partnership, each venturer has the right to possess the venture's property for business purposes. Thus, in the situation where one venturer contributes a manufacturing plant and the other supplies raw materials, the manufacturing partner may not prevent the supplier from proceeding past the delivery dock. Also, any property purchased with profits of the venture belongs to all the co-venturers proportionately. As a corollary to the partnership-property rule, no partner is permitted to sell or otherwise alienate (*e.g.*, by mortgage) partnership property without the consent of the other partner(s).

The interest in the partnership protected by law is the right of the partners to receive proportionate shares of the profits and to share proportionately in any distribution of them at dissolution. Of course, partners may agree to a different form of distribution of profits. Partners are also entitled by law to proportionate control over the management of the business. Even if the partners agree among themselves that only one will manage, that arrangement is not binding to a third party who does business with the nonmanaging partner. As a corollary to this rule it is generally held that any partner may bind the partnership to a contract which is reasonably designed to be for the business purpose of the partnership. The effect of the rule is that one venturer may bind the other without the other's consent. Using similar reasoning, a negligent act by a partner in the scope of the partnership's business creates liability for the partnership for which all partners are responsible.

One major consideration in determining whether a joint venture should exist as a partnership is the rule that each partner is individually liable, without limitation, for the liabilities of the partnership. If a tort liability, for instance, exceeds the value of the venture, the venturing entities would be liable individually and together on the unsatisfied portion of the judgment, even after the dissolution of the venture. The same rule applies to liabilities on contracts formed for a purpose related to the partnership's business. Of course, partners may insure against liabilities and cross-indemnify one another for the liabilities each may create for the others.

A form of business which limits the partners' potential liability is the limited partnership. In this form of business, one general partner retains all the rights and liabilities as described above. The other partners are known as limited partners and their exposure to liability is limited to the extent of their investment. The price the limited partners pay for this limited liability, however, is that they have no right to manage the business. Thus, the limited partner is almost relegated to investor status. The absence of management control will often make the limited partnership an inadequate form for the venturers to take. Arguably, the absence of mutual control makes the limited partnership and the joint venture mutually exclusive types of businesses by definition.

The joint venture may be, and very often is, separately incorporated. The corporate form offers several benefits. Share ownership provides a convenient method for delineating ownership interests and rights of control. The shareholders of a corporation are responsible for the corporation's liability only to the extent of share ownership. In the case of a joint venture, the venturers would become shareholders of their joint project and be at risk of loss only to the extent of their investment in it. On the issue of control, the incorporated venture will act through its board of directors. When incorporating the venture, the venturers will have great flexibility in establishing a board which meets its particular needs for delegation of the authority to make decisions for the corporation. When the venture is operating in the corporate form, only the appropriate corporate officers may make contracts which bind it, and thus there is less risk that one venturer will establish a liability unknown to another. Also, the venture's property will be the property of the corporation and, thus, may only be sold or disposed of through an act of the corporation, in which the shareholders (the venturers) would be likely to participate.

On the downside, corporation law is more complex and regulated than is partnership law. Also the shield from liability is not impenetrable. The venturers may be individually liable for the debts of the venture if the venture is incorporated without sufficient capital. Also, when the venture operates as a corporation its profits are taxed once as its income, and then when profits are passed on to the venturer as stockholder dividends, they are taxed again as income for the venturer.

Given the divergent consequences which follow the selection of a business form, the venturers should weigh several factors before selecting one. They should consider the venture's potential exposure to liability and determine whether it is so significant that a form which will limit it should be selected. They should also consider the extent to which they desire the authority to act on the venture's behalf, and similarly, the extent to which they wish their co-venturers to possess that same authority. They should also consider the amount of input they want to have into management decisions of the corporation, and indeed whether they want hands-on management control.

Antitrust

If a joint venture violates antitrust laws, it faces the possibility of civil and criminal penalties, and even the dissolution of the venture. Given these dire consequences, the last thing the venturers want is uncertainty as to the venture's status under the antitrust laws. Unfortunately, that is what they are most likely to get. Inconsistencies in interpretation between the Department of Justice and the Federal Trade Commission, the two bodies charged with enforcing antitrust laws, along with ever-changing enforcement policies and the possibility of private lawsuits make it very difficult to predict whether any given joint venture will attract an antitrust action. If a planned venture raises any of the general antitrust concerns discussed below, the venturers will do well to undertake a full analysis of the issue prior to formation. In-depth analysis will be required on an individual basis because the spectrum of potential joint ventures is so broad that it is impossible to generalize about their status as a class. This discussion focuses on the general types of antitrust-law concerns.

In a recent speech delivered at the American Bar Association's National Institute on Joint Ventures, Robert Pitofsky, Dean and Professor of Law at Georgetown University Law Center, provided a framework of antitrust analysis of joint ventures. That analysis was reprinted in an article in 1986 in the *Georgetown Law Journal*. Professor Pitofsky points out that joint ventures are an uncertain subject of antitrust enforcement. He goes on, however, to suggest that since the primary purpose of the antitrust laws is to curtail activities which have an anticompetitive effect on the marketplace, the joint-venture analysis generally involves a balancing between the anticompetitive effects of a joint venture and the economic efficiencies that it achieves. Below are some of the potential anticompetitive effects which Pitofsky discusses. Would-be venturers should examine their proposed alliance to see if it will produce any of these anticompetitive effects.

The principal antitrust concern with respect to the formation of a joint ventures is the possibility that the venture will reduce competition in its market. (The determination of the appropriate market is a complex legal issue beyond the scope of this handbook.) In determining whether the venture will lessen competition, courts will look to what the parent corporations would have done had it not been for the joint venture. An antitrust challenge is most likely where, as a result of a joint venture, a single entity is in a marketplace in which there had been two separate competitors. In order for a venture of this kind to withstand an antitrust challenge, the venturers have to show that the efficiencies produced by the combination could not be achieved independently by the two ventures acting separately, and also that those efficiencies outweigh the elimination of competition between the two parties. In some cases, however, even such a joint venture may not raise concerns if it is limited in time or scope in such a way that the anticompetitive effects are limited.

Another potential anticompetitive arrangement, which produces somewhat of a gray area, is the situation where one of the joint venturers is already established in a marketplace and the other is not but could possibly enter the market at some point. The participation of the second joint venturer means that it will never enter the market separately, and, thus, will no longer be perceived as a company which threatens to enter. That threat of potential competition is generally considered to be a competitive asset in the marketplace. Nonetheless, current antitrust analysis treats the "in-the-wings company" situation very leniently. It is not very likely, although it is possible, that a joint venture of this type will run afoul of the antitrust laws.

Another type of anticompetitive effect, different from reduced competition between the parents, is known as the "stifling effect" on the market. The effect of a joint venture may be that each parent will refrain from market activity in which it would have engaged had it not been for the venture. Since the joint-venture parents will very rarely compete with the venture itself, nearly all joint ventures will have this stifling effect. That is, a company is not likely to enter a joint venture to produce a certain product and then produce the same product itself. The enforcing agencies, therefore, tend to recognize that disallowing joint ventures because of the stifling effect would greatly inhibit the development of joint ventures. Their response, therefore, has been to wait and see whether the stifling effects of the joint venture at some later point develop into problems of monopolization or other anticompetitive activity.

MURDOCK LEARNING RESOURCE CENTER

The third potential antitrust problem of joint ventures is that they provide great potential for the facilitation of collusive activities between the parents. In the course of organizing or operating the venture, the parents may exchange internal information regarding prices, production capacity, sales volume, and other information pertaining to the venture. The exchange of internal information of that sort is often the means of collusion between parties, and such an effect by a joint venture may attract the attention of antitrust enforcing agents. Under the antitrust laws, the opportunity to conspire is treated as circumstantial evidence supporting the inference of collusion, but it not adequate in itself to show collusion.

Antitrust concerns also arise out of the agreements which the joint venturers make between themselves in forming the joint venture. Those agreements almost always limit or specify the ways in which the ventures will compete with one another and with the venture. While this type of agreement may be illegal in isolation, it is generally permitted to the extent that it is necessary to further the purposes of a venture if the agreement is no broader in scope than is required. For instance, the type of agreement as to scope discussed earlier in this chapter, in which venturers agree to cooperate in future market developments, might be illegal if made between two nonventuring businesses but will generally be considered valid between co-venturers. Venturers therefore have to be careful in drafting their joint-venture agreements. Agreement provisions which exceed the required scope for the venture may be struck down separately as antitrust violations, but they may also jeopardize the entire venture itself.

As noted above, the anticompetitive effects in any case will be balanced against the various procompetitive effects which the joint venture may accomplish. These include joint bargaining power, the use of existing assets, joint operation in producing new facilities, and other restrictions relating to achieving efficiencies. The foregoing discussion of antitrust concerns and joint venturers is painted with a very broad brush. Almost any contemplated joint venture will raise some sort of question regarding its anticompetitive effects. While the 1980s saw a very relaxed, in some cases almost nonexistent, approach to antitrust enforcement with regard to joint ventures, the underlying law remains significantly broad to encompass joint-venture transactions. Based on the general discussion above, joint ventures should examine the effects of their proposed venture, and in many cases will want to undertake a more detailed analysis of antitrust compliance.

Dispute Resolution

Even the most optimistic of joint venturers are hard-pressed to deny that at some point, regarding some issue, the venturing parties will find themselves in dispute. As the management chapter indicates, one of the key ingredients in a successful venture is the like-mindedness of the parents. But, when tough issues surface which upset the overall harmony of the venture, a mechanism should be in place to assure that the venture's operation is not disrupted. In establishing such a dispute-resolution mechanism, the parties should appreciate that not all disputes are created equal and different categories of disputes require different planning.

One category of potential dispute involves disagreement over the operation or management of the day-to-day business of the joint venture. Often a joint venture will have a management team composed of personnel from each of the parent companies. One sure way to avoid disputes between these two management groups is to clearly delineate the responsibilities of each, and the areas in which each set of managers has final say. But, when disputes do arise between management personnel, they should be handled in-house, relatively quickly, and pursuant to a set procedure. One possible procedure is to involve the parent companies in breaking the impasse. In many cases the venturers themselves will have a broader perspective on the problem and will be likely to be able to resolve it amicably. In cases where such an amicable resolution is not possible, there should be some voting procedure involving a neutral party to resolve the dispute. If the venture is separately incorporated, the neutral party may be a director who is appointed mutually, at the outset, by the joint venturers. The incorporated venture could have a board of directors with equal representation of the two venturers, and an additional person appointed by them jointly. In any event, the final say on management issues should lie with either one person, or with a committee with an odd number of members. Since a management impasse could grind the joint venture to a halt, disputes involving management issues require procedures which are certain of result, and can be rapidly implemented.

A second type of dispute in which the venturers might find themselves involves their respective rights to the profits and so forth of the joint venture. These rights may arise by virtue of the joint-venture agreement, or through fiduciary duties imposed by law. (See the Fiduciary Duties section of this chapter.) A dispute of this nature does not usually interfere with the day-to-day operations of the joint venture. Generally, the venturers will be able to sort out the rights between themselves while the venture itself continues operating. For that reason disputes of this nature may be resolved by a more thorough procedure. The parties may always resort to the court system to resolve any disputes based on their contract or their common-law duties. However, many joint venturers, as well as partnerships and corporations, find some form of alternative dispute resolution more appropriate for disputes of this nature. The joint venturers may agree ahead of time to arbitrate disputes between themselves, involve a third-party mediator to facilitate negotiation, or select some similar procedure. Usually, if a contract provides for arbitration or some other form of dispute resolution, that provision in the contract will be an affirmative defense to an action at law based on a dispute to which the provision applies. That is, the court will require the parties to resolve the dispute pursuant to their agreed-upon means. An ever-increasing number of free enterprise fora for the private resolution of disputes are available to facilitate such an arrangement. These services are often less time-consuming, less expensive, and produce more satisfactory results than litigation in the court system.

In establishing the right to arbitration or to alternative dispute resolution, the parties should keep in mind that the court system will only require arbitration if it can find clear evidence that the parties agreed to arbitrate the particular dispute in question. In negotiating an arbitration provision, therefore, the parties must clearly delineate the types and nature of disputes to which the arbitration remedy will apply.

The third and most drastic category of potential disputes arises when the venturers disagree on a fundamental issue regarding the future of the joint venture. In the least complicated case, one venturer will want the joint venture to continue operations and the other will want operations to cease. In anticipating that dispute, the venturers may simple provide that, should it arise, one party has a right to buy the interest of the other. But more complex disputes may arise if one venturer would like the venture to enter new product markets or geographic markets, or expand the venture's scope in some other way, and the other venturer does not agree. The only workable way to deal with disputes of this nature, albeit not a satisfactory one in all cases, is for the venturers at the outset to make the consequences of nonagreement so dire that they force themselves to agree. Namely, the venturers may agree at the outset that if such an impasse as to the future of the venture occurs, they will dissolve the venture. Alternatively, they may provide that one venturer will have the right to buy the share of the other. The major weakness with this dispute-resolution strategy is that it gives a strong advantage to a venturer who decides that he would like to see the venture dissolved, or would like to buy his partner's or sell his share of the venture.

Joint venturers can expect at the outset that somewhere along the line they will disagree on some issue. There are strategies available for handling these disputes so that they do not cripple the joint venture. Venturers should plan such dispute-resolution tactics at the outset, to avoid that consequence.

Fiduciary Duties

By the act of entering into a joint venture, the venturers impose fiduciary duties upon one another. The extent of these duties was eloquently stated by one of our nation's great jurists, Judge Benjamin Cardoza, in 1928. In the case of *Meinhard v. Salmon,* Judge Cardoza said:

> Joint adventurers, like co-partners, owe to one another, while the enterprise continues, the duty of the finest loyalty. Many forms of conduct permissible in a workaday world for those acting at arms' length, are forbidden to those bound by fiduciary ties. A trustee is held to something stricter than the morals of the marketplace. Not honesty alone, but the punctilio of an honor the most sensitive, is then the standard of behavior. As to this there has developed a tradition that is unbending and inveterate. Uncompromising rigidity has been the attitude of courts of equity when petitioned to undermine the rule of undivided loyalty by the "dissentegrating erosion" of particular exceptions. . . . Only thus has the level of conduct for fiduciaries been kept at a level higher than that trodden by the crowd.

Such an exacting standard can be often violated and not always intentionally so. In a recent article, Professor Zenichi Shishido, of the Seikei University in Japan, concluded that fiduciary duty problems in joint ventures arise in three general types of situations: self-dealing, corporate opportunity conflicts, and disclosure conflicts. The author noted that often fiduciary duty problems arise because there will be directors from the parent corporations who also serve as directors of the joint venture. Such directors owe fiduciary duties to both the joint venture and the parent company simultaneously. When the interests of the parent and the joint venture conflict, the interlocking director is put in contradictory fiduciary duty positions. By agreement, the parent companies may significantly reduce at the outset the risk of fidicuary duty violations between them in the course of the operation.

Self-dealing conflicts arise when a joint venture does business with a parent company. If the deal is overly favorable to either the parent or the joint venture, the director sitting on both boards will almost by definition have breached his fiduciary duty to the entity which got the less favorable terms of the deal. More importantly, if the parent company got the favorable terms, its co-venturer has a very strong argument that the deal was designed to pass joint-venture profits along to the self-dealing venturer in opposition to whatever agreement was in place for the distribution of those profits.

Professor Shishido cited the joint venture between General Motors and Toyota as an example of a joint venture with a possible self-dealing conflict. Toyota has the exclusive right to supply parts to the joint venture, while GM has the exclusive right to purchase and distribute finished cars. Toyota could be in the position to charge the joint venture high prices for parts thus reducing the profit pool on the finished product, while General Motors may be in a position to buy the finished car at lower prices and in that way affect the profits of the joint venture.

The second type of fiduciary duty problem is the business-opportunity dilemma. In this situation the parent and the joint venture do not deal with one another, they compete for the same business. If the parent corporation has access to a business opportunity, it is likely to want to seize it for itself, but the fiduciary duties imposed by law may require it to offer the opportunity to the joint venture. The determination of which company may take the opportunity involves some analysis. Part of the solution may be a clear definition of the scope of the joint venture, as discussed in the first section of this chapter. But even with such a clear definition of scope, technological developments, market developments, and so forth may lead to a situation in which a business opportunity is appropriate both for the parent and the joint venture. Typical situations involve the opportunity to purchase a business which will be attractive to the joint venture and the parent, and the opportunity to enter markets in which neither the parent nor the joint venture currently compete.

The third problem created by the duties of loyalty imposed on the joint venturers involves the duty of fiduciaries to share information. The problem arises when a director of a joint venture has information about the joint venture or the parent company, or when the parent company has sole access to information that is necessary in the operation of the joint venture. The interests of the joint-venture conflict with those of the parent company, because the disclosure of information may be beneficial to one and harmful to the other.

Professor Shishido again cites the General Motors/Toyota joint venture as an example. When the joint venture determines the price for the Nova which it produces, the joint venture has an interest in the cost information regarding Toyota's product, the Corolla. Disclosure of that information, however, is contrary to Toyota's interests. The interlocking directors on the Toyota board and the joint-venture board are in an inherently contradictory position. That is, disclosure will harm Toyota whereas nondisclosure will harm the venture.

Professor Shishido argues in his article that the law should recognize the position that the interlocking directors are put in, and reduce the fiduciary duties owed to the joint venture. Until the law takes that course, venturers, at the outset, may modify the duties between themselves. For instance, the joint venturers may agree that before any self-dealing contract between one parent and the joint venture is executed, the terms of the contract will be approved by the other parent companies. Similarly, they may provide for a ratification vote when such a contract is in effect. To reduce disclosure problems the companies may agree to a list of mandatory disclosures prior to creating the joint venture. Similarly, the best solution to resolving corporate-opportunity conflicts is to create express agreements prior to forming the venture. (See the discussion of scope in this chapter.) Beyond this, the parties may put in place a system for compensating the joint venture when it is harmed by the usurpation of a joint-venture opportunity by one of the parents.

In summary, joint venturers should carefully examine the types of business in which they are involved, the nature and scope of the joint venture's business, and the areas in which these interests might compete. Since the law will impose fiduciary duties upon the parent companies with regard both to the venture and to one another, they should try to facilitate those duties in their joint-venture agreement.

CONCLUSION

Potential participants in a joint venture must recognize at the outset the legal ramifications of the formation of the venture. They should know that they are entering into a potentially adversarial relationship with one another. The parties may realistically anticipate the legal issues which will arise in the course of the venture. At the outset, they should reasonably formulate methods for dealing with future issues, and for avoiding or resolving internal disputes. They may also anticipate the liabilities that the venture will face in terms of outside parties, regulatory agencies, and the antitrust laws. These, too, may be resolved at the formation of the venture by proper planning and structuring. Having anticipated and planned for external and internal conflicts, the venturers minimize the impact should those eventualities occur.

CHAPTER 3

ACCOUNTING CONSIDERATIONS

Barry P. Robbins
Price Waterhouse

ACCOUNTING FOR THE VENTURE INVESTMENT

The Financial Accounting Standards Board (FASB) currently has a major project on its technical agenda entitled, ''The Reporting Entity, Including Consolidations and the Equity Method.'' Conceptual issues of when to use full consolidation, the equity method and pro-rata consolidation, and many application problems, are to be considered. As part of the project, the FASB has established a special task force to advise the board on accounting issues related to joint-venture investments. Until new accounting standards in this area are issued by the FASB (not expected until at least 1989), the following guidelines are appropriate. Joint venturers should, however, monitor the status of this major FASB project.

There are presently four possible ways, under U.S. generally accepted accounting principles, for an entity to account for its ownership interest in another entity: consolidation, equity method, cost method, and pro rata consolidation. The selection of a particular method is not a free choice; the appropriate method depends on the relationship between the investor and the investee.

Consolidation

The circumstances under which consolidation is appropriate are set forth in Statement of Financial Accounting Standards No. 94, ''Consolidation of All Majority-Owned Subsidiaries,'' (FAS 94) which was issued by the FASB in October 1987. FAS 94 states that the consolidation method generally should be followed when the investor owns a majority voting interest in the common stock of the investee. The only exception to this rule is when the control usually embodied in ownership of a majority voting interest is either temporary or does not rest with the majority owner (for instance, when the subsidiary is in legal reorganization or in bankruptcy). Although FAS 94 addresses only corporate investments, its principle of control over the operating and financing policies of the investee is usually applied to determine if consolidation is appropriate for investments in noncorporate entities as well.

Under the consolidation method, the specific assets and liabilities of the investee are included in the balance sheet of the investor, and the specific revenues and expenses of the investee are included in the investor's income statement. The investor's financial statements become consolidated financial statements. That portion of the investee's net assets and earnings allocable to other investors is shown in the consolidated financial statements as minority interest (a quasi-liability in the balance sheet; a quasi-expense in the income statement).

Equity Method

The equity method of accounting for an investment in another entity is appropriate in those circumstances in which the investor has the ability to exercise significant influence over the investee, but does not control the investee. Most joint-venture arrangements give each investor significant influence, but give no single investor unilateral control. Accordingly, the equity method of accounting will generally be appropriate for most joint-venture relationships.

Accounting Principles Board Opinion No. 18, ''The Equity Method of Accounting for Investments in Common Stock,'' (APB 18) is the authoritative accounting literature on this subject. It states that ''investors should account for investments in common stock of corporate joint ventures by the equity method.'' (This assumes that the investor does not have unilateral control.) Often the equity method is also used for investments in noncorporate joint ventures, such as partnerships. In all cases, a careful review of the joint-venture agreement is necessary to understand precisely the rights of each of the joint venturers. Only with this knowledge can the appropriate accounting method be determined.

The equity method is, essentially, an extension of the consolidation concept. Generally, the investor's net income for the period and its shareholders' equity at the end of the period are the same, whether an investee is consolidated or accounted for by the equity method. The difference between the two approaches lies in the details reported in the financial statements. The carrying amount of an investment under the equity method is initially recorded at cost and reported as a single-line item in the investor's balance sheet. Adjustments are made to the carrying amount to recognize the investor's share of the earnings or losses of the investee subsequent to the date of investment. The amount of the increase or decrease is included in the determination of net income by the investor, and this amount is generally reported as a single-line item in the investor's income statement. Dividends received by the investor are applied as a reduction of the carrying amount of the investment.

Cost Method

The cost method of accounting for an investment in another entity should be followed in situations where the investor neither controls nor has the ability to exercise significant influence over the investee. Due to the nature of most joint-venture arrangements, this accounting method is rarely appropriate. However, there may be circumstances in which the control or significant influence normally possessed by the investor has been lost, due, for example, to severe and prolonged foreign exchange restrictions imposed on the joint venture by a foreign government. The cost method would then be appropriate.

Applying the cost method is fairly easy. The investor records its investment at cost, and reports the investment as a single-line on its balance sheet, similar to an investment carried under the equity method. Unlike the equity method, however, the investor recognizes as income the dividends received that are distributed from the net accumulated earnings of the investee since the date of acquisition by the investor. In other words, the investor recognizes its share of investee earnings only when such earnings are distributed by the investee. Dividends received in excess of earnings subsequent to the date of investment are considered a return of investment and are recorded as reductions of the cost of the investment.

Pro Rata Consolidation

In the case of noncorporate joint ventures in which the investor owns an undivided interest in each asset and is proportionately liable for its share of each liability (i.e., no legal entity exists between the investor and the assets and liabilities of the venture), the presentation in the investor's financial statements should reflect the investor's pro rata share of each of the venture's assets, liabilities, revenues and expenses (rather than the one-line treatment called for by the equity method). This is referred to as pro rata consolidation.

INITIAL RECORDING OF THE JOINT-VENTURE INVESTMENT

In this section, it is assumed that the investor follows the equity method of accounting for its investment in the joint venture (the most common situation).

As noted above, the investor initially records its joint-venture investment at cost. When the contribution to the joint venture is cash, the accounting is easy—the investment equals the amount of cash contributed.

Sometimes, however, appreciated noncash assets, such as real estate or mineral properties, are contributed to a newly formed joint venture in exchange for an equity interest when others have invested cash or other "hard" assets. The fair value of the noncash assets is usually used in (a) establishing the contributor's ownership percentage or participation in the joint venture and (b) the joint-venture financial statements. Generally, the cost at which the investment is initially recorded is the investor's carrying value of the noncash assets contributed, not their fair value. It is sometimes argued, however, that the investor contributing noncash assets and not having a continuing involvement (i.e., not acting as general partner, manager, lessee, financier, debt guarantor, or in a similar capacity) has effectively realized a part of the appreciation as a result of its interest in the venture to which others contributed cash or other "hard" assets.

Accounting practice is unsettled in this area. Statement of Position 78–9 of the American Institute of Certified Public Accountants, "Accounting for Investments in Real Estate Ventures," (paragraph 30) prohibits recognition of profit on contribution of appreciated real estate.

However, the same economic results are achieved if the investee sells its own shares to third parties at a price above the investor's average carrying amount per share; the investor would recognize a gain in such a case. Proposals to recognize gain on contribution of assets to a joint venture should be considered carefully. Income should not be recognized on receipt of an interest in a joint venture if some or all of the investor's interest was received for know-how or future services to be rendered.

In situations where appreciated noncash assets are contributed to a joint venture but the gain is not recognized upon contribution, the gain should be recognized in the future as the noncash assets are used by the joint venture. For example, assume that Company A contributes a plant with a net book value of $400,000 and a fair value of $1,000,000; Company B contributes $1,000,000 cash. Each investor receives a 50 percent interest in the joint venture. Company A's inherent gain of $600,000 would be recognized over the estimated useful life of the plant, as used by the joint venture, to the extent the gain is not recognized upon contribution.

It is, of course, possible that a loss in value of a noncash asset will be indicated by an investor capital contribution thereof. Suppose that an investor contributes a plant carried at $10,000,000 for an undivided one-third interest in a joint venture to which two other venturers each contribute $8,000,000 in cash. This situation indicates that the investor contributing the plant should recognize a loss of $2,000,000. The $16,000,000 cash contribution for a two-thirds interest in the joint venture is evidence that the value of the one-third interest received for the plant is only $8,000,000.

TRANSACTIONS WITH A JOINT VENTURE

From time to time, the investor may sell assets to the joint venture (e.g., inventory or fixed assets) or the venture may sell assets to the investor. The accounting issue raised in these situations is the extent to which profit on such sales should be eliminated in the investor's financial statements.

When an investor sells assets to the venture, complete elimination of the intercompany profit is appropriate if the investor is in a position to (or does) exercise effective control over the business policies of the investee, because the intercompany transactions in such cases are not normally considered at arm's length even though they are expressed in terms of objective market prices. If the investor does not exercise effective control over the investee, profit should be eliminated to the extent of the investor's ownership interest in the investee. In all cases, any deferred profit should be recognized when the venture sells the assets (e.g., inventories) to third parties or uses the assets (e.g., fixed assets) in operations.

Since an investor cannot recognize profit on a sale of assets to itself, the investor should defer its proportionate share of the profit realized by the venture on a sale of assets to the investor. The deferred profit should be treated as a reduction in the carrying amount of the purchased property and recognized as the asset is depreciated or sold to a third party.

VARYING PROFIT SPLITS

In some instances, noncorporate joint-venture agreements may designate different splits among the venturers of GAAP profit and loss, taxable profit and loss, distributions of cash from operations, and distributions of cash proceeds on liquidation. Also, one or more of the splits may change with the lapse of time or the occurrence of specified events.

Because of varying profit splits, the accounting for a venturer's equity in venture earnings must be considered with care. Particular attention must be paid to the possibility that the split of profit and loss specified in the agreement may be solely for tax purposes or that it may not be substantive. The profit split specified in the agreement is not substantive when the split of cash distributions, both from operations and in liquidation, is determined on some basis other than the profit split. The specified GAAP profit split is substantive only when cash distributions in liquidation are based on the balances in the venturers' capital accounts after all previous profits and losses, including profit or loss on liquidation, have been recorded. Even when the GAAP profit split will be ultimately reflected in cash payouts upon liquidation, the earnings accruing to the investor may have to be reduced to an estimate of present value, if the investor must await liquidation at some indefinite future time.

Most arrangements with varying profit splits are partnerships. For tax purposes, distributive shares of taxable profit and loss are reported by the individual investors. Equity in investee earnings must be determined on a pre-tax basis. A realistic approach to determining the share of the investee's pre-tax income (loss) accruing to an individual investor under GAAP is to consider how any reported increment (decrement) in net assets will ultimately affect cash payments to the investor, whether over the life of the venture or in liquidation.

ADJUSTING JOINT-VENTURE FINANCIAL STATEMENTS

APB 18 makes clear that "earnings or losses of an investee" and "financial position of an investee" must be determined in accordance with accounting principles generally accepted in the United States (U.S. GAAP) for purposes of applying the equity method. There are three types of adjustments to U.S. GAAP which should be considered:

1. Foreign accounting principles which differ materially from U.S. GAAP. In such cases, the investor should arrange for investee financial statements prepared in accordance with U.S. GAAP or it should obtain the information necessary to adjust the investee statements to U.S. GAAP.

2. Investee financial statements prepared in accordance with accounting principles of a regulatory agency, whose principles differ from GAAP. Such statements should be adjusted to GAAP for purposes of applying the equity method in a similar manner to the adjustments described above.

3. Investee financial statements prepared in accordance with GAAP which use accounting principles that differ from those followed by the investor. Normally the financial statements of a minority-owned investee prepared in accordance with GAAP need not be adjusted when the investor follows alternative GAAP in accounting for similar items in its financial statements. There may be circumstances, however, in which the investee adopts accounting principles principally for the purpose of minimizing income taxes. The investor may believe that alternative accounting principles more fairly present its equity in the income and net assets of the investee. In such cases, adjustments may be made by the investor (not reflected in the investee financial statements) to reflect the more appropriate principles in determining its equity in income of the investee. Each situation should be carefully considered.

LAG IN JOINT-VENTURE REPORTING

There may be situations in which a joint venture, accounted for by the equity method or consolidation method, cannot prepare financial statements (or have them audited) quickly enough for use in the investor's financial reporting. This may occur, for example, with joint ventures in foreign countries. Both Accounting Research Bulletin No. 51, "Consolidated Financial Statements," and APB 18 provide for this circumstance. APB 18, paragraph 19g, states: "If financial statements of an investee are not sufficiently timely for an investor to apply the equity method currently, the investor ordinarily should record its share of earnings or losses of an investee from the most recent available financial statements."

The word *ordinarily* was intended to permit the use of financial statements of the investee as of a date earlier than the date of the "most recent available" financial statements if the earlier date is the investee's fiscal year end or a date for which audited financial statements are available. The difference in fiscal periods should normally not be more than three months and, when a lag is necessary, recognition should be given, by disclosure or other method, to the effect of any known intervening events which materially affect the financial position or results of operations.

JOINT-VENTURE LOSSES

An investor's share of losses of an investee may exceed the carrying amount of an investment (including advances made by the investor) accounted for under the equity method. Two alternative accounting procedures must be considered for possible application in these situations: (1) recognize the investor's share of investee losses in excess of the carrying amount of the investment or 2) discontinue recognition of the investor's share of investee losses when the investment is reduced to zero.

Judgment will usually be required as to whether losses in excess of carrying amount should be recognized. APB 18 states, "The investor ordinarily should discontinue applying the equity method when the investment (and net advances) is reduced to zero and should not provide for additional losses unless the investor has guaranteed obligations of the investee or is otherwise committed to provide further financial support for the investee." Thus, while stating a general presumption that losses should not be recognized in excess of the investment, it is clearly recognized that recognition of losses in excess of the amount of the investment is appropriate in some circumstances. Examples of these circumstances include: (a) legal obligations (e.g., as guarantor or general partner), (b) quasi-legal obligations, based on such factors as business reputation, intercompany relationships, and credit standing, (c) a presumption supported by past performance that the investor would make good venture obligations, (d) public statements that the investor intends to support venture operations, (e) the imminent return to profitable operations by the venture seems assured.

The investor's balance sheet credit arising from recognition of losses in excess of investment should be classified as a liability. When investee losses in excess of investment are not recognized and the investee subsequently reports net income, the investor should resume applying the equity method only after its share of that net income equals the share of net losses not recognized during the period the equity method was suspended.

In some cases, there may be evidence that realization of the underlying net assets of the investee may be permanently impaired because of the trend of operating losses of the investee, inability to operate at a normal capacity, or other considerations. APB 18 does not prohibit a write-down of the investment under such circumstances. However, such instances are rarely encountered because the financial statements of the investee, which are the basis of determining the equity of the investor in the net assets of the investee (under the equity method of accounting), must be stated in accordance with, or adjusted to, U.S. generally accepted accounting principles, and such statements are, therefore, presumed to present fairly the financial position and results of operations of the investee.

BOOK/TAX DIFFERENCES

Differences will often arise between the investor's accounting treatment of joint ventures for financial reporting purposes and for tax purposes. In these situations, the need for deferred tax accounting must be considered, in accordance with Statement of Financial Accounting Standards No. 96, ''Accounting for Income Taxes'' (FAS 96).

Most corporate joint ventures are accounted for by the equity method for financial reporting (''book'') purposes and by the cost method for tax purposes. The difference that will thus arise between the carrying amount of the joint-venture investment between book and tax is a temporary difference, as defined by FAS 96, which may have to be included in the calculation of the deferred tax liability or asset. The book carrying amount of the investment will exceed the tax amount if the venture has undistributed earnings. These undistributed earnings, recognized for book purposes but not for tax purposes, must be included in the deferred tax calculation unless sufficient evidence shows that the joint venture has invested or will invest the undistributed earnings indefinitely or that the earnings will be remitted in a tax-free liquidation.

If this is not the case, the undistributed earnings must be included in the deferred tax calculation, which may require estimates of the years in which the temporary difference will reverse. Such estimates should be based on the expected form of distribution. Dividends should be scheduled for reversal in the expected year of remittance and provision should be made for any foreign withholding taxes. If sale or liquidation of the joint venture is contemplated in some future period, reversal of the remaining cumulative temporary difference should be considered to occur in that period. Related tax attributes, such as foreign tax credits, should also be scheduled.

FAS 96 requires the following disclosures for temporary differences, such as joint-venture undistributed earnings, which are not included in the deferred tax calculation:

- A description of the temporary difference and the types of events that would cause the difference to become taxable.
- The cumulative amount of the temporary difference.
- The amount of the unrecognized deferred tax liability if determination of that liability is practicable, or a statement that determination is not practicable, and the amount of withholding taxes that would be payable upon remittance of those earnings.

When joint ventures are conducted in partnership form, the equity method of accounting generally is used for both book and tax purposes. Differences between the book and tax carrying amounts of the investment can still arise, however, due to different book and tax accounting methods used by the venture. The differences in carrying value thus created are temporary differences under FAS 96 that must be included in the deferred tax calculation. Estimates of the years of their reversal will depend on the nature of the specific differences between book and tax accounting methods used by the joint venture.

DISCLOSURE REQUIREMENTS

Generally, there will be no separate disclosure requirements for joint ventures that are consolidated in the investor's financial statements. However, APB 18 sets forth guidelines regarding disclosures which should be made in the financial statements of an investor when it accounts for investments under the equity method. The introduction to the disclosure requirements of paragraph 20 of APB 18 states, ''The significance of an investment to the investor's financial position and results of operations should be considered in evaluating the extent of disclosures of the financial position and results of operations of an investee.'' Thus, the exercise of judgment is required as to the extent of disclosure which should be made based principally on the significance of the investment in relation to overall financial position and results of operations of the investor. The introduction to the disclosure section also indicates that investments may be appropriately combined or grouped–either wholly or in part—for disclosure purposes.

The disclosures discussed in APB 18 that should be considered relative to joint ventures are as follows:

- Name of joint venture and percentage of ownership by the investor. Normally, the name of the joint venture and the percentage owned would be given only for individually significant joint ventures or those which are publicly held. The ownership percentage should be given when separate financial statements of a joint venture are presented and, generally, should be disclosed as a range where there are numerous individually immaterial investments in joint ventures.
- Accounting policies of the investor with respect to joint-venture investments.
- Difference, if any, between the amount at which an investment is carried and the amount of underlying equity in net assets and the accounting treatment of the difference.
- Summarized information as to assets, liabilities, and results of operations or separate financial statements—either individually or grouped—of joint ventures.

Regulations of the Securities and Exchange Commission (SEC) are more explicit in this regard. In Accounting Series Release 302, the SEC codified two separate disclosure requirements regarding unconsolidated majority-owned subsidiaries and 50 percent-or-less-owned entities accounted for by the equity method (which includes joint ventures). The SEC rules preclude the exercise of judgment by quantifying specific materiality threshholds at which such data must be disclosed by public companies. The SEC disclosures involve, (1) footnote disclosure of summarized financial information for the above-named entities for both annual shareholder reports and SEC filings, and (2) separate financial statements of such entities to be filed as financial statement schedules in SEC filings only. The need for the disclosures is determined, based on tests which attempt to measure the materiality of the entities to the registrant. The SEC's footnote disclosure requirements for summarized data are set forth in Rules 4–08(g) and 1–02(aa) of Regulation S–X. The separate financial statement requirements of the schedule appear in Rule 3–09. The disclosure threshholds are based on S–X Rule 1–02(v), which is the SEC's definition of a significant subsidiary. The threshold for the summarized data requirement is the 10 percent materiality criteria included in Rule 1–02(v). For determining whether full statements are needed, the 10 percent measure is replaced with 20 percent. A significant subsidiary is defined in Rule 1–02(v) as an entity that meets any of the following criteria:

1. *Investment test* - the registrant's and its other subsidiaries' investment in and any advances to the subsidiary (or 50 percent-or-less-owned entities, including joint ventures) exceeds 10 percent of consolidated assets.
2. *Asset test* - the registrant's and its other subsidiaries' proportionate share of total assets of the subsidiary exceeds 10 percent of consolidated assets.
3. *Income test* - the registrant's and its other subsidiaries' equity in the income from continuing operations before income taxes, extraordinary items, and cumulative effect of accounting changes exceeds 10 percent of such consolidated income or, in certain instances described in Regulation S–X Rule 1–02(v), the average of such consolidated income for the most recent five years.

These tests must be applied individually and in the aggregate for all 50 percent-or-less-owned entities accounted for by the equity method. If summarized financial information is required, it must include current assets, noncurrent assets, current liabilities, noncurrent liabilities, redeemable preferred stock, minority interests, net sales or gross revenues, gross profit (or costs and expenses applicable to net sales or gross revenues), income or loss from continuing operations, and net income or loss. Generally, such information would be aggregated for all 50 percent-or-less-owned entities accounted for by the equity method.

In some situations, the credit of the joint venturers effectively supports the borrowings of the joint venture. Such support can take the form of a direct guarantee, an indirect guarantee, or can arise from the terms of a take-or-pay contract. Certain disclosures are required in the investor's financial statements in these circumstances. Statement of Financial Accounting Standards No. 5, "Accounting for Contingencies," requires disclosure by the investor of its guarantee of indebtedness of the venture. A similar disclosure requirement for indirect guarantees is contained in FASB Interpretation No. 34, "Disclosure of Indirect Guarantees of Indebtedness of Others." Finally, Statement of Financial Accounting Standards No. 47, "Disclosure of Long-Term Obligations," requires the following disclosures for unconditional purchase obligations such as take-or-pay contracts:

(a) nature and term of the obligation,

(b) amount of the fixed and determinable portion of the obligation as of the date of the latest balance sheet presented in the aggregate and, if determinable, for each of the five succeeding fiscal years,

(c) nature of any variable components of the obligation, and

(d) amounts purchased under the obligation for each period for which an income statement is presented.

JOINT VENTURE RECORDING OF INITIAL CAPITAL CONTRIBUTIONS

The most significant accounting issue the joint venture may need to address is the amount at which to record noncash capital contributions received from the joint-venture owners. Generally, such contributions should be recorded in the joint venture's financial statements at the fair value of the assets on the date of contribution.

There are exceptions to this general rule, however. Noncash assets contributed by an investor who controls the venture should be recorded by the venture at the same amount at which those assets are carried in the books of the investor (predecessor basis). This is because there has been no change in control over those assets. Also, noncash assets should not be recorded at fair value unless such value is readily determinable with a fairly high degree of reliability and recoverability of that value is not in doubt. Thus, intangible assets contributed to a joint venture will often be recorded at predecessor basis (usually zero).

Sometimes, noncash assets contributed to a joint venture, which are recorded at fair value, have a lower tax basis to the venture which carries over from the investor. In these situations, the different bases of the assets for book vs. tax purposes would be a temporary difference for which deferred taxes would be recorded at the date of contribution, if the joint venture is a taxable entity.

INDEPENDENT ACCOUNTANT INVOLVEMENT WITH JOINT-VENTURE FINANCIAL STATEMENTS

Whenever an investor consolidates or uses the equity method to account for a joint venture, the investor's independent auditor may need to perform some testing at the joint-venture level. The extent of testing will depend largely on the significance of the joint venture to the investor's financial statements.

Independent of any such considerations, the investor may desire some degree of assurance as to the financial results provided by the joint-venture personnel or the adequacy of control systems. Sometimes, there are intangible benefits to just having an independent auditor "be around from time to time."

There are essentially three levels of service an independent accountant can provide with respect to an entity's financial statements: audit, review, and compilation.

An audit examination performed in accordance with U.S. generally accepted auditing standards is the highest, or most comprehensive, level of service that can be provided. The objective is to perform procedures, sufficient in depth and breadth, to enable the accountant to express an opinion as to whether the financial statements are fairly presented in conformity with U.S. GAAP. Procedures include physical inspection of assets, direct confirmation with third parties, examination of written documentation, inquiries of company personnel, and evaluation and testing of internal control systems, among others.

Many joint ventures would benefit from the level of assurance associated with an audit relationship. Such benefits include evaluation of the internal accounting control system, including testing of compliance therewith, and offering recommendations for improvements. In addition, the greater level of knowledge associated with the audit relationship can be expected to provide the auditor with a sound basis for meaningful suggestions concerning operational and business matters.

An audit examination is ordinarily more desirable when: (a) there is an absentee owner or other stewardship function, or (b) financial statements of the joint venture are expected to be used in the foreseeable future to obtain debt or equity funds.

In some cases, owners are active in the day-to-day management of a joint venture and have firsthand knowledge and direct control over the business. Such individuals may not require an audit but desire some degree of assurance on the financial statements. Typically, such ventures would not need financial statements for third parties or, where third parties are involved, they find review reports acceptable.

The objective of a review of financial statements is to provide the accountant with a reasonable basis for expressing limited assurance that there are no material modifications that should be made to the statements in order for them to be in conformity with GAAP. A review does not contemplate a study and evaluation of internal accounting control, tests of accounting records, and responses to inquiries by obtaining corroborating evidential matter through inspection, observation, or confirmation as would an audit. Rather, review procedures generally are limited to inquiries of management personnel and analytical procedures.

A compilation is the least in-depth service an accountant can provide with respect to financial statements. The objective of a compilation is to present, in the form of financial statements, information that is the representation of management (owners) without undertaking to express any assurance on the statements. The procedures involved in a compilation generally are very limited. It is unlikely that this level of service would be useful to a joint venture or its owners.

CHAPTER 4

JOINT VENTURING IN THE HEALTH INDUSTRY

John E. Buelt
Price Waterhouse

THE CHANGING HEALTHCARE INDUSTRY

Challenges Facing Healthcare Providers

During recent years, deregulation and increasing competitive pressure have had a dramatic effect on the healthcare industry. The federal government has also allowed the national health planning laws to expire and thus has eliminated both the burdens of compliance and the market protection of regulation. Providers who have successfully hurdled the regulatory barriers of entry into new services no longer have those same regulatory barriers to protect their markets from other competitors. State by state, Certificate of Need (CON) laws are being repealed or their threshold levels are being increased to provide greater access by competitors. This deregulation encourages stiff market competition. The federal government's institution of a prospective payment system for Medicare inpatients, for example, has led to a decline in the use of traditional inpatient services and has led to competition among hospitals for a share of a declining market.

Searching for alternative sources of revenue, hospitals have begun to build integrated systems in response to competitive challenges. The lesser of the integrative approaches to system growth includes participation in networks and alliances, contract management, and joint ventures. More highly integrated responses for system growth include limited affiliation, leased hospitals, full affiliation, merger/consolidation, and acquisitions. Market preservation and protection are primary objectives of these activities.

Traditionally, physicians have been key partners in joint-venture activities with hospitals, and they continue to be most prominent in health industry joint ventures. The physicians' influence is due largely to their role as "gate-keepers" of admissions to hospitals. While they still retain great influence over services required by patients, physicians, too, are experiencing significant changes in their practices.

An increasing supply of physicians and a freeze on physician fees by some third-party payers are limiting their incomes. Increasing competition for patients has prompted many physicians to band together into single- and multi-specialty groups to achieve economies of scale and other benefits not available to solo practitioners. For aspiring and beginning physicians, the cost of medical education continues to rise. The medical student, the medical school, and the teaching hospital are all paying these increased costs, since fewer of them can be passed on to third-party payers of healthcare.

Other developments affecting hospitals and physicians are insurance coverage revisions and the growth of contract medicine, health maintenance organizations (HMOs), and preferred provider organizations (PPOs) as alternatives to traditional fee-for-services healthcare payment. For example, the number of HMOs (428) in 1985 is double that of 1981. In the past three years, enrollment in HMOs has increased 22 percent to nearly 17 million people.[1]

The major growth of PPOs (from only 13 in 1980 to 413 as of June 1, 1986) occurred primarily from 1983 to 1985.[2] Therefore, many of these PPOs have only two to three years of operational experience. The emergence of HMOs and PPOs provides an alternatively priced option to corporate benefits managers. Increasingly, businesses are steering employees

---

[1]Group Health Association of America, *GHAA's National Directory of HMOs 1986*, (Washington, D.C.), page 4.

[2]American Medical Care and Review Association, *Directory of Preferred Provider Organizations and the Industry Report on PPO Development, June 1986*, (Bethesda, Maryland), page vi.

to low-cost providers and lobbying for legislation to contain healthcare costs. The rapid growth of alternative healthcare providers, including the free-standing emergency treatment centers, outpatient diagnostic clinics, free-standing surgicenters, and mobile diagnostic and therapeutic technology—such as CAT (computerized axial tomography) scans and MRI (magnetic resonance imaging) and lithotripsy—are also presenting new challenges for physicians and hospitals, as well as new opportunities for joint venturers.

The Environment for Healthcare Joint Ventures

In response to these challenges, hospitals and physicians are forming new strategic relationships by joining together to provide healthcare services and increased economic and other benefits to each other. The accomplishment of any of a number of specific organizational and operating needs may be accomplished by a well-planned joint venture.

Other new joint-venture partners are also emerging. Hospitals with low occupancy rates are redirecting resources—space, equipment, capital, and personnel—to ventures with specialized groups. These arrangements provide chemical dependency treatment, skilled nursing care, physical therapy, and rehabilitation services. Some hospitals are initiating joint ventures with nursing homes, retirement housing and lifecare facilities, and a variety of eldercare programs to position themselves to serve the graying U.S. population.

Technology in healthcare changes rapidly. These advances and dynamic complexity require constant vigilance to remain competitive and current. Knowledgeable joint venturers may be in a position to help physicians and hospitals respond quickly to establish a market niche, using the most current technologies.

There are concerns, however, and these include increased scrutiny by the U.S. Internal Revenue Service of the new ventures and expanding business activities of providers. In particular, the question of inurement for private benefit in tax-exempt organizations is coming more into question. Planning for antitrust issues has become increasingly important to joint venturers, as they consider the specific activities and goals of their enterprise. The avoidance of Medicare fraud and abuse violations is also a complex and important consideration. One should also not overlook the significant up-front costs of a joint venture and the increasing difficulty in raising capital for new services and activities.

CONSIDERATIONS FOR JOINT VENTURING IN HEALTHCARE

Advantages

Joint ventures are agreements or organizations in which participating parties share the rewards—and risks—of business. A venture capitalist or partner with key knowledge or skills is likely to be a joint-venture partner with hospitals and/or physicians. A venture arrangement allows participants to share project costs, reduce financial risks, and provide funds and expertise necessary to enter new markets or protect or expand existing product lines. A venture may serve to block a competing initiative, as well as to enhance the existing delivery capacity. The sharing of knowledge, expertise, and experience can limit the start-up difficulties generally associated with a new business, and can shorten the amount of time required to become operational. It can also consolidate referral networks, and provide an opportunity for hospitals and doctors to expand beyond their traditional markets. In addition, joint ventures can minimize capital requirements or develop new sources and reduce operating costs. Participation in joint venturing may have the advantage of building closer relationships, which could in turn make future joint activities more likely. This cooperative association and experience may provide the basis for further system growth. Management knowledge gained through joint venturing can improve the likelihood of successfully developing either vertical or horizontal system integration.

Risks and Concerns

A joint venture is not without risks, however, and should not be viewed as a ''solution'' to all difficulties facing healthcare providers. Rather it should be viewed as a framework for providers to channel their efforts to achieve certain goals. Common management concerns should be anticipated and assessed. Is the venture likely to succeed? What impact might it have on participating organizations' staff, structure, systems, and style? Will the venture result in a benefit to the community?

Some disadvantages arise simply from incurring the risks of a new business. The hospital, a group of physicians, or an entrepreneurial business venturer must consider proposed start-up uncertainty and costs, the high rate of failure, and excessive demands on management time and talent.

Joint venturers must also consider medical staff relationships. What will be the impact of selective participation decisions? Is there any preceived favoritism and competition created among the staff by the venture? Will there be a problem with not-for-profit corporation inurement or benefits to individuals? What do the state laws say about the corporate practice of medicine?

It is important to define the balance of management control within the venture. What are the key operating issues and control factors? Will significantly different "corporate cultures" create management issues or leadership concerns? Who will control professional reputations and standards? How will disputes among partners be resolved? Are there clear procedures established for dissolving the venture? Are any financial risks incurred unequally? Do the parties understand and agree to the timing of the business commitments, and is there sufficient financial strength and staying power available to see the venture through unforeseen start-up difficulties?

Successful entrepreneurs can anticipate both the problems and the rewards. Successful entrepreneurs have a sense of timing, priority, and preparation needed to act. And, successful entrepreneurs have a bias toward action. They make a decision, commit resources, and follow through. Finally, they have learned through experience to recognize success or failure, and are not timid about responding to either.

Selecting a Joint-Venture Partner

When initiating a joint-venture activity, a number of important issues must be addressed:

- What are the objectives of the joint venture?
- Are these objectives consistent with the overall organizational plan and mission of participants?
- What is the most appropriate organizational form for the joint venture?
- What legal, regulatory, and tax issues should be considered?
- What selection criteria would assist in identifying an appropriate partner?

As the possibility of a joint venture is explored, the first step is to define objectives. Why is the joint venture under consideration? What specific objectives or outcomes can be achieved?

For hospitals and physicians alike, one of the most common objectives in undertaking a joint venture is to hedge against competition from new providers. Hospitals may have certain specific reasons including:

- Earning additional revenue and/or establishing additional sources of referrals.
- Establishing or enhancing the link between the hospital and its medical staff.
- Finding alternatives to long-term debt as a method for financing capital projects.
- Cutting costs by combining resources and expertise.
- Improving payor mix by attracting patients with more favorable means of payment.
- Diversifying into businesses that will grow as demand for hospital inpatient services declines.
- Becoming involved in activities that others might be able to provide, such as ambulatory care facilities.

The objectives of physicians participating in joint ventures parallel those of hospitals to some extent, but also include the following:

- Identifying investment opportunities and increasing the potential for return.
- Realizing special tax benefits.
- Protecting and/or enhancing patient base.
- Minimizing the risks of undertaking substantial capital projects alone.
- Capitalizing on the hospital's strong presence in the local health-care market, thereby increasing the chances of success of a new medical venture.

The objectives of an entrepreneurial venture partner other than the hospital or physician will be complementary or similar, and may also include the following:

- Exploiting significant product knowledge or expertise specifically germane to the contemplated venture.

- Obtaining advantageous capital investment opportunity.
- Expressing a vested economic interest in maintaining services or jobs in the community.

Joint-venture participants should devote considerable attention, both individually and as a group, to identifying their specific joint-venture objectives. Once defined, these objectives will then be useful in developing criteria against which organizational structures and specific activities may be evaluated.

IDENTIFYING APPROPRIATE ACTIVITIES

What types of activities should be considered for a joint venture? Sometimes an activity is identified, or a market opportunity is observed, that spurs the development of a joint venture. At other times, participants may identify a number of objectives and determine that certain joint-venture activities are an appropriate means of meeting one or more of these objectives.

The success of a joint venture is more likely if the chosen activities coincide with the primary goals and activities of the participants. The search for appropriate activities should begin with market evaluation and an assessment of the participants' joint capabilities. In addition, joint-venture activities should be viewed as a means of furthering the mission of the participants. This orientation will foster support from participating organizations and others.

For example, one of the earliest hospital-physician joint ventures was the physician office building. This was originally viewed as an extension of the hospital and as a means of maintaining strong relationships with desirable physicians through the provision of inexpensive office space and a convenient location. In recent years, a wide range of joint-venture activities, both medical and nonmedical, has been attempted, with real estate and facility ventures remaining prevalent. Joint ventures to provide specific services have become increasingly popular and will increase as third-party-payer policies continue to favor nonhospital treatment modalities. Ancillary and clinical-type facilities are among the most common activities (see Table 4-1).

TABLE 4–1
Typical Joint-Venture Activities

Physician office building
Medical Malls (conveniently grouped services)
Urgent care center
Imaging Center
Remote radiology units
Birthing facilities
Lifecare/Retirement living facilities
Laboratory services
Durable medical equipment supplies
Home health care
Wellness Promotion
Nursing care facilities
Preferred Provider Organizations (PPOs)
Health Maintenance Organizations (HMOs)
Peer Review Organization (PRO)

EVALUATING ALTERNATIVE STRUCTURES

After identifying appropriate joint-venture activities, the next step is selecting the organizational structure(s) that will best facilitate their proper management and operation. These three basic structural models, with many variations, exist for the healthcare joint venture:

1. **Contractual arrangement** - the venture is completely defined in a contract between the parties involved.
2. **Limited partnership** - one venturer acts as the general partner, and the other venturer(s) participate as limited partners.
3. **Separate corporation** - a corporation, jointly owned by the venturers.

The major benefits and concerns associated with each of these structures are shown in Exhibits 4-1, 4-2, and 4-3.

It should be noted that joint ventures of tax-exempt hospitals and taxable organizations require scrutiny in order to avoid jeopardizing the hospital's tax-exempt status. In particular, both private inurement and substantial unrelated business activities can cause a hospital to lose its exempt status. Therefore, although a 501(c)(3) organization can enter

EXHIBIT 4–1
Contractual Arrangement

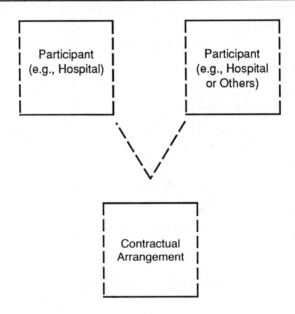

Benefits
  Relatively easy to set up; no new partnerships or corporations are formed.
Concerns
  The ultimate risks of the venture are shared by the contracting parties,
    because no legal entity is created.
  All assets and revenues remain the property of the individual contracting
    parties. As a result, tax benefits, such as depreciation, are severely limited
    and cannot be directed from tax-exempt to taxable partners.
  It may not have as much impact as a stand-alone venture.

directly into a joint venture, it is often advisable to structure a parallel
organization to participate directly in the venture.

   The form of joint venture appropriate in a particular situation can
only be determined by a comprehensive investigation of the objectives
of participating parties and relevant tax, legal, and regulatory considerations. Proper structuring of the venture will benefit all parties involved.

   Typical tax issues to be considered in joint-venture operations are
listed in Table 4-2. Use of a qualified and experienced tax advisor may
minimize the risk of incurring untoward tax consequences, and can help

EXHIBIT 4-2
Limited Partnership

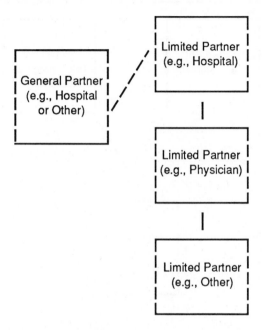

Benefits
    The general partner typically offers management, operations, and data-processing abilities.
    Limited partners have limited financial liability.
    Partners can take full advantage of tax credits and deductions.
    A partnership may increase ability to make exempt securities offerings.
Concerns
    Partnership complicates governance.
    Each state's Medical Practice Act will determine whether physicians may be
    hired or must work under contract.

to maximize the potential tax benefits. A detailed discussion is presented
in the book, *Joint Ventures between Hospitals & Physicians: A Competitive Strategy for the Healthcare Marketplace.*[3]

---

[3]Linda A. Burns and Douglas M. Mancino, *Joint Ventures between Hospitals & Physicians: A
Competitive Strategy for the Healthcare Marketplace,* (Homewood, Illinois, Dow Jones-Irwin, 1987.)

EXHIBIT 4–3
Separate Corporation

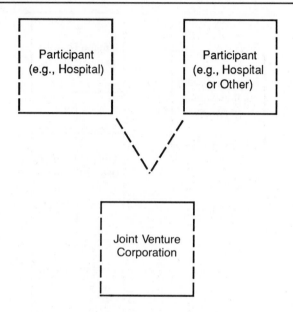

Benefits
  A separate corporation is a distinct entity, and, therefore, is more likely to be
    run as an independent business.
  A new corporate entity generally has equal board representation and capital
    contribution from venturers; thus, neither party would be viewed as
    dominant.
  A corporation offers investors protection from creditors because of limited
    liability.
  A variety of corporate structures exist, each offering different benefits.

Concerns
  A corporation is generally organized as a for-profit, taxable entity, which may
    result in double taxation of physician venturers at both the corporate and
    personal levels.
  A corporation may require state security registration.
  A corporation is more complicated to develop than a partnership or
    contractual arrangement.
  A corporate entity limits availability of deductions and tax credits to
    individual venturers.

TABLE 4–2
Tax Planning Issues Affecting Joint Ventures[4]

Choice of business entity
   Contractual model
   Partnerships
   Corporations
   S corporations
   Comparative tax advantages

Operational considerations
   Cost recovery deduction
   "At risk" limitations

Tax reform act of 1986
   Passive investment loss limitation
   Limitation on use of cash method of accounting
   Taxable year rules

Alternate depreciation system
   Tax-exempt entity defined
   Tax-exempt use property
   Tangible property other than nonresidential real property
   Real property
   Treatment of tax-exempt use of real property
   Service contract rules
   Joint ventures and tax-exempt status
   Inurement
   Private benefit
   Use of corporate subsidiaries
   Planning concerns

Joint ventures and the unrelated business income tax
   Contract joint ventures
   Corporate joint ventures
   Partnerships

OTHER CONSIDERATIONS

Develop a Business Plan

The successful development of a joint venture is a difficult and time-consuming process requiring careful strategic planning, detailed financial

---

[4]Burns and Mancino, *Joint Ventures between Hospitals & Physicians: A Competitive Strategy for the Healthcare Marketplace,* (Homewood, Illinois, Dow Jones-Irwin, 1987), pp. 102–128.

and operational analysis, and ongoing management commitment. A detailed business plan is needed to bring all these matters together.

As a first step, the venture participants should undertake the systematic identification and assessment of proposed new venture opportunities in order to maximize benefits. Written criteria assist in the evaluation process and might include the following:

- How closely does the activity relate to delivery of medical services in the participants' market area?
- Will the activity protect or enhance the market position of the healthcare providers involved?
- Will the activity provide a defined return on investment within a specified time period?

Once a joint venture is determined to be consistent with the agreed-upon criteria, the next step is to determine in detail the economic consequences, physician needs, equipment requirements, location availability, and target market of the proposed venture. A feasibility study will help accomplish these objectives (see Table 4-3). Most joint-venture participants will require such a study to obtain information regarding the risks associated with the venture as well as the strategic, business, and marketing plans. Investors also require such an analysis before committing funds to the project.

Industry Analysis
An understanding of the industry will assist in forming the underlying strategic assumptions on which to base business projections. How can

TABLE 4-3
A Feasibility Study Should Contain

Industry analysis
Service area identification
Demand analysis
Market analysis
Organizational analysis
Physician profile
Complaince analysis
Financial analysis
Legal/regulatory analysis

the venture business activity be described? Are these services growing? Why or why not? Who is involved? What are the categories of services.

Service Area Identification

Who are the customers? Where are they located? What is the population within a convenient distance from the proposed service site(s)? What are the demographic characteristics (age, sex, income, etc.) of those to be served?

Demand Analysis

What factors and trends can be identified and interpreted to assist in projecting future demand for planned services? Who are the competitors? What do they provide? Where are they located? What share of the market do they control? Is there excess service capacity, or can a new entrant provide services for unmet demand?

Market Analysis

What are the significant characteristics of the targeted service population? Why would they prefer to buy services from the joint venture and not the competition? What reputation do participants have or could they develop? What position does the competition have in the minds of potential customers? How can the service offered be differentiated so as to appeal to the market segment most desirable to capture?

Organizational Analysis

What is the proposed governance structure of the joint venture? Will the anticipated management style and leadership be appropriate for this venture? What staffing, space, equipment, and personnel will be required? Are there systems designed to operate this venture? Will human resource benefits common to the venture be imposed on either joint-venture partner organization? What information systems and resources are needed to successfully manage this business?

Physician Profile

What physicians will participate in this venture? Are there any limitations or considerations relating to professional qualifications and certifications, age, income, practice patterns, or service specialty that will influence inclusion in the venture? Will the physicians' current referral patterns and hospital affiliations be a factor in their participation?

Compliance Analysis

Many agencies have the responsibility of overseeing various aspects of healthcare services. Voluntary compliance with these organizations strongly influences the acceptance and financial viability of the organization. For example, the Joint Commission on Accreditation of Healthcare Organizations; the local Provider Review Organization; Medicare and Medicaid participation standards; Blue Cross participation agreements; federal requirements for safety (OSHA), equal opportunity, and employment (EEOC, ERISA); and local and state licensure requirements all need to be reviewed for compliance. This is only the beginning of the list.

Financial Analysis

What costs and revenues have been identified and what basis can be used to project these for the future? Does the projection indicate financial feasibility? What cash flows are projected? Has the financial sensitivity impact of key assumptions been assessed? What impact would there be if a key assumption, such as demand or utilization, were underestimated by 25 percent? What are the financial effects of start-up delays? Can the joint venturers absorb unanticipated up-front costs? And if so, how much can be absorbed and at what potential effect on the success of the venture? What are acceptable financial ratios during the project phases, and what monitoring and control systems will be used? These and many other financial considerations should be identified and anticipated.

Legal/Regulatory Analysis

Given the goals and objectives of the venture, what is the legal structure most appropriate for this venture? Will the venture be in compliance with laws or regulations relating to antitrust, taxation, corporate practice of medicine, etc? The range of issues and problems, challenges, and opportunities should be understood as an aid to planning the venture. Specific legal structures and interpretations or advice can be developed during the implementation of the venture.

Strong leadership is crucial. For example, a hospital has an administrative hierarchy in place, which may be used during planning and development phases. The medical staff hierarchy, on the other hand, is generally clinically oriented and may contain individuals who are less interested in and capable of acting as leaders in business negotiations. Physician participants may, therefore, wish to elect appropriate representatives to work with hospital management during the planning and evaluation process.

Marketing

Marketing the joint venture's services will consume a significant amount of time and should, therefore, be coordinated by whichever party has greater skill in this area.

Financial

The development of a joint-venture organization creates a range of new financing opportunities for healthcare providers whose traditional source of capital has been issuance of long-term tax-exempt bonds. Sales of stock, partnership interests, and other equity participation for physicians provide access to significant amounts of private capital.

Third-Party Payment Issues

An important consideration in developing joint ventures that provide healthcare services is whether third-party payment will be available for services provided. In particular, four major issues should be considered:

- Will the activity be covered by Medicare, Medicaid, and other third-party payers?
- What type of payment may be expected? Some of the payment methods in use today include reasonable cost and reasonable charge reimbursement; the prospective payment system (Medicare), and "cost-related" prospective payment systems such as those currently in effect for end-stage renal disease (ESRD) facilities.
- What reassignment prohibitions and exceptions will apply?
- What certification requirements or standards must be met?

In addition, in states with rate-setting or rate-review controls, it is important to consider the potential effect of such controls on the operations and revenue of a joint-venture organization.

Medicare/Medicaid Fraud and Abuse Considerations

In addition to prohibiting violations of assignments and misrepresentation relating to benefits or payments, Medicare and Medicaid prohibit any kind of remuneration in return for the referral of patients or the purchase of reimbursed services. Potentially fraudulent practices include the sharing of venture proceeds in proportion to referrals and the payment of kickbacks and rebates from suppliers. Physician-compensation agreements must be carefully structured to avoid violation of the fraud and abuse laws.

Certificate of Need

Although the number has decreased in recent years, a number of states still have Certificate of Need (CON) laws that regulate the creation of new healthcare facilities and services, the expansion of existing healthcare facilities, and capital spending above a statutory threshold limit. Expenditures by physician groups, including expenditures for establishment of healthcare facilities, are often excluded from state CON programs, although expenditures by hospitals and hospital subsidiaries are generally subject to review. Depending on how a joint venture is structured, certain activities may require CON approval prior to proceeding. A thorough evaluation of state CON laws is essential before proceeding with a joint venture.

Tax

Tax considerations play an important role in structuring a joint venture. Focusing in particular on the involvement of a tax-exempt hospital, the joint venture must be evaluated from several perspectives:

- Will a hospital's participation in a joint venture jeopardize its tax exempt status? Private inurement, unrelated business income, and investment-tax credit potential must all be evaluated in determining an appropriate joint-venture structure.
- Will the new entity be exempt or taxable?
- To what degree can an exempt hospital participate in joint-venture activities with taxable organizations or individuals?
- What are the personal tax implications for the participating individuals?

Securities Laws

The choice of joint-venture structure may be affected in part by applicable federal and state securities laws. For example, applicable state securities laws will generally treat shares in a for-profit corporation or interests in unlimited partnerships as a security, but may not accord similar treatment to membership in a nonprofit corporation. Both federal and state securities laws require registration of nonexempt securities and full disclosure of all material information to potential investors, often through written offering materials. Early evaluation of applicable securities law considerations during the design phase of the joint venture can help to avoid later problems.

Issues of Antitrust Laws

The healthcare industry was, for a long time, outside the regulatory purview of state and federal antitrust laws. However, since 1975, this exemption from scrutiny has generally no longer held. The tying relationships of joint ventures which mix, exchange, or coordinate the use of assets from two separate parties, are typically aimed at entering or improving geographic or product markets. These joint-venture relationships may be structured vertically, horizontally, or as a diversification. Antitrust violations could be asserted if joint-venture activities result in any of the following anticompetitive effects:

- Reducing potential competition.
- Eliminating actual competition.
- Preempting competition of suppliers or customers.
- Creating anticompetitive collateral restraints.

Consultation with appropriately qualified legal counsel during the planning and implementation of the venture will minimize the risk of incurring legal challenges based in antitrust law. Not only is it important to act within the law, the joint venture also must not appear to be in collusion by its actions or conduct.

A detailed discussion of typical antitrust issues most prevalent in joint ventures is presented by Douglas M. Mancino, J.D., in the book, *Joint Ventures between Hospitals & Physicians: A Competitive Strategy for the Healthcare Marketplace.*[5]

Corporate Practice of Medicine Prohibition

Many states prohibit the practice of medicine by any corporation or business entity other than one established under that particular state's

---

[5]Burns and Mancino, *Joint Ventures between Hospitals & Physicians: A Competitive Strategy for the Healthcare Marketplace,* Dow Jones-Irwin, (Homewood, Illinois, 1987) pp. 143–158.

professional corporation act, in order to prevent a licensed physician caring for a patient from being controlled by a corporation or unlicensed individual. In these states, it would be illegal for a business entity to employ physicians to practice medicine on behalf of the corporation. Prior to developing organizational and contractual arrangements involving physicians, joint-venture participants must carefully examine relevant state statutes to determine whether such a prohibition exists.

KEYS TO SUCCESS

Successful joint-venture activities have common characteristics. In particular, they:

- Help to further the mission(s) of the participants.
- Involve an activity related to the primary activities of the participants.
- Are fully evaluated from marketing, utilization, and financial perspectives prior to implementation.
- Are structured to provide equitable benefits to all participants, with no single participant viewed as the ''winner'' or ''loser.''
- Operate as a business according to a business plan approved by all participants.
- Have strong leadership.
- Have an adequate information systems to provide accurate and timely data for decision-making.
- Recognize physicians' need for clinical autonomy and balance this against the need for integration.

Unsuccessful joint ventures, on the other hand, often display these characteristics:

- Activities far removed from the primary activities, expertise, and goals of the participants.
- Development without adequate participation and input from all participants.
- Lack of proper planning or evaluation.
- Operation as part of the participant's organization rather than a separate business entity.
- Inequitable benefits among the participants.

CHAPTER 5

JOINT VENTURING IN THE CONSTRUCTION INDUSTRY

Robert H. Garb
Bechtel Power Corporation

INTRODUCTION

In the construction industry, joint-venture groupings are a nationally and internationally recognized and common form of cooperation for the fulfillment of construction contract obligations. For our purposes, an appropriate definition of such groupings would be a "business alliance of limited duration formed by two or more unrelated businesses or professional entities for the purpose of furnishing engineering, consulting, procurement, construction and construction management services by consolidating the skills and resources of the participants."[1] Such arrangements are normally contractual, i.e. expressed by written contracts, but they can be implied from the acts of the parties.[2] Although joint-venture groupings in the construction industry are generally formed to accomplish a single project, often one of large magnitude, more "permanent" types of joint ventures or business alliances are being formed in the construction industry to cover two or more firms cooperatively working together as

---

[1]Robert F. Cushman, and John P. Bigda, (eds), *Construction Business Handbook,* 2nd Ed. (New York: McGraw-Hill, 1985), p. 5-2.

[2]Justin Sweet, *Legal Aspects of Architecture, Engineering, and the Construction Process,* 3rd Ed. (St. Paul: West Publishing Company, 1985), p. 30.

opportunities present themselves. This type of agreement is called either a Teaming Agreement, a Protocol Agreement, a Memorandum of Understanding, or a Cooperative Agreement. One pattern in these continuing arrangements is that each job in which the parties elect to participate will be covered by a separate joint-venture agreement. Another format is one in which the parties determine, as each job develops, who will work as the prime contractor and who will work as the subcontractor, and then have a prime contractor-subcontractor relationship between themselves evidenced by a subcontract so that on any particular project they do not act as co-venturers.

ADVANTAGES OF A JOINT-VENTURE RELATIONSHIP

The use of a joint-venture relationship in the construction industry has become a convenient and necessary means of providing the concentration of economic resources, skill, and knowledge required to negotiate, bond, and complete a large-scale construction project. A construction contractor considering whether to bid on a major project would most likely first look at the size of the project and consider its own resources—manpower, management, materials, equipment, bonding capacity, special expertise, local knowledge, and financial capability—and then consider the effect that committing some of these resources to the major project would have on the rest of its organization. Even if the construction contractor determined that it could manage the project alone, this concentration of resources may adversely impact its ability to compete for future work. In this regard, joint-venture groupings may be particularly advantageous in countries whose construction industries consist of small and medium-sized enterprises. In Austria, for example, small and medium-sized firms predominate, since only about 10 percent of all construction enterprises can be classified as "industrial-scale" firms. As a result, Austria has had many years of experience with joint ventures in the performance of relatively large-scale construction projects.[3]

Another motivating factor in forming a joint-venture grouping in the construction industry is the opportunity such groupings would offer to

---

[3]Manfried Straube, "Joint Venture Groups—Effects on the Construction Contract," *International Business Lawyer,* (March 1985), p. 131.

foreign involvement. In fact, combining with a local co-venturer may be the only way for a foreign construction firm to pre-qualify for a particular tender. Many doors, which would otherwise be closed to foreigners, are open to a venture which includes a local organization. Also, substantial tax and customs duties concessions may be available to joint ventures having local partners. Since the resident partner in the host country presumably knows the prospective clients as well as the laws and customs of its country as they relate to the desired construction market, the assumption is that the proposed joint venture will have a smoother initial entry into such market. The Austin Company, headquartered in Cleveland, formed a joint venture with Kawasaki Heavy Industries Ltd. based in Tokyo to compete for work on Japan's estimated $8 billion Kansai Airport. Recognizing the current attitude of the Japanese government with respect to non-Japanese firms being allowed to bid on public sector projects, the Austin Company working alone would have been unable to bid for this work. The joint venture's bid included the design and construction of support facilities and the provision of an integrated computer system.[4] Award of this type of design and construction work to U.S. firms in joint ventures with Japanese firms, or U.S. firms standing alone, has become a central focus in the present debate over fair trade between Japan and the United States.

Still another motivating factor for forming a joint venture in the construction industry occurs when a firm has an outstanding and recognized expertise in one or more areas of a complex construction project but needs another firm to complement its skills. In working together, they hope to be able to tackle a broader market with combined business strength exceeding that of either partner. Examples of these types of joint ventures are seen in combinations between an architect and an engineer (horizontally co-venturing) or between one or both of such professional firms and a constructor (vertically co-venturing). In 1986, the New York City-based architectural firm of Turner International Industries, Inc. was solicited by a British contractor, R. M. Douglas, to enter into a joint venture to construct a $128 million convention center in Birmingham, England. A major challenge of this project was in having to deal with underground rail lines that ran beneath the site. Furthermore, the structure would have to be isolated from the sound and vibration of the trains. After interviewing about a dozen U.S. architectural firms for the project, Douglas selected

---

[4] "U.S.-Japanese Firms Joint Venture for Kansai—", *ENR* (March 12, 1987), p. 5.

Turner because of its expertise in building over underground railroad lines. Turner had demonstrated this special capability in the construction of Madison Square Garden in New York City.[5]

Sometimes it is an advantage for construction firms in basically the same fields to work together on a specific project. As noted above, the construction contractor will decide that due to the size of the project, combination with one of its competitors is a practical necessity. In some cases, however, the client will make that decision for the contractor, and several contractors who expected to be competing with each other for a big project may suddenly find themselves directed by the client to team up instead. Although initially the parties forced to work together may view the arrangement negatively, there is an educational value in this opportunity to observe a competitor on such intimate terms.

Financial concerns are another major impetus for creating a joint venture. One of the venturers may not have the ability to attract desirable financing to bid on a particular job. An initial reason for Bechtel, a U.S. engineering and construction firm, to team up with Japan's largest construction contractor, Kumagai Gumi Ltd., in 1985 to construct Manitoba Hydro's Limestone Dam Project on the Nelson River was the inexpensive financing Kumagai could contribute to the work.[6]

A joint-venture grouping in the construction industry may also be prompted by the need for risk sharing. Several years ago, Bechtel participated in a bid for a large power plant project in a Middle Eastern country, which incorporated bids received from two subcontractors, one for the turbines and one for the boilers. The bid was unsuccessful, ranking fifth amongst seven tenderers. Several years later, Bechtel was given the opportunity to resubmit its bid. The parties quickly recognized that a more competitive price could be achieved if the bid was submitted by a consortium comprised of Bechtel, as sponsor, and the two former subcontractors. Since risks, such as performance guarantees and liquidated damages for schedule delays, could be shared under such an arrangement, the two former subcontractors were able to lower their risk contingencies and submitted more competitive prices.

However, in subsequent negotiations concerning the desired format for a joint-venture agreement formalizing their relationship, the two former subcontractors refused to agree to contribute their share of Bechtel's

---

[5]"Yankee Ingenuity Helps U.K.", *ENR*, (October 23, 1986), p. 16.
[6]"U.S.-Japanese Team Speeds Canadian Dam", *ENR*, (October 23, 1981), p. 20.

forecasted marketing costs as the sponsor of the proposed joint venture. The two former subcontractors noted that they were also expected to incur substantial business-development costs in securing the project and that a more equitable formula was to have each party assume, for its own account, its own marketing costs. Since no agreement was reached on this issue, one former subcontractor dropped out of the project and Bechtel submitted a bid based on a prime contractor-subcontractor relationship with the other subcontractor.

Besides risk sharing, another advantage to international construction joint ventures is the ability to obtain government subsidies. For example, Pakistan and India will help a construction joint venture provided it includes one of their national companies as a true partner.[7]

A final incentive is a particular country's legal requirements. For example, China and Yugoslavia require that a unit of a national construction corporation be a partner in any construction contract in which a foreign firm desires to participate. All bidders involved in Saudi Arabia's Riyadh University's construction in the early 1980s were under a Saudi mandate to form a binational joint venture.[8] These legal requirements may have evolved in order to provide an incentive (or compulsion) for foreign construction firms to impart their technology and know-how to local construction firms. The objective is to decrease a country's future dependence on foreign expertise. Another basis for such laws would be to maximize utilization of underemployed local talent, such as engineers.

CURRENT TRENDS

The increasingly large scale of many of the world's present construction projects, with their unprecedented problems and risks, makes joint cooperation among contractors necessary. The initial explosive growth of a world economy buoyed by rising oil prices, followed by a worldwide leveling off of economic activities with increased risks, has made joint venturing necessary.[9] Construction firms now broker joint-venture partnerships as the vehicle to obtain complex multinational financing.

---

[7]"Joint Ventures Win Big Contracts", *ENR*, (April 30, 1981), p. 28.

[8]*Ibid.*, p. 25.

[9]Straube, "Joint Venture Groups—Effects on the Construction Contract", *International Business Lawyer*, (March 1985), p. 131.

Currently there is a trend toward having construction joint-venture groupings comprised of two or more venturers from different countries combined to perform a project in a third country, often a third-world country. Hochtief, A.G. led a West German-Italian joint-venture group in obtaining a $1.46 billion hydro project in northern Iraq in the early 1980s. During the same time period, West Germany's Thyssen Rheinstahl Technik and the U.S. firm of M. W. Kellog teamed up as a joint venture to win a $1 billion chemical plant award in southern Sumatra, Indonesia. Thyssen was the general contractor and Kellog was the engineer and the provider of the construction services.[10]

As the Middle East weathers the present world-wide oil glut and a period of declining revenues, the Pacific Rim emerges as the new land of opportunity for international construction projects. This area is secure, currently free of war, industrious, openly solicitous of joint-venture arrangements with foreign firms and, most importantly, well financed. Singapore, Taiwan, Hong Kong, Thailand, and the People's Republic of China are all developing airports, railroads, subways, or other forms of mass transit. From New Zealand to Japan, from Brunei to Jakarta, the region is flush with major construction projects.[11]

As is particularly true in Japan, Korea, and the People's Republic of China, the only manner in which a U.S. contractor can effectively secure construction work today in many of the Pacific Rim countries is to join with a local "sponsor" or "joint-venture partner." For example, it was earlier noted that the Japanese government is unreceptive to having non-Japanese firms bid on public sector projects, therefore, joint venturing with Japanese partner(s) becomes essential.

Besides the obvious marketing advantage, the following are some of the other current advantages in forming a joint venture with a Japanese partner:

- A foreigner is at a disadvantage in recruiting good construction personnel in Japan; therefore, a local partner is essential in this regard.
- In the tax area, there is generally less scrutiny of the relationship when a U.S. company and a Japanese affiliate are involved in a project.

---

[10]"Joint Ventures Win Big Contracts," *ENR*, (April 30, 1981), p. 28.

[11]Michael J. Ladino, *"Vital Issues in International Construction Contracting,"* International Construction Law (November 7–8, 1985), pp. 2–3.

- There may be advantageous technology input from the local partner.
- It becomes important in terms of relationships with the Japanese customer.

PRECAUTIONS IN FORMING A JOINT VENTURE

As noted earlier, often the only way for a U.S. construction firm to prequalify for an international tender is to combine with a local co-venturer. Since outright bribery is widely practiced in many foreign business communities, any multinational joint venture involving a U.S. construction firm must withstand the scrunity of the Foreign Corrupt Practices Act (FCPA) 15 USC Section 78dd–1,2.

The FCPA prohibits certain conduct by U.S. firms acting through their representatives in their dealings with foreign officials, politicians, and agents. Generally, the giving of or promising to give any sort of gift, donation, or anything of value to the above category of persons, directly or indirectly, with the intention of influencing the outcome of a business decision is strictly prohibited.

Influence is an all-encompassing term as used in the FCPA, which includes actions and reactions with respect to a business opportunity in which the ultimate objective is to obtain or retain business, or simply to direct business to a particular person. The Attorney General of the United States can initiate either criminal or civil actions directly against a company, alleged to be in violation of the FCPA, and against any of its officers, directors, stockholders, or employees. Violations by individuals are punishable by fines, imprisonment, or both.

In order to avoid the possibility of having FCPA problems, it is prudent for U.S. construction firms, who participate in a multinational joint venture, to insert a clause in their joint-venture agreement that requires the non-American co-venturer(s) to recognize the U.S. venturer's obligations under the FCPA and to agree to so conduct their respective joint-venture activities so as not to place the U.S. firm in violation of its FCPA obligations. In order to enable the non-American co-venturer(s) to become familiar with the U.S. venturer's obligations under the FCPA, it is desirable to incorporate a summary of the pertinent provisions of FCPA as an attachment to the joint-venture agreement.

In choosing a local co-venturer, one must evaluate its standing in the local business community, as well as its experience, financial capability, and particular strengths for the proposed undertaking. The choice of the co-venturer is not only critical for completion of the particular assignment and avoidance of potential FCPA problems as noted above; but, initially, the wisdom of the selection could impact the client's decision to retain the particular proposed joint venture.

In third-world countries, local co-venturers in major construction work will often be affiliated with the government. In these situations, it is particularly important that the understandings of the parties to the venture be carefully documented, due to the continuous turnover in government personnel.

Additional precautions in forming a construction industry venture are issues regarding loss of control, joint liability, and increased management time and effort. If the joint venture proves unworkable, it could result in unsatisfactory means of resolving disputes or terminating the relationship. It may well be that a company will be in a better net position if it does the construction work itself.

Given the potential for problems, one should first determine if a host country's business environment really requires a joint venture with a local co-venturer in order to gain access to the host country's construction market. It may be that the business environment is flexible, and that naming a local firm as the designated construction subcontractor or as a licensee in a construction technology-transfer licensing arrangement will be all that is required for a successful bid.

One particular disadvantage for prospective construction industry venturers is the partnership attribute of a joint venture wherein each co-venturer can bind the other. Thereafter, for any commitment made by either co-venturer, both venturers have assumed liability to third parties. Assume for example, a joint-venture agreement provided that both venturers had to give their consent before the joint venture could enter into any contractual commitment. Further assume that, despite this provision, one of the parties to the joint venture enters into a subcontract, on behalf of the joint venture, with a third party to perform the civil works on the project. If the third party then has a dispute under the civil-works subcontract and sues both parties, this would be an acceptable procedure in most countries that recognize joint-venture groupings. The subcontractor could successfully argue that it was unaware that both venturers had to consent to any binding contracts with the joint venture and that it had a valid contract with both venturers.

In international construction joint ventures, the diversity of cultural backgrounds frequently results in a tenuous working relationship. In the situation of the Bechtel-Kumagai joint venture, the Bechtel management personnel who worked with Kumagai found that the biggest difference between them was that in Japan, contractors, not owners, were responsible for quality control. As a result, Japanese firms like Kumagai tend to be more meticulous, adding to the costs.[12]

To overcome cultural disparity, the joint-venture agreement must be carefully drafted to define the partners' relationship and the rights and responsibilities of the parties involved. In this manner, the agreement between the domestic venturer and the foreign venturer will be as important as the construction contract for actual performance of the work.

There is also the problem of joint and several liability, especially for the co-venturer with the deeper pocket whom the client would most likely look to in the event of any deficiency in the performance of the services. However, there are ways to minimize this exposure; first, through the use of a subsidiary corporation of lesser net worth as the firm's participant in the joint venture; and second, by a spreading of the risks through subcontracts for all or most of the services. These subcontracts would contain indemnification provisions wherein the subcontractors agree to defend and hold harmless the joint venture from any liability arising from their particular portion of the services. Of course, by spreading risks, one is also reducing the revenues to be gained by undertaking such work oneself. Furthermore, no matter how careful the joint-venturer participants may be in assessing the subcontractors and transferring the legal liabilities to them, the client will still look to the joint venturers for ultimate responsibility.

POSITIONING THE JOINT VENTURE

Assume that, after weighing the advantages and disadvantages of forming a particular construction-industry joint venture, the decision is made to form such a venture. The primary objective will then be to form a joint venture which attracts a client or clients. However, one must recognize that this activity may only get the joint venture to the negotiating table. Once at the negotiating table one may find that the client's real needs

---

[12]"U.S.–Japanese Team Speeds Canadian Dam," *ENR* p. 21.

may require further tinkering with the planned joint-venture arrangement. The original joint-venture arrangement should have some flexibility to allow for this potential need to regroup and revise certain provisions. One way to accomplish this flexibility is to have the initial arrangements be recorded in the form of a simple Memorandum of Understanding covering the precontract stage, i.e. the bid stage, and then having this document superseded by a formal Joint-Venture Agreement upon project award. If the project is not awarded to the proposed joint venture, the relationship contemplated by the Memorandum of Understanding should then automatically terminate.

It is the usual practice in the construction industry for each co-venturer to bear its own costs associated with bidding activities and, thereafter, share in the responsibility for the proposal and subsequent construction contract.

In reviewing a proposed joint venture the following issues should be noted:

1. When considerations of local law are given as the basis for the need for the formation of the joint venture, does such law in fact require the joint venture?
2. Has the correct form of business entity arrangement, i.e., partnership, corporation, or other arrangement, been selected for the joint venture?
3. If guarantees for either financial or technical performance are involved, has the assumption of these risks been properly allocated among the co-venturers?
4. If a party is intended to be the leader of the joint venture, has that party retained effective management control?
5. If a party has a minority interest in the joint venture, has that party protected itself on substantive matters of interest, e.g. having a veto regarding fundamental issues?
6. Is the manner in which the joint venture intends to contract for project execution of the construction work acceptable to all parties involved, i.e., a contract with one of the co-venturers as the general contractor, or subcontracts with each of the co-venturers?
7. Does the proposed joint-venture arrangement reflect appropriate termination provisions?

As noted in Item 2 above, one of the important issues in positioning the joint venture is in the selection of the correct form of business entity arrangement. It is a major consideration for U.S. tax purposes as to whether the joint venture will be considered a partnership or a corporation. The following four factors are generally considered in making this determination:

1. Continuity of life.
2. Centralization of management.
3. Limited liability.
4. Free transferability of interests.

If the proposed joint-venture arrangement has two or fewer of the above-outlined characteristics, it is treated as a partnership for U.S. tax purposes. If the proposed joint-venture arrangement is considered as a partnership for U.S. tax purposes, there are the following potential advantages:

- Earnings are not doubly taxed by the United States, as are corporate earnings.
- Partners can elect individually to deduct foreign taxes or to credit them.
- Each partner may deduct current losses, whereas deduction of corporate losses is often deferred until liquidation.
- Problems caused by dividend income are avoided.
- Problems with tax-credit limitations caused by tax structures when there is a local participant in the joint venture are avoided. In Saudi Arabia, for example, only the foreign participant's share of the profits are taxed, not the Saudi participant's share. If a Saudi entity, treated for U.S. tax purposes as a corporation, were owned 50/50 with a Saudi citizen in calculating the deemed-paid U.S. foreign tax credit, the U.S. shareholder would be treated as having paid only one-half of the taxes of which it bore the entire economic burden. On the other hand, a joint venture treated as a partnership could make a special allocation of the taxes to the U.S. partner as necessary to reflect the actual burden of the tax.[13]

If the proposed joint-venture arrangement is considered as a corporation for U.S. tax purposes, there are the following potential advantages:

---

[13]John L. Gornall, Jr., "Tax Status and Planning for Joint Ventures in International Construction Contracts," *Tax Management International Journal*, (December 1977), p. 31.

- Deferral of U.S. taxes upon foreign construction earnings until actually repatriated to the United States. As a business objective, deferral only makes sense if the cumulative effective tax rates in the country of incorporation and county of construction are substantially less than the applicable U.S. rates.
- Greater flexibility than partnerships in choice of accounting methods and tax years.
- Greater ability to segregate activities, for example, engineering work done in the United States is done by the U.S. parent, while on-site construction work is done by an overseas subsidiary.[14]

Effective tax planning can be achieved by providing the site country's tax/legal advisors with a concise description of the activities to be carried out by each co-venturer and a brief statement of the home-country tax considerations most important to each co-venturer. Utilizing this information, the site country's advisors can then describe the local tax system and successful contractual devices previously utilized and recommend advantageous methods of operations. Then, each home-country tax/legal advisor can work back through his own laws to achieve the best combined-site-country/home-country tax result.

The critical issue in successfully positioning a planned joint venture is to make a thorough and thoughtful investigation of the potential co-venturer. It should not be assumed that weaknesses in the proposed participant can be completely resolved by contractual language and the structuring of the joint venture. Therefore, at the outset a detailed evaluation should be made of the proposed co-venturer's project-execution capability to confirm that the proposed co-venturer could make a meaningful contribution to the joint venture. A clear understanding should be reached with the co-venturer regarding the extent and nature of its participation.

No single set of rules or guidelines can be developed as to how best to develop and operate a joint venture to undertake construction work in the United States or abroad. It should be recognized that joint ventures are treated differently in various countries. Compare for example the U.S. definition of a joint venture, namely, a partnership formed for a limited purpose, with Saudi Arabia's Royal Decree No. 38 which defines a joint venture as…"a partnership not divulged to others, without a juridical

---

[14]Gornall, Jr., "Tax Status and Planning for Joint Ventures in International Construction Contracts," *Tax Management International Journal*, (December 1977), pp. 31–32.

status, nor subject to advertising formalities.'' However, there are certain general themes of construction-industry joint ventures that emerge.

INTEGRATED AND NONINTEGRATED AGREEMENTS

In general, the format of joint-venture agreements in the construction industry falls within two categories referred to herein as either integrated or nonintegrated agreements:

Integrated Agreement

This is a type of joint venture agreement wherein the parties essentially agree to perform their work as if it were performed by a single corporation having several shareholders. All monies received would go into a joint-venture bank account, and the parties would share profits and losses on a particular project in accordance with a previously agreed upon sharing ratio. Normally, this type of an agreement is used when the parties to the proposed joint venture intend to perform their work on an integrated basis, i.e. by having both parties' personnel work together under the supervision of one or more of the co-venturers in accomplishing the project's objectives.

Nonintegrated Agreement

This is a type of joint-venture agreement wherein the parties, for the most part, undertake their respective portions of the work separately. Often this arrangement is entered into by co-venturers who have specialized areas of expertise or assigned work responsibilities, such as, for example, an engineer and a contractor; or a turbine supplier and a construction contractor. Frequently, these types of arrangements are known as ''Consortium Agreements'' or in most South American countries as ''Consortios.'' The parties will sometimes send their invoices to the leader or sponsor of the joint venture who will in turn forward them to the client under the cover of a transmittal letter using the joint-venture letterhead. All monies received will be disbursed to each of the joint venturers based on the invoices they submitted, and there will be minimal sharing, if any, of profits and losses. Sometimes the client will agree, in its contract with the joint venture, to pay each of the co-venturers directly for its specific portion of the work. Although each party will generally be responsible for its portion of the work, there will have to be some agreed upon sharing arrangement in areas of common interest, such as, for example, engaging a local lawyer regarding legal requirements, or for common business-development costs expended in securing the job. If the client does not recognize, in the contract with the joint venture, that it will look only to the particular co-venturer for that portion of the work for which only he is responsible, the joint-venture agreement should then indicate that each co-venturer will indemnify and hold harmless the other party from any liability associated with its designated portion of the work. The nonintegrated type of agreement is normally used when parties to a joint venture each have discrete scopes of work and the joint venture is being formed merely to satisfy a particular requirement necessitating a joint bid.

In both integrated and nonintegrated agreements, the joint venturers usually will assume joint and several liability for their work in the prime contract with the client associated with the particular construction project. However, in the case of the nonintegrated agreement such liability will generally be reallocated through cross-indemnities inserted into the joint-venture agreement, so that it becomes the full responsibility, or at least the primary responsibility, of the party who gave rise to such liability. In order to ensure oneself that the cross-indemnities are truly valid and meaningful, one should be careful to examine the financial strength of one's proposed co-venturer(s).

Table 5–1 which appears on page 89 is an example of a matrix of liability associated with the assumption of liquidated damages for late completion taken from a nonintegrated agreement between two construction industry co-venturers, in which the party who gave rise to the liability did not in every instance have to bear the full responsibility but had to bear the greater proportion of such liability.

In an integrated agreement, a joint venture will normally address how the joint venture is to be managed and structured: i.e., two firms on a 50/50 basis, or a 51/49 basis, or a 80/20 basis or somewhere in between? Or should there be three or more firms? And how will they share the workload and profits and losses? The percentage in which co-venturers' shares in profits and losses may not be the same. Sometimes the local partner may take a disproportionate share of the venture's profits when it is recognized that its resources may not be sufficient to bear a substantial portion of any losses. In contrast, however, the local partner's special contribution of local skills may justify a greater profit share.

TABLE 5–1
Matrix of Liability

Category of joint-venture liability	Allocation among co-venturers
Delayed completion—assumption of liquidated damages: attributable to fault of particular co-venturer or third parties acting on behalf of a particular co-venturer.	Paid first by the co-venturer(s) causing or responsible for such a delay, in proportion to the degree to which such co-venturer caused or contributed to the delay, up to a maximum for each such co-venturer of an amount equal to 10 percent of the final contract price including escalation applicable to the scope of work of such venturer. The excess there of, if any, is borne by all the co-venturers, including the co-venturer at fault, in accordance with their respective proportionate value.*
Delayed completion—liquidated damages: where there is an inability to determine which co-venturer caused or contributed to the delay.	Shared among the co-venturers in accordance with their respective proportionate value* on a "without-prejudice" basis until the determination of fault is arbitrated or otherwise determined.
Delayed completion—liquidated damages: due to a third party not acting on behalf of any co-venturer.	The co-venturers shall assist one another in seeking redress from such third party or relief from the client under a force majeure provision or other articles of the prime contract with the client. Failing such recovery then, to the full extent necessary, the co-venturers shall share in accordance with their respective proportionate value.*

*Proportionate value as used in the above matrix means for each co-venturer, the percentage or fraction represented by the ratio of the price of the co-venturer's scope of work to the sum of prices of all the co-venturers' scope of work.

Other questions to be addressed in an integrated agreement arrangement could include whether the local partner in an international-construction joint venture should be included as a full-sharing member of the team or should it essentially be a dormant partner, an agent rather than a true partner? Is the joint venture complete in itself or will it rely on subcontractors, and if so, how many subcontractors? How is the day-to-day management of the joint venture to be structured? How much say in the management should be given to the minority venturers?

OPERATIONAL FEATURES

The following features are critical to the operational success of construction-industry joint ventures:

- A limited number of co-venturers, preferably no more than three.
- A balance of ambition between the co-venturers and a commonality of view regarding risks.
- The ability to achieve synergisms by capitalizing on the strengths of individual co-venturers.
- Adequate delegation of authority to the on-site joint-venture team.
- Dedicated off-site support to the on-site joint-venture team by appropriate management representatives from each of the co-venturers. (However, caution should be taken that such representatives not overadminister the joint venture to the point it looses efficiency.)
- A strong and experienced project manager.
- A sound financial plan.
- Protection of technology transfer to the co-venturer(s).

As to the operational feature of having a sound financial plan as noted above, take for an example an integrated agreement with several co-venturers to perform a major construction project in a developing nation. An important initial issue will be the need for a substantial infusion of cash for mobilization costs associated with the integrated work force, including camp construction and the assembly of a fleet of purchased and leased equipment. The leader of the venture will estimate the required funds and the co-venturers will be called upon to furnish their proportionate shares. The joint-venture agreement should spell out these cash-call procedures. The cash should be deposited in a joint-venture bank account with agreement that the co-venturers can draw upon the interest until the funds are actually required.

If there is uncertainty as to the financial ability of the co-venturers to timely and fully meet these cash calls, it is recommended that, to avoid an impasse or the inability of the venture to function, the co-venturers furnish to the venture in advance, bonds, letters of credit, or cash in an amount necessary to fund the expected cash requirements of the job.

Other infusions of cash into an integrated joint venture will most likely be needed from time to time throughout the term of the joint venture as it performs its activities. In this regard, the joint-venture agreement should have very specific provisions which permit calls for additional capital and which include a time period as to when these contributions should be made and penalties for failure to participate in an appropriate and timely manner. Typically, the integrated joint-venture agreement provides that in the event of such failures, the nondefaulting co-venturers are required to fund the deficit and are entitled to interest on such advances. Furthermore, the nondefaulting co-venturers are generally given an option to convert such debt to additional profit participation in the venture. The defaulting co-venturer's share of the venture's profits is reduced proportionately, but not its share of the losses.

As to the protection of technology transfers, this should require special attention, especially where the joint-venture partner is a potential competitor. In such cases, future improvements in construction technology conceived by one co-venturer during the term of the joint-venture relationship should not be granted to the other co-venturer. In most cases, a U.S. co-venturer can be protected with regard to patented technology. Specifically, one can incorporate into the patent license the termination of the co-venturer's right to use the patents if the joint venture is terminated. However, as to unpatented technology, the situation is different. At the outset, the co-venturer should be committed in the joint-venture agreement to secrecy in regard to the know-how transmitted, and such co-venturer should be committed not to use the know-how at any time without prior approval of the co-venturer who owns such know-how. These clauses should be stipulated as surviving the termination of the joint-venture agreement. There should also be an attempt to provide for a limitation on the transfer of computer programs to ''access only'' with no right to source codes and no physical transfer of software.

DECISION-MAKING AND MANAGEMENT

In the construction industry, joint ventures are generally organized either through sponsorship or through the committee method. In the sponsorship method of organization, one of the designated joint venturers has the power to make a decision for both venturers. This allows for prompt decision making. The sponsor who has the majority of the responsibility for the project is typically given the authority for the day-to-day supervision and management of the work, including authority to appoint the project manager; to enter into purchase orders and subcontracts associated with the work; to receive payment on behalf of the joint venture; and to pay all obligations of the venture.

An issue associated with the sponsorship arrangement is the amount of the sponsor's fee. If the sponsor is to have a substantial share in the joint venture's profits and most, if not all, of its expenses are to be reimbursed by the capital being contributed to the joint venture, such firm should not be entitled to a fee. However, if the situation is the opposite, the sponsor should request and receive a fee, typically based on the profitability of the venture.

A variant of the sponsorship method is to have an advisory committee comprising senior representatives from each co-venturer's organization and/or outside consultants to give general advice and direction to the project manager and to try to resolve any areas of dispute which may arise.

Under the committee method of organization, the joint venture is run by majority or unanimous vote of the committee. Generally, the only time when a co-venturer would lose his right to vote would be when such co-venturer is in default in meeting some obligation, such as, for example, failing to meet a cash call. The recommended procedure in such cases is to allow the defaulting co-venturer's representative to continue to attend the committee meetings to be kept apprised of the project's activities, but to suspend the defaulting party's right to vote until the default is cured.

If a more than a two-co-venturer arrangement uses the committee method of organization, it is recommended that only several fundamental decisions require a unanimous vote. To mandate too many decisions by unanimous vote could impede the performance of the joint venture. The following is a suggested listing of decisions requiring such unanimous consent:

- Admission of a new co-venturer.
- Assignment of a co-venturer's interest to a third party.
- Agreements for any of co-venturers to perform construction services for the venture.

- Agreements to purchase and/or lease construction equipment from any of the co-venturers.
- Disbursements to the co-venturers in excess of their capital contributions.
- Tax elections.

The proposed joint-venture agreement should contain a comprehensive listing of those fundamental decisions requiring unanimous committee vote.

In the committee method, it is best to have only one representative and one alternate appointed from each of the co-venturers, so that the committee does not become unwieldy. A more senior appointee is typically found to have the greatest personal commitment to arriving at a consensus. A joint venture should seek to avoid a situation in which the committee members in the field always have to refer decisions to the home office for approval.

A construction-industry joint venture can also be organized through a combination of the committee and the sponsorship methods. In this case, the sponsor would report to a management committee comprising representatives from both venturers; however, the committee would only serve to provide policy rulings, overall direction, and dispute resolution. The sponsor would typically be obligated to make periodic reports to the committee as to the status of the work.

Should the joint venture do without the sponsorship or committee methods, the project will be likely to experience delays and other difficulties in administration. The co-venturers will have to negotiate any management issue that might come up during the operations of the project.

Under both the sponsorship and committee methods of organizing construction-industry joint ventures, there is typically a project manager selected from one of the co-venturers. The project manager reports to the joint-venture sponsor or committee, and is responsible for day-to-day management. The project manager provides leadership and coordinates communication between the venturers.

If the committee method of organization is used, it is best to give the project manager authority to make a decision in the event of deadlock by the committee. This way the project will be able to proceed even though a final management decision has not as yet been made. In construction contracting, time is of the essence. Frequently any decision is better than no decision at all.

MANAGEMENT CONTROLS

Normally one of the first actions in the implementation of a construction-industry joint venture is to put into place a system of management controls, as a framework for conducting relations between the partners and for internal management. It is important to recognize that, during the period of contract performance, members of the construction joint venture will exercise different skills which become critical at different times during the project. One participant may be an expert on concrete; another on the mechanical or electrical work; and another on roofing. The joint venture must preserve flexibility in order to vary technical leadership and direction to accommodate these changing needs. However, management leadership should remain unchanged for efficient and continuous administration.

The joint venture should adopt procedures implementing a clear internal financial reporting system, which would indicate to each co-venturer costs incurred as compared to the operating plan, and what payments have been billed to and received from the client. Such reporting should also give an individual accounting of all deviations from the operating plan greater than a certain percentage or volume. Each of the co-venturers should be given the authority to inspect and audit the joint-venture books.

One of the cardinal operating features of a construction joint venture, whether on an integrated or nonintegrated basis, is that the work must go on. When the co-venturers are unable to agree, there should be a summary procedure for permitting the work to continue. This can be accomplished by designating a person, not necessarily an arbitrator, to whom a dispute will be referred. It can be an outside, respected individual or a senior management person from one of the co-venturers who can make the decision. The joint venture can then proceed in accordance with that decision. If any of the co-venturers is dissatisfied with the decision, the matter can be referred to formal dispute-resolution procedures, preferably arbitration proceedings, since disputes among construction industry co-venturers don't lend themselves readily to resolutions in courts of law. The joint-venture agreement should indicate that the arbitration should take place in a neutral locale and the decision issued should be final and binding.

Finally, one should not enter into any joint venture for construction work without developing an exit strategy. If, in the planning stages, you haven't provided for a way to get out, don't get in. The first level of an exit strategy should be a determination of the length of the joint venture. Since joint-venture groupings in the construction industry are generally formed to accomplish a single project, the desired term of such a joint venture should be the foreseeable duration of the project, including the period necessary to perform any warranty, maintenance, or other contingent obligations that continue after the client's acceptance of the project.

Another part of a required exit strategy would be to address the issue of default. In event of default, whoever is the leader of the joint venture should be entitled to terminate the defaulting co-venturer's participation in the joint venture. The following represents a typical listing of events of default that could be inserted in a construction-industry joint venture agreement:

- Failure of any of the co-venturer's to prosecute the work with promptness and diligence in accordance with the construction contract after written warning by the project manager.
- In the case of an integrated agreement, the failure to advance working capital when required.
- The charging by a co-venturer of any cost not related to the performance of the construction contract, or the completion of the project, or otherwise authorized under the terms of the joint-venture agreement.
- The adjudication that a particular co-venturer is bankrupt or insolvent, or a general assignment by any co-venturer for the benefit of creditors, or the appointment of a receiver for any co-venturer, or participation by any co-venturer in any reorganization, composition, or arrangement resulting from insolvency.
- Any material breach of the joint-venture agreement.

In an integrated agreement, the co-venturer whose participation is terminated remains liable for any losses incurred by the joint venture, as determined by the percentage of its participation in the joint venture. The defaulting party should not be entitled to receive payment of any part of the fee under the construction contract, which has not already been distributed. After deducting the co-venturer's share of any losses, the defaulting co-venturer should be entitled to the return of that portion of the working capital it has contributed to the joint venture. If there is the possibility that the joint venture could end up with ''blocked currency'' accounts in a foreign jurisdiction, like Brazil or Venezuela, for example, the interim investment and future disposition of such accounts should be specified.

CONCLUSION

The above-mentioned listing of potential defaults by a co-venturer coupled with the earlier discussion in this chapter of the numerous disincentives for forming a construction-industry joint venture should demonstrate that the decision to proceed with a joint-venture arrangement to perform work on a construction project should only be made after a careful consideration of alternative ways of doing business. Unless one or more of the advantages listed clearly necessitates the formation of a joint venture, one will generally be in a better position, in terms of profit, liability, and effective completion of the construction tasks, if one can work without a joint arrangement. Even when one is able to negotiate satisfactory provisions in the joint-venture agreement, regarding the establishment of cash-call procedures, use of the sponsorship method of organization, implementation of an efficient system of management controls, incorporation of provisions for resolution of disputes and termination, and so forth, one cannot always rely upon them in the event of a dispute. One might not even be able to get a court to require a co-venturer to specifically comply with these types of provisions. In any event, enforcement will be costly, time-consuming, and generally unsatisfactory. In light of this, it is clear that the selection of the proposed co-venturer is the critical factor in the success or failure of the construction-industry joint venture.

CHAPTER 6

JOINT VENTURING IN REAL ESTATE

Richard J. Behrens
Price Waterhouse

The history of venture arrangements can be traced back to the days when merchants and investors banded together to share the risks and rewards of seafaring, trading expeditions. In this country various venture arrangements have been widely used for many years in the financing, mining, and oil and gas industries as well as for real estate developments. In the aftermath of the stock market's "Black Monday," real estate has regained the spotlight as a viable long-term investment, and joint venturing—the sharing of risk—is emerging as a widely accepted vehicle for this investment.

There are several characteristics of real estate investments that are common to both joint ventures and other forms of real estate activities. This chapter will present three fundamental concepts and then apply those concepts to the frequently found forms of joint ventures. In addition several legal, accounting, and tax considerations unique to real estate joint ventures will be discussed.

FUNDAMENTAL CONCEPTS

The underlying principle of virtually all commercial real estate transactions involves the existence of nonrecourse debt or some form of limited liability. Very few of us could—and those who could are smart enough

not to—accept personal liability in connection with the large-dollar transactions which are common to the commercial real estate business. Thus,
separate entities are created for each party's investment in each transaction. Shell corporations and limited partnerships are frequent structures.
Practice in the commercial real estate industry involves the use of nonrecourse debt. This principle requires the lender to agree that it has no
recourse to the borrower's assets other than the specific property designated in the transaction. The limited liability concept will be further
developed as we see it in practice.

The second fundamental concept in real estate is leverage. To illustrate, assume that $10 of capital will be a sufficient down payment to
purchase $50 worth of property. In the case of commercial property, the
selling price is normally determined as a multiple of the cash flow of the
property. For example, cash flow (often referred to as net operating
income) of $5 per year at a 10 percent "discount rate" (a concept anal-
ogous to the price/earnings ratio) produces a current-valve purchase of
price of $50. But if only $40 was borrowed, as above, then the $5 of
cash flow is available to service the $40 of debt. Since the capitalization
rate is significantly influenced by prevailing interest rates, the relatively
limited amount of equity has a significant effect on the ability of the
project to service the debt. It is therefore an axiom in the real estate
business that the availability of capital is just as important to the developer
as the current market demand for the product. With a fixed capital base
(or favorable financing such as a cash flow mortgage) a developer has
the ability to wait for the market to turn. Leverage and its permutations
will appear frequently as a factor of the joint venture transactions to be
discussed later in this chapter.

The third fundamental factor to real estate transactions is that wealth
is generated over relatively long periods of time. This third factor is not
always true; many stories are told about the profit in "flipping" land en
route to the title company. However, the great wealth of many families
can be traced to long-term real estate holdings which have been judicially
developed over decades. This is not, generally speaking, an industry for
the short-term player.

JOINT-VENTURE CONSIDERATION

Recognition of the need for external assistance, e.g. expertise, funding,
or other contributions (such as signing a lease to occupy a building), is

the starting point in the formation of a venture. This is both a strength and a weakness of the joint-venture format. The strength is that this form of business combination is very flexible; the nature of the project and the partners' respective capabilities determine the precise form of the venture. However, since joint-venture structures are rarely identical to each other, difficulties arise in interpretation because the underlying purpose that brought the parties together is different. Hence, generalizations about joint-venture formats are difficult. It is essential that each party recognize and mutually value the contribution of the other parties. Real estate developers create wealth by combining real estate products (land, construction, leasing, and operations) into a single product—income producing properties. When one component of that equation is missing, the opportunity for a joint venture exists.

The most significant emerging trend in real estate joint ventures is the recognition that the numerous areas of expertise needed for successful development are frequently not available within a single organization, and that the concepts of motivation and commonality of interest dictate that equity interest be held by a broader range of participants than has historically been the case.

The most common impetus in joint-venture formation is the developer/builder needing capital. Here the two parties have clearly different areas of expertise, and, thus, their relationship is relatively easy to establish. Note, however, that a multibillion-dollar segment of today's real estate market exists because many lenders did not understand that they were being transformed from real estate lenders into real estate principals. The key to success from the lender's perspective is to know whether the funds advanced are in substance a loan, a participating mortgage, or an equity investment. This is the "acquisition, development, and construction loan" issue. The American Institute of Certified Public Accountants (in its February 1986 "Notice to Practitioners") and the Securities and Exchange Commission (in its August 1987 and December 1987 releases of Staff Accounting Bulletin No. 71 and No. 71A) have attempted to focus on the differences among these types of cash advances which often utilize similar loan documents.

To avoid costly misunderstanding, the developer should understand the lender's expectations regarding: (a) what collateral and guarantees secure the loan, (b) what other sources of financing, if any, are to be utilized in the project, (c) how principal and interest payments are to be funded (amount and timing), and (d) the lender's participation in expected residual profits. The lender's expectation issue is important to a discussion of joint ventures, since it is a clear example of the wisdom that a successful venture has at its base a clear—preferably written—agreement among the venturers as to each party's responsibilities and expectations.

Other joint ventures are formed because of non-capital needs of the developer of the property. Co-development is a venture between developers. For example, an urban office building project might match a national developer who directs the architect and a general contractor as well as arranging for financing with local real estate experts who would provide site selection, local tenant contacts, and leasing expertise. Co-developers for a suburban office park might be, again, a national developer who deals with feasibility analysis and project master-planning, while the local people are involved in leasing and operations.

Another rationale for formation of a joint venture is the necessity for or appropriateness of the developer sharing the increase in value added by a lessee. This general concept reflects several different motivations from the developer's point of view and emphasizes (to the prospective lessee) the need to understand the rationale motivating the lessor joint-venture partner. A developer's motivation may be any combination of a desire to do the following:

(a) keep a large tenant from leaving a building located in a market where rents are declining;

(b) attract and keep a tenant the developer otherwise could not obtain without giving up an ownership interest;

(c) develop a project which could not otherwise proceed as an "all-speculative" project;

(d) defray lease-up risk or the risk of carrying an investment in land and construction by accelerating the lease-up process;

(e) support a project already under construction by securing a large tenant; or

(f) lead a quality tenant to an unestablished project so that the balance of the project becomes more viable.

These are subtle but significant differences, the key to which, in the developer's mind, is whether the granting of equity is justified in view of the decrement in risk to the project's success associated with obtaining the new tenant. Note that often the driving force for these initial concessions is a decrement of risk rather than a measurable increase in profit potential.

Let's review an example of the decrement-of-risk aspect of joint venturing. Assume that a 100,000 square foot building costs $10 million to build, including all hard costs (land, bricks and mortar) and soft costs (interest, taxes, fees, etc.). Without a tenant, the sales value of the project is far more questionable—and probably at a lesser value—than if a paying tenant were under lease. So if a lessee were to need 100,000 square feet of space at the time the building was available, the developer should be willing to "give" a portion of the equity solely for obtaining a fair-market-value lease, which would result in secured cash flow for the project. The worth of the property is positively affected by the secured cash flow of the project. Assume the tenant signs a long-term lease which produces $10 per foot of net operating income: $10 per foot multiplied by 100,000 square feet at a capitalization rate of 10 percent produces a present value of $10 million-apparently equal only to the assumed cost. The difference is that the cash-flow valuation is far more preferable to a lender than a valuation based on cost. In addition, secured cash flow over the project's early years provides a base which covers operating cost and services debt. At the expiration of the lease, a new, and presumably more favorable, set of economics is utilized by the developer/owner to set future rental levels. Note, however, that the project's major costs—construction and interest—have been fixed. In return for "carrying" the project to this point, the smart lessee has negotiated some form of equity/joint-venture interest.

Three significant points from the developer's perspective are evident from this example. Assuming all lessees at the inception of the lease were negotiating similar terms, the developer/lessor is only giving away a percentage of profit that would otherwise not exist. In addition, the developer is generally involved in managing the property and receiving an annual fee which helps cover overhead. Finally, many permanent-financing lenders do not allow the developer to take the full amount of "development profit" until satisfactory leases are in place.

The decision regarding the precise form of the joint venture should reflect the relationship of the parties and the nature of their contributions to the venture. A corporate joint venture, general partnership, limited partnership, or even co-tenancy may be appropriate. The structure is inherently flexible; the need is to choose wisely.

DIVORCE IN REAL ESTATE

Before consumating the marriage of a joint venture, it is important to establish a mechanism for disbanding the agreement. Real estate is generally a long-term investment; marriages often are not. The value of a project prior to sale is a subjective determination, particularly when operations have not yet been normalized. Thus, many joint-venture agreements have a "shotgun" or "Texas draw" clause which operate in the following way: each joint-venture party has the right at times specified in the agreement (e.g., each anniversary date), or possibly at any time, to cause the termination of the joint venture. This is based on the premise that there is very little value in attempting to force the continued participation of an unwilling venturer. Litigation is time-consuming and often disruptive to the successful operations of a property. In most cases, each venturer makes intangible as well as tangible contributions. Thus, the question should be "how" not "if" the venture is to be disbanded prematurely. Upon notice served to the other venturers, the shotgun clause requires the party initiating the withdrawal to offer a value to the project. After a reasonable time period, say 30 days, the party receiving the notice must respond indicating its intention to either buy the disenchanted party's interest or to sell its own interest. In either case, the price has been fixed in the initial notice. After the response, a further period, say two weeks, will be allowed at which time the closing occurs. The buying party is required to pay cash for the selling party's interest.

The principle is that either party can cause the termination of the venture without fatally jeopardizing the underlying project's operating viability. While this procedure is neutral when the parties are of equal strength, it tends to favor the better-financed party. Generally, it is the stronger party who "pulls the trigger" and sets a price which, they believe, the weaker party cannot afford to pay. Thus, the stronger party can buy the remaining interest in the project at a favorable price. Often the timing of this strategy is to have it occur after the completion of the construction and pre-leasing phases but prior to the normalization of operations. A call-option arrangement eliminates some of these problems but is not practical in a development project, due to the difficulty in establishing, in advance, a fair market value of the project at stated future time periods. In any case, the principle to be addressed at the inception of the joint venture is the mechanism to be established so that the parties in an adversarial environment can avoid damaging the value of the underlying real estate project.

TAXATION

Joint ventures are "pass-through entities," i.e., they are not subject to federal income tax at the entity level, but must pass through to their owners the tax attributes of the joint venture's operations.

In addition to the general taxation aspects of joint ventures, there are only two areas which might be said to have a particular impact on real estate joint ventures: depreciation (a function of the leveraging concept), and at-risk considerations.

Real estate has been a highly visible target for tax reform. Taken in a broader historical perspective however, the thrust of the Tax Reform Act of 1986 (TRA '86) was simply another readjustment of tax policy. The tax orientation of many personal investors in the real estate industry reflects the favorable results of leveraging a purchase price which is then subject to depreciation. As a simple example, let's assume that a $10 million property is purchased with 20 percent equity. The equity holders could previously depreciate the property over roughly twenty years. A 20 percent factor for land value produces, under previous regulations, an annual depreciation allowance of $400,000 or 20 percent per year of the original cash invested. The increase of depreciable lives mandated by TRA '86 brings the annual depreciation down to roughly 13 percent of the same equity investment. Assuming the property has sufficient cash flow to service all operating and debt requirements, the tax impact of returning original principal in seven and a half years compares favorably to other industries, even if it is less favorable than five years as under previous tax legislation.

The "at-risk" provisions of the tax law affect all investors. In the above example, investors were at risk for only $2 million, assuming the $8 million debt was nonrecourse. In many other industries, the investor's deduction would be limited to the amount invested. In real estate, assuming the transaction is properly structured, the investor's basis can include the amount of nonrecourse debt. The at-risk rules have been significantly strengthened so that this favorable aspect is not available as frequently as was the case prior to TRA '86. Careful planning is essential in all tax matters, but particularly so for real estate.

Change is constant, but the key to investing is relative value. The tax aspects of real estate are still attractive when compared to many other industries.

TRANSACTIONS WITH JOINT VENTURES

Transactions with joint ventures reflect the responsibilities and expectations of each joint-venture partner. Let's examine the motivations of four types of venturers. The landowner typically contributes land for a joint-venture interest without active participation in the venture. The joint venture may, in fact, acquire the land under a subordinated-note agreement; thus giving the seller slightly more security as to the ultimate collection of proceeds, while allowing the venture to use the equity in the land to obtain development funding. In return a valuation is fixed on the initial land and an equity-participation rate is negotiated.

Cash investors add an equity layer essential to the debt financing—and debt servicing—process. Numerous joint-venture and limited-partnership structures have been devised to compensate the cash-equity partner. For example, preferential cash distributions of net operating income are frequently made to the cash investor, in preference to distributions of such profit to the land contributor or developer. Allocation of the tax results of operations was, prior to TRA '86, a matter of wide diversity in practice. Application of the "substantial-economic-effect" concept limits the flexibility of partnerships and joint ventures. For tax purposes, the allocation of results of operations must be in a manner consistent with the true economic relationship among the partners, i.e., artificial allocations—even if agreed to by the parties—will not be recognized. This problem occurred in the past when one group of investors—individuals—were allocated a greater proportion of losses with the agreement of another group of investors—say, tax-exempt pension plans or corporations with net operating losses. Substantial economic effect also requires that, at the termination of the partnership, capital accounts of the partners be normalized. Thus, a partner who has been allocated cumulative losses may be required to receive allocated taxable income without receiving a related amount of cash in order to bring its capital account out of a negative balance to zero. Note that real estate projects usually will have operating losses in earlier years followed by a period in which (as operations improve) cash flow is positive but taxable income is reduced by depreciation. Thus, the return to investors is a delicate combination of the tax effects of their investment and the actual operating results of the project.

The developer usually contributes services and intangibles in return for its joint-venture interest. The analogy has been made that a good developer is the glue necessary for all the pieces to be properly assembled: another is that a good developer is the chef who is an essential ingredient in the cooking process. So much for analogies. The developer's joint-venture interest is determined by the value added and risk assumed, and this will vary substantially among joint ventures.

We have previously referred to the fourth major player in the joint venture, the lender. Here too, the precise nature of involvement varies substantially among joint ventures. The principal message of this section is that the significant role of each joint-venture partner cannot be stereotyped. It must be negotiated for each joint venture, so that each party in the agreement understands the responsibilities and expectations of each other venturer.

SALES OF REAL ESTATE

Accounting for sales of real estate is governed by Financial Accounting Standards Board Statement No. 66. The overriding principle is that profit recognition is appropriate only when the earnings process has been completed, i.e., when the risks and rewards of ownership have been transferred and collection of the sales proceeds is reasonably assured. The existence of a joint-venture structure often complicates a clear understanding of this principle. The general rule is that, to the extent an investor enters into a transaction with a joint venture in which the investor has an equity interest, the transaction is tainted to some degree with regard to profit recognition.

Since the purpose of this chapter is to focus on the joint-venture aspects of real estate, rather than accounting for joint ventures in general, this segment will only summarize the specialized areas of real estate transactions which commonly cause questions about profit recognition. These are three: buyer's initial investment, buyer's continuing investment, and seller's continuing involvement. Permutations of these principles are constantly being reviewed as ''innovative'' transactions are developed. Accounting rules are sometimes inflexible in response to perceived abuses in past practice. In summary, a favorable response to the following three questions generally provides comfort that profit recognition is appropriate:

1. Have the risks and rewards of ownership truly been transferred?
2. Is the buyer motivated and committed to complete the transaction?
3. Has the seller completed performance of all of its obligations to and association with the property?

JOINT-VENTURE FINANCIAL STATEMENTS

The financial statements of joint ventures have a more limited purpose than many other financial statements prepared in accordance with generally accepted accounting principles. This is better understood in demonstrating the varied interests of the venturers. Assume a joint venture is formed among a landholder, a cash-equity partner, a developer, and a lender. The land is valued at the fair market value of $1 million at date of contribution—determined principally by mutual concurrence of the venturers—but cost the contributing venturer $300,000. Cash-equity investors contribute $1 million. The lender provides an $8 million loan at prevailing terms, and the developer oversees construction of an income-producing property. Each party has a negotiated portion of profit upon ultimate sale and may also have similar or differing interests in periodic operating cash flow. Often, however the cash equity partner will ask that it receive a return, say $80,000 (8 percent), on the first available net operating income. Then, the land contributor may ask to receive the next $80,000 as a preferential distribution.

A careful analysis of the interests above shows that each venturer will have a different interpretation of the results of operations. In this case, ignoring any residual profit participation interest, the lender has a significantly diminished concern after its debt service is covered. The cash equity partner may be content with receiving its stated preferential return during the periods of operations. Payment of this same amount, however, when received by the land contributor, represents a significant return on its investment ($80,000 divided by $300,000 or 27 percent per annum). Thus, it is critical to review the economic effects—and accounting results—of each transaction, both from the point of view of the joint venture as a whole and, more importantly, from each joint-venturer's perspective. While all venturers wish the project to succeed, each individual venturer usually has different criteria for what constitutes success.

For example, the financial statements of the joint venture reflect land at $1 million. The amounts reflected in the financial statements of the joint venturer who contributed the land remain unchanged, with the $300,000 amount, previously captioned "land" now captioned "investment in joint venture."

Another excellent example of this point is the procedure for recording, on the books of the investor, losses arising from the initial operations of a real estate project. As mentioned previously, most real estate projects reflect losses in initial periods due to the level of financing and the impact of depreciation. If the joint-venture partner who contributed land receives a 25 percent joint-venture interest (together with the preferred cash-flow arrangement), any losses allocated to the venturer in excess of $300,000—

the investor's cost in the land contributed to the joint venture—will most likely not have to be recorded in such venturer's financial statements. This is true notwithstanding that the investor could probably continue to take such losses in excess of $300,000 for federal income tax purposes, subject to the passive-loss limitation, "at-risk" and "substantial economic effect" rules of TRA '86. This accounting result arises from application of the historical cost convention; only $300,000—the original cost—is at risk. This result also assumes that the joint-venture partner was a limited partner, rather than a general partner. The tax and accounting results are often influenced by factors that may not initially appear significant to the venturers. That is one more reason why it is imperative that the joint-venture agreement clearly state the position and obligations of each venturer.

When venture losses in excess of investment are not recognized and the venture subsequently reports income, the investor should recognize venture earnings only after its share of net income equals that share of net losses not previously recognized during the period in which the equity method was suspended.

Situations may arise in which one or more venturers may be incapable of bearing their share of venture losses. In the event that cash losses are incurred, and if it is probable that an investor is not capable of bearing its share of the losses, the remaining investors often should record their revised proportionate share of venture's losses. Subsequent earnings of the venture should be recorded by those other investors to the extent that such earnings equal the previously recorded excess losses. The critical factor is the manner in which the joint venture's cash losses are being funded. Recognition of the loss by the other venturers, however, does not exempt a financially incapable investor from recording its allocable share, unless relieved from any obligation by agreement or operation of law. The determination of probability as to whether an investor is unable to bear its share of losses should be based on the provisions of Financial Accounting Standards No. 5, "Accounting for Contingencies."

Statement of Position 78–9 issued by the AICPA has adopted a position comparable to that in paragraph 19h of Accounting Principles Board Opinion No. 18 and indicates that "A loss in value of an investment, including loans and advances, other than a temporary decline should be recognized under the accounting principles that apply to a loss in value of other long-term assets. Such a loss may be indicated, for example, by a decision by other investors to cease providing support or to reduce their financial commitment to the venture."

CONTROL

In determining the appropriate accounting for venture interests, it is important to identify which party, if any, is in control of the investee; the legal form of the entity is often not a determining factor.

A controlling investor should account for its income and losses under the principles of accounting applicable to investments in subsidiaries which would usually require consolidation of the venture's operations with appropriate recognition of minority interests.

Paragraph 1 of Accounting Research Bulletin No. 51 states with respect to corporate entities that:

> There is a presumption that consolidated statements are more meaningful than separate statements and that they are usually necessary for a fair presentation when one of the companies in the group directly or indirectly has a controlling financial interest in the other companies.

The Securities and Exchange Commission has issued Rule 3A-02 of Regulation S-X which emphasizes the same point:

> In deciding upon consolidation policy, the registrant must consider what financial presentation is most meaningful in the circumstances and should follow in the consolidated financial statements principles of inclusion or exclusion which will clearly exhibit the financial position and results of operations of the registrant. There is a presumption that consolidated statements are more meaningful than separate statements and that they are usually necessary for a fair presentation when one entity directly or indirectly has a controlling financial interest in another entity. Other particular facts and circumstances may require combined financial statements, an equity method of accounting, or valuation allowances in order to achieve a fair presentation.

The application of consolidation principles to investments in partnerships and unincorporated ventures should not be different from those applicable to corporations; but in each case the provisions of the agreement must be carefully analyzed, together with all the facts and circumstances surrounding the investor's interests to determine if control is present.

If the venture is operating in a foreign country in which realization of venture earnings by the investor is subject to major uncertainties, as in the case of significant exchange restrictions, governmental controls, substantial political, economic, or social disruptions or uncertainties, it might be appropriate not to consolidate such operations or to recognize the investor's share of such earnings until they are remitted as dividends or distributions.

A noncontrolling investor should account for its share of income and losses in real estate ventures by using the equity method. An interpretation issued by the AICPA in November 1971 stated further that "Many of the provisions of the Accounting Principles Board Opinion No. 18 would be appropriate in accounting for investments in...unincorporated entities...." Therefore, as a general rule, investors should account for all unincorporated joint-venture interests (including general and limited-partnership interests) using the equity method.

The cost method, however, is appropriate in certain situations such as: (a) ventures operating in a foreign country where realization is subject to major uncertainties (e.g., exchange restrictions, governmental controls, substantial political, economic or social disruptions), and (b) for limited partnerships where the investor's interest is so insignificant that the limited partner has virtually no influence over partnership operating and financial policies (e.g., a very minor interest in a limited partnership). As with all investments, the owner should assess the recoverability and make appropriate write-downs where necessary. Although not common in the real estate industry, the proportionate-share method may be appropriate where stringent criteria are met for "undivided interests."

With respect to corporations, Paragraph 3 of APB Opinion No. 18 states that "...the usual condition for control is ownership of a majority (over 50%) of the outstanding voting stock. The power to control may also exist with a lesser percentage of ownership, for example, by contract, lease, agreement with other stockholders or by court decree."

With respect to a general partnership, control would generally be the same as indicated for a corporation. However, if voting interests are not clearly indicated, ownership of a majority (over 50 percent) of the financial interests in profits and losses would usually indicate control. On the other hand, majority ownership may not constitute control if major decisions, such as the acquisition, sale, or refinancing of principal partnership assets must be approved by one or more of the other partners.

The rights and obligations of general partners are different from those of limited partners. A general partner may be in control regardless of his ownership or financial interest when the substance of the partnership arrangement or other agreement provides for his control. This may be the case when the general partner decides on major operating and financial policies of the partnership and cannot be removed. If such conditions do exist, a limited partner may not be in control even if it holds over 50 percent of the total partnership interest.

With respect to undivided interests, control is generally not present since each investor owns an undivided interest in each venture asset and is liable for its share to each liability. If this is not the case, such arrangements should be treated the same as a general partnership.

ACCOUNTING

Under the equity method, the initial investment is recorded by the investor at cost. Thereafter the carrying amount is increased by the venturer's share of current earnings and decreased by the venturer's share of current losses or distributions.

Under the cost method, the initial investment is recorded by the investor at cost. Thereafter income is recognized only when distributions are received by the investor from earnings subsequent to the acquisition or when the investor sells its interest in the venture.

The proportionate-share approach may be applied: (1) to noncorporate investments which are, in fact, undivided interests (each participant owns an undivided interest in each venture asset and is liable for a proportionate share of each liability), and (2) where it has become established industry practice. This may be the case for oil, gas, and mining ventures or for similar ventures that are a part of a vertically integrated operation. Generally, this feature of being part of a vertically integrated operation, which makes the proportionate-share approach appropriate, is not found in real estate operations. The proportionate-share approach would be to record the investor's share of each item of income, expense, asset, and liability together with appropriate interentity eliminations.

Application of this approach in balance sheets of real estate ventures should be selective even for legal undivided interests, since the concept of proportionate title may not be valid; i.e., a partner may not be able to exercise his title to a portion of each asset because of agreement or practical business considerations. Another problem in using this method is that the interests of the other venturers are not disclosed, and the statements may imply, erroneously, that all assets are under the unrestricted control of the investor.

CONCLUSION

The economic principles that enable real estate to be a source of long-term wealth are often enhanced by careful application of the joint-venture concept. The parties should understand the nature of the proposed project and be able to deal with changes in joint-venture partner attitudes. Ultimate realization of the earnings process—receiving unencumbered cash from third parties—represents the true measure of success.

CHAPTER 7

JOINT VENTURING IN THE INFORMATION AND TECHNOLOGY INDUSTRY

John R. Griffiths, Esq.
Crist, Griffiths, Schulz & Biorn
Patricia J. Van Horn, Esq.
Crist, Griffiths, Schulz & Biorn
Irving S. Rappaport, Esq.
Associate General Counsel Apple Computer, Inc.

Perhaps nowhere has technology moved so far, so fast, as it has in the computer and data communications industries in the 1980s. The personal computer has revolutionized computing, placing it affordably in the hands of families, schools, and small businesses. The operational capacity of personal and minicomputers has expanded, making them capable of sophisticated design applications, desk-top publishing, spread sheets, and graphics. The larger mainframes and the new ''supercomputers'' can perform computations at previously undreamed-of speeds. Networking programs allow personal computers and minis to communicate with one another in a way that was once reserved for larger machines capable of utilizing powerful multiuser, multitasking operating systems.

Consumer expectations have risen to keep pace with the industry. Voicemail has become a part of the standard office-automation package in many large offices. Major manufacturers have automated their product design and assembly, seeking increasingly more sophisticated software to create the prints and prototypes and to run the robotics involved in those processes. The medical profession has automated and computerized its diagnostic equipment. A new generation of ''minisupers,'' which have the speed and power to rival mainframes, are multiuser capable, and can be used for mathematical, scientific, and business applications, is appearing on the market. Operating systems which are capable of use in a number of human languages are coming to the fore. The permutations of computer-driven technology seem endless.

Taken together, the expanded potential and the expanded demands for new applications have created a high-tech environment in which new products sometimes appear obsolete before they are introduced. In this environment, private enterprise, working within itself or together with universities and government agencies, is making increasingly frequent use of the joint venture to spread out research and development costs and marketing costs and to extend the useful life of products by exposing those products to a broader group of users. These joint ventures accomplish a variety of ends.

Example: A manufacturer of minicomputers with multiuser capabilities enters into a joint venture with the manufacturer of a peripheral which allows the minicomputer to accomplish voice simulation and add voicemail to its total office-automation system. Each party to the joint venture is responsible for the development of its own component to interface with one another; each manufacturer is responsible for marketing the combined system to its existing, new, and potential customers, effectively doubling the sales force of each organization and doubling the exposure of the combined product in the market place.

Example: A U.S. manufacturer of computer hardware and bundled software forms a joint venture with a group of companies in the Far East for the purpose of licensing the manufacture and marketing of products outside the United States.

Example: A major manufacturer of minicomputer hardware and system software enters into a joint-development effort with a leading manufacturer of personal computers. Although both companies have preexisting networking capability for their own products, the two companies agree that each of them will develop certain portions of the software necessary to permit the systems and networks to communicate with one another. The development agreement focuses only on the technology, leaving open the potential for a future marketing joint venture of the newly developed communication system, as well as for the related products of the two companies.

Example: A major university enters into a joint venture with a computer manufacturing company, licensing to the manufacturer its design of and rights to a new super computer with a revoluntary chip-based central processing unit.

Example: The developer of a personal computer operating system with multiuser, multitasking ability and the developer of the most commercially successful variant on that operating system enter into a joint-venture/licensing agreement, under which they combine their two systems into an identical system in which they both market under the same trade name, hoping, by this device, to force standardization in the market place and to gain a preeminent position in that market place.

Example: A Japanese industrial giant enters into a joint venture with a small, but emerging, U.S. computer hardware manufacturer to develop and market a new workstation. The U.S. company gains financial strength and industrial clout from dealing with a recognized international firm. The Japanese company gains a head start in breaking into a competitive U.S. market in which its joint venturer is already established as a force in the development of workstations.

The examples, in short, are endless. The forms the joint ventures take vary from highly structured corporate formations with complex cross-licensing agreements to loose statements of intent to cooperate. The ends, however, are uniform. Through their cooperative efforts, the joint venturers gain a competitive edge: they cut their costs of development, manufacture or distribution; they gain access to new technology; they broaden the visibility of their own product and, hence, its acceptance in the market place.

All of this is not, however, without its price. Because joint venturing in the high-tech fields of computers and data communication is so linked to research and development in areas considered proprietary and confidential, joint venturing in these areas gives rise to some questions which do not commonly arise among joint venturers in other industries. How does one share his proprietary information with his joint venture partner, without having that information, lose its proprietary or secret nature? Who owns the new, jointly developed technology? What research and development costs are tax deductible by the joint venture itself, or by each of the joint venturers? What form of business organization is preferable and what are the consequences of choosing one over the other?

This chapter will address these questions and others more broadly applicable to joint venturing in any field or industry with the view toward giving those contemplating entry into this arena a sense of the legal implications of joint venturing and the questions which should be resolved among the joint venturers before they commit to the project.

THE FORM OF THE JOINT VENTURE—LEGAL PRINCIPLES COMMON TO ALL

The law does not require any particular form or formality of contract to establish a joint venture. In fact, since, as a general rule, oral contracts are as valid and binding as written ones, joint venturers could theoretically embark upon their new relationship with a verbal agreement sealed with the traditional handshake. There are exceptions to this rule, however. The exception which is most likely to apply to joint-venture agreements in high-tech fields is the one which requires agreements which will be in force over extended periods of time (in most states, one year or longer) to be in writing. Given the long lead-time for the research and development effort required if the venturers are to reap any benefits from their enterprise, a written agreement is advisable. The form of the agreement can be molded, however, to fit precisely the needs of the project it is intended to formalize.

The most highly formalized sort of joint venture is one in which the venturers form a separate corporation to carry out their enterprise. An entirely new corporate entity can be formed, or a joint venturer can buy into an existing company. If the latter vehicle is chosen, it may be necessary to amend the bylaws of the corporation in order to allow the new venturer-shareholder to acquire stock. If all of the authorized stock has been issued, for example, amendment of the bylaws to authorize additional shares will provide the new venturer with an investment vehicle. In order to make certain that the enterprise is truly managed jointly, the joint-venture agreement should provide for equal representation on the corporation's Board of Directors, a mechanism for approval of all remaining shareholders in the event that one shareholder wishes to sell his stock, and a mechanism for maintaining parity in stock ownership. Since a corporation is a legal entity existing separate from its owners, the written agreement should also cover the issues of transfers to the corporation of assets belonging to the joint venturers. For example, if one of the joint venturers owns a patent which is critical to the common enterprise, the written agreement should cover the circumstances under which the corporation should be licensed to utilize the patent. If unpatented technology is to be transferred to the corporation, the written agreement should establish a mechanism for protecting that technology by maintaining its secrecy. The agreement should also address the issues of ownership of any technology developed by the corporation; i.e., is it to be the property of the corporation or is it to be transferred to the joint venturers.

Many of the same questions arise in less highly structured venturers. For example, imagine a joint venture of two well-established hardware/software developers. Each of the two wishes to keep its own corporate and product identity, but a large potential market exists for enhancements that would permit the integrated use of the products of the two companies. The two companies might enter into a joint venture in which they agree to strive to develop such product enhancements. The development, however, will be done not by a new joint entity, but by the existing corporations each working in-house toward a common goal. Once the goal is reached and the new product enhancements are available, each company will market them to its own customer base with the hope of broadening that base by making available products which will allow the customer the increased flexibility that results from the integrated use of the two product lines. In a venture such as this, ownership and management questions are minor. However, the written joint-venture agreement must address such areas as technology sharing, development responsibility, and ownership of new technology.

No matter what form is selected, there are some nearly universal legal principles that apply to all joint ventures. First, joint venturers are treated fundamentally as partners in a general partnership. In fact, in a litigation context, courts rarely trouble themselves about determining whether a particular litigant is a general partnership or a joint venture. The provisions of the Uniform Partnership Act are applied to both where appropriate.[1]

---

[1]*Ziebak v. Nasser,* 12 Cal.2d 1 (1938).

In any partnership or joint venture, the joint venturers owe one another the duties of fiduciaries. They must render to one another complete and true information on all things regarding the joint venture; account to one another for the profits of the venture; and share business opportunities that are within the scope of the venture.[2]

In their relationships with third parties, joint venturers may not be bound so completely by general partnership law as they are in their dealings with one another. For example, general partners are held to be one another's agents, with the authority to bind one another contractually by acts which are related to the partnership enterprise. Early cases, in an attempt to distinguish between general partnerships and joint ventures, found that joint ventures were more limited in breadth and scope than partnerships.[3] However, later courts have recognized that a joint venture may be as broad-based as a partnership, or more so, and have determined questions of one joint venturer's ability to bind another contractually on a case-by-case basis. These courts have reasoned that no matter how broad or narrow the scope of the venture, one joint venturer must be found to have authority to bind the other contractually if the contract is one that is reasonably necessary to the carrying out of the venture's business.[4]

Where tort liability is concerned, members of a joint venture are treated exactly like general partners. All members of the venture are liable for torts committed by any member if those torts are done in furtherance of the business of the enterprise. This is true whether the tort was committed negligently[5] or intentionally.[6]

All of these legal principles apply no matter what form of joint venture is adopted. In fact, it has been held that even where the joint venturers adopt a corporate form in an attempt to limit liability, that form may be examined to determine whether in fact the corporation is a mere agency for the purpose of carrying out the joint venture. If innocent third parties would be injured by recognizing the corporate form, the courts will look through that form and put the parties back in the positions they

---

[2]*Nelson v. Abraham*, 29 Cal.2d 745 (1949). *MacIsaac v. Pozzo*, 81 Cal.App.2d 278 (1947).
[3]*Keyes v. Nims*, 43 Cal.App.1 (1919). *Nelson v. Abraham, supra.* 203.
[4]*Smalley v. Baker*, 262 Cal.App.2d (1968).
[5]*Hupfield v. Wadley*, 89 Cal.App.2d 171 (1948).
[6]*Grant v. Weatherholt*, 123 Cal.App.2d 34 (1954).

occupied under the original joint-venture agreement for purposes of as-
signing liability.[7] Therefore, if questions of limitation of liability are a
major concern, care should be taken to draft the agreement in order to
state the business of the venture as narrowly as possible, and to establish
in the agreement a system of safeguards under which the business of the
venture will be conducted. In corporate forms, this can be accomplished
by guaranteeing equal stock ownership among the venturers and equal
representation on the Board of Directors. In more loosely organized entities, it is still possible to institute such safeguards. For example, the
agreement might provide that the consent of more than one venturer, or
the consent of a majority of the venturers, would be required before the
enterprise can be bound.

Potential joint venturers in the high-technology industries, however,
will typically have different concerns. Such enterprises generally involve
high-level research and development, technology sharing, and questions
of ownership of newly developed technology. If a sufficient level of trust
and confidence exists among the venturers to solve these more intricate
questions, general concerns of creation and sharing of venture-wide liability should be easily solved. The important thing is that they be addressed and not ignored.

RESEARCH AND DEVELOPMENT: THE TAX
IMPLICATIONS OF COST SHARING

Empirical evidence suggests that one of the main reasons to enter into a
joint venture in the high-technology industries is to spread the cost of
developing new products or applications. Because, even though under
the new tax law (the Tax Reform Act of 1986), tax deductions and credits
may be available for costs of research and development, the joint venture
should be carefully structured to assure that these tax benefits fall where
they are most useful. We caution you that a review of this chapter is not
intended to substitute for consultation with a tax specialist. However, an
awareness of these principles may assist you in choosing the form that
the joint venture is to take.

Two different tax benefits are potentially available for research ex-
penditure. Section 174 of the Internal Revenue Code allows deduction

---

[7]*Elsbach v. Mulligan*, 58 Cal.App.2d 354 (1943).

or amortization of expenses. IRC Section 41 establishes a tax credit. Although different rules apply, certain expenditures may be eligible for both. Under Section 174, if the rules are met, the taxpayer may elect to deduct research or experimental expenses paid or incurred in connection with a trade or business *or* he may amortize the costs over a period of not less than 60 months, beginning with the month he first receives benefit from the result of the research.

The research and development credit found in Section 41 was added to the code by the Economic Recovery Tax Act of 1981 and extended to 1989 by the Tax Reform Act of 1986. It was originally a nonrefundable 25 percent credit (reduced to 20 percent by the Tax Reform Act) for certain research and experimental expenditures incurred in carrying on a trade or business. In addition to the credit for *in-house* experimentation and research, the taxpayer is entitled to credit for 65 percent of amounts it pays to others for contract research conducted on its behalf, and for 100 percent of amounts paid to universities or other qualified institutions to conduct basic research. The taxpayer is allowed the credit only to the extent that the current year's research expense exceeds the average annual amount of such expenditures in a specified base period (generally the three tax years immediately preceding the year in which the deduction is claimed). If the taxpayer is a new business, it can still qualify for the credit. The base period is assumed to be the three immediately preceding tax years, and the amount expended in each of those years is presumed to be zero.

Research is defined similarly under the two sections. Generally, it is expenditures incidental to the development or improvement of an experimental or pilot model, a plant process, a product, a formula, an invention, or similar property. In order to qualify for the Section 41 credit, it must be undertaken through a process of experimentation, must be technological or scientific in nature, and must be related to a permitted purpose (e.g., experimentation designed to lead to cosmetic changes in a product does not qualify).

There are some fundamental differences in the rules promulgated under the two sections. For example, certain overhead items are eligible for deduction or amortization under Section 174, but not for the Section 41 credit. Research must be done inside the United States to be eligible for the credit. Although the taxpayer's involvement in the trade or business must be active (as opposed to passive investing)[8] to qualify for the benefit

---

[8]*Green v. Commissioner,* 83 T.C. 667 (1984).

of either section, expenditures undertaken in connection with developing businesses (as opposed to presently profitable ones) are eligible for the Section 174 deduction, but not the Section 41 credit.[9]

The rules applying to both sections have some nuances of special interest to those involved in high-technology industries. The first relate to costs of developing computer software; the second, to the costs involved in obtaining patents.

Under Section 174, software development costs have not been treated as research costs. However, the Internal Revenue Service has stated that software development so closely resembles the kind of research and experimentation that comes within Section 174 that it is entitled to similar accounting treatment.[10] When Congress enacted the R & D tax credit in 1981, it was aware that the IRS had never actually decided whether software-development costs qualified as expenditures entitled to Section 174 benefits. Thus, earlier procedures promulgated by the IRS were specifically referred to in committee, and Congress established its intent that software development costs would be eligible for the R & D credit under the same rules that apply to other research costs.

In 1983, the Treasury Department proposed regulations to use in determining whether specific software development costs were eligible for benefits under either Section 174 or Section 41. These proposed regulations provided that the expenditures must relate to software which is new or significantly improved and the operational feasibility of which is clearly in doubt. The proposed regulations limited the eligible expenditures to programming costs, a limitation which excludes from eligibility the important preprogramming stages of software development.

During the Conference on the 1986 Tax Reform Act, however, the Treasury Department assured the conferees of its intent to modify the 1983 regulations, and on an expedited basis. The conference report noted and relied upon that assurance, and the Treasury followed up by issuing a notice that its final regulations would clarify that, under Section 174, software development costs would " . . . qualify as research expenses eligible for the credit under the same standards as applied to the costs of developing other products and processes."[11]

---

[9]*Snow v. Commissioner,* 416 U.S. 500 (1974).
[10]Rev. Proc. 69–21.
[11]Notice 87–12, I.R.B. 87–4.

Still in doubt is the tax treatment of software developed for the taxpayer's internal use. When regulations are finally adopted, it appears that they will require, if the cost of developing internal-use software is to be eligible for benefits, that the software be innovative, developed at significant economic risk to the taxpayer, and not commercially available to the taxpayer.[12]

The questions as to tax treatment of the costs involved in obtaining a patent are clearer. Under Section 174, the costs of obtaining a patent, including legal fees incurred in making and perfecting a patent application, are eligible expenditures.[13] This is also true of the costs of obtaining a foreign patent if the taxpayer already holds U.S. patents or patent applications on the invention.[14] However, the cost of acquiring another person's patent, model, production, or process are excluded from Section 174 eligibility.[15]

Under Section 41, however, patent perfection costs are probably not eligible, because they appear to be more in the nature of noneligible administrative or overhead expenses.

Having established these principles, the next important question from the point of view of the joint venturer is, "Who is the taxpayer?" Since research and development expenditures can be substantial, the tax benefits to the joint venture itself or to the entities who are venturers are potentially great. Care should be taken to structure the venture so as to allow maximization of benefits. In structuring the venture, the following rules should be borne in mind:

1. The Section 174 deduction applies not only to costs incurred in research undertaken directly by the taxpayer, but also to expenditures incurred by the taxpayer for research performed on his behalf by another person or entity.[16] However, *the taxpayer must own the technology being developed before it can qualify for the deduction.*[17] Therefore, if it appears that tax benefits can be maximized by having the venturers, as opposed to the joint venture itself, take the deduction, the venture should be structured to permit the venturers to own the newly developed technology.

---

[12]Conf. Rep. No. 841, II-73 and II-74.
[13]Regs. Section 1.174-2(a)(1).
[14]Rev. Rul. 68-471, 1968-2 C.B. 109.
[15]Regs. Section 1.174-2(a)(1).
[16]Regs. Section 1.174-2(a)(2).
[17]TAM 8725001.

Care must be taken, however, to structure the venture so that it is the trade or business of the venturers themselves and that they are not transformed into mere passive financiers for the trade or business conducted by the joint venture. One way to accomplish this end might be to form a two-step venture. In the first place, joint venturers X and Y would enter into an agreement to jointly finance research. The developed technology would be jointly owned by them and not by the partnership or other institution which performed the research. In phase two of the venture, X and Y would agree to jointly develop and market their new product.

If the goal is to preserve tax benefits for the joint venturers, the corporate form for the venture seems less workable. If X and Y formed a corporation to experiment with and develop new technology and each invested money and obtained stock, they probably would not be eligible for tax benefits because they would have become financing vehicles (i.e., passive investors) for the venture. The venture would be in the trade or business of developing the product and not the venturers as individuals. Therefore, the tax benefits would flow to the venture.

2. As long as the taxpayer claiming the benefits is involved in the trade or business to be benefited by research and development efforts, the Internal Revenue Service will recognize Section 174 deductibility of payments made to a coordinating intermediary (i.e., a partnership or foundation which, in turn, contracts with third parties to conduct research on the taxpayer's behalf.[18] This is true even if the taxpayer's business is an indirect beneficiary of the research. For example, deductibility has been upheld in a situation in which an airline paid an aircraft manufacturer to design, develop, fabricate, and test a prototype aircraft. The direct beneficiary of the research effort was the manufacturer which would develop the plane for sale in its business. However, the airline benefited indirectly, since the new aircraft would be available for purchase and use in its business.[19]

3. For Section 41 purposes, the expenses of taxpayers under common control will be treated in the aggregate as the expenditures of a single taxpayer. The payments by one entity to another for purposes of conducting research will, therefore, not entitle the payor to a credit. However, the payee will be eligible for the credit for in-house research expenditures

---

[18]Rev. Rul. 73-20; TAM 7937004.
[19]1969-2 C.B.

as the funds are expended.[20] This should be borne in mind carefully by corporate joint venturers who contemplate the formation of a separate corporation, related to one or more of the venturers, to conduct the joint venture.

4. If the taxpayer pays a third party for contract research, only 65 percent of those expenditures are entitled to credit under Section 41. However, 100 percent of the funds are eligible for the credit if the payment is to a university and the research done qualifies as "basic" research. This can make universities attractive joint-venture partners in some instances, if the confidentiality problems discussed below can be overcome.

WHO OWNS THE KNOW-HOW: KEEPING YOUR SECRETS SECRET

The tax questions addressed above assume a joint venture in which the venturer's primary goal is the development of new technology or knowledge. Equally frequently encountered in the high-technology fields are ventures in which the product has, at least in part, been developed, and the business of the venture is to market the product or market it after further enhancements. In either case, one or more of the venturers may be turning over to the new business some form of protected intellectual property. Care must be taken to maintain that protection in the hands of the new entity and to protect any enhancements or new technology or know-how developed by the joint venture. If one of the functions of the joint venture is having a beneficial interest in the new technology experimentation and research, ownership takes on extra importance. The venture must be structured so as to maximize tax benefits without sacrificing the trade secret or other protection to which any newly developed processes or technology may be entitled.

There are three basic ways to protect intellectual property: patent, copyright, and trade secret. The first two are purely creatures of statute, and allow a developer to make its invention or creation public and, at the same time, protect it from unauthorized use. Trade-secret protection is quite different. It has developed in common law rather than by statute. In order to accord his or her ideas, know-how, and processes trade-secret

---

[20]Prop. Regs. Section 1.44F- 6(e)(2).

protection, the owner must keep them strictly confidential. Prospective joint venturers who are already owners of protected know-how must take care to avoid permitting their copyrighted or patented property to be used by co-venturers without proper authority. Perhaps even greater care must be taken to avoid disclosing materials which are trade secrets to a co-venturer without taking the necessary steps to maintain their confidentiality.

PATENTS

Patents are traditionally used to protect inventions. Any person who invents or discovers " . . . any new and useful process, machine, manufacture, or composition of matter, or any new and useful improvement thereof. . . . "[21] may obtain a patent. Acquiring the patent is a complex process and applications are generally prepared and prosecuted by attorneys licensed and admitted to practice before the U.S. Patent and Trademark Office.

Novelty is the basic condition which makes an invention patentable.[22] In addition, the material sought to be patented must not be obvious at the time the invention is made to a " . . . person having ordinary skill in the art to which the subject matter [sought to be patented] pertains."[23] Finally, mere ideas themselves may not be patented. For example, in order to patent a mathematical formula, the formula must be applied to or imbedded in a specific method or process.[24]

Once the patent is obtained, it gives the inventor an absolute and exclusive right to exclude others from making, using, or selling the invention for the 17-year life of the patent. At the end of that 17 years, the patented product or process is dedicated to the public and may be freely used by anyone.[25] During the life of the patent, the patent holder may permit others to manufacture, use, or sell his invention by granting a license. If a joint venture is formed to, for example, manufacture or sell a patented invention, the patent holder should include, in the joint-

---

[21]35 U.S.C.§101.
[22]35 U.S.C.§102.
[23]35 U.S.C.§103.
[24]*Gottschalk v. Benson*, 409 U.S. 63 (1972). *Diamond v. Diehr*, 450 U.S. 175 (1981).
[25]35 U.S.C.§154; 35 U.S.C.§271.

venture documents, a grant of license, either to the venturers as a group or to the joint venture itself, to make specific uses of the invention. The license should be written and should be carefully drawn to assure that the patent holder retains all rights that he does not, in fact, intend to license. Bear in mind, however, that joint venturers owe one another fiduciary obligations, and generally cannot hold to themselves business opportunities which would benefit the venture. If, for example, the business of a joint venture is to manufacture and sell an invention in the United States, the patent holder would probably be required to grant an exclusive license for domestic manufacture and sale to the venture. If he retained the right to license domestic manufacture and sale to another entity, that would constitute an impermissible conflict with the business of the joint venture. However, the inventor might retain for himself the right to license the manufacture and sale of the invention *outside* the United States, since this would not conflict with the venture's business. However, all such restrictions and reservations should be clearly disclosed to all joint venturers and set out in the license agreement.

COPYRIGHT

Because of the general rule that mere ideas may not be patented, patent protection has been difficult to obtain for an authorization or formula used in computer software. Applications for patent protection directed solely to a mathematical algorithm or formula underlying a software invention have been rejected as attempts to patent an idea. However, patents on software can be obtained where the software elements recited in a patent claim are placed in a hardware context. As a result therefore, copyright has been a more common form of protection sought for software developments, and, in fact, the Copyright Act was amended, effective January 1980, to expressly define computer software as a type of published work eligible for copyright protection.[26]

Only the precise form of a work of authorship is eligible for copyright protection, not the idea underlying the work.[27] The work may be either

---

[26] 17 U.S.C.§101.
[27] 17 U.S.C.§102(b).

published or unpublished,[28] and copyright protection is achieved simply by affixing the required copyright notice to all copies of the work. The notice should include either the word *copyright* or the universally recognized *C* in a circle, should state the year of first publication, and the name or recognizable abbreviation of the name of the owner,[29] i.e., *C* in a circle 1988 ABC Corporation.

In order to perfect copyright protection, the claimant must file an application for registration and deposit a copy of the work with the U.S. Copyright Office prior to filing any action for infringement of copyright.[30] A work deposited with the copyright office is available for public inspection, which has raised some justifiable concern regarding confidentiality among software developers. Because of this concern, the U.S. Copyright Office has allowed registration of software by deposition of only portions of the source or object code,[31] as long as special relief from the usual full deposit requirement has been granted on petition.[32]

The author of copyrighted material is the owner of the copyright. If a joint venturer is the owner of a copyright on material which is essential to the venture, he may protect his interest either by turning over copies of his work with the notice attached to the venture (and thereby maintaining ownership of the copyright), or by transferring ownership to the venture or venturers as a group. The copyright gives the owner the exclusive rights to reproduce, copy, distribute, perform, and make derivative applications of the copyrighted work for a period equal to the life of the author plus 50 years.[33]

Generally, copyright registration is quick and simple as compared to the much slower patent process. In high technology, where the speed of development gives new products a relatively short competitive life, copyright protection may be more useful than patent protection. However, in some instances where the particular development may have broad applicability, a patent may be very powerful protection and worth the extra time and effort. In certain situations seeking both patents and copy-

---

[28]17 U.S.C.§104.
[29]17 U.S.C.§401.
[30]17 U.S.C. 411.
[31]Prop. Reg., 51 FED. REGISTER 34667, (Sept. 30, 1986).
[32]37 C.F.R. 202.20(D) (1986).
[33]17 U.S.C. 106.

rights in combination may provide the strongest protection possible and should be carefully explored. Of course, if a joint venture, as opposed to the individual venturers, creates new inventions and/or works, then the venture is entitled to own the patent and/or copyright.

TRADE SECRETS

Patent and copyright protection both offer a developer of new products and processes statutory forms of protection obtained through large federal bureauracies. Trade secrets, on the other hand, are largely maintained through self-help. It is essential to trade-secret protection that the developer of the invention or work be eternally vigilant to maintain secrecy, since even inadvertent disclosure may destroy the secrecy claimed for the invention or work.

A wide variety of kinds of know-how is entitled to trade-secret protection. However, the laws of most states, as summarized in the Uniform Trade Secrets Act (which has been adopted in 16 states, including California) provides that in order to be a legitimate trade secret, the information must be:

1. Not known to the general public or ascertainable through sources generally available.
2. Of economic value to the owner.
3. Kept as a secret by the owner.

Trade secrets are protected by secrecy and are enforced in the final analysis via litigation. Once suit is filed, the trier of fact will examine, on a case-by-case basis, the claims of secrecy to determine whether these criteria are met. However, protection is available for many types of information which may not be susceptible to copyright or patent protection. Among these are:

1. Lists of suppliers of the components which make up a newly developed product.
2. Expression of the concept, algorithm, or formula which is the basis of a new product or development.
3. Lists of buyers and their needs, or distributors, or other type of marketing channel for the product to be developed.
4. Sales, marketing, and other business or product plans.

While these kinds of information could not be accorded protection under copyright or patent laws, they may legitimately be trade secrets if they are not, in fact, the subject of public knowledge. In order to maintain that protection, however, the owner of the secret must keep it confidential and should be able to prove that he has taken objective steps to protect the confidentiality of the information. These steps should include, at a minimum, the following:

1. Require employees and co-workers to execute confidentiality agreements which acknowledge that certain information belonging to the employer is the secret property of the employer, and that that information will not be disclosed or used outside the organization either during or after employment.

2. Control access to the information and make that control provable by doing such things as numbering copies, requiring persons viewing the information to sign logs showing what they have viewed and when they have returned copies, and ascertaining that confidentiality agreements have been signed by everyone (employee or not) allowed to view the secret information in locked rooms or files.

3. Label secret writings identifying them as trade secrets and subject to confidentiality agreements.

4. When employees, co-workers, or consultants end their relationship with the company, conduct formal exit interviews, formalized in writing, to be signed by the departing individual, reminding the individual of his duty to maintain confidentiality and requiring him to return all confidential documents in his possession.

All of these principles should be carefully applied if the owner of trade secrets enters into a joint venture, the business of which requires controlled disclosure of the secret to others. The venturers and their employees and consultants should all be required to conform to the procedures outlined above. If it is otherwise desirable, the owner of the secret may sell or lease his secret to the venture, or license it to the venture for the purpose of carrying out certain processes. If this is done, however, the agreement of sale, lease or license *must* contain covenants requiring the venture to take certain steps (such as those outlined above) in order to protect the secret information. If this is not done, the owner may find when title to the secret reverts to him at the end of the license or lease period, that the information has lost its secret character and is available for public use.

Of course, the same protective steps can be followed by the joint venture itself when it develops information which may be accorded trade-secret treatment. If the venture is to be the developmental arm of the business, then it, as opposed to the venturers, will own the secret information. The venture will have the burden of maintaining the confidentiality of the material and may have an asset to resell to one or more of the individual venturers if they decide to continue in the business on their own at the conclusion of the joint venture.

Some special problems arise when one is joint venturing a research and development project with a university. As set forth above, there are tax benefits to such arrangements, at least for the next few years (a Section 41 credit on 100 percent of expenditures rather than 65 percent). However, universities, assuming that they are not prohibited by their charter or bylaws from entering into joint-venture contracts with private industry, will often insist upon ownership of any technology developed in the joint project,[34] thus possibly stripping all tax benefits from the private-industry venturer, unless that venturer can argue that its business maintains an indirect beneficial interest in the technology.

Another even greater problem to be faced in joint venturing with universities is that most of them have open research policies which may be destructive of a private joint venturer's carefully maintained trade secrets. Even if the university is willing to agree to some level of secrecy in the joint-venture agreement, nonparties will not be bound by the agreement and tenured faculty members engaged in research are frequently less tractible than employees in private industry about agreeing to maintain secrecy for the benefit of their employer.[35] All of these factors must be weighed against the benefits, both tax benefits and benefits involving instant access to valuable expertise, of joint venturing with a university.

Clearly, joint ventures in high-technology fields are complex creatures. No matter how simple the structure which the venturers may wish to adopt, the question of tax benefits, confidentiality of information, and ownership of technology cannot be avoided. These should be faced head-on at the beginning of the venture, if the business is to run smoothly and expensive litigation is to be avoided.

---

[34]Gilliland, *Joint Venturing University Research: Negotiating Cooperative Agreements,* 40 THE BUSINESS LAWYER 971 (1985).
[35]Gilliland, *id.*

LOOKING OVER YOUR SHOULDER—THE
ANTITRUST IMPLICATIONS OF JOINT VENTURING

Just when you thought you had an agreement which resolved all of the technical problems outlined above, a new spectre looms ahead: Will your joint venture cause you to run afoul of the antitrust laws? This is a question worth examining carefully in certain instances (for example, a proposed venture between horizontal competitors) since violations can result in criminal penalties or treble-damage awards.

The case of *Penn-Olin Chemical Corp.*, 378 U.S. 158 (1964) is demonstrative of the dangers. There, two chemical companies formed a joint venture to manufacture and sell a certain chemical compound in an area in which neither of them had sold previously. The Supreme Court held that the venture would run afoul of the antitrust laws if the trial court determined that the venture would eliminate potential competition. The Court indicated that the following factors should be considered:

> . . . the number and power of the competitors in the relevant market; the background of their growth; the power of the joint venturers; the relationship of their lines of commerce; the competition existing between them and the power of each in dealing with the competitors of the other; the setting in which the joint venture was created; the reasons and necessities for its existence; the joint venture's line of commerce and the relationship thereof to that of its parents; the adaptability of its line of commerce to noncompetitive practices; the potential power of the joint venture in the relevant market; and appraisal of what the competition in the relevant market would have been if one of the joint venturers had entered it alone instead of through Penn-Olin; the effect, in the event of this occurrence, of the other joint venturer's potential competition; and such other factors as might indicate potential risk to competition in the relevant market.

The Department of Justice investigates alleged antitrust violations for the U.S. government. That agency has stated that it will examine three major issues in inquiring into the legality of a particular joint venture. These are:

1. Whether the joint venture itself is an unreasonable restraint upon competition. (This will involve an inquiry similar to the one outlined by the Court in the Penn-Olin case.)

2. Whether the joint venture, even if proper in itself, utilizes any collateral restraints on competition which must be struck down.

3. Whether the venture constitutes what is known as a "bottleneck monopoly" of an area which is so vital to business as a whole that it must be opened to all on nondiscriminatory terms.[36] An example of this sort of venture has been recently in the news. The developer of UNIX, a widely used computer operating system, has entered into a joint venture with a major manufacturer of UNIX-compatible workstations, the object of which is to standardize the operating system's format. Competing manufacturers have complained that these standardizations, if not equally available to them, may put them out of business, thus stifling competition among the manufacturers.[37]

CONCLUSION

High-technology joint venturing is a thicket of great potential perils and great potential benefits. To enjoy the maximum rewards with minimum risks, do your work up front. Carefully consider the purpose that you wish to achieve, the identities of your joint venturers, the structure of the relationship, and the ownership of the technology to be developed. As with any new business, early planning can only minimize the possibility of costly litigation.

---

[36]Hills, ANTITRUST ADVISOR, Second Edition (1978) at Page 213.
[37]"Industry News: Unix/Xenix Marriage," UNIX/WORLD, (May 1987).

CHAPTER 8

JOINT VENTURING IN THE TELECOMMUNICATIONS INDUSTRY

Willard W. Brittain
Price Waterhouse

The literal definition of telecommunications is communication over long distances. Today's telecommunications industry incorporates those who provide the information content of the communication and those who provide the transmission conduit for the communication. It includes software providers (programming data bases, information services, etc.), equipment manufacturers, common carriers, and a host of products and specialized services.

Often, the telecommunications industry is also thought of and segmented by transmission media. Wire media consists of Open wire, Twisted pairs, Coaxial cable, and Fiber-optics cable. Radio media consists of Shortwave, Microwave, Mobile radio, Aeronautical radio, Maritime radio, Broadcasting (AM, FM, and TV), and Earth-space (e.g., satellite communications).

Some of the major providers of "transmission" services include the regional Bell operating companies (RBOC's), independent local exchange carriers (GTE, Contel, Centel), long distance carriers (AT&T, MCI, U.S. Sprint), and cable television operators (TCI, ATC, Continental).

The telecommunications industry is fertile ground for joint ventures. Primary motivating factors have been the regulatory environment, changing demand, and technological development.

REGULATORY ENVIRONMENT

The U.S. telecommunications industry has been subject to regulation since The Post Roads Act of 1866, which granted the Postmaster General the authority to set rates for government telegrams. The Communications Act of 1934 established the Federal Communications Commission (FCC), and broadened the regulatory coverage. The FCC became the consolidation point for regulatory authorities previously scattered throughout various agencies. Its major objective, as is that of the legislation, is to "make available, so far as possible, to all the people of the United States, a rapid, efficient nationwide, and worldwide wire and radio communication service with adequate facilities at reasonable charges."[1]

The most far-reaching "regulatory" impact on today's telecommunications industry has resulted from the 1974–1983 AT&T antitrust suit and divestiture agreement. In 1974 the Justice Department charged that AT&T, Western Electric, and Bell Laboratories were in violation of the Sherman Antitrust Act as a result of conspiring to prevent, restrict, and eliminate competition from other telecommunication common carriers, private telecommunication systems, and manufacturers and suppliers of telecommunication equipment.

The initial remedy sought was AT&T's divestiture of its local telephone companies or withdrawal from the long-distance telephone market and divestiture of Western Electric, its manufacturing subsidiary. After seven years, a settlement (the Modification of Final Judgment, or MFJ) was reached under which AT&T agreed to divest itself of the local operating companies. A divestiture plan calling for the establishment of seven regional companies was developed and took effect on January 1, 1984.[2]

Among the critical provisions of the settlement as modified were:

1. All relationships between AT&T and the divested companies had to essentially be severed and remain that way.
2. Consumer Premises Equipment (CPE) lines of business could be retained by AT&T.

[1]The Communications Act of 1934, as amended, 50 Stat 189, Section I (1937). "The Communications Act of 1934, As Amended and Other Selected Provisions of Law," (U.S.G.P.O., 1983).
[2]Datapro Research Corporation, *U.S. Telecommunications Regulation—A Changing World* (Delran, New Jersey, 1983), 101–110.

3. The divested companies must provide all interexchange carriers with equal access.
4. No information services or interexchange services could be provided by the divested companies.
5. No divested local company could manufacture or provide telecommunications products or customer premises equipment.

In 1987, as part of the review of the divestiture, Judge Greene reaffirmed the basic principle that telephone companies are to be limited to transporting information for other parties. Thus, again precluded from the information business, the regional operating companies are, as anticipated, appealing Judge Green's latest findings.

In addition to federal regulation, there is also significant regulation of the telecommunications industry at the state and local levels.

By precluding certain players from various segments of the telecommunications marketplace, regulation has encouraged joint venturing. Only with joint ventures and other forms of strategic alliances can the benefits of expanded markets and technology sharing be attained in certain instances. For example, BellSouth has teamed with Telenet Communications Corp. for information services in Atlanta and Gainesville, Florida.[3]

Recent regulatory changes have also had a major impact on joint venturing in the cable television sector of the telecommunications industry. The Cable Communications Policy Act of 1984 (the Act) fully deregulated rate-setting and established guidelines for franchising and refranchising. It did, however, retain certain restrictions which have helped encourage and set the structure for joint ventures between cable operators and local telephone companies, such as those examined later in this chapter. More specifically, these restrictions require that:

1. A number of channels for lease, depending upon the number of activated channels of the system, must be made available to third parties.
2. A cable system cannot be owned by a licensee of a local broadcast station serving a portion of the same community.
3. Local newspapers and other electronic media be prohibited from ownership of cable systems.

---

[3]John Burgess, "Deciding Regionals' Data Role," *The Washington Post,* 10 January 1988, Sec. F, p. 1.

4. Basic service rates no longer be subject to regulation. (Premium service rates were already unregulated).
5. Operators be granted franchise agreement modifications when the operator can demonstrate that certain promised services have turned out to be commercially impracticable.
6. Specified criteria set forth in the Act be used when a franchise renewal is under consideration. In part by limiting the nature of the considerations, the Act makes *not* granting a renewal very difficult.[4]

CHANGING DEMAND AND TECHNOLOGY

As noted by many observers, the United States is in the information age in which the effective gathering, packaging, and delivery of information is a cornerstone of our economy. There has been what seems like an unending series of new demands and technical developments for delivering more information faster, at less cost, and with less degradation.

A case in point is the fiber optics technology, which uses light pulses instead of electrical pulses for signaling. Fiber-optics technology has the very desirable characteristics of providing end-to-end digital capabilities, low-cost installation, low signal loss, and tremendous capacity. The Integrated Services Digital Network (ISDN) services available with fiber include advanced voice, data, traditional telephone, cable television, home energy management, remote meter reading, and other services. BellSouth is providing those services through its joint venture with the developers of the private mixed-use community of Heathrow, Florida.[5]

Another relatively recent technology being applied successfully is cellular radio. The cellular radio technology has replaced the old car telephone with a relatively low-cost, high-transmission-quality service, capable of handling large numbers of users. The high-quality transmission is achieved with the cellular concept in which there is a handoff from one cell (transmission point) to another as the user moves about the city.

The popularity of the cellular service in combination with regulatory restrictions has helped spawn numerous joint ventures. Two cellular li-

---

[4]National League of Cities and U.S. Conferences of Mayors, *Cable Franchising and Regulation, A Local Government Guide to the New Law* (Washington, D.C., 1985), II-1 to II-5.
[5]*Information Week*, "Fiber Optics: Business Lights the Way," (December 1987), p. 30.

censes were awarded by the FCC in each market area, one to a "wireline" (local telephone company) and the other to a "nonwireline" entity. The nonwireline entity can be a telephone company from outside the area. In fact, a number of telephone companies have pursued that opportunity, frequently with local joint-venture partners.

LIGHTNET JOINT VENTURE EXAMPLE

Lightnet is a joint venture formed in August 1983 between CSX Corporation, a major railroad and transportation company, and Southern New England Telecommunications (SNET), one of the seven regional Bell operating companies. Lightnet provides telecommunication services through a fiber optics network now serving 63 markets coast to coast. It specializes in interstate private line, business-to-business communications, through the sale or leasing of capacity to common-carrier resellers and through direct marketing to businesses. Dow Jones, the publisher of this book, for example, has contracted with Lightnet for private-line data-communications services. Lightnet provides a high-speed service between the Dow Jones World Financial Center Headquarters site in New York City and Dow's printing plant in Chicopee, Massachusetts.[6]

The basic impetus for the joint venture was CSX's desire for profitable alternative uses of its railroad right-of-ways. Burying fiber-optic cable along CSX railroad tracks was just such a use. For SNET, the joint venture provided a logical, effective mechanism for further application of its fiber-optics expertise.

Lightnet has achieved its 10,000 mile, coast-to-coast network in part through another joint venture. Lightnet has linked up its 5,000 mile, east-of-the-Mississippi network with the 5,000 mile, west-of-the-Mississippi network of Williams Telecommunications (WilTel).[7]

CSX and SNET each have a 50 percent interest in the joint venture, consistent with their respective capital contributions. A portion of CSX's

---

[6]Interview with Debra Arrington, Director, Corporate Communications and Government Relations, Lightnet.

[7]Joan Tyner, "Lightnet Teams with WilTel to Create National Fiber Networks," *The Baltimore Sun*, 13 August 1987, Business Section.

capital contributions has been in the form of the right-of-way access it is providing. SNET capital contributions have all been in cash.

Lightnet's operations were co-located initially with SNET in New Haven, Connecticut. Lightnet is now located in Rockville, Maryland with its own full complement of managerial and administrative staff.[8]

The joint venture appears to be a success. Profitability was achieved in 1986 after only three years of operation, and there is an optimistic profitability outlook for the future.

Another significant joint venture in the fiber-optics sector is the National Telecommunications Network, which is a consortium of seven other fiber-optics networks and a competitor of Lightnet.[9]

CABLE TELEVISION EXAMPLE

Some of the best examples of complex joint ventures in the telecommunications industry are in the cable television sector. For example:

1. Major cable companies who compete regularly against one another on various fronts have joined together to purchase the cable systems of other major operators. These alliances appear to have been formed because of the magnitude of the financing required to purchase the systems.
2. Major cable operators and programmers have also entered into joint ventures. The substance of the transactions is that the cable operator receives an equity interest in the programmer under favorable terms in return for access to the operator's subscribers.
3. There are joint ventures for the cable systems in several major cities involving the franchisee/owner, the local telephone company, and a major cable operator. An example of this type of joint venture is provided below.

---

[8]Interview with Debra Arrington, Director, Corporate Communications and Government Relations, Lightnet.

[9]Tyner, "Lightnet Teams with WilTel to Create National Fiber Networks," *The Baltimore Sun,* 13 August 1987, Business Section.

MAJOR CITY CABLE JOINT VENTURE

The Franchisee and the Telephone Company

The franchisee is often a locally controlled entity. For the franchisee, the local telephone company offers financing capacity and construction and system maintenance expertise. The telephone company also lends a high-tech (fiber optics), but stable, image to the highly competitive franchise award process.

Generally, the telephone company will construct, construct and own, or construct and lease back the broadband distribution plant (headend electronics, trunk cable, and feeder cable). The connection between the broadband facility and the wiring and equipment in the house, which is called the drop, is provided and maintained by the franchisee. For the telephone company, the joint venture offers the chance for further utilization of its technical capabilities and work force and for learning more about broadband services such as cable. As noted earlier, the telephone company is precluded currently from providing cable service under the Cable Act and the Modified Final Judgement. The telephone company also derives additional revenue from the unused capacity it may have in its existing fiber-optics trunks.

There are, however, significant "tension points" between the cable company and the local telephone company which must be overcome. Foremost is the issue of exclusive use of the broadband facility. The franchisee, of course, wants exclusive use of the entire capacity. The telephone company, on the other hand, would like to control at least a portion of the broadband capacity so that it is well positioned for a fast start, should the regulatory environment be relaxed to allow it to enter the cable television and information services businesses. Exacerbating the tension point is the fact that the local telephone company will continue to provide data-transmission services and the cable operator will be seeking that business.

A related tension point is the extent of the telephone company's involvement in the system financing, by either leasing the broadband facility to the cable operator or by providing favorable construction and permanent debt financing. The franchisee would prefer to have the system financed by a third party, independent of the local telephone company. As the financing source, the local telephone company gains powerful leverage in the venture should there be a default or a need to renegotiate financing terms.

The Franchisee and the Major Cable Operator

The franchisee and a major cable operator enter into an agreement under which the cable operator manages the system for the franchisee. Close examination will indicate that it is not a typical contract/manager relationship, but more like a joint venture. The major cable operator has often been involved with the franchisee throughout the proposal and selection process and probably provided seed capital. The operator may be an equity partner, provide financing guarantees, or have rights of first refusal for purchase of the system.

The joint-venture incentives of the two parties are straightforward. The franchisee needs the operator's expertise and credibility to win the franchise, obtain financing, and operate the system. The cable operator receives an attractive management fee, participates in the appreciation of the system, and has an excellent vantage point from which to access the desirability of the system for possible purchase in the future.

ACHIEVING SUCCESSFUL JOINT VENTURES

As described earlier in this chapter, the regulatory environment is a major determinant of the participants and structure of joint ventures in the telecommunications industry. Similarly, fast-changing demand and technology are major determinants. In general, however, the factors and techniques for achieving successful joint ventures in other industries are applicable to the telecommunications industry. A "successful" joint venture in this discussion is one which, assuming it is pursuing a sound economic enterprise, results in the relatively harmonious achievement of the objectives of its participants.

THE JOINT-VENTURE ESTABLISHMENT PROCESS

The process for establishing the joint venture is often not given enough attention. It is critical that it be well planned if a successful joint venture is to result. A well-planned process is characterized by:

1. A sound business plan to help ensure that the joint venture is pursuing an economic enterprise.
2. Thorough analyses of the tax and financial statement implications of the proposed structure.
3. A full review of the proposed structure and terms by key executives.
4. A review of the proposed structure and terms by managers and administrators who will have to implement them.
5. A realistic and thorough assessment of implementation time frames and costs.
6. A review by the appropriate experts to address potential regulatory pitfalls.
7. Fair sharing by the partners of the cost of the venture.

Equitable Balance of Contributions, Risks and Rewards

The foremost factor in structuring a successful joint venture is establishing and maintaining an equitable balance of contributions, risks, and rewards as perceived by the parties to the venture. Without an equitable balance there is a high probability that the relationship will deteriorate over time and cause the venture to achieve less than maximum performance. The balancing which must take place is depicted in Exhibit 8-1.

Provisions for Consideration in Joint-Venture Structuring

Every joint venture is unique. However, there are a number of often-overlooked provisions which, when tailored to the situation at hand, can help balance the contributions, risks, and rewards of the parties to the venture.

Purchase of Other Partners Interest
Provisions of this type allow one partner to purchase another partner's interest through either (1) the right of first refusal or (2) a forced sale. A forced sale is generally triggered when a partner defaults on an agreed-upon obligation. The purchase price can be determined by formula, independent offers received, or third-party appraisals.

Resolution of Disputes Prior to Arbitration
It is often wise to include procedures for having executives resolve the disputes internally before arbitration.

EXHIBIT 8–1

Joint Venturing in the Telecommunications Industry (Balancing Joint Venturing Contributors, Risks and Rewards.)

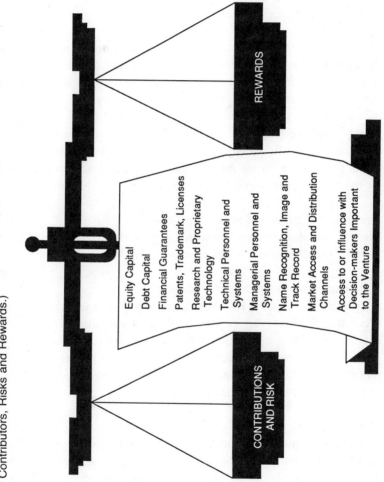

REWARDS

CONTRIBUTIONS AND RISK

Equity Capital

Debt Capital

Financial Guarantees

Patents, Trademark, Licenses

Research and Proprietary Technology

Technical Personnel and Systems

Managerial Personnel and Systems

Name Recognition, Image and Track Record

Market Access and Distribution Channels

Access to or Influence with Decision-makers Important to the Venture

Performance-based Profit Sharing, Bonuses, or Penalties
Provisions of this type increase or reduce the financial rewards of the various participants based on achievement of specified performance standards. In establishing such incentives, one must be careful not to inadvertently build in undesirable incentives. Most misused are cost-containment incentives, which discourage investment in revenue enhancement and possibly higher profitability.

Preparation and Approval of Annual Budget and Multiyear Plans
Partners to the venture should review budget and longer-term plans. However, this involvement should be designed so it does not bog down the venture in an endless planning and review cycle.

Specification of Required Financial and Other Reporting
The content and frequency of reporting to the parties should be spelled out in the venture documents. Exhaustive requirements must be balanced by the resources required for preparation.

Acceptable Activities Outside the Venture
These provisions address involvement by the parties in related ventures outside the joint-venture structure at hand.

Designation of Independent Accountants
All parties should have full confidence in the joint venture's independent accountants. Moreover, cost savings can sometimes be achieved if the accounting firm is also independent accountant for a major party to the venture, and, therefore, familiar with consolidation and other financial reporting issues. Thus, it may be desirable to designate the firm by name in the joint-venture documents.

Oversight Body
Major joint ventures can often benefit from the establishment of a management oversight body formed specifically for the venture. It provides a good sounding board for the joint-venture managers and most importantly provides them a clear reporting line.

Managing Partner
Depending on relative ownership percentages, areas of responsibility, and other factors, it can be appropriate to have one of the joint-venture partners designated as the managing partner with full operating responsibility.

CONCLUSION

The telecommunications industry is ripe for joint ventures because of the regulatory environment, fast-changing demand, and technology. The process for developing a joint venture is key to its success. The right process helps insure economic soundness and an effective balancing of contributions, risks, and rewards among the parties. Finally, there are a number of often-overlooked provisions and techniques for structuring the joint venture which, if tailored to the situation at hand, can also help ensure its success.

CHAPTER 9

JOINT VENTURING IN THE MANUFACTURING INDUSTRY

Thomas S. Nowinski
Clark, Klein, & Beaumont
D. Kerry Crenshaw
Clark, Klein, & Beaumont

WHAT MOTIVATES THE FORMATION OF JOINT VENTURES IN THE MANUFACTURING INDUSTRY?

Technology

More than any other factor, the exploitation of technology in one form or another drives the formation of joint ventures for manufacturing. Typically, one party to the venture will have conceived and developed (or partially developed) a particular manufactured product or manufacturing process having a potentially significant market. If that party lacks the production and/or marketing resources to realize the full potential of the product or process, and also lacks the financial ability to create such resources on its own, it may seek out a joint-venture partner who has the requisite characteristics.

This is the traditional ''Mr. Idea/Mr. Money'' theme, and there are numerous variations on the theme. One such variation is illustrated by the celebrated joint venture between General Motors Corporation and Toyota to build automobiles in California, by way of a new co-equally owned corporation called New United Motor Manufacturing, Inc., or NUMMI (the GM-Toyota enterprise provides a wealth of illuminating detail in the field of manufacturing joint ventures, and will be referred to frequently throughout this chapter). One of the purposes of this venture was, of course, to take advantage of the concededly superior manufacturing methodology Toyota had developed in Japan. General Motors had more in mind, however, than simply using that methodology to produce one particular subcompact automobile. Rather, a primary objective of GM in this venture was to *study* Toyota's methodology for future application to GM's other assembly facilities. Thus, although a joint venture is by definition limited in scope, General Motors hoped to gain for itself some rather permanent advantages by its combination with Toyota.

Marketing Expertise

Not every manufacturer has a marketing research arm. A company may have the manufacturing capability to produce huge quantities of a technically superior product, but may have no idea what type of product is needed or how that product should be marketed. Thus, the impetus for forming a joint venture may come from a nonmanufacturer that has discerned a market for a particular product, developed a performance specification for it, and perhaps has even begun to test the market for the product with potential customers. Having discovered or created a market for the product, that company may then seek out a joint venture partner with the technical capability to design, develop, and manufacture the product in profitable numbers.

Furthermore, there are industry segments in which market entry would be difficult for a newcomer because of high entry costs or because the market is insular in other ways. In the GM-Toyota venture, for example, Toyota was able to benefit immediately from the established and powerful General Motors dealer-distribution network as a ready-made market for the automobiles manufactured by the venture. This easy market entree may be contrasted with the enormous logistical and financial difficulty involved in setting up a distributor network for a completely new entry such as Yugo or Hyundai. Even Honda, a marketing giant, faced significant obstacles of this type in bringing to market the product of its new Acura division.

Risk-spreading

Sharing the risk of developing a particular product is a traditional motivation for forming a joint venture, but it has particular applicability in the manufacturing industry. The cost of research and development, tooling, and manufacturing machinery to produce a new manufactured product may run into millions of dollars. The balancing of risks against potential rewards may make such a development financially unfeasible unless there are two or more solvent participants willing to accept a share of the cost.

Production of Raw Materials

A manufacturer may not need any help in developing, producing, or marketing products, but may find it crucial to have a guaranteed source of the raw materials or components from which its products are manufactured. Many years ago, for example, Henry Ford decided that the best way to insure a steady supply of quality steel to manufacture his automobiles was to build his own steel mill.

Few manufacturers are willing to undertake this type of capital commitment today, but the concept survives in joint ventures between manufacturers and suppliers for the production of certain specialized materials and components. What this represents is a version of vertical integration that can be significantly less costly to the manufacturer than building its own facility, while offering the supplier an assured market for its output.

In the extractive industries joint ventures have been quite common throughout this century. Even though Henry Ford built his own steel mill, he found it desirable to seek partners for the iron ore mines necessary to support the mills. The huge outlays of capital required for development of long-lead-time projects, such as mining of metallic ores and exploration for hydrocarbons, have prompted a sharing of risks in those industries almost on a routine basis.

Examples of this are found in the marketplace in the drilling of offshore oil and gas claims leased from governments around the world. Perhaps the high point of this type of risk sharing was the highly innovative arrangement between Standard Oil of Ohio and British Petroleum during the 1970s. Sohio held leases to exploit the north slope of Alaska. British Petroleum supplied the initial capital under a formula by which it gained an increasing interest in Sohio's common stock proportionate to the success of the exploitation. Eventually, British Petroleum's interest in Sohio under this arrangement reached the level of majority control, providing Sohio not only with capital but with protection from bust-up takeovers during a critical period in its development.

Other Factors

The list of factors which may compel the formation of manufacturing joint ventures is as varied as the participants themselves. The GM-Toyota venture offers one additional illustration of this point. At the time the venture was formed, "voluntary" trade restraints prohibited Japanese manufacturers from exporting to this country more than a stated number of automobiles. These restraints did not apply to vehicles assembled in the United States. Several Japanese manufacturers had taken advantage of this exception by constructing and staffing manufacturing facilities here, an extremely costly and time-consuming enterprise. Toyota was able to avail itself of the same exception at a much smaller cost by entering into a venture to utilize GM's existing facility.

ADVANTAGES AND DISADVANTAGES

The advantages and disadvantages of joint ventures in the manufacturing industry are likely to be typical of those of joint ventures generally. The advantages tend to track the motivations discussed in the previous section for forming the venture in the first place. The disadvantages are not unlike those that plague such ventures in other segments of the industry.

Thus, for example, a primary advantage of joint venturing in manufacturing is the venturers' ability to bring to market a product which neither of the venturers could successfully have managed alone, because one or the other lacks manufacturing capacity, marketing prowess, or design expertise. A joint venture may permit the development of new products or processes which one company working alone could not afford to manage. Finally, as is illustrated by the GM-Toyota venture, it may permit the introduction of new fundamental concepts of manufacturing methodology into a tradition-bound industry.

A second category of advantage to joint venturing involves the marketing of the finished product. As previously noted, one of the parties to the proposed venture may already possess a sophisticated distributorship network through which the venture's products can be marketed. This feature makes that party an attractive venture partner to the party with manufacturing skills but limited marketing expertise. A joint venture is not the only solution for the latter party, however. If the product is sufficiently sophisticated and self-contained, a franchising operation is a possible solution.

Assume, for example, that a manufacturer has a process rather than a product which it wishes to market. One method for doing so is to franchise the entire operation. Thus, Bandag, Inc. has developed a process for remanufacturing truck tires, and it manufactures the machinery and materials used in the process. Rather than participate in the retail end of the operation, i.e., by selling recapped tires, Bandag franchises the entire remanufacturing operation and thereby profits both from the sale of its machinery and the use of that machinery.

A universal disadvantage of joint ventures is the potential for "culture clash" in the management of the venture, and manufacturing joint ventures are no exception. This is especially true where a design-oriented, "creative" firm enters into a venture with a no-nonsense manufacturing company to exploit the intellectual property of the former. By contrast, the likelihood of a clash is probably less severe where the venturers are of approximately equal sizes and are drawn from the same industry segment.

Different factors may account for differences in "culture." The GM-Toyota venture is again a prime example. The differences between U.S. and Japanese approaches to management and manufacturing are well known and have been extensively debated. The operating agreement between the two companies permits Toyota to appoint the chief executive officer and the chief operating officer, and one might assume that this arrangement comprises a tacit agreement that the Japanese management philosophy will be permitted to predominate. Nevertheless, the venture must operate in this country, and GM will remain a highly visible presence in its operation. GM may have made a corporate decision to permit its management style to be submersed, but it remains to be seen how well individual managers will adapt to that decision.

Another potential difficulty with a manufacturing joint venture is product-oriented. When a product designer enters into a venture with a manufacturer, the two may have different goals. The designer may be interested primarily in the further development of the product, and may view the joint venture as a means to that end. The manufacturer, by contrast, may be motivated principally by a desire to establish a high volume of production and sales of the existing product as quickly as possible, in order to derive the maximum potential profit in the shortest practicable time frame. This is the type of issue that requires careful consideration in the planning stages, leading to detailed agreement on goals and objectives.

CONSIDERATIONS IN SELECTING A JOINT-VENTURE PARTNER

Joint venturers in the manufacturing industry, like joint-venture partners elsewhere, strive to achieve a certain "fit" in forming the venture. This consideration has several facets, and the venturers have more control over some than they do over others. In the area of management style, for example, which has already been mentioned, there is only so much that can be done. Every venturer would prefer to have a partner with a similar outlook as to what constitutes good management and how management decisions are made. The exigencies of the situation may require, however, a combination of corporate "personalities" that are very much different, because it is the product that is the primary focus of the venture.

Nowhere is the question of "personality" more thoroughly evident than in the increasingly popular joint-venture negotiation between a U.S. and a Japanese manufacturing company. With the move of several Japanese automobile manufacturing plants to the United States, many of their traditional Japanese suppliers have followed their customers to the United States, in the same manner as the U.S. original equipment automotive suppliers followed General Motors, Chrysler, and Ford to Europe in the 50s and 60s. When the Japanese company decides to seek a joint-venture arrangement for its U.S. operations, the U.S. company typically faces many difficult cultural problems. While the U.S. party is frequently interested in adopting the benefits of "Japanese-style management," the reality of this is sometimes unsettling to the U.S. businessman.

The U.S. business executive is accustomed to relentless pressure for quarterly results, particularly if the U.S. company is publicly held. This pressure creates problems which are novel to the Japanese partner, who is accustomed to taking a very long-term view of investment and relationships. As a result, many negotiations for these joint ventures founder on such questions as management authority and the process of making major decisions. The consensus-seeking Japanese tend to recoil from a power-directed system of decision making, and the U.S. partner, which views itself as being accountable to a public audience of shareholders, is equally reluctant to place management control in the hands of an unknown process for reaching decisions.

Another aspect of ''fit'' that a potential venturer in the manufacturing segment must take into consideration, whether the venture is domestic or international, is that of ''technological fit.'' The venturers should have a common understanding of how the manufacturing process works, and should share a common technical language relating to the subject matter of the venture. This is an area that requires a most careful exploration by the technical staff on both sides. It may require each party to disclose a good deal of information that would otherwise be regarded as confidential—manufacturing processes, patent rights, sources of supply, and the like. There will naturally be a certain level of resistance to this process. The parties' legal counsel can help overcome this reticence through well-considered confidentiality agreements. Nevertheless, if either party finds this type of scrutiny too much to bear, it is not a likely prospect for a successful joint venture.

An obvious but important characteristic of a good venture partner is financial staying power. Each party must carefully evaluate the capital requirements for the project and make a frank appraisal of its own and the other party's ability to contribute its share. An undercapitalized joint venture has no better prospects for success than an undercapitalized new business of any other type.

A manufacturing joint venture is likely to require a good deal of unskilled or semiskilled labor. This requirement leads inexorably to the issue of labor relations. If either of the venturers is party to a collective bargaining agreement, an argument may be made that the joint venture is some type of extension of that party, and that there is therefore a duty to bargain with the union under the National Labor Relations Act.

Once again, the General Motors-Toyota joint venture supplies a useful illustration of this point. The venture was formed to manufacture automobiles in a GM plant in Fremont, California, which GM had closed a few years earlier. When the plant was shut down, some 6,000 GM employees were laid off. When the joint venture was announced, a question arose immediately as to whether the venture was a ''successor employer'' to GM, whether the venture could be compelled to hire from the ranks of the laid-off employees, and whether the venture could be compelled to bargain with the UAW respecting those employees. Ultimately, the UAW was recognized as bargaining agent for the workers and a three-year labor agreement was negotiated.

PROBLEMS AND PITFALLS

The most obvious problems with a joint-venture arrangement are those that flow naturally from the roles of the joint venture partners. In a joint venture between a contributor of technology and a contributor of manufacturing capacity, the potential concerns come from opposite directions. The technology partner will wish to assure itself that the other party has the financial, physical, and/or marketing capacity to transform the technological concept into a profitable product. The manufacturing partner, on the other hand, will wish to be sure that the other partner has all of the necessary rights to the technology, and that the technology has reached the necessary stage of development to insure that a marketable product can be produced.

One potential pitfall that sometimes escapes attention is that of geographic proximity of the parties to the physical location of the venture operation. Even assuming that the venture is adequately managed in regard to its operations, manufacturing is nevertheless distinctly a "hands-on" activity. A venturer who is far from the scene may easily lose track of the evolution and development of the product and/or process, and as a result may not be able to anticipate and deal with significant problems as they arise.

LEGAL CONSIDERATIONS

At the National Institute on Joint Ventures, held in New York in November 1985, the eminent antitrust lawyer, Paul McGrath, related the wonderful anecdote of the pig and the chicken who formed a joint venture to produce bacon and eggs. After the joint-venture agreement was painstakingly negotiated and exhaustively documented, and after the documents had been signed and the appropriate celebrations had, the pig began to have second thoughts in realizing that he was unlikely to survive implementation of the venture. When he telephoned the chicken with his misgivings, the chicken replied: "Well, that's just the story of joint ventures. In every joint venture, somebody gets slaughtered." McGrath concludes that the chicken, or perhaps his lawyer, was a markedly superior negotiator.[1]

---

[1] 54 Antitrust LJ 971 (1986).

McGrath's view of the joint-venture experience may be unnecessarily cynical, but it points up the necessity of taking both the long and short view in negotiating the joint venture. A carefully negotiated and drafted joint-venture agreement is an absolute necessity, not only for the success of the venture itself, but often for the continuing good health of the venturers as well.

Choice of Entity

The first decision the venturers must make is how the venture should be structurally organized. In the manufacturing industry, the corporation is the vehicle of choice for a number of reasons, all of which relate to possible exposure to liability. There may, for example, be potential product liability ramifications inherent in the product being manufactured. The manufacturing process itself may involve significant risks in the nature of workers' compensation claims. The process may also generate by-products which potentially violate the laws regarding air and water pollution. It is natural to assume that the venturers would wish to interpose a separate corporate entity between themselves and these possible sources of exposure. Assuming the entity is adequately capitalized and/or insured for the nature of the undertaking, this strategy provides the desired insulation from potentially catastrophic liability resulting from the venture's activities.

Nowhere is the risk associated with a lack of adequate capitalization more clearly illustrated than in the 12-year environmental saga of Reserve Mining Company. This case, which has been the subject of extensive commentary in business publications and legal journals, evolved from a joint-venture corporation which maintained only minimal capital because a unique (and since reversed) ruling of the Internal Revenue Service permitted the corporation to act as a "cost company," passing through all of its costs to each of its 50 percent owners, each of whom took an equal share of the annual output of the company's production. When environmental problems in the disposition of solid wastes became a highly publicized issue, the 50-50 partners were forced by the courts to ante up hundreds of millions of dollars to solve those problems, and the fact that Reserve Mining was a separate corporate entity availed it naught. Ultimately, the company was reorganized as a partnership.

Where issues of liability are not paramount, the partnership form of organization presents some attractive possibilities. A partnership is a considerably more flexible entity than a corporation: the parties can agree in their partnership agreement to do virtually anything the law otherwise permits. This flexibility can be extremely advantageous in arranging the distribution of cash flow and tax attributes to match the contributions of the respective partners. These advantages are frequently obtained while at the same time the partners are enjoying the advantages of the corporate form, by having their wholly-owned subsidiaries act as partners in the venture.

Once a decision has been reached as to the type of entity to be used as a vehicle for the enterprise, the venturers must decide on the "citizenship" of the new organization. Most often, external factors will determine the geographic location of the venture entity, and that location will be the natural jurisdictional situs of the entity. This is not an automatic decision, however, especially for a corporation, since the corporate laws of the several states vary widely. The organizers of a corporation may prefer to use a Delaware, Michigan, New Jersey, or New York corporation for the perceived liberality of those states' business corporation codes, even if the corporation will not be physically located in any of those states.

An even more fundamental issue for an international joint venture may be the "nationality" of the venture entity. In other words, it may be possible to characterize a venture between a U.S. and a foreign partner as a creature of the foreign jurisdiction for treaty purposes. Such a characterization may have significant effects on the venture entity's rights and duties. When NUMMI was formed, for example, a question was raised whether the new corporation could be deemed a Japanese company under the U.S.-Japan treaty, and whether such a characterization would permit the corporation to give hiring preference to Japanese nationals in potential violation of U.S. equal-employment-opportunity laws. Although the question itself may be regarded as extreme, it drives home the point that parties to an international venture must be mindful of the provisions of any treaty between the countries of their respective organization.

Joint-Venture Agreement

The text of every agreement will differ, of course, depending on the contributions, duties, and objectives of the joint-venture partners and the venture itself. Nevertheless, there are certain issues which every joint venture agreement must deal with.

Choice of Entity

Will the venture be organized as a corporation or a partnership? Wouɪd a limited-partnership arrangement be appropriate? Under which state's jurisdiction should the entity be organized? Is a non-U.S. entity indicated?

Management Provisions

How will the board of directors be structured? Who will appoint the directors, and how many will be appointed? Should the agreement spell out who will appoint officers as well? Are there events which would change the balance of the power? What happens if there is a deadlock?

It goes without saying that the questions raised under this category are of vital importance to the smooth operation of the venture. In a venture between two companies with radically different "corporate cultures," however, a detailed agreement on these points is even more important. The parties may explicitly or implicitly agree, for example, that the culture of one or another of them will be permitted to dominate the venture. Conversely, the parties may agree to disagree, and attempt to create a third culture which is different altogether.

No matter what type of management arrangement is finally arrived at, one party or the other is likely to feel that it is not "in control" of the venture. This is as it should be, because a perfectly bilateral management scheme is a practical impossibility. Nevertheless, the noncontrol party should insist on including in the joint-venture agreement a laundry list of significant actions which management of the venture may not take without joint authorization. These items may include incurring debt, acquiring or disposing of substantial assets, recognizing a labor union, and making significant changes in the venture's method of operation or market focus.

Capital Contributions

Who will contribute how much in cash? What obligations will the parties have for future contributions? Will any part of the respective contributions be treated as loans? Is it feasible to use preferred stock? In what circumstances can a party recover all or a portion of its contributions?

Licensing Arrangements

In a venture between a contributor of technology and a contributor of manufacturing capacity, the technology partner will often seek a profit "override" by way of licensing the technology to the joint venture in exchange for an "above-the-line" royalty. Deciding whether such an arrangement is appropriate, and at what levels of compensation, requires a careful analysis of the economics of the venture. To borrow an analogy from another industry, investors with a "profit participation" in motion picture productions often find that all of the "profit" has escaped from the venture by way of guaranteed payments, and that a "profit participation" applied to nothing yields nothing.

Termination and Withdrawal Provisions

A joint venture is by definition formed for a limited purpose, and for that reason alone may have a limited duration. In addition, however, each party will probably wish to have, under some set of circumstances, the ability to "pull the plug" on the venture, or at least to disengage itself from further activities. This requires that each party think carefully about the types of events that would make continuation of the venture undesirable. This is not strictly a negative concept. A party may, for example, wish to exit a venture once certain financial goals are met. Providers of venture capital frequently operate this way.

If the venturers agree that the venture will be terminated entirely if certain events occur, the venture's business will presumably be wound up in an orderly fashion if termination pursuant to the agreement comes to pass. On the other hand, if one or more parties has a "put," i.e., a right to be bought out under certain circumstances, the agreement must provide for the economics of that event. At one end of the spectrum, a party that withdraws may be paid off immediately in full for its interest in the venture. At the other, the agreement may require a withdrawing party to pay an "exit fee" to escape. In the middle is a variety of arrangements and strategies for deferring, discounting, or enhancing payment for the withdrawing party's interest, and for financing that payment.

Dispute Resolution

Every lawyer attempts to capture in the agreements he or she prepares every possible contingency that may arise in the performance of those agreements. However, the infinite variety of human conduct makes this an unreachable goal. For this reason, contracts frequently contain provisions which govern the resolution of disputes that may arise between the parties. Such provisions are particularly appropriate to joint-venture agreements.

A joint-venture agreement commonly specifies the jurisdiction whose laws govern interpretation of the agreement, and often reflects as well the parties' agreement to submit disagreements to particular tribunals or courts of law. Such provisions are in general not so much dispute resolution mechanisms as they are reflections of the relative bargaining strength of the parties—the dominant party is permitted to incorporate *its* state law and refer disputes to *its* state courts.

While these provisions are better than no procedure at all, a better alternative is an agreement to submit disputes to arbitration. Most manufacturers are aware of the American Arbitration Association and its facilities, and are usually receptive to the notion that arbitration is less expensive and time consuming than litigation.

Registration and Regulatory Requirements

Intellectual Property Rights

If the joint venture is formed to exploit technological developments that are patentable but have not yet been patented, the venture partners will first wish to determine whether a patent application should be filed, who will be responsible for filing the application, who will bear the cost of registration, and who the owner of the patent will be. The same process applies equally to other intellectual property issues. If the product or process involves computer software that is amenable to U.S. copyright laws or a product that will be marketed under a name that can be registered under U.S. or state trademark statutes, the joint-venture partners must identify and assign responsibility for compliance with the particular requirements that are at issue.

Doing Business in Foreign Jurisdictions

Another registration issue that may arise is that of qualification to do business in another state. This question has two facets. First, if the venture entity is a creature of the laws of a particular state, it will need to register as a foreign entity in any other state in which it intends to "transact business" as that phrase is defined by the laws of the particular state. Second, if the joint-venture entity is a creature of the laws of a state other than that in which one or more of the joint-venture partners is located, those partners themselves should determine whether it is necessary for them to register to do business in the state in which the venture is formed.

Environmental Issues

A third category of regulatory issues that must be addressed arises under the heading of environmental requirements. All other things being equal, manufacturing operations are more likely than enterprises of other types to produce by-products that might be characterized as violating the laws regarding air or water pollution. The venture partners must consider whether federal, state, or local laws or regulations require permits for the discharge of effluents of the type that will be produced in connection with operation of the venture.

ACCOUNTING AND TAX CONSIDERATIONS

Accounting and tax questions affecting joint ventures in the manufacturing industry are not greatly different from those raised by joint ventures generally, except to the extent manufacturing ventures tend to be highly capital-intensive. This characteristic raises issues in two areas. First, the acquisition of plant and equipment generates deductions for depreciation, which translates to a noncash tax expense that has the potential for generating a corresponding level of tax-free cash flow. If it is assumed that the venture will be sufficiently short-lived that this cash flow need not be contributed to a reserve for replacement of the depreciating assets, the partners may wish to devise a method for taking advantage of this cash flow on a current basis.

Mentioning acquisition of assets, however, brings up the preliminary question of whether the venture should own assets at all, or conversely whether it should lease manufacturing space, machinery, and other hard assets necessary to the manufacturing process. The tax and cash flow results of an entirely leased enterprise will be quite different from those of an operation in which all assets are owned by the venture, especially if the lease has "finance" characteristics which take the place of on-balance-sheet borrowing the venture otherwise would have incurred.

INSURANCE CONSIDERATIONS

Insurance may be more important to a manufacturing joint venture than to ventures of other types, primarily because of liability issues that have been referred to previously. So, for example, the venture is likely to be required to purchase product liability insurance to insulate itself from liability for the failure of products it produces. (The need for insurance of this type, and the cost and difficulty of procuring it, may come as a shock to a venturer which until that time has been engaged solely or primarily in pure design or research.) Likewise, workers' compensation insurance is a necessity in an enterprise involving manufacturing processes. Finally, because of the plant-intensive nature of most manufacturing concerns, casualty insurance and coverage for environmental contamination will become relatively more significant and more expensive issues for a manufacturing joint venture than for enterprises of other types.

OTHER CONSIDERATIONS

Antitrust

The potential antitrust issues raised by joint ventures in general have been studied in some depth, but are probably not as well known to most lawyers as other aspects of antitrust law. One possible antitrust consideration, for example, is whether the venture is being used to exploit assets (particularly patents) in such a way as to bar potential competitors from entering the field. The entire process of granting patents is anticompetitive by its very nature, of course, but this characteristic is usually accepted as a necessary evil which is outweighed by the societal good of encouraging technological innovation. When a joint venture uses patents as an offensive weapon against competition, however, this policy justification cannot be maintained.

   Another potential issue of concern to antitrust regulators is that of the "spillover" effect of cooperation between putative competitors in a joint venture. The concern is frequently raised that when competitors combine to form a joint venture, they will not be able to stop at the cooperation necessary to get the venture up and running. Rather, it is feared, they will begin to discuss an entire gamut of forbidden topics such as fixing prices or dividing markets entirely outside the scope of the venture itself. In those joint ventures which necessitate the filing of a Hart-Scott-Rodino Act premerger notification form, the Federal Trade Commision and the Department of Justice have sometimes required elaborate "Chinese wall" procedures as a condition of refraining from seeking injunctive relief against proceeding with the venture.

   A third concern often mentioned in the antitrust context is that a potential entrant into a particular market will, in essence, take the easy way out by forming a joint venture to enter the market rather than doing so by internal expansion. A variant on this hypothesis is the possibility that one party will co-opt an actual or potential competitor by forming a joint venture with that competitor.

None of these concerns is entirely spurious, and there are no doubt potential anticompetitive effects lurking in every joint venture. The primary regulatory agencies—the Justice Department and the Federal Trade Commission—bear the responsibility of sorting out the procompetitive aspects of a joint venture from its anticompetitive aspects, and deciding which predominate. The FTC undertook an exhaustive review of the GM-Toyota venture on these issues, and determined that the venture should be permitted to proceed. It should be noted that the Hart-Scott-Rodino premerger notification guidelines have been extended to cover formation of unincorporated joint ventures in an effort to make the job of the regulatory agencies easier.

Labor Relations and Collective Bargaining

Depending upon the particular industry segment, and on the particular physical location of the joint-venture facility, the venture partners may be able to exert some control over whether the employees of the joint venture will be represented by organized labor. As has previously been seen, however, the parties' wishes may not be the most significant factor. Legal doctrines applicable to labor-management relations may cause the venture to be regarded as an extension of or successor to one or another of the venturers. As an example, the chairman of Toyota stated very clearly at the outset of the venture that he did not want the NUMMI facility to be unionized. The UAW was, nevertheless, recognized eventually as bargaining agent for the NUMMI. After extensive collective bargaining, a three-year agreement was reached with the union which calls for unprecedented "affirmative measures," including reduction of management salaries and return of subcontracted work, before any union employees can be laid off.

CHAPTER 10

JOINT VENTURING IN THE BANKING AND FINANCIAL SERVICES INDUSTRIES

Jack S. Older
Rogers and Wells

Joint ventures are often undertaken by banks and affiliates of banks for the same reasons that joint ventures are undertaken by ordinary business corporations. These reasons include such matters as expansion of markets, entry into new fields, acquisition of expertise, and sharing of risks. On the other hand, banks often enter into joint ventures for reasons that may not be considered important by the ordinary business corporation. In many instances, the bank may enter into a joint venture in order to derive additional profit from a large and well-developed customer base whereby the other party to the joint venture can market a new service to the bank's customer base. In other instances, banks enter into joint ventures because they wish to take advantage of entrepreneurial skills which are not developed in the ordinary course of the banking business.

It is well recognized that the banking industry is perhaps the most heavily regulated segment of U.S. society because a safe and sound banking system is essential to a healthy economy. As a result, the ability of banking organizations to enter into joint ventures is severely circumscribed by a host of statutory and regulatory complexities. The first level of complexity arises from the fact that there are several different forms of banking organizations which are subject to differing forms of regulation.

The differing forms of organization include national banks, state-chartered commercial banks (often referred to as banks and trust companies), federal savings and loan associations (and federal savings banks), state-chartered savings and loan associations, and state-chartered savings banks. A national bank or a state-chartered commercial bank may be the subsidiary of a bank holding company, whereas a federal savings and loan association or a state-chartered savings and loan association may be the subsidiary of a savings and loan holding company.

Bank holding companies are regulated primarily by the Board of Governors of the Federal Reserve System (the Federal Reserve); national banks are regulated by the Office of the Comptroller of the Currency (OCC); state-chartered commercial banks and state-chartered savings banks are regulated by state banking departments as well as by the Federal Deposit Insurance Corporation (FDIC) which insures the deposits of such banks as well as the national banks; federal savings and loan associations and federal savings banks are regulated by the Federal Home Loan Bank Board (FHLBB) and state-chartered savings and loan associations are regulated by state banking departments or state savings and loan supervisors as well as the FLHBB which acts as the operating head of the Federal Savings and Loan Insurance Corporation (FSLIC), which insures the deposits of both federal and state-chartered savings and loan associations.

Each of the regulators mentioned above is charged with the enforcement of specific laws which prescribe the activities of the banking organizations under its supervisory jurisdiction. To a greater or lesser degree, each of the statutes enforced and administered by the regulatory agencies limits the investment authority of the banking organizations within its purview. The applicable limitations relate to the type of investment, the amount of investment, and the structure of the investment. Therefore, in determining whether a banking organization should enter into a joint venture with another party, it will be necessary to determine whether, under the law applicable to such a banking organization, such banking organization may invest in the contemplated venture, whether there are any limitations on the amount of such investment, and whether there are any restrictions on the form of such investment.

Apart from specific statutory or regulatory restrictions and limitations, the bank regulatory agencies will generally take into account the safety and soundness of any bank investment or transaction. In this regard, the agencies may try to insure that a banking organization does not allow itself to be exposed to risks beyond its control, so joint-venture agreements are often reviewed by the agencies with such considerations in mind.

Moreoever, the agencies may seek assurances that a banking organization will not feel compelled to honor the obligations of a partnership of which it becomes a partner, even though it is not legally required to honor such obligations.

BANK HOLDING COMPANIES

The Bank Holding Company Act of 1956 generally prohibits a bank holding company from acquiring the ownership or control of any company which is not a bank. However, there are a number of exceptions to this rule, the most important of which is the exception which permits the bank holding company to acquire the shares of any company the activities of which are found by the Federal Reserve to be so closely related to banking as to be a proper incident thereto. The Federal Reserve has issued regulations which provide that certain activities are so closely related to banking as to be a proper incident thereto and may be engaged in by a bank holding company or a subsidiary of a bank holding company by filing certain notifications or making certain applications. These activities include, but are not limited to, the following:

1. Making and servicing loans.
2. Acting as investment or financial advisors for real estate investment trusts and investment companies as well as providing advice to state and local governments.
3. Leasing personal or real property or acting as agent, broker, or advisor in leasing such property provided that (a) the lease serves as the functional equivalent of an extension of credit to the lessee, (b) the property to be leased is acquired specifically for the leasing transaction under consideration or an earlier leasing transaction, (c) the lease is on a nonoperating basis, (d) the effect of the transaction (at the inception of the initial lease) will yield a return that will compensate the lessor for not less than the lessor's full investment in the property plus the estimated total cost of financing the property over the term of the lease, (e) the maximum initial lease term must not be greater than 40 years, and (f) at the expiration of the lease (including renewals or extensions), the lessor must liquidate or release all interest in the property.

4. Providing to others data processing and data transmission services, facilities, data bases, or access to such services, facilities or data bases by any technological means if such services, facilities, or data bases are financial, banking, or economic in nature.
5. Limited insurance agency and underwriting activities that relate primarily to extensions of credit by the bank holding company or any of its subsidiaries.
6. Performing appraisals of real estate and tangible and intangible personal property.
7. Arranging commercial real estate equity financing.
8. Providing securities brokerage services.
9. Underwriting and dealing in government obligations and money market instruments.
10. Providing advisory and transactional services with respect to foreign exchange.
11. Acting as a futures commission merchant for nonaffiliated persons in the execution and clearance of futures contracts and options on futures contracts relating to financial instruments.

A bank holding company that wishes to engage, through a joint venture, in a nonbanking activity approved by the Federal Reserve must file a notice or application with its local Federal Reserve Bank. Where such entry is de novo, a notice is required, and the applicant may commence the activity 30 days after receipt of the notice by the Federal Reserve Bank unless the Reserve Bank returns the notice as incomplete, notifies the applicant that it can start the activity at an earlier date, extends the 30-day period for an additional 15 days, or refers the notice to the Federal Reserve Board. Where such entry involves the acquisition of an existing company, a formal application must be filed with the Reserve Bank. When a notice or application involving an approved nonbanking activity is received by a reserve bank, it must promptly send notification to the *Federal Register* for publication inviting comment for a period of not more than 30 days.

A bank holding company that wishes to engage in a nonbanking activity that has not been set forth in the Federal Reserve Regulations as an activity which is so closely related to banking as to be a proper incident thereto, must file an application with its Federal Reserve Bank. Such application must contain evidence that the proposed activity is so closely related to banking as to be a proper incident thereto. If the Board finds that the applicant has demonstrated that the activity is closely related to banking so as to be a proper incident thereto, it will publish notice of the application in the *Federal Register* for comment. If the Board does not so find, it will not publish notice of the application, and it must inform the applicant of the reasons for its decision.

There are specified time periods in which a Federal Reserve Bank must act upon a notice or application or refer it to the Board. An expedited procedure can be followed where certain criteria regarding small acquisitions apply, but it isn't clear whether this procedure is available in the case of a joint venture.

In evaluating a notice or application, the Board must consider whether the applicant's performance of the activity will produce benefits to the public such as greater convenience, increased competition, or greater efficiency; and whether these benefits outweigh possible adverse effects such as undue concentrations of resources, decreased or unfair competition, conflicts of interest, and unsound banking practices. The board will also evaluate the applicant's financial and management resources, including its subsidiaries and any company to be acquired. It will also consider the effect of the proposed transaction on the applicant's resources.

A number of joint ventures involving approved nonbanking activities have been approved by the Federal Reserve. These activities include data processing services, investment advisory services, insurance activities, lending services, leasing and securities brokerage activities. In many instances the joint ventures involve partnerships between bank holding company subsidiaries and nonbanking companies.

NATIONAL BANKS

National banks have very limited investment authority, and their ability to invest in subsidiaries is also very limited. Even with respect to those banking activities in which a national bank may invest directly, there is substantial case law which holds that a national bank cannot become a general partner whereby it becomes exposed to unlimited liability.

Although a national bank may invest in subsidiary corporations which can engage in joint ventures, the types of subsidiary corporations are limited to statutory subsidiaries and operating subsidiaries, as well as companies which are formed to manage or liquidate property received for debts previously contracted.

Statutory subsidiaries include safe deposit companies, entitles organized for the purpose of encouraging private investment in low- or moderate-income housing, certain other housing corporations, agricultural credit corporations, small business investment companies, corporations that own bank premises, bank service corporations, Edge corporations, and Agreement corporations which engage in international and foreign banking and foreign banks. Operating subsidiaries are corporations through which a national bank may engage in activities which are part of the business of banking or incidental to the business of banking. A subsidiary of a national bank will not qualify as an operating subsidiary unless the bank owns at least 80 percent of the corporation's voting stock.

If a national bank wishes to acquire or establish an operating subsidiary, it must submit a letter to the deputy comptroller of the district in which the bank's principal office is located detailing the proposed activities of the operating subsidiary and stating whether the activity of the operating subsidiary will be conducted at some location other than the main office or a previously approved branch of the bank. The OCC has 30 days in which to notify the bank of any objections to the acquisition or establishment of the operating subsidiary. If no objection is received within the 30-day period, the bank may acquire or establish the operating subsidiary. The same procedure regarding notification applies when a national bank seeks to perform new activities in an existing operating subsidiary. Under the OCC's regulations, each operating subsidiary is subject to examination and supervision by the OCC in the same manner and to the same extent as the bank which has acquired or established the operating subsidiary.

The OCC has permitted operating subsidiaries of national banks to become general partners in joint ventures with other operating subsidiaries and with commercial enterprises. However, in exchange for its approval of a bank's proposed entry into a joint venture through an operating subsidiary, the OCC has often imposed conditions. Such conditions may include provisions in the partnership agreement which give a bank subsidiary the right to veto certain decisions by the partnership, in order to prevent the partnership from engaging in activities which are not permissible for national banks or in activities that may expose a national bank to excessive risk. Furthermore, the OCC may impose conditions which limit a bank's investment or further investment in the enterprise.

A major issue which has recently been decided by the U.S. Supreme Court is whether an operating subsidiary may engage in permissible activities at locations beyond those in which the parent national bank may conduct its business. The Court decided that where the operating subsidiary does not conduct the business of accepting deposits, making loans, or paying checks, it may establish offices outside of the state in which the parent bank has its principal office. This decision would appear to apply to joint ventures entered into by the operating subsidiaries of national banks.

FEDERAL SAVINGS AND LOAN ASSOCIATIONS

Federal Savings and Loan Associations (S&Ls) are permitted to enter into joint ventures through service corporations which engage in certain specified preapproved activities or an activity specifically approved by the FHLBB after its review of an application. The activities in which service corporations of S&Ls or the joint ventures of such service corporations may engage are the following:

1. Originating, investing in, selling, purchasing, servicing, or otherwise dealing in loans which the parent S&L may make.
2. Performing certain analytical, administrative, or operational services primarily for financial institutions. These services include, but are not limited to, credit analyses, appraisal, administration of personnel benefit programs, liquidity management, accounting and internal auditing services, the operation of remote service units, and the purchase of office supplies, furniture, and equipment.
3. Real estate services including the maintenance and management of real estate, real estate brokerage for the property of the joint venture, the acquisition of real estate for development, the acquisition of improved real estate for rental or resale, and the acquisition, maintenance, and management of real estate used for offices of a stockholder of the venture.
4. Investment in certain securities.
5. The preparation of state and federal tax returns for individuals or not-for-profit organizations.
6. Insurance brokerage or agency for liability, casualty, automobile, life, health, accident, or title insurance, but not private mortgage insurance.
7. Providing fiduciary services as a trust company.
8. Issuing notes, bonds, debentures, or other obligations or securities.

9. Issuing credit cards, extending credit in connection therewith, and otherwise engaging in or participating in credit card operations.
10. Acquiring personal property for the purpose of leasing such property.
11. Providing data processing services for the S&Ls which own the joint venture.
12. Any activity reasonably incident to those listed above.

The aggregate amount which a federal S&L may invest in the capital stock, obligations or other securities of service corporations is generally 2 percent of the assets of the S&L. In addition to the amount invested in the securities of service corporations, a federal S&L may lend certain additional amounts to service corporations if it meets its minimum regulatory capital requirements. With respect to each joint venture in which a service corporation of a federal S&L owns either 10 percent or less of the capital stock or is a limited partner which has contributed 10 percent or less of the joint venture's capital, a federal S&L may lend an amount up to its regulatory capital. Where a federal S&L owns more than 10 percent of the venture through a service corporation, then the aggregate, amount which it may lend is limited to 50 percent of its regulatory capital.

As indicated above, a federal S&L may engage in the listed activities preapproved by the FHLBB without filing any notice or application with the FHLBB. Where a federal S&L proposes to enter into an activity which is not on the preapproved list of activities, it must file an application in letter form with its principal supervisory agent (the regional Federal Home Loan Bank) and obtain the approval of the FHLBB. Under this procedure, the FHLBB has approved applications by federal S&Ls to organize and invest in a service corporation providing securities brokerage services. The FHLBB has also ruled that its approval is not required prior to a service corporation investing in a real estate investment trust which engages only in preapproved activities.

STATE-CHARTERED SAVINGS AND LOAN ASSOCIATIONS

The investment authority of state-chartered S&Ls is determined under state law. Accordingly, there continues to exist great diversity regarding the investment authority of state-chartered S&Ls, depending upon their state of incorporation. For example, the states of California and Florida have been reputed to have very liberal laws regarding investments by S&Ls chartered in them. As a result, the FHLBB as the operating head of the FSLIC which insures the deposits of both federal and state-chartered S&Ls became concerned about the ability of certain state-chartered S&Ls to invest unlimited amounts in nonbanking activities (*e.g.*, real estate syndication). It is the responsibility of the FSLIC to make sure that all insured S&Ls operate on a safe-and-sound basis.

The response of the FHLBB and FSLIC was promulgation of regulations limiting the authority of all insured institutions to make investments in equity securities, real estate, service corporations, operating subsidiaries, and certain land loans and nonresidential construction (collectively these investments are referred to as "equity-risk investments"). For an S&L which has tangible equity capital of at least 6 percent of its total liabilities, the amount of its equity-risk investment may not exceed three times its tangible capital. For an S&L which meets its regulatory capital requirements but has tangible capital of less than 6 percent of its total liabilities, equity-risk investment may not exceed the greater of 3 percent of its assets or two and one-half times its tangible capital. An institution that fails to satisfy its regulatory capital requirement is not permitted to make any equity-risk investments except as may be specifically approved by its principal supervisory agent.

Certain institutions with investments exceeding the limits of equity-risk investment on December 10, 1984 were grandfathered in their existing equity-risk investment. An insured institution seeking to make equity-risk investments in an amount, at a threshold level, or of a type other than is generally permitted under the regulations must file an application with its principal supervisory agent and with its state supervisor. The application must contain certain specified financial information with regard to the investment, and it must include a business plan which deals with diversification of equity-risk investments. The regulations also include the factors which the principal supervisory agent is required to review in determining whether the overall policies, condition, and operation of the applicant afford a basis for supervisory objection. These factors include the institution's trends in performance and the controls established by the institution with respect to the proposed investment. The principal supervisory agent must also consider whether the investment will increase the applicant's risk of default or the financial exposure of the FSLIC, whether the institution and its subsidiaries are appropriately diversified, and whether the applicant's policies are inconsistent with economical home financing.

If the principal supervisory agent makes an adverse determination regarding an application to make equity-risk investments, the institution may file a petition for reconsideration with the FSLIC.

SAVINGS AND LOAN HOLDING COMPANIES

Both federally chartered and state-chartered S&Ls may be the subsidiaries of a savings and loan holding company. If such a holding company owns only one S&L, it is known as a unitary S&L holding company, and such a holding company may itself or through its other subsidiaries engage in any business it desires to undertake. For example, the Ford Motor Company is a savings and loan holding company, and so too is Sears, Roebuck and Company. It should be noted, however, that transactions between an S&L and its parent holding company, or the affiliates of such a holding company, are largely prohibited. Moreover, if the S&L holding company on a consolidated basis derives more the 50 percent of its income and its net worth from the types of activities an S&L may engage in, the S&L holding company will be considered nondiversified, and a nondiversified S&L holding company is subject to severe limitations with respect to incurring indebtedness.

STATE-CHARTERED SAVINGS BANKS

The authority of state-chartered savings banks to make investments and to enter into joint ventures is governed by state law, and in this regard is similar to the authority of state-chartered S&Ls. However, most state-chartered savings banks have their deposits insured by the FDIC rather than the FSLIC, and as a result they are not subject to the same degree of limitation in making equity-risk investments.

The largest state-chartered savings banks are found in New York, New Jersey, Pennsylvania, Washington, and the New England states. Many of these states have adopted laws which permit state-chartered savings banks to invest a fairly large percentage of their assets in diverse economic enterprises. For example, New York has for many years permitted savings banks to make so-called "leeway" investments. Pursuant to such authority, a savings bank may invest up to 5 percent of its assets in anything which it is not otherwise authorized to invest in, other than the common stock of a commercial bank or a life insurance company.

Within the aggregate limitation of 5 percent of assets, no single leeway investment can exceed 1 percent of a savings bank's assets.

In addition to the broad authority to make investments pursuant to leeway authority, a New York savings bank may invest up to 10 percent of its assets in one or more service corporations, provided that all of the stock of such service corporations is owned by one or more savings banks. The activities of such service corporations may include the following:

1. Originating, investing in, purchasing, selling, servicing, or otherwise dealing in, directly or through participation, loans of any type which may be made by a savings bank.
2. Providing services primarily for other financial institutions such as accounting, auditing, clerical, consulting, data processing, investment advisory, or managerial services.
3. Providing insurance brokerage or agency services.
4. Providing travel agency and tax preparation services.
5. Providing real estate services such as brokerage, appraisal, inspection, or property management.
6. Providing courier services.
7. Sponsoring, organizing, and advising open-end mutual funds.
8. Providing securities services such as brokerage or investment advice.
9. Leasing personal property to customers.
10. Engaging in factoring.
11. Acquiring investment securities.
12. Issuing letters of credit.
13. Issuing credit cards and engaging in credit-card operations.
14. Acquiring improved and unimproved real property for the purpose of subdividing, developing, constructing improvements thereon, and reselling, leasing, or operating such property for the production of income.

It is also clear under New York state law that savings banks as well as subsidiaries may participate in joint ventures as either general partners or limited partners.

Furthermore, it is also interesting to note that, in the case of leeway investments, a savings bank is not required to submit an application or file a notice with the banking department before it commences such an investment. As long as the savings bank takes care to make sure that the investment fits within the purview of the law, it is permitted to undertake the investment without supervisory approval. On the other hand, a savings bank must give the banking department prior notice of its intention to make a capital investment in a service corporation which will engage in the activities listed above. Such notice must be given 45 days prior to the making of such investment, and if the superintendant of banks does not object in writing, within 45 days after the receipt of a completed notice, the savings bank may make the contemplated investment. Savings banks that wish to make a capital investment in a service corporation which will engage in any activity requiring the specific approval of the New York Banking Board must submit a written application, and such application must be approved by a three-fifths vote of the banking board.

It should also be noted that certain federal savings banks which converted from a New York state charter to a federal charter were permitted pursuant, to the Garn-St Germain Act of 1982, to retain investment authority under New York law as it existed at the time of their conversion. Accordingly, there are a number of federal savings banks in New York which still retain leeway investment authority.

As a result of leeway authority, a number of large savings banks in New York, both state-chartered and converted federally chartered banks, have made investments in companies that have been the subject of leveraged buyouts. In many cases, such investments were structured to maximize the federal tax benefits of net-operating-loss carryovers available to such savings banks. However, in 1986 the IRS regulations relating to partnerships were changed to make it more difficult for banks with net operating losses to avail themselves of certain partnership structures designed to offset the income of industrial companies against the large net-operating-loss carryovers accumulated by banks during the early 1980s.

Although leeway authority has permitted savings banks in New York to invest in virtually any type of economic enterprise other than a commercial bank or a life insurance company, many banks have been hesitant to avail themselves of the opportunity to make broader investments because they often lack the management expertise and entrepreneurial skill required to make such investments successful. As a partial response to such a problem, it has been suggested that a savings bank undertake broader investments with carefully selected partners using the limited-partnership format. In such a structure, the savings bank would be the limited partner and the general partner would be the company with the requisite experience and entrepreneurial skills; and the limited-partnership agreement would provide for the submission by the general partner of annual budgets and annual business plans which would be reviewed with the limited partner on a quarterly or monthly basis. Such a structure would permit a savings bank to gain the benefits of a desirable investment with limited liability and an opportunity to maintain oversight while a more entrepreneurial partner could gain the benefits of the savings bank's financial resources.

The most significant limitations includes in FDIC regulations involve the establishment or acquisition of subsidiaries engaged in securities activities. The FDIC regulations which have been adopted for reasons of safety and soundness provide, in general, that an FDIC-insured bank make clear to the public that any subsidiary or affiliate engaged in the securities business is an entity separate and apart from the bank. The regulations require a bank that shares a common name and logo with a securities subsidiary or affiliate to make certain disclosures to the public. In addition, the regulations prohibit a bank to share common officers or a majority of directors with securities subsidiaries or affiliates, and there are other requirements regarding separate space, separate records, and separate conduct of business.

STATE-CHARTERED COMMERCIAL BANKS

State-chartered commercial banks also derive their authority to make investments and engage in joint ventures from state law. For the most part, the investment authority of state-chartered commercial banks is more limited than that of state-chartered savings banks. For example, in New York a state-chartered commercial bank is not permitted to undertake leeway investments, but instead, its authority to make equity investments is severely limited and generally subject to approval by the New York State Banking Board. However, it should be noted that most state-chartered commercial banks of significant size are subsidiaries of bank holding companies, and in such a structure, new enterprises are undertaken by subsidiaries of the holding company within the limitations described above.

ALTERNATIVE STRUCTURES

Although there has been a gradual expansion of the authority of banking organizations to undertake joint ventures in both banking-related and in nonbanking fields, there still are many obstacles to such ventures. These obstacles have led banks to seek other avenues for obtaining profit from businesses which they cannot otherwise enter. Perhaps the best example of this phenomenon has been the efforts of banks to enter insurance underwriting and agency activities. National banks have been severely limited by the restrictions on operating subsidiaries, but they have obtained rulings from the OCC which permit them to lease space on their banking floors to insurance agencies under rental arrangements, which allow them to share in the profits of such operations. These so-called percentage-rental arrangements provide some of the same benefits that a partnership structure may have offered. In many instances, banks have sold their customer lists to providers of life, health, and accident insurance. Under these arrangements, insurance companies often pay certain amounts for lists provided by banks and additional amounts if conversions to sales exceed certain levels. It should be noted that under the FHLBB regulations for federal S&Ls, a federal S&L is prohibited from divulging its customer list to any third party without permission from its customers.

Apart from such alternative structures as leases or sales of customer lists, banks wishing to enter new fields may, for legal or business reasons, revert to alternatives tried in the past. For example, rather than make equity investments in new enterprises, banks may feel more secure in making loans to new enterprises whereby the loan contains features which may permit a bank to profit from the success of the venture. Items such as equity kickers, percentage rentals and warrants have been used with varying degrees of success in prior ventures by banks.

For those banks which are permitted to invest in certain activities but are wary of making such investments, it may be possible to structure loan transactions using convertible notes. Such a structure would permit a bank to commit its funds conservatively and await the results of operations before committing itself to becoming an equity investor.

CONCLUSION

It is possible to structure joint ventures among the subsidiaries or affiliates of banking organizations and other banking organizations or nonbanking organizations. However, in the case of commercial banks, whether they are part of a holding company structure or not, the range of activities for joint venturing is generally limited to those activities which are closely related to banking and a proper incident to banking. Moreover, care must be observed in following the appropriate notification or application process. In the course of following such procedures, the structure of a joint venture often becomes a matter of negotiation with the regulator, in order to assure the regulatory agency that the venture will be conducted without exposing the bank or its affiliates to excessive risks and without going beyond the limitations of permitted activities. Any attempt by bank holding companies, national banks, and state-chartered commercial banks to participate in joint ventures which involve activities that are not closely related to banking will be difficult, time-consuming, and costly.

State-chartered thrift institutions often present broader opportunities for participation in joint ventures, but many of these institutions have been more conservative and cautious in moving beyond the bounds of banking activity. In the case of state-chartered savings and loan associations, the FHLBB has played a significant role in limiting the expansion of joint-venture activity by focusing attention on the insurance risk to the FSLIC.

Although the opportunity for joint ventures in the banking industry appears to be somewhat limited and great care must be exercised in undertaking such ventures, there are ample opportunities for joint venturing in the banking industry, and it is likely that the growth of such opportunity will increase gradually in the future.

CHAPTER 11

JOINT VENTURING IN THE TRANSPORTATION INDUSTRY

Paul A. Cunningham, Esq.
Pepper, Hamilton & Scheetz
Richard S. Kopf, Esq.
Bechtel Investments, Inc.

INTRODUCTION AND OVERVIEW

Joint venturing has been prevalent in the transportation industry for well over 100 years. In the mid-1800s, for example, railroads entered into joint ventures involving the construction and ownership of passenger stations and bridges, and also formed jointly owned terminal railroads to provide switching services at major hubs.

The long history of transportation joint ventures does not indicate that joint-venture opportunities in the industry have been exhausted, or that joint-venturing activity is moribund. To the contrary, the joint-venture form has been widely used in recent years, involving imaginative ways of pooling transportation resources and exploiting new technology.

The opportunities for joint venturing are of many types, including: (1) "intramodal" arrangements between transportation firms providing the same type of service (*e.g.*, railroads, airlines, motor carriers, shipping, and pipelines), (2) "intermodal" arrangements involving firms providing different types of transportation service, and (3) perhaps most interesting of all, "interindustry" arrangements in which a transportation firm joins with a company in another industry to provide a service—such as a fiber-optic communications—traditionally not offered by transportation firms.

Opportunities also exist for private/public joint ventures between transportation firms and units of state or local governments wishing to develop their jurisdictions' transportation infrastructure.

In the transportation industry, as elsewhere, firms enter into joint ventures in order to achieve economies of scale and scope, expand capital spending and research and development, draw on complementary strengths or expertise, share risk, and obtain resources or expand operations more quickly than would otherwise be possible. Several of these factors appear to be especially pronounced in the transportation context. Joint ventures have frequently been used to create equipment pooling arrangements which allow the spreading of capital costs and the realization of economies of scale. Other transportation joint ventures may seek to realize synergisms through the combination (or, more frequently, the coordination) of several companies' transportation networks into a larger network.

Because most sectors of the transportation industry are dominated by a small number of companies, joint venturers must be especially sensitive to the antitrust laws. If the joint venture restricts access by competitors to essential facilities that it controls, or if the joint venture is otherwise structured or operated in an anticompetitive manner, the joint venturers may risk an antitrust challenge by government or private parties.

The transportation industry in the United States has historically been subject to extensive economic regulation because of the industry's perceived importance to the public interest. While the scope of such regulation has waned in recent years with several deregulatory initiatives, joint venturers must still comply with many regulatory requirements. Railroads, motor carriers, and inland water carriers are principally regulated by the Interstate Commerce Commission (ICC); ocean shipping and interstate water carriers are principally regulated by the Federal Maritime Commission; airlines are subject to limited regulation by the Department of Transportation (DOT); and pipelines are regulated by the Federal Energy Regulatory Commission (FERC). Other federal regulatory agencies may also have a limited role in the regulation (economic, safety, and environmental) of transportation firms, as do state and local governments.

The following discussion describes the many types of joint venturing activity by transportation firms, and identifies some of the key antitrust and economic regulatory issues that are likely to need to be addressed early on by potential joint venturers. Because labor costs and labor relations are often critical to the viability and success of transportation firms, we also discuss briefly some of the special labor laws that govern several sectors of the transportation industry.

ANTITRUST CONSIDERATIONS

General Principles

A joint venture involves collaborative activity between two or more firms, which are frequently competitors, that may be challenged under the U.S. antitrust laws. The most important statutory provisions are Section 1 of the Sherman Act, which prohibits contracts, combinations, and conspiracies in unreasonable restraint of trade; Section 2 of the Sherman Act, which proscribes monopolization or attempted monopolization of particular markets; and Section 7 of the Clayton Act, which generally prohibits combinations between actual or potential competitors that may substantially lessen competition or create a monopoly.

As noted above, antitrust issues figure significantly in the transportation industry because many sectors are dominated by a small number of firms. Collaborative activity by two or more of these firms, if not carefully limited, may have the potential for restraining competition.

Throughout the first half of this century, joint ventures were routinely attacked under the antitrust laws by the Department of Justice and private parties, and were frequently found to be unlawful. Some of these cooperative efforts were thinly disguised price-fixing agreements; others involved restraints of trade (such as the allocation of markets) ancillary to the legitimate goals of the enterprise; and yet others restricted access to a "bottleneck" or "essential facility" (such as a railroad bridge that had to be crossed to enter a particular market) in order to thwart competition.

Such blatantly illegal joint ventures are rarely found today. Instead, the legality of joint-venture activity increasingly requires a careful balance between efficiencies that such arrangements make possible and any offsetting restraint on competition. Congress has specifically acted to encourage certain types of research and development joint ventures by passing the National Cooperative Research Act of 1984, which reduces or eliminates the antitrust risks entailed by such ventures. That act is applicable to the transportation industry.

Congress has long recognized the potential benefits of transportation joint ventures. As explained next, transportation regulators are authorized by statute to approve particular arrangements and grant antitrust immunity, notwithstanding a modest restraint on competition, if the broader public interest is served. Thus, in view of general antitrust trends as well as those laws specifically applicable to transportation, the antitrust laws should be viewed as accommodating to properly structured joint ventures.

Government Review and Approval of Proposed Transportation Joint Ventures

Once the business decision is made to conduct activity through a joint venture, it must be determined whether the formation of the joint venture requires review by the applicable regulatory agency or the Department of Justice. The principal considerations in this regard are outlined next.

Agency Review and Antitrust Immunity

Most transportation common carriers are today regulated by one or more federal agencies or departments. Certain types of joint ventures require prior regulatory approval, and are immune from attack under the antitrust laws once such approval is obtained. While the various statutes require that the regulators consider the competitive consequences of such joint ventures when deciding whether to grant approval, the overriding standard is the "public interest."

Recent deregulatory initiatives have significantly affected this process. Generally, Congress has narrowed the type of joint ventures which can be immunized, and regulators have been encouraged to apply more rigorous antitrust standards when determining the public interest.

The ebb and flow of deregulation will continue to impact the nature of regulatory review and the extent to which a particular transportation joint venture can be immunized. At this point, for example, agency review and immunity for shipping joint ventures appears firmly embedded in applicable laws and regulations. On the other hand, absent Congressional action, DOT will soon cease to have any authority to immunize intercarrier agreements among domestic airlines.

The regulatory review process, and the availability of antitrust immunity, is illustrated by ICC regulation of "pooling" arrangements. ICC-regulated common carriers may not agree with each other to pool or divide traffic or services, or any part of their earnings, without the approval of the ICC. Once obtained, such approval immunizes the transaction from the antitrust laws. From an antitrust perspective, such immunity protection should generally encourage carriers, where feasible, to structure a joint venture in a manner that qualifies it as a pooling arrangement.

The participants in any pooling joint venture must recognize that by seeking ICC approval they do not necessarily avoid review of the arrangement by the Department of Justice. The department has become increasingly active in this area and may submit comments to the ICC respecting antitrust issues. For example, the department recently moved to reopen an ICC proceeding regarding the antitrust immunity of the Trailer Train Company, which is a joint venture of rail carriers that pool trailer railcars. While the department's comments are influential, the ICC will make the final determination and is not bound by the views of the Department.

Department of Justice and FTC Reporting Requirements
When nonimmunized business activity is to be conducted through joint-venture entities that are incorporated, the formation of the joint venture may have to be reported to (1) the Department of Justice, which would review the agreement for compliance with the antitrust laws, and (2) the Federal Trade Commission (FTC), which enforces Section 5 of the FTC Act and proscribes "unfair methods of competition" (a standard essentially comparable to that applied by the Department of Justice under the Clayton and Sherman Acts). However, under the applicable regulations (known generally as Hart-Scott-Rodino regulations), only incorporated joint ventures of relatively substantial size need be reported.

A decision by the Department of Justice or FTC to allow a joint venture to proceed does not provide the venture with antitrust immunity. Indeed, private parties have successfully attacked some mergers which were reviewed under the Hart-Scott-Rodino filing procedure.

Department of Justice Business Review Procedures
Parties to joint ventures that are not immunized, or that are not subject to Hart-Scott-Rodino, may wish to describe the proposal to the Department of Justice and request that the Department state whether it would challenge the agreement as a violation of the antitrust laws. The Department's responses are referred to as Business Review Letters. In general, the business review process is less costly than most formal proceedings, and the Department's responses are usually reasonably prompt. While a favorable letter would not bind private parties and can be disclaimed later by the Department in light of new facts or circumstances, as a practical matter the business review letter provides reasonable as-

surance that the contemplated joint venture will not be held unlawful under the antitrust laws.

The business-review-letter approach has been pursued by transportation companies with good results. In 1983, the Burlington Northern Railroad Company and Road-Rail Transportation Company were advised that the Department had no intention of challenging a joint-venture agreement regarding the development and use of an experimental vehicle for use on both rail tracks and service roads. Similarly, favorable letters from the Department of Justice have been received respecting joint-venture proposals for (1) the exchange of shipper credit information and (2) airline reservation systems.

Structuring a Joint Venture that Highlights Procompetitive Elements

In view of the possibility that transportation joint ventures may be subject to antitrust challenges by private parties, even if government review has been requested or sought, every arrangement must be carefully structured to reduce antitrust risks to the extent consistent with the joint venture's purposes. The joint venturers should seek to limit the venture's activities to those elements which are clearly procompetitive.

In particular, it is typically best that joint ventures be limited to a specific period of time and not continue in perpetuity; the joint venture should not unreasonably limit competitors' access to an "essential facility" or "bottleneck"; and actual or potential competitors participating in a joint venture should not facilitate or encourage the exchange of peripheral information, such as price data, among themselves. To assure compliance with the antitrust laws, it is good practice for joint venturers to issue written rules governing the conduct of employees participating in the joint activity.

JOINT VENTURING IN SURFACE TRANSPORTATION

Joint-Venture Activity and Trends

Joint ventures frequently offer an attractive method of increasing efficiency in surface-transportation industries, including railroads, motor carriers, and inland and ocean shipping. As noted at the outset of this chapter, joint ventures have been used for over a century in the rail industry.

Surface-transportation industries generally utilize many methods of interfirm coordination short of a "pure" joint venture involving the creation of a jointly owned, separate business entity. Coordinated activities among the railroads, for instance, have included the development of uniform operating procedures, agreements on standardized technology, (standard gauge rail and track design), joint routes and rates for traffic moved by two or more railroads, car accounting (permitting a rail carrier's cars to move on lines owned by other carriers), switching operations, and a common bill of lading. Recently, there has been a flurry of activity among transportation firms to facilitate intermodal movements of containerized or trailer-load freight between oceangoing vessels, railroads (using double-stack railcars and other special equipment), and motor carriers.

The joint venture form has been used by surface-transportation firms in a wide variety of circumstances, ranging from equipment pooling to research and development projects. Recent joint ventures include the following:

• In order to increase railcar supply and promote efficient car use, railroads have created equipment joint ventures to pool boxcars, flat cars, and other rail cars. In some pools, like Trailer-Train, the joint venture buys railcars and hires them to participating railroads, which then share the earnings. In other pools, the joint venturers donate their own equipment and share its use.
• Railroads have formed joint ventures to share data. The National Railroad Industry Trade Group, formed in 1987, is operated by Dunn and Bradstreet in a way that permits members to exchange credit information on shippers without fear of antitrust prosecution.
• Several major railroads together own a feeder railroad that gathers freight from a remote shippers and hauls it to main-line tracks.
• Fifteen railroads in the United States and Canada have teamed together to develop advanced train-control systems.
• A manufacturer of railroad construction materials has formed a joint venture with a railroad development firm to create, structure, and finance regional railroads.
• In the early 1980s, 33 motor carriers and equipment suppliers created a joint venture, the Mega Task Force, to develop new products to increase productivity in the trucking industry. The Mega Task Force developed a

prototype semi-trailer tractor, designed to have an extended life expectancy; but the product was not a commercial success due to its high cost. Currently, the Mega Task Force is concentrating on safety projects and truck maintenance.

• In 1983, Leaseway Transport, a contract carrier, and Duplex, a fire truck manufacturer, established a joint venture to build state-of-the-art city delivery trucks. Two prototypes of the truck were built and proved to be quite efficient. Another 25 trucks were assembled and delivered, but production was discontinued in the face of foreign competition.

• In 1980, Conrail and the Commonwealth of Pennsylvania cooperated in a venture to rehabilitate the Philadelphia Pier 124 South in order to improve coal export operations. Conrail, which owned the pier, deeded it over to the commonwealth, and invested approximately $21 million. In turn, the commonwealth floated approximately $24 million in general obligation bonds to fund necessary improvements and agreed to lease the pier back to Conrail until the bonds are paid off.

• Ocean carriers frequently enter into joint ventures to provide service by combining their operations in designated geographic areas. For example, in February 1988, two carriers proposed to jointly own and operate an ocean common carrier to provide service between Florida ports and ports in Ecuador, Costa Rica, Mexico, and Panama. Other cooperative efforts include the cross-chartering of ships.

• Railroads have entered into several types of interindustry joint ventures, which are discussed below.

There are undoubtedly many other areas, so far unexplored, in which surface-transportation joint ventures could be advantageous. For example, economies of scale and other efficiencies might be realized through joint ventures for the construction, ownership, and maintenance of railroad tracks, motor carrier terminals, and port facilities, or airports.

Federal and State Jurisdiction Over Surface-Transportation Carriers

As noted earlier, the ICC regulates railroads, motor carriers, and inland water carriers, and the Federal Maritime Commission (FMC) regulates interstate water carriers and ocean carriers (operating between the United States and foreign countries). An "interstate water carrier" regulated by the FMC differs from an "inland-water carrier" regulated by the ICC in that the former's service between states is limited to the Great Lakes and seaport-to-seaport service.

Potential joint venturers also need to consider whether their plans will trigger state regulation. If the joint venture will engage in intrastate transportation services, regulatory approvals may be required from a state public utility commission or department of transportation.

Regulatory Approvals

Intramodal or intermodal joint ventures among regulated railroads, motor carriers, or inland-water carriers require prior ICC approval only if they involve a pooling or division of traffic, services, or earnings. A joint venture is considered to involve a pooling or division if (1) the participants are competitors, (2) the participants' resources (*e.g.*, traffic, earnings, equipment capital, or information) are consolidated (pooled) and/or allocated (divided) among the participants on a pro rata or some other agreed-upon basis, and (3) there will be an actual or potential reduction in or restraint on competition.

The FMC's jurisdiction over cooperative efforts among ocean and interstate water carriers extends not only to pooling agreements, but also to most cooperative working arrangements between such carriers. All such agreements must be filed with the FMC, but the precise requirements and standards for approval vary depending on whether the agreement is among ocean carriers or among interstate water carriers.

Gaining ICC Approval of Joint Ventures Involving Pooling
Joint venturers subject to ICC jurisdiction must obtain prior ICC approval, or an exemption from regulation, before implementing a pooling joint venture. As a general matter, joint venturers seeking ICC approval must demonstrate that the written agreement underlying their proposal (1) will be in the interest of better service to the public and (2) will not unreasonably restrain competition.

Motor carriers can obtain pooling approval from the ICC under the standards stated above. In addition, they can obtain automatic approval if they meet certain conditions. Specifically, the ICC must approve any motor carrier pooling agreement that is submitted 50 days in advance of its effective date if (1) it is not of major transportation importance, and (2) will not unduly restrain competition.

Railroads have the option of seeking an "exemption" of a proposed pooling agreement from ICC regulation. This requires a showing that such regulation is not necessary to carry out the national rail transportation policy and that the proposed venture is either of limited scope or that regulation is not needed to protect shippers from the abuse of market power.

The approval and exemption procedures mentioned above also apply to any substantive modification of a pooling arrangement or agreement. In addition, the ICC may exercise continuing oversight by imposing conditions (such as reporting requirements) on its approval of the transaction, and it may also reconsider its approval or revoke an exemption on its own motion or that of third parties.

Firms that are subject to ICC jurisdiction will also need to consider generally applicable ICC regulations that may have significant bearing on the contemplated joint venture. For example, a railroad that plans to issue securities in connection with a joint venture, or to assume an obligation or liability related to securities to be issued by one of its joint venturers, must obtain ICC approval or an exemption.

FMC Approval of Joint Ventures

Under the Shipping Act of 1984, ocean carriers are required to file most types of joint-venture agreements with the FMC. Unless the FMC rejects a proposed agreement for failure to comply with specified conditions, the agreement automatically takes effect 45 days after filing. The FMC retains oversight over automatically approved agreements and may seek injunctive relief if it determines that the agreement is likely, by a reduction in competition, to produce an unreasonable reduction in transportation or an unreasonable increase in transportation cost.

Interstate water carriers must seek and obtain FMC approval before implementing or modifying any cooperative agreement with other such carriers. It is unlawful to implement an unapproved agreement, and modifications and cancellations to a previously approved agreement are lawful only when and as long as approved by the FMC.

Antitrust

As we have said, transportation firms subject to ICC regulation may obtain antitrust immunity for joint ventures involving pooling arrangements.

Such antitrust immunity, if granted, will generally also insulate carriers from state and municipal law to the extent necessary to carry out the ICC-approved transaction and to hold, maintain, and operate property.

Ocean carriers will generally receive antitrust immunity for agreements filed at the FMC and not rejected during the 45-day notice period. But there are important limitations on such immunity. For example, antitrust immunity extends only to agreements with other ocean carriers, and not to any agreement with air, rail, motor, or nonocean water carriers with respect to transportation in the United States. It also does not extend to any agreement by ocean carriers to establish, operate, or maintain a marine terminal in the United States.

The FMC can confer antitrust immunity by approving the cooperative agreements of interstate water carriers. But this immunity is also subject to limitations. For example, the immunity extends only to specified antitrust statutes (the Sherman Act and the Wilson Tariff Act) and may provide no protection from liability under other antitrust statutes.

Foreign Ownership

The ICC does not restrict foreign ownership of railroads, motor carriers, or inland-water carriers within its jurisdiction, and foreign entities are generally not restricted from participating in joint ventures with such transportation firms. However, foreign participation in a joint venture may be problematic with respect to activities that are ancillary to the joint venture's transportation operations. For example, railroads may hold common-carrier radio licenses (issued by the Federal Communications Commission) that are not permitted to be held or controlled by foreign interests.

Foreign participation in joint ventures involving ocean and interstate water carriers may be restricted if, for example, the joint venture will involve federally subsidized, U.S. flag carriers registered in the United States. Depending upon the nature of such carriers' government subsidies and operations (*e.g.*, domestic, coastwise, or foreign), DOT permission may be required before any interest in a vessel is transferred to an alien.

JOINT VENTURING IN THE AIRLINE INDUSTRY

Until 1978, the airline industry was heavily regulated by the federal government, and cooperative agreements between airlines were greatly restricted. As a result, airline joint ventures were virtually non-existent.

In 1978, the Airline Deregulation Act substantially deregulated the industry. The Department of Transportation (DOT) was left with some residual authority over the airlines. While air carriers are not required to obtain DOT approval for most types of intercarrier cooperative or pooling arrangements, many have chosen to do so because of the antitrust immunity that is conveyed by DOT approval. If DOT finds that an agreement is anticompetitive, it may still approve if the agreement is found to serve an important transportation or public need which cannot be realized by any reasonably available, less-anticompetitive means.

Absent Congressional action, joint ventures among domestic air carriers will not be able to obtain antitrust immunity from DOT after December 31, 1988, and will be subject to the general strictures of the antitrust laws. International agreements, however will still be able to be reviewed and immunized by DOT.

The Airline Deregulation Act ushered in an era of competition between the airlines. Indeed, competition was so vigorous that airlines eschewed cooperative arrangements—let alone joint ventures—with their business rivals. Only a few ''pure'' joint ventures have been implemented or seriously explored. These include the following:

• In 1982, Braniff International (then in Chapter 11 bankruptcy proceedings) tentatively agreed with Pacific Southwest Airlines (PSA) to operate an airline as a joint venture. It was planned that Braniff would lease 25 to 30 of its planes to the joint venture, which would then operate this fleet under the PSA name (using Braniff facilities and 1,500 former Braniff employees). The joint venture was never implemented because, among other factors, a federal court ruled that Braniff had improperly transferred airport landing slots without necessary approval from the Federal Aviation Administration.

• In 1986, DHL Airways and United Parcel Service formed a joint venture to transport small packages between the United States and Japan. The DHL/UPS venture ultimately disbanded after DOT, in accordance with an international agreement, selected Federal Express to be the sole U.S. company with landing rights in Japan for the delivery of small packages.

• Northwest Airlines and Trans World Airlines jointly own a computer reservation system. Benefits of the joint venture include economies of scale for the computer service, more resources for expansion and improvement of the system, and an increased sales force. European airlines are also utilizing joint ventures to operate computer-reservations systems.

• A group of more than 60 airlines formed SATO Inc. to provide airline ticketing facilities and travel services to the federal government and military installations. The Department of Justice has issued favorable business review letters to SATO.

• In numerous cases, manufacturers of aircraft or aircraft components have created manufacturing or research and development joint ventures.

There are several areas in which airlines have sought to coordinate their activities, albeit in a form short of a pure joint venture. At least four computer-reservation systems (CRS) are owned by individual carriers (United, Texas Air, Delta, and American Airlines), and CRS services are made available, for a fee, to competing airlines. Several of these competitors have charged that the CRS-owning carriers have manipulated the reservation systems to favor themselves, and these allegations have been investigated by federal regulators.

In addition to these investigations, CRS activities have come under attack in the courts. In perhaps the most important suit to date, several airlines have filed an antitrust action in California against American and United alleging that those carriers are engaging in monopolistic pricing by charging other airlines access fees which are unrelated to the cost of CRS usage.

Another significant example of interairline cooperation involves "code-sharing" agreements between national and regional airlines. Code sharing is a marketing alliance in which two carriers (usually consisting of a regional and national airline) agree to utilize the same "designator code" to identify flights in computer-reservation systems. By using a major airline's designator code, a regional carrier is likely to increase ticket sales as the national airline's passengers are directed to the regional carrier for connecting flights. National airlines also benefit from code sharing with regional carriers as the regional airlines "feed" them passengers from sparsely populated areas. When airlines agree to code share, they will frequently implement other cooperative arrangements, including the sharing of airport facilities and discounts or preferences on supplies.

Code sharing may also be useful between domestic and international air carriers. One such arrangement was recently established between a U.S. and foreign carrier, but is presently under review by DOT for compliance with DOT's code-sharing policies.

Foreign investors should be aware that U.S. law limits the percentage of interest and control that foreign entities may have in U.S. air carriers. These limitations should be carefully explored in the early planning stages of a joint venture.

JOINT VENTURING IN PIPELINES

Pipeline joint ventures are usually formed when several oil or gas producers developing petroleum reserves in one area seek to arrange for transportation to market. It is generally not economic to build more than one pipeline, and a joint venture is sometimes the most convenient mechanism for sharing financing and operating risks. Also, pipeline joint ventures prevent a single owner-operator from gaining control of the only transportation access to an area with petroleum reserves. (Joint ventures have also been considered for the construction of coal slurry pipelines, but the number of such projects has been greatly limited by right-of-way and environmental difficulties.)

Gas Pipelines

Joint-Venture Activity
Joint ventures were used in the initial construction of major gas pipelines in 1920s and 1930s. In recent years, major *onshore* pipeline projects have generally not been constructed or initially operated in joint-venture form. However, one principal exception is the not-yet-built Alaska Natural Gas Transportation System. On the other hand, *offshore* gas pipelines have often been developed as joint ventures.

Joint ventures are also used from time to time by gas pipeline firms to build and operate facilities interconnecting two or more pipeline systems, although such links are usually owned and operated by a single company. In addition, most recent Canadian border-crossing gas projects have been joint ventures of U.S. (and in some cases Canadian) transportation firms.

Regulatory Requirements
As indicated above, gas pipelines are subject to economic regulation by FERC and state authorities. Federal and state licensing and rate-setting requirements generally are not affected by whether a gas pipeline is owned

or operated in the joint-venture form. All interstate natural gas pipelines (regardless of ownership form) are subject to the Natural Gas Act, including its provisions governing certificates of convenience and necessity (Section 7), import/export licenses (Section 3), and rates (Section 5). Federal and state safety and environmental regulations are generally not affected by the joint-venture form. State economic regulation typically does not vary with the form of ownership.

Liquids Pipelines

Joint-Venture Activity
Liquids pipelines (primarily carrying crude oil and petroleum products) are frequently constructed and operated by joint ventures in this country. The owners are typically (but not exclusively) oil producers who share interests in producing areas, and seek a convenient form to finance, construct, and operate an economically scaled marketing facility. An outstanding example of such a project is the Trans Alaskan Pipeline System, which is owned by a joint venture of eight major oil companies holding production interests in the Alaskan Prudhoe Bay oil reserves.

Railroads, ocean shipping, and barge interests which compete directly in the transportation of petroleum liquids have frequently joint ventured in liquids pipelines. However, it should be recognized that such pipelines are nonmovable, and tied to sources of supply and marketing outlets. Risk factors are specialized, and investment recovery tends to be relatively inflexible and long-term. Because of the integrated nature of the industry, liquids pipelines can be a favorable investment opportunity, through joint ventures or otherwise, for individuals or companies otherwise involved in oil production, refining, or marketing activities.

Regulatory Requirements
FERC does not impose any licensing requirements on the construction or operation of liquids pipelines. Such pipelines are subject only to light rate regulation by FERC; have favorable debt financing; and partly as a result have proven highly profitable in past years. Individual states may license construction or regulate right-of-way acquisitions. The joint-venture form generally does not affect the impact of federal and state regulation, including safety and environmental regulation of liquids pipelines.

Joint-venture companies that build or operate liquids pipelines can be organized either as stock companies, or as tenancies in common in which the multiple owners hold undivided interests in the pipeline facilities and a jointly owned or hired contractor is responsible for operational management. In the latter form, each owner is a common carrier subject to regulation as such by state authorities.

Antitrust Issues in the Liquids-Pipeline Industry

During the past 10 years, Congress and antitrust enforcement agencies carefully scrutinized the state of competition in the oil pipeline industry, but little resulted in the way of legislation or litigation. At an early stage, attention focused on Congressional proposals for divestiture of oil company ownership of crude and petroleum-product pipelines. Later on, attention shifted to the question of whether the industry was sufficiently competitive to permit removal of FERC rate regulation.

In a May 1986 report, the Department of Justice recommended that all crude pipelines, and all except five petroleum product pipelines, be deregulated, but Congress has not acted on this recommendation. Since such pipelines are common carriers under federal law, access by shippers or buyers ordinarily does not raise substantial competitive issues. As a result, the investor is likely to encounter antitrust law questions primarily in the merger or acquisition area under the Clayton Act.

Foreign Ownership

There are no significant restrictions on foreign ownership of natural gas pipelines or liquids pipelines in the United States. Indeed, the Trans Alaskan Pipeline project had substantial foreign ownership from its inception.

INTERINDUSTRY JOINT VENTURES

In recent years, transportation firms have recognized that they are well positioned to use their resources to provide goods or services traditionally offered by other industries. In doing so, they have sometimes utilized joint ventures to facilitate their diversification into other lines of business.

Several railroads, for example, have entered into joint ventures with other firms to build and operate cogeneration facilities which produce electric power. These arrangements are attractive because railroads frequently need steam and electricity for internal consumption, a federal statute provides incentives for the development of cogeneration facilities, and the joint-venture form enables the railroad to team with firms that also have substantial energy needs or that have expertise in cogeneration development and operation.

The joint-venture form also appears to have great promise in the area of fiber-optic technology. Railroads or pipelines have found that their rights-of-way may have great value to telecommunications carriers seeking to develop and operate fiber-optic communications networks, and that a joint venture is one means for the railroad or pipeline firm to participate in a potentially lucrative business. These joint-venture opportunities are worthy of some discussion because they offer an excellent paradigm as to how a joint venture may span two regulated industries (here, the transportation and telecommunications industries).

From a telecommunications carrier's perspective, fiber-optic cable offers significant advantages over microwave radio, copper wire, and other traditional transmission media. At the same time, this technology is attractive to transportation firms because installation, operation, and maintenance of a fiber-optic transmission system will interfere only minimally with transportation operations. Plowing equipment can bury fiber-optic cable directly into the ground, obviating the need to dig trenches, or to construct ducts or erect poles. Once installed, fiber-optic cable requires infrequent maintenance.

Use of railroad or pipeline right-of-way corridors for fiber-optic cable offers the transportation firm an opportunity to earn additional revenue from dormant or underutilized assets, with minimal disruption to its own business activity. The construction of a fiber system along transportation right-of-way corridors also provides the transportation firm with an opportunity to obtain access to state-of-the-art telecommunications facilities at minimal or no cost.

As noted above, right-of-way corridors controlled by transportation firms may provide great value to telecommunications companies. Railroad right-of-way corridors, for example, link major metropolitan areas throughout the nation, and often run directly into central business districts and to the premises of major telecommunications customers. Those corridors are particularly attractive to long-distance telecommunications carriers seeking to construct regional or national networks.

Regional and metropolitan area transportation firms (*e.g.*, commuter lines), on the other hand, potentially can provide telecommunication carriers with access to concentrations of large users *within* metropolitan areas. These transportation firms control corridors that are well suited for local telecommunication "bypass networks" that are being developed to compete with local telephone companies. A joint venture among several local transportation firms, each serving a geographically distinct area of a region, might be particularly advantageous in creating a synergistic, area-wide right-of-way network to be offered to telecommunications firms seeking to develop a local bypass network.

Transportation firms have structured their participation in telecommunications ventures in a variety of ways. Some, including Amtrak, have elected merely to lease their rights-of-way to telecommunications carriers in exchange for cash payments and, in some instances, the right to use a specific amount of capacity on the fiber network. Other transportation firms have opted to participate as active joint venturers with telecommunications carriers. One of the best-known enterprises of this nature is LightNet, a joint venture between Southern New England Telephone Company, a local telephone company, and CSX, a railroad holding company.

Once a transportation firm decides to participate in a telecommunications joint venture, two principal types of regulation must be considered: (1) transportation-agency regulation of the firm's diversification into another business, and (2) telecommunications-agency regulation of the services offered to third parties by the joint venture.

These types of joint ventures will present transportation regulators with novel and challenging issues. For example, regulators will have to consider how assets used in the joint venture, and revenues derived therefrom, should be treated for ratemaking purposes. Regulators may also address the corporate form in which the transportation firm participates in the venture—e.g., whether a holding company subsidiary should be used to separate the venture from the core, regulated transportation business.

Novel issues will also arise in connection with the regulation of the telecommunications services offered by the joint venture. A transportation firm that merely owns and operates a fiber-optic communications system for its own internal use can do so virtually free of regulation. To the extent that that capacity is marketed to third parties, however, it may be subject to regulation by both federal and state authorities.

In the current regulatory climate, it is possible to structure an offering of telecommunications services to a limited number of third parties so as to avoid regulation by the Federal Communications Commission (FCC), which is the federal agency that regulates interstate telecommunications. LightNet, for instance, has marketed fiber-optic capacity on its interstate system to unaffiliated common carriers and to private entities on a long-term lease basis virtually free of federal regulation. Should a fiber-optic venture elect to market services to a broader customer. base, it may be subject to light regulation by the FCC as a common carrier.

To the extent that a fiber-optic venture offers intrastate telecommunications services to third parties, those offerings may be subject to regulation by state public utility commissions. The nature and scope of that regulation will vary substantially among the states. State regulators may seek to impose rate regulation on such offerings, and may even preclude a venture from offering certain types of services. It is not unusual for state regulators to regulate telecommunications services more extensively than the FCC.

LABOR ISSUES

No analysis of transportation joint ventures would be complete without some discussion of the labor law issues which are peculiar to the transportation industry. Specifically, any joint venture involving either a railroad or an airline will trigger the many obligations and procedures of the Railway Labor Act (RLA), which is markedly different from the labor statutes governing other industries.

The RLA was passed in 1926, and resulted from a cooperative, legislative effort by the railroads and the unions. Designed to protect employee rights while promoting uninterrupted transportation service, the RLA imposes a multitude of restrictions on both employers and unions.

Under the RLA, disputes between employers and employees are categorized as either "major" or "minor," and the procedures and administrative bodies empowered to enforce these procedures vary depending on the particular category involved. The National Railroad Adjustment Board, or System Boards of Adjustment (for airlines), handle so-called "minor" disputes—those growing out of employee grievances or out of the interpretation or application of labor agreements. The National Mediation Board has jurisdiction over "major" disputes, usually arising in the context of stalemated contract negotiations.

The procedures for resolving "major" disputes can be protracted. The RLA provides a scheme of compulsory mediation, voluntary arbitration, and emergency boards to be selected by the President. In some circumstances, the parties to a labor dispute may resort to "self-help" (*i.e.*, unilateral imposition of the employer's final offer, or a strike).

Transportation firms covered by the RLA are more susceptible to secondary picketing than are non-RLA employers. In a 1987 case, the U.S. Supreme Court ruled that unions cannot be enjoined from picketing rail employers who are not actual parties to a labor dispute, once the actual parties have exhausted RLA procedures. Thus, a completely disinterested carrier faced with picket lines set up by the striking employees of another company may not be able to obtain relief in the courts.

CONCLUSION

The transportation industry is rich with opportunities for efficiency-enhancing joint ventures. The diverse types of joint ventures already implemented most likely account for only a fraction of the projects that firms could jointly undertake for mutual advantage.

At the same time, potential joint venturers must be cognizant of the sometimes unique regulatory and legal issues bearing on the transportation industry generally, and transportation joint ventures in particular. Careful consideration of these issues is likely to minimize the possibility that the otherwise well-conceived joint venture will be derailed by legal obstacles.

CHAPTER 12

JOINT VENTURING IN THE WASTE DISPOSAL INDUSTRY

Merrick C. Walton
Hoover, Bax, and Shearer

INTRODUCTION

Prior to World War II, the business of collection, transportation, treatment, storage, and disposal of waste materials was, for the most part, a highly localized and entrepreneurial industry. Regulation of the industry was likewise mostly local, or at best statewide. The steadily increasing urbanization and continued industrialization of the United States in the postwar era, however, coupled with a growing awareness of the environmental injury caused by the uncontrolled burning or simple burial or lagooning of waste materials, led to the adoption of a variety of state and federal legislation that was intended to protect the environment and which dramatically altered both the technology and the economics of the waste disposal business. Accordingly, although entry into at least the collection and transportation phases of the business remained relatively easy and inexpensive, large vertically integrated companies began to grow and to increase their market power in many areas of the United States, especially in the large urban markets.

The largest companies actively engaged in the industry today are for the most part publicly traded, well financed, and competitively aggressive. Although they collectively control a relatively small percentage of the total solid waste disposal market on a nationwide basis, they have achieved a certain degree of dominance in many major cities where the

195

density of their collection routes or control of substantial disposal site capacity sometimes makes it difficult for new entrants to compete profitably. Likewise, their relatively greater financial resources have enabled a few companies to obtain significant market shares, at least in some regions of the country, in the more capital-intensive hazardous waste business. In many instances, however, joint ventures among smaller entities, especially where one of the venturers owns or operates a disposal site, have nevertheless managed to become effective competitors. The larger companies themselves are also frequent joint venturers, moreover, especially in areas in which they lack disposal capacity of their own or in which political, legal, and social considerations dictate the involvement of a local partner. Yet another factor in favor of joint venture formation may be the need to assemble a variety of expensive equipment and expertise for a single job, such as the cleanup of a hazardous waste disposal site. In these situations, the venture may be formed to couple the financial resources and technological expertise of the larger disposal company with, for example, the existing earth-moving and transportation capabilities of local contractors. Still another occasion for the use of the joint venture arises when it is necessary or desirable to continue existing ownership of a tract of real property used as a disposal site, or to operate under a permit already issued to one of the prospective venturers. Finally, there may be even more pragmatic and mundane reasons for formation of joint ventures in this industry, such as the parties' inability or unwillingness to associate themselves generally for the long term despite their immediate needs to share resources. This industry, like politics and some other endeavors, indeed makes strange bedfellows, and the joint venture is often an appropriate vehicle. Joint venturing in this industry, however, has specific pitfalls as a consequence of the impact of environmental regulation and liability on the venture agreement itself and on the venture's contractual relationships with vendors and customers. While the basic contractual problems, as well as the antitrust, tax, and accounting considerations that affect joint ventures generally apply with equal force to ventures engaged in the waste industry, the latter are subject to some liability risks that often require especially careful negotiation and skillful draftsmanship in structuring the venture's internal and external relationships. This chapter will focus primarily on those matters that are unique to this particular industry, with special attention to some contractual provisions designed to address those unique and, even to many legal or accounting professionals, somewhat obscure issues.

ENVIRONMENTAL REGULATION AND LIABILITY

Federal, state, and local regulation of waste disposal activity has coalesced into a more or less consistent pattern at virtually all levels of government. Unlike some industries in which the basic license to do business is easy to obtain (or even unnecessary beyond something akin to a "store license"), participants in the waste disposal chain are classified into a number of fairly rigid categories from generator of the waste to disposer, and there are specific licensing and permitting requirements for each category. Likewise, liability for the activities in question is either explicitly spelled out in the applicable statute, as in the case of most hazardous waste cleanup legislation, or flows, at least to some extent, more from the nature of the activity and the classification of the actor than from traditional concepts of negligence. In addition, federal and state financial responsibility requirements will apply in ways determined by the characterization of the participants as well. The statutory imposition of financial responsibility requirements and liability depending solely on status can be quite rigid and rather draconian in result. Therefore, those forms of business organizations such as the corporation or partnership, in which the identities of the owners are, at least for some purposes, wholly or partially ignored in favor of recognition of an entity whose characteristics are prescribed by statute, may not provide sufficient flexibility to enable the parties to adjust their relationships with each other in the manner contemplated by the terms of the "deal," or to enable the parties to apportion the risks satisfactorily in accord with their respective resources, economic expectations, or control over the operations of the business. In these situations, the joint venture may be the ideal vehicle for parties who consider each other indispensable for the task at hand but do not wish to share either a particular risk, or control over the activity that generates the risk, over the long term.

Even in those jurisdictions that decline to recognize other meaningful distinctions between partnerships and joint ventures, there still seems to be some semblance of agreement that joint ventures are organized either for single projects or for specific, limited purposes; whereas partnerships are more generalized associations for the purpose of engaging in a particular business. Other jurisdictions, however, at least pay lip service to the proposition that a joint venture is a distinct type of entity with its own unique characteristics. Case law in this author's home state, for example, defines a joint venture as being based on an express or implied agreement containing four essential elements: (1) a community of interest in the venture, (2) an agreement to share profits, (3) an agreement to share losses, and (4) a mutual right of control or management of the enterprise.[1]

The same line of precedent holds that parties agreeing only to share profits in a joint enterprise are not liable for the debts of the venture since the parties have no agreement to share losses, and, therefore, no joint venture or partnership exists.[2] Although it is arguable that a venturer who has the degree of ownership or control that is generally contemplated in such a relationship should be liable to third parties without regard to the terms of the generally undisclosed agreement among the venturers, this line of precedent at least leaves open the possibility that the character- ization of the entity as a joint venture, and the absence of an agreement to share losses, will provide some degree of liability protection. The advantage of the joint venture in the waste disposal business, therefore, is not derived so much from its "special purpose" nature as from the fact that creation of a joint venture may not necessarily result in the creation of precisely the same kind of separate and distinct legal entity as is the case in a true partnership. This fact may in turn engender substantially greater flexibility in allocating risks in general and environ- mental liabilities in particular.

The three principal sources of environmental liability are violations of regulatory statutes and permits, statutorily required hazardous waste site cleanup, and toxic torts. As noted above, virtually all of the envi- ronmental regulatory schemes currently in effect divide participants in the waste generation-to-disposal process into fairly rigid functional cat- egories (generator, transporter, disposer, etc.). Either the regulatory sys- tems themselves or judicial decisions interpreting them impose different degrees or types of liability depending on this same categorization. The various federal environmental statutes include the Clean Water Act,[3] the Clean Air Act,[4] the Solid Waste Disposal Act[5] (SWDA), the Resource Conservation and Recovery Act[6] (RCRA) which is actually a series of

---

[1]*See, e.g., Coastal Plains Development Corp. v. Micrea, Inc.*, 572 S.W.2d 285, 287 (Tex. 1978).
[2]*Id.* at 288.
[3]33 U.S.C. §§ 1251 *et seq.* (1986).
[4]42 U.S.C. §§ 7401 (1983).
[5]42 U.S.C. §§ 6901 *et seq.* (1983 & Supp. 1987).
[6]*Id.*

amendments to the SWDA, the Toxic Substances Control Act,[7] the Safe Drinking Water Act,[8] the Comprehensive Environmental Response, Compensation, and Liability Act of 1980[9] (CERCLA) and the Federal Insecticide, Fungicide, and Rodenticide Act.[10] Other, more general statutes, such as the Hazardous Materials Transportation Act,[11] also have application to this industry. Liability can result from the violation of any of these statutory provisions, and the violator generally is, potentially at least, subject to both criminal and civil sanctions. Liabilities also can follow from the violation of specific operating permit requirements. RCRA establishes a cradle-to-grave tracking system for hazardous waste—from generator to disposer—and imposes different regulatory and permitting requirements at each stage of that process; whereas CERCLA, on the other hand, simply lists the persons who may be held liable for releases of hazardous substances into the environment. Contractual arrangements are not effective to alter this imposition of liability; the statute says as much:

> No indemnification, hold harmless, or similar agreement or conveyance shall be effective to transfer . . . from any person who may be liable . . . to any other person the liability imposed under this section.[12]

The courts have interpreted this provision literally.[13] Although contractual provisions are not effective to avoid the imposition of liability to the

---

[7]15 U.S.C. §§ 2601 *et seq.* (1982 & Supp. 1987).

[8]42 U.S.C. §§ 300f *et seq.* (1982 & Supp. 1987).

[9]42 U.S.C. §§ 9601 *et seq.* (1983 & Supp. 1987) (often also known as the ''Superfund Act'').

[10]7 U.S.C. § 136 *et seq.* (1980 & Supp. 1987).

[11]49 U.S.C. §§ 1801 *et seq.* (1976). This is transportation safety regulation only; there is no economic regulation of most waste materials, at least at the federal level. The Interstate Commerce Commission lacks jurisdiction over interstate transportation of *nonradioactive* hazardous wastes. *ICC v. Browning-Ferris Industries*, 529 F.Supp. 287 (N.D. Ala. 1981); *see also* ICC Declaratory Order, 47 Fed. Reg. 29,402–5 (1982) (overruling an inconsistent ICC staff position); *compare Long Island Nuclear Service Corp.*, 110 M.C.C. 398 (1969) (ICC asserts jurisdiction over transportation for hire of radioactive waste materials). The list of statutes in the text is by no means an exhaustive list, however, even of the federal laws that affect this industry. There are, for example, a number of statutes that are not generally thought of as environmental statutes but which impose similar liability or cleanup obligations. *See, e.g.*, Occupational Safety and Health Act of 1970, 29 U.S.C. §§ 651 *et seq.* (1985); Surface Mining Control Reclamation Act of 1977, 30 U.S.C. §§ 1201 *et seq.* (1986); Uranium Mill Tailings Radiation Control Act of 1978, 42 U.S.C. §§ 7901 *et seq.* (1983).

[12]CERCLA § 107(e)(1), 42 U.S.C. § 9607(e)(1)(1983).

[13]*See, e.g., United States v. Ward*, 618 F.Supp. 884 (D.N.C. 1985).

government or to third parties, however, such provisions are nevertheless enforceable as between the parties themselves.[14] On the other hand, since liability is imposed largely as a consequence of the status or functional involvement of the particular person or entity in the process of generation, transportation, treatment, and disposal of the waste rather than according to more customary concepts of negligence or even traditional forms of strict liability, the most effective way to avoid a particular liability is simply to avoid falling within the particular category to which that liability attaches.

Probably the most expensive and sensational environmental liability a venture can incur is liability for the cost of remedial action for hazardous waste releases at disposal sites the venture has owned, operated, or used. The liability will depend on the nature and extent of the venture's involvement in the waste transportation and disposal chain. Section 107 of CERCLA classifies responsible parties into four broad categories: (a) the generator of the waste; (b) any person who exercised control over the waste and arranged for its disposal; (c) a transporter of the waste that selected the site for its disposal; and (d) the owner of operator of the disposal site itself.[15] There is no escape at either end of this spectrum; the liability of persons or entities in those two categories is imposed based on sheer status, and that status is clearly not susceptible to direct contractual alteration. Likewise, that status results from a conscious engagement in a particular business activity over the long term, and is virtually impossible to change once attained. A generator of waste is liable in perpetuity, apparently, for harm caused by its waste materials. The liability of the owner or operator of the disposal site is not quite so simple: CERCLA, as originally enacted, imposed liability for cleanup costs on both the person or entity that owned or operated the site at the time of disposal, regardless of whether it had subsequently sold the property, and on any subsequent purchaser or operator without regard to participation in or knowledge of the disposal practices that created the problem.[16] The Superfund Amendment and Reauthorization Act, however, has created a defense for subsequent owners who purchased the

---

[14]CERCLA § 107(e)(1), 42 U.S.C. § 9607(e)(1)(1983). *Cf. also Caldwell v. Gurley Refining Company,* 755 F.2d 645, 651–62 (8th Cir. 1985) (allowing indemnity even in absence of express contract, based on misrepresentation concerning prior disposal activities).

[15]42 U.S.C. § 9607(a)(1983).

[16]*Id.*

property without actual or constructive knowledge of the prior disposal of hazardous materials at the site.[17]

Additionally, the courts have held responsible parties to be jointly and severally liable, although CERCLA does not explicitly deal with this issue.[18] Therefore, one party may be held to be liable for the entire cleanup costs if others are judgmentproof. This application can be particularly harsh if the one solvent party is a current owner who had no connection with the generation, transportation, or disposal of the hazardous waste that creates the environmental harm, and yet by virtue of current ownership is required to pay for all cleanup activities.

The two intermediate categories, on the other hand, are more specific to a particular waste stream, do not generally create the same risk of successor liability, and are somewhat more "volitional" on a short-term basis. They are, moreover, also considerably more susceptible to variation by contract. For example, a generator of the waste cannot change its identity as such by the terms of a contract, but a person contracting with the generator to dispose of the waste can avoid the specific liability that is based on the selection of the disposal site simply by specifying in the contractual document that the choice of disposal site is reserved exclusively to the generator (or to some other party). Likewise, co-venturers may allocate these risks and the concomitant liabilities inter sese in their governing document, by specifying which of them is to have control over specific aspects of the business. It is in this area, in particular, that the terms of the joint-venture agreement may provide great flexibility.

THE JOINT-VENTURE AGREEMENT

At this juncture, therefore, it is appropriate to consider, first, some specific language that may be incorporated into the joint venture itself to allocate these various risks and, thereafter, to consider some mirror-image provisions for use in the venture's other contracts. The precise nature of these contractual provisions will be dictated by the circumstances of the venturers and the specific phase of the business in which they wish to

---

[17]42 U.S.C. § 9601 (35) (Supp. 1987).

[18]See, e.g., United States v. Chem-Dyne Corp., 572 F.Supp. 802 (S.D. Ohio 1983); and compare United States v. Wade, 577 F.Supp. 1326 (E.D.Pa. 1983) (joint and several liability appropriate unless defendants establish reasonable basis for apportionment) with United States v. Shell Oil Co., 605 F.Supp. 1064 (D.Colo. 1985) (joint and several liability permitted but not mandated).

engage, as well as by the nature of the role of each venturer in that activity. The owner of patents covering technology to be employed by the venture will have objectives that differ from those of the owner of a disposal site. Although it is impossible to cover every combination and permutation in this brief chapter, there are some basic provisions that provide the starting point for drafting of all such agreements. The initial step in this process is to negate the mutual agency which partnership law might otherwise impose. A typical contractual provision intended for this purpose might read more or less as follows:

> This Agreement does not, and is not intended and shall not be construed to, create any partnership between the parties. The parties further agree that, in entering into this Agreement, they do not intend to organize any entity which would create any form of mutual agency between them or to create, allocate or assume, other than to provide for indemnification to the extent of, as specifically provided for in this Agreement, any joint liability in connection with their respective activities carried on pursuant to this Agreement. Accordingly, neither party shall be deemed to be an agent or legal representative of the other for any purpose other than the purposes of this joint venture set forth expressly in other provisions of this Agreement, nor shall either party have any authority or power to act for, or to undertake any obligation or responsibility on behalf of, any other party except as expressly herein provided. No party by reason of this Agreement shall acquire or be deemed to have any interest in any property, real or personal, owned by any other party or in any other business venture engaged in by any other party, whether or not similar to the purposes of this joint venture, except as is otherwise expressly herein provided. Each party severally agrees to indemnify and hold each other party harmless from any and all liabilities, obligations, claims or losses resulting from (i) any representation that it is the partner or agent of the other, or (ii) any of its actions beyond the express purposes set forth in this Agreement, or (iii) the lawful performance of its respective obligations as set forth in this Agreement. The signature of each party, or of a duly authorized representative of each party, shall be necessary to bind such party to any agreement, contract, indenture or other instrument in writing on behalf of the joint venture. The provisions of this section shall survive the termination of this Agreement.

The agreement should also specify which of the venturers has responsibility for obtaining environmental and other permits, as in the following provision:

[Venturer] shall obtain and maintain, in the name and on behalf of the joint venture [Optional: or any one or more of the venturers (as may be necessary or appropriate) but for the exclusive benefit of the joint venture], all necessary governmental permits, approvals and authorizations for the development and operation of the joint venture, including without limitation [specify those known to be required], and shall indemnify and hold each other party harmless from any liability resulting from the failure to obtain or maintain in force any such permit, approval or authorization.

Finally, it may be appropriate to limit the ability of any one venturer to obligate the other venturers:

Each party shall assist the others and the joint venture in obtaining contracts with third parties for [transportation, disposal, etc.] of waste; provided, however, that no party shall, without the written consent of the others, have the power to enter into any contract on behalf of any other party hereto; provided further, however, that the execution of any contract by a party or by its duly authorized representative shall be deemed to constitute the written consent required hereby.

Although unique circumstances may dictate the need for more specific or more detailed language dealing with issues of concern in a particular situation, the three provisions set out above provide at least a foundation for the concept that certain risks and liabilities are *not* to be shared but are to be rigidly allocated in a predetermined fashion.

The allocation of liability among co-venturers is relatively more difficult to accomplish with respect to liability to third parties and governmental entities, however, than it is between the venturers themselves. That is, although the governmental entity may be able to impose liability for remedial measures on all of the venturers without regard to any attempted allocation of risks among them, the venturers have considerably more flexibility in adjusting their own liabilities to each other. The applicable section of CERCLA provides, in pertinent part, as follows:

Nothing in this subsection shall bar any agreement to insure, hold harmless, or indemnify a party to such agreement for any liability under this section.[19]

---

[19]42 U.S.C. § 9607(e)(1) (1983). The quoted sentence immediately follows the sentence set forth in the text at note 12.

Although judicial authority interpreting this section is sparse, the few cases that have reached the subject have indicated that indemnity obligations can be enforced among the parties themselves but will not be effective, as the statute suggests, to shift liability in a response or expense recovery action by the government.[20] Accordingly, such an indemnity clause should always be included in the joint-venture agreement to reflect whatever arrangement has been concluded among the venturers with respect to this issue. A fairly typical, mutual indemnity provision might read as follows:

> Each party shall each defend and indemnify the venture and each other party from and against any claim asserted by, or any liability to, any person, including without limitation, any agency, branch or representative of federal, state, or local government, on account of any personal injury or death or damage, destruction or loss of property, or substantial contamination of the environment, resulting from or arising out of (i) the indemnifying party's sole negligence, (ii) the indemnifying party's respective share of concurrent or joint negligence of the parties, (iii) the indemnifying party's intentional, unauthorized or unlawful acts or omissions, or (iv) the indemnifying party's breach of any obligation or responsibility imposed on that party by the provisions of this Agreement. For purposes of the preceding sentence, "negligence" shall be deemed to include both acts and omissions, or willful misconduct, and the negligence of a party shall include the respective negligence of its officers, employees, agents (including subcontractors) or representatives. Nothing in this Agreement shall be deemed or construed to limit, in any way, any right of action which may be asserted by any party against publicly or privately created funds established for the purpose of satisfying, in whole or in part, claims asserted by persons referenced herein. In the event that any third party, including without limitation any governmental agency or any person or entity acting pursuant to orders of or contract with any governmental agency, asserts any claim, demand or cause of action arising out of performance of this Agreement, each party agrees to maintain, for the joint and mutual benefit of the parties and the Venture, any rights that such party may have resulting from a cause of action against, or contract with, any person or entity who may share liability.

Depending on the role and resources of each venturer, the naked obligation to indemnify may not be enough. Accordingly, the indemnity provision should be coupled with an appropriate insurance clause:

---

[20]*Id.; see* note 14 *supra.*

Each party represents and agrees that it has, or will cause to be maintained during the term of this Agreement, for the protection of the joint venture and the other parties hereto, insurance that provides coverage for its respective obligations [including the indemnity obligations] and actions hereunder in at least the amounts that such party customarily maintains for its own protection [or the types and amounts of coverage may be specified]. Each such policy shall name the joint venture and each other venturer as an additional insured to the extent of any liability for which the venture or any other venturer is entitled to indemnity pursuant to the terms of this Agreement. The provisions of this section shall survive the termination of this Agreement and shall apply to all judgments, claims or penalties arising from acts or omissions occurring prior to such termination.

Other provisions of the joint-venture agreement that require consideration in this context include those specifying which venturer has responsibility for ongoing compliance with permit conditions, financial responsibility requirements, and environmental statutes and regulations in general. A venture engaged in waste transportation will have insurance needs that differ greatly from those of a disposal site owner; while both of those parties' needs will remain relatively stable, however, the venture that is a cleanup contractor may be required to vary its coverages from job to job. If the venture operates a disposal site, the agreement must also address the often troublesome issue of responsibility for closure of the site and for long-term, postclosure monitoring and maintenance. Such provisions generally should be tailored to the particular facts and circumstances relating to the site and its permits, and will almost always require consultation with legal counsel and technical experts who are familiar with permit conditions, site characteristics, and the specific regulatory requirements that are applicable in the particular situation.

CONTRACTUAL RELATIONSHIPS OF THE VENTURE

The complexities of the environmental laws also impact the venture in many ways that transcend the joint-venture agreement itself. After formation of the venture, strict attention to the environmental laws is likewise required in connection with the operations of the venture and in structuring its contractual relationships with other parties, in order to minimize both long- and short-term risks of environmental liability. Just as the allocation of risks among the venturers based on the categorization of persons liable under the environmental laws is a matter for consideration in the drafting of the joint-venture agreement, the allocation of these same liabilities among the venture and its suppliers and customers, or the shifting of risks among such persons through insurance and indemnity provisions, demands equally careful consideration. For example, just as the venturers may agree that one venturer will assume a particular liability by virtue of assumption of a paticular role in the operations of the venture and that such venturer will indemnify the other venturers against that liability, the joint venture engaged in waste transportation, for example, may agree with its customer (typically a generator of hazardous materials) that the customer will select both the disposal site and the disposal method and will enter into direct contractual arrangements with the disposer, thereby enabling the venture to avoid, for example, being in that category of persons liable under CERCLA as transporters who select disposal sites.[21] A typical site-selection clause, which could be used either by a transporter or a broker with access to more than one site, might read as follows:

> Customer shall select the site for disposal of the waste; [Optional: provided, however, that [the venture] shall have the right to veto such selected site.] In the event that either (i) the present means of disposal or (ii) the present disposal site utilized in disposing of the waste becomes unavailable for the disposal of such waste as a result of events which prohibit such disposal or increase the cost of transportation and disposal so as to render transportation and disposal at current rates prohibitive, [the venture] shall have the option of (a) terminating this Agreement upon ten (10) days written notice to Customer or (b) renegotiating the selection of the disposal site and the transportation and disposal rates in effect at that time. For purposes of this Agreement, the term "unavailable" includes, but is not limited to, situations in which, in the reasonable judgment of [the venture] the disposal facility in question becomes unable to accept or dispose of the waste in question in a lawful or environmentally sound manner. If, after thirty (30) days the parties are unable to reach agreement on new transportation and disposal rates, either party may terminate this Agreement after ten (10) days written notice; provided, however, that in the event this Agreement is terminated for either reason set forth above, Customer shall pay to [the venture] the excess costs incurred in the period between the date of ter-

---

[21]42 U.S.C. § 9607(a)(4) (1983).

mination and (i) notice of termination or (ii) notice of the desire to renegotiate, whichever is greater.

Likewise, to obtain some measure of protection against the often substantial expense of mere involvement in litigation while these issues are
being sorted out, the venture may wish to require that its customer indemnify it against that particular liability as well as others. A typical
contractual provision intended to accomplish this purpose might read as
follows:

> Customer hereby agrees to indemnify and hold [the venture] harmless from
> any and all loss, damages, suits, penalties, costs, liabilities and expenses
> (including, but not limited to, reasonable investigation and legal expenses)
> arising out of any claim for loss of or damage to property, including [the
> venture's] property, and injuries to or death of persons, including [the
> venture's] employees, caused by or resulting from Customer's (i) negli-
> gence or willful misconduct; (ii) Customer's selection of the disposal site;
> (iii) delivery to [the venture] of waste that does not conform to the de-
> scription contained in this Agreement; or (iv) breach of any provision of
> this Agreement or violation of any law or regulation. Where [the venture]
> and Customer are both entitled to indemnity but Customer's obligation to
> indemnify is predicated in whole or in part on Customer's delivery of
> nonconforming waste, [the venture] and Customer agree, by way of ap-
> portionment of their respective responsibilities, that the amount of in-
> demnity payable by Customer shall be equal to that amount of damages
> which would not have arisen but for such breach by Customer. Nothing
> herein shall be interpreted or deemed to limit, in any way, any right or
> action which may be asserted by any party against publicly or privately
> created funds established for the purpose of satisfying, wholly or in part,
> claims asserted by persons referenced herein. In the event that any third
> party, inclusive of any governmental agency, asserts any claim, demand
> or cause of action arising out of the performance of this Agreement, [the
> venture] and Customer agree to maintain, for their joint and mutual benefit,
> any rights that either may have resulting from either (i) an action against
> or (ii) a hold harmless or indemnification agreement with, any transporter,
> disposal site operator or any other party who may share liability.

At this juncture it should be reemphasized that such a provision does not
ever prevent the filing of suit against the indemnitee; it merely provides
a mechanism whereby the indemnitee may recoup its expenses and any
money judgment it is required to pay (assuming the indemnitor is solvent
or adequately insured). If the contractual provision concerning selection

of the disposal site is sufficiently clear and unequivocal, however, and if its effect has not been diluted by the subsequent course of dealing between the parties, the venture should be able ultimately to extricate itself from such litigation without undue difficulty, assuming that this is the sole basis on which the venture's liability is predicated. Mere indemnity is an incomplete solution, however, especially where there may be some doubt about the indemnitor's ability to honor the indemnity obligation. Likewise, an individual venturer may require or demand additional liability protection, or additional security may be needed for the property of the venturers or the business of the venture itself. For this reason, the indemnity provision should be coupled with an insurance requirement stated in more or less the following terms:

> Customer agrees to furnish to [the venture], upon request, certificates attesting to the existence of workers' compensation insurance providing statutory benefits and comprehensive automobile and general liability insurance with policy limits of not less than $1,000,000 each person, $5,000,000 each occurrence for bodily injury and $1,000,000 each occurrence for property damage liability; environmental impairment insurance with policy limits of not less than $3,000,000 per occurrence and $6,000,000 annual aggregate; and sudden and accidental insurance with policy limits of not less than $5,000,000 combined single limit. Each such certificate shall contain a designation of [the venture] and [each venturer] as an additional insured, and a statement of the insurer's obligation to notify [the venture] at least ten (10) days prior to cancellation of any policy described therein.

Note that the "additional insured" language requires that the venturers be individually named as additional insureds along with the venture. This is especially important in those jurisdictions in which the venture is viewed essentially as a partnership, and treated as an entity separate and distinct from the venturers themselves. The limits of liability are somewhat arbitrary, of course, and must be tailored to each situation depending on factors ranging from the nature of the risk to pure considerations of bargaining power.

These indemnity and insurance issues are not unique to the waste-disposal business, of course, but they are especially acute because of the significant potential for injury to human health as well as long-term impairment of the environment. Environmental impairment liability insurance is extremely expensive, if it can be obtained at all. Even when it is possible to obtain the insurance at more or less reasonable premium cost, the policy typically will provide only third-party coverage and will specify a large self-insured retention, or deductible amount. Accordingly, considerable attention should be given both to the venture's own insurance arrangements and the insurance provisions in its contracts with customers and suppliers.

Of course, customers and suppliers, and especially operators of disposal sites, will be seeking to shift as much liability as possible to the entity with which they are contracting. It is not an understatement to say that the entire process of contracting for waste disposal services is fraught with peril for all participants. The effort to avoid liability to third parties, including governmental entities and potential tort plaintiffs, becomes especially complex in the joint-venture context, however, since the venturers' internal risk allocation must be superimposed on the mosaic of risk-shifting mechanisms incorporated in the contractual documents.

For example, a party contracting with the venture itself, or nominally with one of the venturers, may demand a variety of indemnities, insurance, or guarantees from other venturers. Suppose ABC Trucking Corporation forms a joint-marketing venture with X, an individual with numerous contacts and considerable experience in the brokerage of hazardous waste transportation and disposal. The actual disposal is to be subcontracted to a hazardous waste landfill company. Leaving aside for the moment considerations of disposal site selection, which party should enter into the contract with the customer who is presumably the generator of the waste? As an individual, X would prefer to avoid any direct contractual relationship with the customer, and intends not to give any indemnity, provide any insurance, or personally guarantee the performance of ABC. The customer deals only with X, however, and may ask some pointed questions when presented with a contract in the name of ABC. Moreover, if ABC is thinly capitalized or has a questionable reputation for environmental compliance, it can be anticipated that there will be, at a minimum, considerable negotiation over the insurance and indemnity provisions of the contract. Although ABC and X may have adjusted their own relationship through the terms of the joint-venture agreement, that adjustment is of little, if any, consequence to the customer and may in fact conflict with what the customer perceives to be in its own best interest. This conflict can create considerable tension both between the venture and its customer and among the venturers, depending on the manner in which the venturers are compensated and the profits (and losses) of the venture are allocated. For example, if X is compensated with something akin to a commission in the form of a percentage of gross sales, but does not share either in the indemnity obligation or the payment of insurance premiums, it may exert considerable pressure on ABC to accept contractual provisions that are not in ABC's own best interest. In fact, depending on X's authority to act on behalf of the other venturers, he may even be able to commit ABC to those contractual provisions without ABC's knowledge or informed consent.

If the joint-venture agreement contains provisions (such as those suggested above) negating mutual agency and limiting X's authority to bind ABC contractually, however, the problem is at least partially solved. Nevertheless, X may have apparent authority to obligate ABC to third parties who lack notice of the terms of the joint-venture agreement. In these circumstances, even carefully worded insurance and indemnity provisions may still be an incomplete solution, and this source of potential controversy underscores the importance of thorough trust and understanding between venturers and of close attention, in drafting the joint-venture agreement, to every aspect of the relationship.

PERMITS

Another aspect of the waste disposal business that poses special problems for joint ventures is the matter of permits. Every hazardous waste treatment, storage, and disposal facility (TSDF) generally must have at least one federal permit and probably several state and local permits or other approvals as well. The issuance of the so-called "Part B" TSDF permit under RCRA requires the submission of a voluminous and complex application, exhaustive review of that application by the Environmental Protection Agency (EPA) or an equivalent state agency operating under authority pursuant to RCRA, opportunity for public comment, and almost certainly a public hearing of some sort.[22] In addition, depending on the location of the facility and the nature of the operations conducted there, the owner and operator of the facility may be required to obtain air permits, water permits, and a variety of state and local permits, ranging from zoning variances or other land-use permits to state environmental

---

[22]*See generally* 40 C.F.R. Parts 264 and 265 (1987); these are the regulations that govern RCRA permits.

permits that mirror the federal permits. Proximity to a flood plain may require construction of levees and therefore issuance of levee permits, whereas proximity to a navigable body of water or a wetlands may require dredge-and-fill permits. Issuance of most, if not all, of these permits will generally require some form of public hearing, and all will require, at a minimum, publication of notice and the opportunity for public comment. In some instances, preparation of environmental impact statements will be required. Likewise, the application process often involves a lengthy inquiry into the applicant's track record in similar endeavors elsewhere. None of the foregoing is to imply that the application process is necessarily different for a joint venture than for any other applicant.

There are, however, at least two respects in which the fact that the applicant is a joint venture or one of its venturers may raise questions that complicate the process. The first such area is the question of the identity of the applicant. Should the venture be the applicant, or should the permit be obtained in the name of one of the venturers? The answer to this question may depend on factors ranging from ownership of specific property to be used by the venture to the particular experience, expertise, or resources of the prospective applicant. Those who oppose the siting of a disposal facility at the particular location, and therefore oppose the issuance of permits for the site, may assert variously that the application for the permit in the name of one of the venturers is intended to shield the others from liability (perhaps quite correct), to avoid inquiry into the environmental track record of one of the other venturers (also sometimes correct), or to avoid certain longer-term liabilities such as closure costs, expenses of postclosure monitoring and site maintenance, or toxic tort and cleanup claims occasioned by a serious environmental accident or long-term impairment resulting from gradual and undetected leakage from the site. In fact, waste-disposal enterprises are seldom structured as joint ventures for these latter reasons, and when they are the attempt usually fails because of federal and state financial responsibility requirements that must be met before the permit will be issued. Nevertheless, these sorts of motivations may be imputed whenever the joint-venture form of entity is employed, and this factor may add acrimony and complexity to the permitting process.

The second such problem relates not to the original application but to difficulties that may be encountered when there is an attempt to transfer the permit to a new person or entity. Most jurisdictions require at least some form of public notice and scrutiny of an application for transfer of a permit, if not a public hearing and reapplication process similar to that involved in the issuance of the original permit. Although the *complete* change of control of a corporation holding a permit may trigger this same process, the buyout of one of several stockholders, or the withdrawal of one of several partners, generally will not affect the permit (unless, of course, the withdrawing party is essential to the entity's ability to meet its financial responsibility requirements or is otherwise essential to or has guaranteed the performance of the entity). If the permit is issued in the name of a withdrawing venturer, however, the withdrawal of that venturer will almost certainly trigger the aforesaid requirements, and will reopen any preexisting controversies concerning the financial and environmental responsibility of the venture, as well as give opponents the opportunity to raise any new concerns that have come to light since issuance of the original permit. Any of these eventualities will involve at least some degree of scrutiny of the joint-venture agreement. The lesson here is to be prepared to discuss the arrangements among the venturers and to have rational explanations for the nature of those arrangements. It will not be possible to avoid having the joint-venture agreement become public, even absent any of the above controversies, since one or more of the permit applications will involve disclosure of all contractual arrangements affecting the operation of the site.

THE OPPORTUNITY

Notwithstanding these numerous pitfalls, there is ample reason to consider formation of new ventures for involvement in the waste transportation and disposal industry. Although the regulatory and contractual issues are complex, the magnitude of the opportunities appears ample to justify the risks. Although even the various federal agencies with responsibility for environmental matters do not always agree on the scope of the problem, even the most casual observer would agree that problems of waste disposal and hazardous waste clean-ups continue to loom large. In 1980, the EPA estimated that at least 57 million metric tons of hazardous waste were generated annually in the United States.[23] At the same time, EPA estimated that 90 percent of the hazardous wastes produced in the United

---

[23]U.S. Environmental Protection Agency, *Everybody's Problem: Hazardous Waste* 1 (1980).

States were being disposed of by "environmentally unsound methods," and that there were approximately 2000 "abandoned or uncontrolled dump sites" requiring some form of remedial action.[24] The disposal costs for hazardous materials in 1980 ranged from $2 to $2,000 per ton, depending on the type of material and the method of disposal.[25] In 1984, the EPA was estimating that there were still some 1800 sites that required remedial action, at a total cost of some $23 billion.[26] A still more recent estimate by a congressional agency indicated that there might be as many as 10,000 such sites, however, and that an amount in the area of $100 billion would be required for that remedial action.[27] These estimates may still be low, and some informal estimates of actual hazardous waste generation in the United States at the present time tend to indicate that the actual volume of hazardous waste generated annually in the United States is as much as four to five times the 1980 EPA estimate.

The foregoing statistics deal only with the matter of hazardous waste generation and site cleanups. The somewhat related but less risky solid waste disposal market is also large and equally lucrative, and there are significant market niches in both aspects of the waste disposal industry that can be filled by entities other than the large waste disposal companies. In fact, although the financial responsibility and capital investment requirements for new disposal facilities for either hazardous or solid waste may exclude many ventures from this aspect of the business, there are substantial other opportunities for new entrants and many of those opportunities are in relatively low-risk aspects of the business. Specific phases of the waste disposal industry that can be readily exploited with relatively low initial capital investment range from solid waste collection and transportation to at least some types of hazardous waste site assessment and even cleanup. The latter, in particular, often provide opportunities for engineering professionals to collaborate with earth-moving and transportation contractors to form a venture that contracts with governmental agencies or groups of responsible parties to handle the cleanup of a particular site. In addition, even the largest waste disposal companies often lack the specific manpower, equipment or expertise for particular

---

[24]*Id.* at 10, 15.

[25]*Id.* at 15.

[26]U.S. Environmental Protection Agency Office of Solid Waste and Emergency Response, *Extent of the Hazardous Release Problem and Future Funding Needs* (1984).

[27]U.S. Congress Office of Technology Assessment, *Superfund Strategy* (1985).

projects, and many of those companies frequently engage subcontractors for that purpose or to provide specific expertise in the design and construction of new disposal facilities. There is no reason, however, why a joint venture could not be substituted for the subcontract arrangement in many instances.

Accordingly, despite the considerable risks inherent in this industry, through appropriate planning and careful negotiation of appropriate venture relationships new entrants into the waste disposal business can exploit opportunities with an acceptable degree of risk while existing participants in the industry can maximize their utilization of existing expertise, facilities, and equipment by joining forces with others whose resources complement their own. This appears to be an industry that is still growing rather than declining or remaining static, and which seems to be relatively recessionproof in many respects. Although recycling, technological advances, and even shifts from manufacturing to service economies may in time reduce the amount of waste requiring disposal, it cannot be doubted that significant volumes of both solid and hazardous wastes will continue to be produced each year. In addition, if the governmental estimates are correct, considerable additional funds remain to be spent on remedial action at problem sites. With close attention to the regulatory issues and careful planning and draftsmanship to minimize liability risks, joint venturing in this industry should continue to have considerable profit potential.

PART 2

INTERNATIONAL JOINT VENTURES

John D. Carter
Bechtel Corporation

While my co-editor, Scott Hartz, highlights the major attributes of the joint venture organization in his introduction to Part I, I will highlight some uniquely appealing features of the joint venture on the international business front.

Perhaps most important in international work is the flexibility of the joint venture. Key technical or financial strengths can be combined for one project and can include partners that have no interest in long-term affiliations. Local contributions of smaller firms can be utilized, and pricing advantages can be realized through the use of less expensive local resources.

On the other hand, longer-term relationships can be beneficial, particularly where specific market opportunities exist. Teaming with local contractors may be required to satisfy special tax incentives, export credit requirements, and technology transfer policies. There may also be special tax benefit considerations that can only be captured by a local company.

The frequent "project" orientation of the joint venture requires special attention to detail in setting up the venture. Often, there is no long-term commitment or incentive to work out practical problems if they are not addressed in the documented organizational framework.

The identification of key issues is a challenge on the international front because of different legal systems and a variety of legal questions. Expert advice and a clear understanding of roles, responsible parties, financial and performance issues requires the assistance of experts skilled in several disciplines, as well as the strategic advice of experienced practitioners.

We believe this section on international joint venturing provides the right framework of skill and experience to identify the issues and suggest workable solutions to common problems.

CHAPTER 13

TAX ASPECTS OF FOREIGN JOINT VENTURES[1]

David F. Kleeman
Price Waterhouse

INTRODUCTION

International joint ventures encompass those ventures carried on within the United States as well as those carried on abroad, but this chapter will focus only upon joint ventures conducted abroad and the U.S. income tax issues which relate to them. Although an understanding of the taxation of a foreign joint venture by the foreign country in which it is located is important, this chapter will not specifically address foreign tax issues. Other U.S. taxes such as excise taxes, customs duties, and property taxes will not be discussed either, although they must be properly addressed by a U.S. venturer in the planning and decision-making process.

The net earnings available to a U.S. venturer in a foreign joint venture can be substantially affected by the taxation of the foreign venture's operations. The venturer will need to be aware that the earnings of the foreign joint venture may be subject to tax by both the United States and the foreign country or countries in which the venture is located. Consequently, earnings from the joint venture are potentially subject to double taxation. Tax treaties and a credit for foreign income taxes are generally

---

[1]This discussion reflects the U.S. Internal Revenue Code of 1986 as amended through December 31, 1987.

available to avoid double taxation of the venture's foreign earnings. The venture may also be subject to other taxes (*e.g.*, net worth or capital taxes) imposed by several taxing jurisdictions for which treaty relief or a foreign tax credit is not available.

The venturer should also be aware of the various alternatives available to terminate a joint venture and the tax consequences of each of them. The U.S. tax ramifications will depend on the alternative chosen and could have an important impact on the ultimate return realized on the venturer's investment in the joint venture.

ESTABLISHING A FOREIGN JOINT VENTURE

General Considerations

Of substantial importance to any U.S. entity contemplating a foreign joint venture is whether the United States has ratified a tax treaty with the nation in which the venture is to be based. The United States has ratified tax treaties with more than 30 nations, including nearly all of the developed countries.[2] A primary benefit of tax treaties is that they mitigate the problem of international double taxation arising when a venture is subject to tax in more than one country.

The selection of the type of legal entity used to conduct the foreign joint venture is an early decision which must be made by the venturers. In choosing the type of entity, venturers should take into consideration the U.S. tax consequences as well as the foreign tax ramifications. In addition, the venturers will need to determine if a particular legal entity under foreign law will be taxed as a partnership or as a corporation for U.S. tax purposes. For example, an entity which is a corporation under the laws of a foreign country may be considered a partnership for U.S. tax purposes.

The venturers must also determine how the foreign joint venture will be financed. Financing is generally provided by either debt, equity, or some combination of debt and equity. Since the selection of either debt

---

[2]The United States presently has income tax treaties with Australia, Austria, Barbados, Belgium, Canada, China, Cyprus, Denmark, Egypt, Finland, France, Germany, Greece, Hungary, Iceland, Republic of Ireland, Italy, Jamaica, Japan, Republic of Korea, Luxembourg, Malta, Morocco, Netherlands, New Zealand, Norway, Pakistan, Philippines, Poland, Romania, Sweden, Switzerland, Trinidad and Tobago, U.S.S.R., and United Kingdom.

or equity will have differing U.S. tax consequences, this question must be fully explored prior to funding the venture.

Type of Entity

Partnership

A foreign joint venture can be conducted as a partnership organized under the laws of the United States or of a foreign country. A partnership is not a taxable entity for U.S. tax purposes, and this is true in many foreign countries as well. There are, however, circumstances in which the United States will tax the partnership as if it were a separate taxable entity (*i.e.*, corporation) resulting in U.S. tax consequences not originally anticipated by the venturers. Thus, the legal characteristics of the entity under foreign law must be closely reviewed and compared to the U.S. tax rules regarding partnership status.

U.S. Partnership. Income and deductions of a U.S. partnership are determined for U.S. tax purposes at the partnership level and flow through to the partners retaining the same character. Thus, U.S. venturers using a U.S. partnership to conduct a foreign joint venture will be subject to current U.S. tax on their portion of the earnings of the joint venture. The partnership agreement frequently sets forth the allocation of partnership items between the partners including ordinary income, deductions, capital gains and losses, tax credits, and partnership indebtedness. Special allocations may be used to maximize the economic rewards to each venturer and to properly take into account each venturer's economic contribution and assumption of risk in the venture. Partnership allocations (particularly special allocations) must have "substantial economic effect" in order to be accepted by the U.S. tax authorities. Substantial economic effect simply means that for each item of income or deduction which is allocated, the venturer to whom the allocation is made must have received the related economic benefit or burden related to such item.

Foreign Partnership. A U.S. venturer needs to be aware that the U.S. taxation of foreign partnerships is based on U.S. tax rules. The foreign taxation of the partnership is based on the tax laws of the country in which the partnership conducts its business. Thus, a foreign partnership may be treated as an incorporated entity (*i.e.*, foreign corporation) or as an unincorporated entity (*i.e.*, partnership) for U.S. tax purposes irrespective of its characterization in the foreign country. In order for a foreign partnership to be treated as a corporation for U.S. tax purposes, it must have more corporate than noncorporate characteristics. There are six major indicia of a corporation for U.S. tax purposes which distinguish a corporation from a partnership. These characteristics are:

1. Presence of associates.
2. Business objective and division of gains therefrom.
3. Continuity of life.
4. Centralized management.
5. Liability limited to corporate property.
6. Free transferability of interests.

Of these six characteristics, the four characteristics that generally distinguish a partnership from a corporation are unlimited liability, limited life, restrictions on the transfer of partnership interests, and decentralized management. If three of these four characteristics apply to the foreign partnership, the partnership will be treated as a corporation for U.S. tax purposes.

Branch of U.S. Corporation

The U.S. venturers may want to consider organizing a U.S. corporation and conducting the foreign joint venture through a branch or division of this entity. An important aspect of this decision from a U.S. tax perspective is the fact that the income earned by the foreign joint venture will be subject to U.S. tax when the income is earned. In fact, the earnings of a foreign joint venture conducted through a foreign branch of a U.S. entity will normally be taxed currently by both the U.S. and the foreign country.

Controlled Foreign Corporation (CFC)

The U.S. taxation of joint venture earnings conducted by a controlled foreign corporation (CFC) will differ significantly from the taxation of a foreign corporation which is not controlled by a U.S. shareholder. The primary difference to the U.S. venturer relates to the potential application of the Subpart F rules in the controlled foreign corporation situation. Depending on the nature of the income generated by the CFC, the U.S. venturer may lose, under the Subpart F provisions, the ability to defer U.S. taxation on the foreign joint venturer's earnings. Absent the Subpart F rules, the earnings would not be subject to U.S. tax until actually remitted to the venturer.

A foreign corporation qualifies for U.S. tax purposes as a CFC if *more* than 50 percent of either the voting power or value of its stock is owned by U.S. shareholders. The term U.S. shareholder means a U.S. person who owns 10 percent or more of the total combined voting power of all classes of stock of the foreign corporation. The definition of a U.S. person includes a U.S. corporation, U.S. partnership, U.S. citizen or resident alien, and any U.S. estate or trust. A U.S. person does not include residents of Puerto Rico, the Virgin Islands, or other U.S. possessions. The rules relating to the recognition of income by a U.S. venturer under the Subpart F or foreign personal holding company provisions are discussed more fully later in this chapter.

Noncontrolled Foreign Corporation

A foreign joint venture may be conducted through a noncontrolled foreign corporation provided the requirements for CFC status are not present. The distinction between CFC and non-CFC tax status is important since the Subpart F rules and various U.S. reporting requirements will not apply in a non-CFC situation. If the foreign corporation is not a CFC, the U.S. venturers will generally recognize taxable income from the venture as a dividend only when the earnings of the non-CFC are actually distributed. The recently enacted passive foreign investment company rules, discussed more fully below, must be considered in the case of a non-CFC receiving passive income.

Financing the Joint Venture

In addition to deciding what type of entity best accommodates the business and tax objectives of the venturers, the question of funding the venture also has significant tax implications. Funding may be accomplished by issuing capital stock, making loans, contributing tangible or intangible property (including cash), or some combination of these alternatives. The U.S. tax implications associated with each alternative are summarized below:

Equity

The venturers may choose to incorporate the joint venture and issue capital stock as the primary means for funding the foreign venture. The issuance of multiple classes of common stock (Class A and Class B) may be considered in order to satisfy conflicting interests of the various U.S. and foreign venturers. In addition, the use of preferred stock having preferential dividend rights, a fixed redemption price, and preferential rights upon liquidation, may facilitate the desired allocation of the economic benefits of the joint venture to the venturers. In essence, preferred stock can often achieve some of the same objectives as the use of a special income allocation in the partnership agreement.

From a tax perspective, the use of equity capital to fund a venture has two major tax consequences. First, there will usually be no foreign tax deduction for dividends paid by the joint venture. Second, the payments to the U.S. venturer with respect to his equity interest in the venture will be taxable as a dividend to the extent the joint venture has current or accumulated earnings and profits. Payments in excess of this amount will be considered a nontaxable return of capital to the U.S. venturer. After the earnings and profits and capital have been fully repaid, any additional payments with respect to the venturer's stock interest will be considered capital gain for U.S. tax purposes.

The U.S. tax rules relating to equity investments in a foreign joint venture may not correspond to the foreign country's tax rules. For example, what may be considered stock under U.S. tax rules may be considered debt in the foreign country. Thus, payments on such an investment would be dividends for U.S. tax purposes and deductible interest for purposes of the foreign tax laws. The U.S. venturers must, therefore, determine any difference in treatment prior to deciding upon the funding for the venture. This difference in treatment between different countries is a tax planning opportunity that can be used to minimize overall taxes.

Debt

Where a joint venture must look to outside sources for financing, the decision to incur indebtedness will often be governed by considerations other than taxes. Where cash or other property is contributed by venturers who are to be stockholders of the joint-venture corporation, the parties may be relatively free to choose between stock and indebtedness. In such circumstances, tax considerations will often be a primary reason for using debt. The tax advantage of debt is that the payor is entitled to a deduction for interest, whereas dividends are not tax deductible. Accordingly, debt financing of a foreign corporate joint venture allows the repatriation of venture profits to the venturers through tax-deductible interest payments.

In addition, profits may be paid to the venturers in the form of principal repayments which are not subject to U.S. tax.

Thin Capitalization

The rules regarding "thin capitalization" relate to the situation where a corporation has been capitalized with a substantial amount of debt and a small amount of equity. One tax advantage of a thinly capitalized joint venture is that by maximizing debt, the resulting interest expense reduces the taxable income of the joint venture for tax purposes.

In an effort to deny the tax deduction for a portion of the interest expense in a thinly capitalized joint venture company, the Internal Revenue Service may contend that shareholder indebtedness should be treated as stock for U.S. tax purposes. As a result, the IRS would contend that some portion of the payment should be regarded as a nondeductible dividend. The debt-equity issue may also arise in the case of principal payments to the debtholder. In this situation, the question arises as to whether debt repayment to a venturer is a bona fide repayment of principal or should again be categorized as a dividend. A final question is the debtholder's right to a bad debt deduction when, for one reason or another, the debt principal is not repaid. If the company has little capital, the debt may be considered equity and a worthless stock deduction may be the venturer's only recourse.

The resolution of the question of whether debt should be treated as equity usually depends on the particular facts and circumstances. In weighing the various factors, the intention of the parties and the treatment of the loan and interest payments on the joint venture books will be important in determining whether indebtedness is treated as debt or equity. Other factors to be considered include the following:

1. Is there a formal written note?
2. Is the debt unconditionally payable either upon demand or at a fixed maturity date?
3. Are the debtor and creditor related or otherwise under common control?
4. Can the debt be converted to equity?
5. Does it bear interest, and if so, is the interest rate fixed rather than fluctuating based on corporate earnings?

6. Is the debt-equity ratio of the corporation in accordance with industry standards?

Transfers of Property

If property (tangible or intangible) is transferred to a foreign joint venture, the tax-free incorporation rules available to a U.S. transferor are limited if there is a foreign transferee. The obvious concern of the IRS is to be certain that the transfer of property out of the United States does not have as one of its principal purposes the avoidance of U.S. taxes. For example, the transfer of appreciated property held by a U.S. venturer in order to form a foreign venture would result in a deferral of U.S. tax on the appreciation of the property until the transferor's interest in the venture was sold or the venture was liquidated. Therefore, the U.S. tax rules restrict the ability of a U.S. venturer to transfer appreciated property to a foreign venture (corporation or partnership) without being subject to U.S. tax on the appreciation at the time of the transfer.

The specific U.S. tax rules governing transfers of property by a U.S. venturer to a foreign joint venture depend upon the type of entity being used to conduct the foreign venture. If a foreign corporation is used, transfers of property are subject to gain recognition under Section 367, and if Section 367 does not apply, to Section 1491 excise taxes. In addition, transfers to a partnership may be subject to Section 1491 excise taxes. The tax consequences of transferring property as a capital contribution to a foreign venture are set forth in detail below.

Cash. The transfer of cash by a U.S. venturer to a foreign joint venture does not result in U.S. tax consequences. The transfer of foreign currency, however, is considered to be a transfer of property and is subject to gain recognition at the time of the transfer.

Tangible Property. The transfer of appreciated tangible property from the United States to a foreign corporation will generally result in current U.S. taxation. The recognition of gain does not apply to property used by the foreign corporation in the conduct of an active trade or business. If recognition of gain is required, the amount will *not* exceed the gain which the U.S. venturer would have recognized had the property actually been sold. If both depreciated and appreciated property are transferred, the losses cannot be offset against the gains in computing the taxable gain resulting from the transfer.

Although the active trade or business exception applies to most business assets, inventory and certain other assets (*e.g.*, passive investment assets) are excluded from the active trade or business definition. Consequently, the transfer of inventory to a foreign corporation will require current gain recognition. To the extent gain is recognized on the transfer, the tax basis of the transferred property to the transferee and the tax basis of the transferor in the joint venture will be increased by such gain.

The active trade or business exception may not fully protect against tax if the transferor to the foreign corporation is a foreign branch of a U.S. corporation. In this case, a special loss recapture rule may require the recovery of any branch losses previously deducted for U.S. tax purposes. A U.S. joint venturer will need to consider this result if the joint venture is eventually to be conducted through a foreign corporation.

Intangible Property. The transfer of intangible property by a U.S. venturer to capitalize a foreign joint venture does not generally result in full current gain recognition. Rather, the U.S. venturer is deemed to have sold the intangible property in exchange for periodic payments (royalties) which must be commensurate with the income actually earned by the transferee on the intangible property. Thus, the U.S. venturer cannot rely on industry norms or unrelated party transactions to justify the amount of the royalty. The foreign joint venture is entitled to reduce earnings and profits for U.S. tax purposes by the amount of this royalty charge.

The recognition of periodic royalty income by the U.S. venturer on the transfer of intangibles is required whether or not such payments are contemplated under the transfer agreement. If royalties are not provided for under the transfer agreement, any royalty income imputed by the IRS will be U.S. source income. If royalty payments are required under the terms of the transfer, such amounts are sourced in accordance with the general sourcing rules. Although a determination of the royalty under the commensurate income standard may be difficult, particularly since the IRS has the benefit of hindsight in making its determination, the taxpayer should receive a foreign tax credit benefit by requiring royalty payments on transfers of intangibles.

Excise Taxes (Section 1491). The United States imposes an excise tax on certain transfers of property by a U.S. venturer to a foreign corporation or partnership as a contribution to capital. In the case of transfers to a foreign corporation, the excise tax applies only in the unlikely event that the rules of Section 367 do not govern the transaction. A U.S. venturer contributing property to a foreign joint venture which is conducted as a foreign partnership may also be subject to the Section 1491 excise tax unless an election is made to apply principles similar to those found in Section 367 to the transfer.

Since most transfers to a foreign corporation are governed by Section 367, the excise tax under Section 1491 is seldom applicable when the recipient of the property is a foreign corporation. In the case of a foreign partnership, it is important to avoid the excise tax since it is imposed at the rate of 35 percent on the excess of the fair market value of the contributed property over the property's adjusted basis. Thus, the tax is currently higher than the maximum U.S. corporate tax rate and is not deductible in computing the regular corporate tax.

Reporting Requirements

A U.S. venturer acquiring an interest in a foreign joint venture or transferring U.S. property to such a venture has special disclosures concerning the transfer which must be included in the U.S. tax return of the venturer for the year of the transfer. These disclosures do not apply if the joint venture is conducted through a U.S. partnership or a foreign branch of a U.S. corporation.

Acquisition of Interest in Foreign Corporation

A U.S. venturer whose interest in a CFC increases or decreases by 5 percent or more must, in the year of such change, complete and file Schedule O of Form 5471, Information Return with Respect to a Foreign Corporation. This is in addition to the other information normally required to be filed on Form 5471. The reporting is for information purposes and is intended to assist the IRS in maintaining current records concerning the ownership of foreign corporations by U.S. persons and identify ownership changes which may result in reportable U.S. gains.

Transfer of U.S. Property to a Foreign Corporation/ Foreign Partnership

A U.S. venturer transferring property to a foreign corporation as a contribution to capital is required to disclose the transfer on his U.S. tax return. The venturer must also disclose the gain, if any, which is required to be recognized pursuant to Section 367. It should be emphasized that the Section 367 disclosure requirements can be relatively substantial and, if they are not complied with, can result in adverse U.S. tax consequences.

OPERATION OF THE JOINT VENTURE

Reallocation of Income and Deductions

A foreign joint venture is frequently controlled by a small group of venturers. In order to fund and operate the venture, these venturers may enter into various transactions with the venture including loans, sale of inventory, and providing technical and management services. The IRS will often review transactions between the U.S. venturers and a foreign joint venture to determine if income is being shifted out of the United States to reduce or avoid U.S. tax. The IRS has the authority under Section 482 to allocate items of income or deduction between the venturers and the joint venture if the allocation results in a truer reflection of the venturer's taxable income. The venturers have the burden of proving that such a reallocation of taxable income does not result in a true reflection of taxable income. Furthermore, the IRS may reallocate income under Section 482 whether or not there has been any intent by the venturers to avoid U.S. taxes.

The Section 482 regulations provide guidelines which can be relied upon to avoid a Section 482 allocation by the IRS. In particular, the regulations discuss in some detail the five types of intercompany transactions set forth below.

Loans and Advances
If funds are loaned from a U.S. venturer to the foreign joint venture (or vice versa) at an interest rate which is less than arm's length, the IRS may impute interest income to the lender. Assuming the lender is not in the financing business, an interest rate which is at least equal to (but not more than 130 percent of) the applicable federal rate (AFR) will be treated as an arm's-length rate. If the interest charge is below this range, the IRS can impute additional interest sufficient to equal the AFR.

The safe-haven interest rules do not apply in cases where the U.S. venturer borrows funds at the situs of the joint venture for the purpose of lending these funds to the joint venture. The term *situs* is defined as the maximum foreign geographic unit throughout which a uniform interest rate prevails. In such a case, the joint venture must be charged the same rate of interest which the lending venturer is paying for the funds, plus the cost of borrowing. Similarly, a loan denominated in a currency other than the U.S. dollar does not qualify for the safe-haven interest rate. A loan of this type must bear interest at a fair market rate based on the foreign currency in which the loan is denominated.

Indebtedness covered by the Section 482 regulations includes any loan or advance of money, including indebtedness arising out of commercial transactions between the U.S. venturers and the foreign joint venture. In the case of accounts receivable arising from sales or services between related foreign entities, interest need not accrue until the first day of the fourth month following the month in which the receivable arises. The taxpayer is entitled to demonstrate that a longer repayment period is appropriate by reference to industry standards or its trade practices with unrelated parties.

In order to avoid adjustments upon audit, interest on intercompany loans and other indebtedness should ordinarily be charged at a safe-haven interest rate. Furthermore, if interest is actually provided rather than being imputed by the IRS, the foreign joint venture will generally obtain a current income tax deduction for such interest in the foreign country.

Performance of Services

If the U.S. venturer performs marketing, managerial, administrative, or technical services for the joint venture at less than an arm's-length charge, the IRS may impute income to the venturer. The following general guidelines apply for this purpose:

- An allocation is required if there is a direct benefit, but not if the benefit is so indirect or remote that an unrelated party would not have made a charge.
- An allocation is required if the benefit is for the joint venture's day-to-day activities or its overall operations, as contrasted with general supervisory services performed by the venturers.
- No allocation is required if the services merely duplicate services for which the joint venture is adequately staffed and is performing itself.
- No allocation is required for a service for which the joint venture would not have paid a fee to an unrelated party.

The regulations provide that except in the case of services which are an integral part of the business of the renderer or the recipient, the arm's-length charge is the *cost* of rendering the services unless the taxpayer can establish a more appropriate charge. If the services are an integral part of the business of either party, the charge is determined with reference to the amount that would be charged in a similar transaction involving unrelated parties. This will usually result in a profit for the renderer.

The cost of providing a service generally includes not only all direct expenses identified with the service (*e.g.*, salaries and traveling expenses) but also any indirect costs. Incremental or marginal costing is not permitted. Indirect costs include building occupancy costs, an appropriate share of overhead from supporting departments, and general and administrative expenses.

Use of Tangible Property
If a U.S. venturer transfers possession or use of tangible property to a joint venture at less than an arm's-length charge, an allocation may be made under Section 482 to reflect an arm's-length rental arrangement. If either party is in the business of leasing that property, an arm's-length rental is required. If neither party is in the leasing business, rental charges based on a formula are acceptable. The formula rental is equal to the sum of (1) depreciation computed on a straight-line basis, (2) 3 percent of the original basis of the asset, plus (3) current operating expenses. The taxpayer retains the right to establish an arm's-length rental based on marketplace criteria.

Use or Transfer of Intangible Property
The Tax Reform Act of 1986 substantially changed the royalty payments which are required between the U.S. venturers and a joint venture with respect to the transfer (or license) of intangibles. As mentioned earlier in this chapter, in the case of any transfer (or license) of intangible property, the income received by the transferor with respect to such transfer must be commensurate with the income realized by the joint venture which is attributable to the intangible. This amount will frequently be greater than an arm's-length royalty. The provision applies to tax years beginning after December 31, 1986 but only to transfers of intangibles made *after November 16, 1985.*

Intercompany Sales of Personal Property
If inventory is sold by the U.S. venturer to the foreign joint venture at less than an arm's-length price, the IRS may adjust the purchase price. The Section 482 regulations describe three methods of pricing inventory

and the circumstances under which each may be used. The three specified methods are:

- Comparable uncontrolled price method.
- Resale price method.
- Cost-plus method.

The above methods are not true alternatives since the regulations require that the first method be used if there are comparable uncontrolled sales. If the first method cannot be used, the resale price method must be used. If certain requirements regarding the resale price method are not met, the taxpayer may then use the cost-plus method.

Comparable Uncontrolled Price Method. The comparable uncontrolled price is the price resulting when the buyer and seller are unrelated. For this purpose, a sale to an unrelated customer is an uncontrolled sale, as is a purchase from an unrelated supplier. Sales are comparable if the physical property and the circumstances involved in the sale are identical, or so nearly identical, that differences can be readily ascertained and the differences quantified (*e.g.,* for place of delivery). The regulations list some of the circumstances which may affect the price. These include quality of product, terms of sale, intangible property associated with the sale, time of sale, level of the market, and geographical market in which the sale takes place. Whether these and other factors render the price noncomparable depends upon the facts and circumstances of each case.

The Section 482 regulations provide that related parties may, for a time, sell at less than a normal profit if it can be shown either that the buyer passes the price reduction along to his customers who are unrelated parties, or that the buyer engages in substantially more sales promotion activities with regard to the new product than with regard to other products.

Resale Price Method. In the event there are no comparable uncontrolled sales to establish the arm's-length price of a controlled sale, and if the circumstances listed below exist, the seller must use the resale price method. Under this method, an arm's-length price is established by taking the actual resale price charged to the customer and reducing this resale price by an appropriate markup for the seller. An appropriate markup is computed by multiplying the actual resale price by an appropriate markup percentage. This percentage is arrived at by reference to the gross profit percentage realized by uncontrolled resellers in similar transactions.

The resale price method must be used if *all* of the following conditions exist:

- There are no comparable uncontrolled sales.
- An uncontrolled sales price is available within a reasonable time before or after the controlled purchase.
- The buyer and reseller have not added substantial value to the product by physically altering it (not including packaging, labeling, and minor assembly).
- The buyer and reseller have not added substantial value to the product by the application of intangible property.

Cost-Plus Method.   The last of the three prescribed methods, the cost-plus method, can be best described as the reciprocal of the resale price method. The starting point is the cost of production or acquisition, to which is added an appropriate markup for the seller. Under this method, the manufacturing costs are presumed to be determinable and the markup percentage is established by looking at both internal and external trade factors. This method is normally used if the seller adds substantial value to the product.

Determining the Taxable Income of the Joint Venture

U.S. Concepts Utilized

The U.S. taxable income/loss of a foreign joint venture conducted through a foreign corporation, foreign partnership, or branch of a U.S. corporation will be determined using U.S. tax rules. Moreover, this applies whether the earnings are currently subject to U.S. taxation or whether they will not be taxable in the United States until the future. Of course, the determination of taxable income in a foreign country is dependent upon that country's tax rules and may be substantially different from taxable income under U.S. concepts. If the earnings of a foreign joint venture corporation are retained abroad, the foreign earnings and profits are determined for U.S. tax purposes under U.S. tax concepts. Thus, the IRS could apply Section 482 to reallocate income on transactions between the foreign joint venture and a commonly controlled foreign entity. In addition, if the foreign joint venture is a party to a recapitalization or reorganization, U.S. tax rules will apply for U.S. tax purposes even if such transactions are completed entirely outside the United States.

Foreign Currency Issues

The Tax Reform Act of 1986 contained new rules for transactions denominated in foreign currency. These new rules will be important to the U.S. venturer since the venture's earnings and profits and related foreign taxes will be translated under these rules and will have an impact on the U.S. taxation of the foreign earnings.

A foreign joint venture's functional currency for U.S. tax purposes is generally the currency of the economic environment in which a significant part of the entity's activities are conducted. A foreign joint venture can elect to use the U.S. dollar as the functional currency if the foreign currency is a hyperinflationary one. A hyperinflationary currency is generally defined as a currency of a foreign country in which there is at least 100 percent inflation over a three year period.

If the U.S. dollar is not the functional currency of a foreign corporate joint venture, either by definition or election, the earnings will be translated into U.S. dollars when the earnings are actually distributed to the U.S. shareholder or deemed distributed under the Subpart F, foreign personal holding company, or passive foreign investment company (PFIC) rules. Actual distributions of foreign earnings will be translated into U.S. dollars at the exchange rate in effect at the time this income is received by the shareholder. Thus, there will be no foreign exchange gain or loss on actual profit distributions. Distributions from a foreign joint venture which are deemed to have been made to the U.S. shareholder under the special U.S. tax rules noted above are translated into U.S. dollars using the weighted average foreign exchange rate in effect during the entire taxable year. In the case of deemed distributions, foreign exchange gain or loss can arise due to exchange rate fluctuations between the time the earnings are deemed to have been distributed and the actual date of distribution. A foreign exchange gain is ordinary income and is sourced in the same manner as the related income.

The U.S. venturer will also need to apply the new foreign currency rules in determining the deemed paid foreign taxes on profit distributions from a foreign corporate venture. These deemed paid foreign taxes reflect the foreign taxes paid by the foreign venture on the distributed income and are available to the U.S. shareholder as a result of the foreign corporation's dividend distributions. Under the new foreign currency rules, the deemed-paid foreign taxes are translated into U.S. dollars using the foreign exchange rate in effect when the foreign taxes were actually paid. If there is a refund of foreign tax, the refund is translated to U.S. dollars using the exchange rate in effect when the tax overpayment was made.

U.S. Taxation of Joint Venture Earnings

The U.S. taxation of foreign joint venture earnings varies depending upon the type of entity which is used to conduct the venture, the ownership of the entity and the character of the income which is generated.

The U.S. tax consequences of each type of entity which can be used for a foreign joint venture is discussed below. Since the U.S. taxation of income from a partnership and a foreign branch of a U.S. corporation will be similar, they are discussed together.

Partnership and Foreign Branch of U.S. Corporation
Partnerships and foreign branches are not separate taxable entities for U.S. purposes. Rather, income and deductions determined at the partnership or foreign branch level flow through to and are taxed to the U.S. partner or, in the case of a foreign branch, to the U.S. corporation currently.

Controlled Foreign Corporation

Cash Versus Accrual Method of Accounting.   Generally, earnings of a foreign venture conducted through a foreign corporation are not taxable in the United States (provided the income is not effectively connected with the conduct of a U.S. trade or business or passive income from sources within the United States) until the income is actually repatriated to the United States in the form of dividends, interest, royalties, or other similar payments. Thus, the timing of U.S. taxation of the foreign corporate venture earnings can be controlled through the distribution of the foreign corporation's earnings.

As previously noted, in certain situations the income of a foreign corporation is includable, in whole or in part, in the taxable income of the U.S. shareholders. This results if the foreign corporation is a CFC for purposes of the Subpart F provisions, a foreign personal holding company, or makes an investment in U.S. property. In most instances, care should be taken to avoid these provisions which result in current U.S. taxation either by limiting the U.S. ownership of the venture or by controlling the nature of its activities and income.

Subpart F Income.   The Subpart F rules requiring the current taxation of the earnings of a foreign corporation apply only to entities that are CFCs. These rules require that all U.S. shareholders include in income, for the taxable year within which the taxable year of the CFC ends, a pro rata share of the income of the CFC which is considered to be Subpart F income. A U.S. shareholder is defined for this purpose as a U.S. person who owns, directly or indirectly, 10 percent or more of the stock in the foreign corporation.

Subpart F income generally includes income from insuring U.S. risks, foreign base company income, and income associated with the CFC's activities within international boycott countries. Of the three categories of Subpart F income, foreign base company income is of most concern to U.S. venturers engaging in a foreign joint venture. Foreign base company income includes personal holding company (passive) income, sales, services, shipping, and oil-related income. Since the Subpart F provisions are quite complex, a detailed analysis of all of these provisions is beyond the scope of this chapter. Consequently, only the personal holding company, sales, and services income will be discussed.

Personal Holding Company Income. Foreign personal holding company (FPHC) income includes dividends, interest, rents, royalties, gains from the sale or exchange of property, and certain gains from foreign currency transactions. Exceptions include dividends and interest received from a *related* person which is organized under the laws of the same foreign country in which the recipient CFC is incorporated and has a substantial portion of its assets used in a trade or business. In addition, FPHC income does not include rents or royalties derived from an active trade or business and received from an *unrelated* party or from a *related* person for the use of intangible property in the same foreign country in which the CFC is incorporated. For this purpose, a person related to a CFC is any individual, corporation, or partnership which controls the CFC or is controlled by the CFC. Control is defined as 50 percent or more ownership of the voting power *or* value of all classes of stock in the case of a corporation and 50 percent or more of the total value of the partnership interests in the case of a partnership.

Sales Income. Foreign base company sales income includes profits from the purchase or sale of personal property, if the property is purchased from or sold to a related person and is manufactured outside *and* sold for use outside the CFC's country of incorporation. Simply stated, a U.S. venturer cannot avoid U.S. tax by manufacturing a product in the United States and selling it to a CFC venture at a small profit, wherein the CFC would then sell the product to the ultimate consumer at a much higher profit.

Services Income. Foreign base company services income results from the performance of services for or on behalf of a related person if such services are rendered outside the CFC's country of incorporation. Services are considered to be performed where the person rendering the service is physically located when the services are performed. Service income does not include income received in connection with the performance of services that are directly related to the sale by the CFC of property which it produces if such services are performed *before* the sale.

Other Issues. Income of a CFC which would otherwise be subject to current U.S. tax under Subpart F is not subject to current tax if the income is subject to a high rate of foreign tax. In order to qualify for this "high foreign tax" exception, the effective foreign tax rate must be at least 90 percent of the maximum U.S. corporate tax rate for that year. Subpart F income is limited to a CFC's current earnings and profits. If foreign income is blocked because of foreign currency restrictions, it is not subject to U.S. taxation under Subpart F until the restrictions are removed.

A U.S. venturer in a foreign joint venture which is controlled by a small group of U.S. venturers could conceivably be subject to taxation in a particular year on the venture's income under both the Subpart F and foreign personal holding company rules. In such a case, the Subpart F rules provide that the venture's income is taxed under Subpart F rather than under the foreign personal holding company provisions.

Investment in U.S. Property. U.S. venturers who participate in a joint venture conducted through a CFC need to be aware of the U.S. tax consequences if the venture invests in U.S. property. In such a case, Section 956 provides that the U.S. shareholders of the CFC will be taxed on their pro rata share of the CFC's earnings and profits invested in U.S. property. In this regard, the definition of U.S. property includes the following:

1. Tangible property located in the United States.
2. Stock of a related U.S. corporation.
3. Obligations of a U.S. person.
4. Right to use in the United States a patent, copyright, invention or design.

The intent of Section 956 is to prevent U.S. shareholders of CFCs from repatriating excess cash to the United States by purchasing U.S. property without incurring U.S. taxation. An example would be loans or advances from the CFC to the U.S. venturers or their controlled enterprises. If it were not for this restriction, the U.S. venturer could use such a loan to distribute the accumulated earnings and profits of the CFC without current U.S. tax consequences. Thus, the Section 956 provisions consider the substance of such a transaction to be a distribution of the CFC's earnings and subject it to current U.S. taxation in the same fashion as an actual dividend.

Passive Foreign Investment Companies (PFIC). A PFIC includes any foreign corporation over 75 percent of whose income is passive *or* over 50 percent of whose asset value consists of assets held for investment. "Look-through" rules apply when characterizing income received by a PFIC so as to preclude PFIC treatment to any holding company receiving payments from active foreign operating subsidiaries. Certain "start-up" foreign corporations are also excluded from the PFIC rules.

If a foreign corporate joint venture qualifies as a PFIC, special tax rules apply when a U.S. venturer either disposes of the joint venture stock or receives a substantial distribution with respect to such stock (*e.g.*, a stock redemption). In such a case, the U.S. venturer is subject to U.S. taxation on the gain from the sale or distribution. In addition, the U.S. venturer must also pay an interest charge on the U.S. tax attributable to the portion of the gain resulting from PFIC earnings accumulated during his period of ownership. The effect is to eliminate the economic benefit of deferring the U.S. tax on joint venture earnings for the period of time the stock was held by the U.S. venturer.

Gain from the sale of PFIC stock is deemed to be earned on a pro rata basis over the holding period of the stock. The tax on the gain is then assessed based on the highest annual U.S. tax rate in effect for each taxable year such income was earned. Furthermore, the gain is ordinary income rather than capital gain. The interest charge resulting upon the sale of PFIC stock can be avoided if the U.S. venturer makes a "Qualified Electing Fund" election to be taxed annually on a pro rata share of the PFIC's earnings. While the PFIC provisions were enacted primarily to reduce tax avoidance by individuals, the broad wording of the statute makes the provisions applicable to corporations as well.

Foreign Personal Holding Company (FPHC). The foreign personal holding company tax provisions are intended to assure that the income of those foreign corporations controlled by five or fewer U.S. individuals, and whose income is primarily passive, is subject to current U.S. taxation. It should be noted that these provisions are separate and distinct from the *domestic* personal holding company provisions. In the case of an FPHC, the U.S. shareholders are subject to current U.S. tax on their pro rata share of the company's annual taxable income, whether or not such income is actually distributed.

The foreign personal holding company provisions do not normally come into play in the case of joint ventures, since the parties involved in the joint venture are normally widely held by individual shareholders and, more importantly, the Subpart F rules take precedence over FPHC treatment.

Noncontrolled Foreign Corporation

Earnings of a joint venture foreign corporation which is not subject to current U.S. taxation under the rules discussed above will be taxed in the U.S. only when such earnings are actually remitted to the U.S. shareholders. The rules for determining what portion of a cash or property distribution by a noncontrolled foreign corporation is subject to U.S. tax follow the same general rules as apply to U.S. corporations. Thus, to the extent the foreign joint venture corporation has current or accumulated earnings, the distribution will be fully taxable as a dividend. In many cases, the dividend distribution will give rise to a deemed-paid foreign tax credit. The importance of deemed-paid foreign taxes on dividend distributions is discussed below. The dividend received deduction which is available for dividends received from a U.S. corporation is generally not available with respect to dividends from a foreign corporation.

Foreign Tax Credit

Purpose

The income tax laws of the United States provide that U.S. citizens and domestic corporations, regardless of their place of residence, are subject to U.S. tax on their worldwide income. In addition, most countries tax income derived from sources within the country regardless of the citizenship or residence of the recipient. The result of this interplay between the tax systems of two or more countries is the potential for double taxation. Consequently, the United States allows a U.S. taxpayer to take a credit against the U.S. tax liability for foreign taxes accrued or paid on income which is also subject to U.S. tax. This credit is subject to certain limitations discussed below.

Who is Entitled to the Foreign Tax Credit?

The general rule for determining who is entitled to the foreign tax credit is to identify the person liable for payment of the foreign income tax. In addition, if a foreign joint venture corporation is subject to foreign income taxes, the U.S. venturers are frequently entitled to a foreign tax credit for these taxes when the corresponding earnings are actually distributed to the venturer. In order to qualify for this "deemed-paid" foreign tax credit, the U.S. venturer must be a U.S. corporation and must own 10 percent or more of the voting stock of the foreign joint venture corporation which pays the foreign income tax.

In the case of a foreign joint venture conducted in partnership form, the partners of the partnership are entitled to a foreign tax credit for foreign taxes paid by the partnership on partnership income. This rule follows the concept of a partnership as a conduit for items of income, deductions, and credits. If a foreign partnership is deemed to be a foreign corporation for U.S. tax purposes, the rules pertaining to foreign corporations will apply.

Direct Foreign Taxes

Direct foreign tax credits refer to credits taken for foreign taxes *actually paid* by a U.S. venturer in the form of withholding taxes imposed on payments from a foreign venture. Reducing or eliminating the foreign withholding tax is possible if the United States has a tax treaty with the country from which the payment is being received. Consequently, a U.S. venturer should explore treaty relief and, if available, obtain the necessary exemption certificate prior to receiving payments of income (*e.g.*, dividends, interest, and royalties) which may be subject to foreign withholding tax.

Direct foreign tax credits also arise if the foreign joint venture is conducted through a branch of a U.S. corporation or through a foreign partnership. In these situations, the foreign tax paid on the venture earnings is creditable by its U.S. venturers. In the case of a venture conducted through a foreign corporation, direct credits most often arise when dividends or interest are paid to the United States and a foreign withholding tax is imposed on the distribution.

Indirect Foreign Taxes

A U.S. corporate venturer receiving a dividend from a foreign joint venture corporation in which such venturer owns 10 percent or more of the voting stock is deemed to have paid the underlying foreign income taxes paid by the foreign corporation on the earnings from which the distribution is made. Assuming the 10 percent voting stock ownership requirement has been met at the time the dividend is paid, a deemed-paid foreign tax credit is even available with respect to dividends paid from income earned by the joint venture prior to the time the U.S. venturer reached the 10 percent stock ownership requirement.

Actual dividends and deemed dividends under Subpart F are considered to come first from the foreign joint ventures aggregate, multi-year pool of post-1986 undistributed earnings and profits (E&P), without regard to year-by-year accumulations. This rule is designed to limit the ability of U.S. venturers to claim deemed-paid foreign tax credits at an effective rate higher or lower than the average foreign tax rate experienced over a period of years.

If a U.S. venturer is entitled to a deemed-paid foreign tax credit on a dividend from a foreign joint venture corporation, the amount of income on which the venturer is taxable in the United States includes the dividend itself (including withholding tax) plus the amount of the deemed-paid tax credit. The inclusion in income of the deemed-paid foreign tax credit is known as "grossing up" the dividend.

Limitation on Credit

The foreign tax credit which is available to offset the U.S. tax liability is limited to the lower of the foreign taxes paid or accrued (including carryovers) or the U.S. tax liability attributable to the foreign source taxable income of the U.S. venturer. The allocation of the venturer's total U.S. tax liability to foreign source taxable income is based on the following formula:

$$\frac{\text{Foreign Source Income}}{\text{Less Foreign Source Deductions}} \times \frac{\text{U.S. Tax Liability}}{\text{(Before Credits)}}$$

In order to compute taxable foreign source income for purposes of the foreign tax credit limitation, a U.S. venturer's taxable income must first be sourced within and without the United States. Deductions directly allocable to income within and without the United States are then allocated to the related income and any remaining deductions are allocated between United States and foreign source based on the gross income of the venturer from within and without the United States. Interest expense, however, is allocated based on assets.

Sourcing of Income. A complete discussion of the income sourcing rules is beyond the scope of this chapter. Detailed U.S. income sourcing rules are provided by statute, however, with respect to dividends, interest, rents, and royalties received from a foreign payor. In addition, the sourcing of gains from the sale of tangible property (real or personal) is also contained in the U.S. tax law. Losses resulting from the sale of tangible property are sourced based on the rules relating to the allocation of deductions rather than those relating to the source of income.

Allocation of Deductions. Once a determination has been made as to the portion of the U.S. venturer's gross income which is foreign source, the expenses, losses, and other deductions which are subtracted from gross income to reach taxable income must be allocated and apportioned between foreign and U.S. source income in order to determine foreign *taxable* income. The allocation rules provide that deductions which are definitely related to a particular item or class of income must be subtracted from that income. A "ratable part" of the remaining deductions must then be applied against foreign source income. Specific allocation rules are provided for the following items:

1. *Interest Expense.* Interest expense must be allocated on the basis of the U.S. venturer's assets. For this purpose, all members of the U.S. affiliated group of corporations are treated as a single taxpayer in determining the allocation of the consolidated interest expense to foreign source income.
2. *Loss on Sale of Property.* Losses incurred on the sale or exchange of property are allocated to the source of income to which the property sold would have given rise. Thus, a loss on the sale of a U.S. research facility which gave rise to substantial foreign royalty income would be charged against foreign source income.
3. *Home Office Expenses (Stewardship Expenses).* Expenses incurred by a U.S. venturer in managing its investment in a foreign joint venture must be allocated to foreign sources.

4. *Legal and Accounting Fees.* Legal and accounting fees are not specifically related to either U.S. or foreign source income and must, therefore, be apportioned between the two types of income.
5. *Research and Development Expenses.* Expenditures for research and development relate primarily to sales income. Accordingly, such expenses are not ordinarily allocated to the particular product which may have directly benefited from the results of the research, but to the sales income from a wider product group.
6. *Other Expenses.* Expenses not directly allocable to any specific income producing activity are to be apportioned as if all members of the U.S. affiliated group were a single corporation, similar to the allocation of interest expense. Gross income, gross receipts, or any other appropriate basis for allocation may be used for this purpose.

Separate Limitation Baskets

There are separate foreign tax credit limitation calculations for a number of different types of foreign source income received by a U.S. venturer. The purpose of the separate limitations is to prevent U.S. taxpayers from combining active business income with passive income in computing the utilization of foreign tax credits. Since active business income is frequently taxed in a foreign country at rates higher than in the United States, whereas passive income may be taxed at rates (*i.e.*, withholding taxes) lower than in the United States, the separate limitations prevent the greater utilization of foreign tax credits which would result if the separate baskets did not exist.

The most important separate limitations are the passive income and the non-CFC entity limitations. For this purpose, income such as dividends, interest, rents and royalties is considered to be passive income. The separate limitation for non-CFC entities applies to dividends received from a foreign venture that is not a CFC, but still qualifies for a deemed-paid foreign tax credit (*i.e.*, a foreign corporation between 10 percent and 50 percent owned by the U.S. venturer). Each such corporation has its own separate foreign tax credit limitation (a per company limitation).

Certain payments (or Subpart F income) from a CFC to a related U.S. person are subject to "look-through" rules whereby payments of interest, rents, royalties, or dividends may be recharacterized as separate limitation passive income or as overall limitation by referring to the underlying character of the earnings out of which such payments were made. Look-through rules also apply to interest, rents, and royalties received from noncorporate foreign entities (*e.g.*, partnerships or trusts) by 10 percent or more U.S. holders if such entities are more than 50 percent controlled by U.S. persons.

An important "de minimis" exception is provided so that the look-through rules will not apply to payments received from a CFC if such CFC meets the Subpart F "de minimis" exception (*i.e.*, Subpart F income does not exceed the lesser of 5 percent of gross income or $1,000,000). Under this exception, separate limitation income received from a CFC in any year will be treated as overall limitation income in the hands of the U.S. venturer.

Foreign source losses arising in any of the separate limitation categories will first proportionately reduce the foreign source income in the other separate limitation baskets *before* being offset against U.S. source income. When the separate limitation in which the losses arose generates foreign source income in a subsequent year, that income (but not the related tax) is recharacterized as income of the category or categories which were previously offset by the loss.

Reporting Requirements

Claiming the Foreign Tax Credit
A U.S. venturer claims the foreign tax credit by completing Form 1116 in the case of a U.S. individual venturer and Form 1118 for a U.S. corporate venturer. Whether the computation of available foreign tax credits is on an accrual basis or, alternatively, on a paid basis, will primarily depend upon the accounting method of the taxpayer.

Information Return with Respect to a
Controlled Foreign Corporation (CFC)
A U.S. shareholder, director, or officer of a foreign joint venture corporation may be required to include certain information regarding the foreign corporation on his U.S. income tax return. The required disclosures are made on Form 5471, Information Return with Respect to a Foreign Corporation. The question of whether a U.S. venturer is required to file Form 5471 and how much information is required to be disclosed on the form will largely depend on the venturer's ownership interest in the venture and whether or not the venture is a CFC. In general, if the

venturer owns at least 10 percent of a foreign venture and the venture is a CFC, rather extensive financial information will have to be disclosed including a current profit and loss statement and transactions with related parties.

State Tax Considerations

The earnings of a foreign joint venture may be subject to state tax if the venture is conducted through a U.S. corporation or partnership. In addition, the income from a venture conducted through a foreign corporation may be subject to state tax at the time the earnings are repatriated to the U.S. venturer. Therefore, state taxation of a foreign joint venture's earnings can represent a significant potential cost which can be minimized or eliminated through proper planning.

Separate Versus Unitary Taxation

States impose a corporate income tax using either the separate entity approach or the unitary business approach. The separate entity approach views each legal entity separately for purposes of determining the imposition of state tax. The unitary approach combines all unitary businesses conducted by a related group of corporations. Although the earnings of a foreign joint venture corporation whose management and operations are outside the United States are not ordinarily subject to state tax until the earnings are remitted to the U.S. venturer, unitary states may impose a current tax on a foreign venture's earnings if the foreign business is considered to be unitary with the business of the U.S. venturer. The ability of unitary states to ignore the separate legal entities and tax the entire unitary business conducted by a commonly controlled group of corporations should be addressed before establishing a business in unitary tax states. It should be noted that many unitary states have recently been adopting a "water's edge" approach whereby only related U.S. corporations are combined for purposes of computing state taxable income.

Delaware Holding Company

The venturer in a foreign joint venture conducted through a foreign corporation should consider holding the stock of this corporation through a Delaware holding company. In general, Delaware does not tax a holding company incorporated in Delaware which receives only passive income from intangible investments (*i.e.*, dividends, interest, and royalties). Thus, the use of such a corporation by a U.S. venturer can avoid state tax on dividends, interest, and royalties from the joint-venture company.

RESTRUCTURING OR TERMINATING THE JOINT VENTURE

Reorganizations

The U.S. tax rules relating to the reorganization of a U.S. corporation also apply to the U.S. tax treatment of a foreign joint venture conducted through a foreign corporation. There are, however, certain tax rules which must be considered in restructuring a foreign corporation without adverse U.S. tax consequences. These restrictions are primarily set forth in the regulations to Section 367. Whenever a foreign reorganization is contemplated, these rules should be carefully reviewed to determine whether a U.S. "toll charge" must be paid in order to obtain U.S. tax-free treatment of the transaction.

Partnership

Winding up a joint venture conducted through a partnership can be accomplished by having the partners agree to terminate the partnership and distribute the partnership assets to the partners. Alternatively, the partners can sell their partnership interests or sell the partnership assets and distribute the cash, thereby terminating the partnership.

The rules for sourcing gain from the sale of a partnership interest treat the partnership interest as an intangible asset. Consequently, any gain or loss will be sourced to the seller's country of residence. Thus, a U.S. venturer will need to determine whether it will be better from a tax standpoint to sell the partnership assets so that gain or loss will be sourced based upon the location of the assets rather than sourced to the country of residence of the venturer.

In determining whether to sell the partnership assets or the partnership interest, a U.S. venturer must compare the tax basis of the partnership assets with the tax basis of his partnership interest. This is an important consideration since it is frequently found that the venturer's tax basis in the partnership interest (outside basis) is significantly different than the tax basis in the underlying partnership assets (inside basis).

Foreign Corporation

The alternatives/methods by which the U.S. venturer may terminate an interest in a foreign joint venture corporation are as follows:

1. Sell the entire stock interest to a third party.
2. Redeem the entire stock interest by selling it back to the joint venture.
3. Liquidate the foreign joint venture.

The sale of a venturer's stock interest to a third party has the same U.S. tax consequences as a redemption of the interest by the joint venture company. Therefore, the U.S. tax consequences to the venturer of a sale of stock and a stock redemption are discussed together.

Sale or Redemption of Stock
The character of the gain resulting from the sale of the stock of a CFC is subject to special rules if the selling shareholder owns at least 10 percent of the company. In this case, any gain from the sale will be characterized as a dividend (ordinary income) to the extent of the pro-rata share of the joint venture's earnings and profits. To arrive at adjusted earnings and profits, any previously taxed earnings and profits (*e.g.*, Subpart F income) are excluded. The dividend portion of the gain results in deemed-paid foreign tax credits to the corporate venturer.

If the U.S. venturer selling the stock is an individual, the amount of gain which is recharacterized as a dividend is determined somewhat differently than for corporations. In essence, there is a special limitation on the amount of taxes which the individual venturer must pay on the portion of the gain which is treated as a dividend.

Liquidation
The venturers may decide that a foreign corporate joint venture should be terminated and the net assets distributed to the venturers. In the case of a U.S. venturer, this results in a transfer of cash, property, and other assets into the United States. One of the distinguishing features of liquidating a foreign joint venture corporation (as opposed to a U.S. cor-

poration), is that a tax-free liquidation is not generally possible. This is due to the fact that the liquidation of a foreign corporation requires immediate U.S. tax recognition of the foreign corporation's previously untaxed earnings and profits. The intent is to prevent the U.S. venturer from using a foreign corporation to avoid U.S. taxation on the earnings and then liquidating the foreign corporation on a tax-free basis. To the extent the foreign venture corporation does not have untaxed earnings for U.S. purposes, the liquidation of the foreign corporation to U.S. shareholders can be accomplished free of U.S. tax.

CHAPTER 14

JOINT VENTURING IN EUROPE

David R. Wightman
Solicitor, Supreme Court of Judicature, England

REASONS FOR JOINT VENTURES

The joint-venture concept is one which has operated in Europe for many years and, indeed, in England the statute law which governs many forms of joint-venture arrangements was passed long ago in 1890. It is therefore surprising that at least in the common-law jurisdictions, the joint-venture concept has not been given a specific legal or statutory definition. Perhaps, one of the reasons for this is the great variety of different forms in which joint ventures manifest themselves—partnerships, limited partnerships, single-venture partnerships, consortia, and corporate joint ventures—either with limited liability, unlimited liability, or a mixture of the two. The form taken by a joint venture is frequently dictated by the reasons for its existence and its objectives and these, of course, are even more varied than the structures themselves.

Until recent years in Europe, there were few instances in which parties were obliged to create joint ventures because of legal or political pressures. In general terms, it was permissible for a foreign entity to carry on a commercial activity in a European country without the necessity of having a local, indigenous partner. However, in some fields of activity this has changed. In the oil industry, for example, the government of the United Kingdom requires the maximum possible involvement of U.K. manufacturers, consultants, contractors, and service companies in the provision of supplies and services to the offshore hydrocarbon industry operating in the North Sea. This policy extends much further than a requirement that U.K. companies be given equal opportunities in tendering processes, and effectively imposes a system in which, with certain exceptions, a foreign company cannot engage in North Sea activities without a British partner holding a controlling interest. One of the intentions being, of course, to provide for the transfer of technology to U.K. companies which can be used not only in the local domestic market but also exploited in overseas export markets for the overall benefit of the U.K. economy. Similar requirements exist in Norway in respect to the Norwegian sector of the North Sea, and it is hardly surprising, therefore, that these regimes have given rise to a proliferation of joint ventures in this field of activity.

The North Sea example illustrates an instance in which a joint-venture structure between a local and a foreign partner is a requirement of the law or of government policy. This situation is not, however, the norm in most European jurisdictions and in the majority of cases the reasons giving rise to the formation of joint ventures are of a commercial rather than a political nature.

As is the case in most other areas of the world, the need for a joint venture is quite often dictated by the size of the project, either because no single partner has the capacity, in terms of finance, manpower, or resources, to undertake the project on his own or because there is a need to acquire technological skills or expertise which are not otherwise available. A current example of this situation is the Eurotunnel project in which a tunnel is to be constructed under the English Channel between Britain and France. This is, of course, a major construction project as well as being, politically, a somewhat sensitive issue. The construction work is being undertaken by a group of five British contractors acting in joint venture with a similar-sized group of French contractors. The size of the project and its complexity dictated the need for the joint venture but it is also worthy of note that political considerations may also have been an influence in the exclusion of any non-French or non-UK participants as main contractors.

Another factor which has given rise to the creation of a number of joint ventures in Europe has been the need to pool resources and efforts in the fields of research and development, particularly in the high-tech industries and those which require substantial capital investment for a limited market. Notable examples of this were seen in the aircraft industry in respect to the development of the Concorde and of the European Airbus. These projects were, of course, unusual in terms of capital investment and government involvement; but the same principles have been applied in numerous smaller joint ventures in the more specialized sectors, involving both cross-frontier partnerships and purely domestic arrangements. The combination of two or more smaller enterprises has frequently resulted in the joint venture having greater opportunities to compete against the larger competitors in the world market, than would have been available to any of the constituent partners on their own.

ADVANTAGES AND DISADVANTAGES OF JOINT VENTURING

Apart from the general advantages referred to above, the potential partners in a joint-venture may be able to benefit from opportunities which are specific to the situs of the joint-venture operation or to the nature of its undertaking. A non-European wishing to establish an operation in a European country may, for example, be able to benefit from local government grants, subsidies, or export incentives which would only be available if he has a local partner. Similarly, the tax rules applicable in the particular country may well favor a joint-venture structure, particularly when considered in conjunction with applicable double-taxation agreements. Obviously, these considerations depend upon the precise details of the proposed joint-venture and will need to be considered on a case-by-case basis. Conversely, any potential joint-venturer will need to consider carefully the disadvantages of surrendering, at least in part, his independence. The very nature of a joint-venture implies that unless one party is prepared wholly to surrender his right to participate in decision making, the operation of the enterprise must be by consensus. Even a minority partner will require some form of protection and consequent control, albeit limited, over the joint-venture decisions. This is particularly so where the joint venture takes the form of an unincorporated partnership where the liability of the partners is joint and several and unlimited. It would be usual in most European joint ventures for the joint-venture agreement to list specifically a number of actions that can be taken only with the unanimous approval of all parties. Matters such as the termination of the joint venture, the disposal of the principal assets of the venture, and the giving of guarantees would normally be included in such a list. On the other hand, the imposition of too many negative restraints will inhibit the positive management which the operation will need to succeed. There is no simple solution to this problem which will cause the downfall of the joint venture if the delicate balance between negative protective controls and the requirements of positive management is disturbed by a disintegration of the goodwill between the partners. Clearly, the composition of the management structure can help to reduce the incidence of such problems and ensure that each partner is properly represented and has a fair say in management decisions. This aspect of the venture will require careful consideration.

Another problem that a potential joint venturer will need to consider is what is to happen if there is a total breakdown in the relationship between the parties. The laws of most European countries provide for some form of dissolution or, in certain cases, for one party to buy out the interest of another party; but generally, these measures produce a somewhat draconian result and require the parties to resort to the courts. While it is possible and, indeed, usual to provide, in the joint-venture agreement, for some form of escape route if the parties have a falling out, the disadvantage of a joint-venture arrangement which goes wrong, should not be underestimated.

In joint ventures which require the transfer of technology or know-how into the venture, the partner making the transfer should realize that if the joint venture is subsequently dissolved, he may well have provided a significant benefit to a competitor or created a competitive situation where one did not exist before. There are, of course, procedures for preventing the misuse of certain types of intellectual property or other similar information; but, although the laws of the countries in Europe will afford some degree of protection, it may not be absolute.

Although taxation has been mentioned as a possible advantage to a joint venturer; it may also be a disadvantage. A non-European partner may well become liable to the tax regime of a European country by entering into a joint venture in Europe, whereas the liability might have been avoided or reduced if the objective had been achieved in some other way, such as a license or distributorship arrangement. Again, each case will depend on its own facts, but the taxation implications of a joint venture can give rise to other problems, particularly in regard to the timing and method of distributing profits. The difficulties need to be clearly identified and resolved at the outset.

SELECTING A JOINT-VENTURE PARTNER

While the rationale behind the creation of a joint venture in the first place or the nature of the venture itself, may dictate the choice of partner or selection from an identified range of potential partners, there are certain general considerations which should be taken into account in making the selection. First, it is obviously essential to ensure that the joint-venture partner is properly qualified and registered to undertake the venture in the required jurisdiction. Returning to the earlier example of joint ventures in the U.K. sector of the North Sea, a potential joint venturer will wish to make sure that his partner is acceptable to the Offshore Supplies Office.

Secondly, an evaluation should be made of the respective tax positions of the partners to identify any potential conflicts. So far as the law permits, a decision should be made on the place of residence of the joint venture for tax purposes and the effect of that decision on the taxation of profits and the availability of losses for tax relief.

Thirdly, in many parts of Europe, the trades' unions exercise considerable control and influence over work practices and the organization of labor. There would be little point, for instance, in a joint-venture arrangement being entered into which would effectively preclude one party's seconded personnel from undertaking their duties because they are not members of a particular trades' union.

Fourthly, it may be necessary to consider the antitrust and monopoly implications of the proposed venture. If the combination of two or more parties into a single joint venture is likely to have an effect on competition in any particular market, there may be registration or disclosure requirements applicable to the arrangement. In the worst cases the joint venture may be forbidden to operate or become liable to substantial fines.

Finally, there are the purely commercial questions as to the potential partner's suitability for the project, some of which are as follows:

- What are his resources, in terms of finance, manpower, technology, etc?
- How are these resources compatible with those of the would-be joint venturer?
- What is his track record and rating for insurance purposes?
- Does his management style and philosophy suit the proposed venture?
- To what extent is the purpose of the venture going to create conflicts with other activities of the partner?

- Are language differences likely to give rise to major communications problems?
- Are local accounting or other technical standards or codes compatible?

The list is, of course, endless but the process of selecting the right partner can only be begun if the rationale and *raisons d' etre* for the venture have been clearly established.

LEGAL AND TAX CONSIDERATIONS

Having decided to opt for a joint venture, perhaps the most fundamental consideration is the legal form in which the venture is to pursue its objectives. In some cases this may be dictated to the parties by law or government policy. If the government requires the local partner to have a controlling interest, it may be that the only suitable vehicle for the joint venture will be a corporate entity. In the absence, however, of any mandatory directive as to the form of the joint venture, the parties should make their choice after considering the following factors:

- Is the joint venture a single-project venture or will it have a continuing purpose?
- Is the venture to be restricted to a specific geographical area?
- Do the parties wish the joint venture to have limited liability, so far as possible?
- Is the venture to employ its own work force?
- How is the joint venture to be funded?
- What are the registration and disclosure requirements applicable to the venture?
- What are the taxation implications?
- Is the undertaking to be the owner of a substantial capital asset?

As mentioned above, there is a wide range of legal forms or entities from which to chose. The precise nature of these entities and the laws governing them vary from country to country in Europe; but the underlying concepts are basically the same and, with the development of the European Community, are being standardized between the member states of the European Community. For the sake of illustration, therefore, the forms of joint ventures most commonly found under English law, may be summarized as follows.

PARTNERSHIP OR CONSORTIUM

This type of arrangement is generally most suitable for a single-venture arrangement or project which can be commenced and completed within a reasonably short period of time, and which is not intended to own or hold a capital asset of any material size. It is used extensively by, for example, contractors wishing to combine forces and resources to bid for a particular contract, or in the development of real property where an owner of a site joins forces with a developer or a financial institution to develop the site. The parties agree on their respective roles in the project, the management and operational structure, the method of funding, and the manner in which profits or losses are to be shared. In common-law jurisdictions, such as the English system, problems can arise with this type of joint venture if it is treated as a partnership either for the single venture or in general. It may be that the parties wish to limit their respective liabilities in the same proportions as their input into the joint venture. There is, of course, no reason why they should not enter into such agreement between themselves as they wish, but despite this, if the arrangement is construed to be a partnership, as far as the outside world is concerned they will be jointly and severally liable for each others' acts and defaults. Similarly, under the law, one partner can act as agent for the partnership and enter into commitments which will be binding on all the partners. Such an act may well constitute a breach of the joint-venture agreement but this may be of little comfort if the defaulting party has not the resources to satisfy the liability. It is, of course, possible to create a joint venture of this type which does not constitute a partnership. In practice, however, this is difficult and impracticable in cases where the joint venture is to enter into a contract with a third party who requires, as a condition of the contract award, joint and several liability on the part of the members of the venture.

In addition to the more technical and legal problems of this type of joint venture, there are the more practical operational difficulties, primarily in the areas of management structure and joint-venture personnel. Most European joint ventures of this type provide for a management board or committee to which the partners appoint their nominated representatives. Unless the interests of the parties remain *ad idem* throughout the course of the project, this sort of structure contains all the seeds of dissent which could arise out of the conflicts of interest between loyalty to the project, on the one hand, and loyalty to the provider of one's salary check, on the other. While a well-prepared joint-venture agreement can help to prevent some of these conflicts from arising, it does seem to be the case that many of the more successful joint ventures are those in which the parties have been prepared to surrender a reasonable degree of authority to one of their number in whom they have confidence, who acts as sponsor and takes the more dominant role.

The position of employees seconded to the joint venture is also a potential, but perhaps less-difficult source of problems. In the majority of cases seconded personnel continue to be employees of the party seconding them, who remains liable for their salaries, Pay-As-You-Earn tax, and social security contributions. There are, however, circumstances in which one party to the joint venture might become liable for PAYE tax on another party's seconded personnel's salaries if the employees are, *de facto,* under his direction and control, and the joint-venture agreement needs to address this eventuality. Similarly, care must be taken to ensure that all statutory insurances, such as employer's liability, and workman's compensation, are adequate to cover seconded personnel while working on a joint-venture project.

Apart from the question of employees' tax, the parties will need to consider their taxation positions in general. In most cases, the partnership or consortium type of joint venture presents no particular problems. There is, of course, the possibility that a nonresident partner may be deemed to be resident for tax purposes in the country of the joint venture but, apart from this, each party will be responsible for any taxation on its share of the venture's profits. If the joint venture is properly structured there should be no question of one party to the venture becoming liable for the other party's taxation liabilities in the event of default.

Finally, most European countries impose a value-added tax on sales or supplies of goods and services. The supplier of the goods or services is obliged to recover the tax from the recipient and account for it to the appropriate authority. Value-added tax paid on the purchase or receipt of goods or services may, in appropriate cases, be set off against tax recovered on sales or supplies. However, in order to obtain the benefit of any such set off, it is necessary that the venture is properly registered with the appropriate authority. Depending upon the nature of the joint venture the rules can be complex, and careful consideration should always be given to this aspect to ensure that the venture is correctly structured and, if necessary, registered as a separate entity from its constituent partners.

CORPORATE JOINT VENTURES

The formation of an independent corporate entity to act as the joint-venture vehicle provides, at least on the face of it, an answer to some of the problems which are encountered with the more amorphous partnership or consortium joint venture. It has a formalized constitution and management structure. It can more readily employ its own personnel who are dedicated to the joint-venture project and who may not be subject to any conflicting interests of the participants in the venture. It has, in appropriate cases, limited liability of its own; and in most countries it has the benefit of applicable statute law providing it with various safeguards and a clear legal framework within which to operate. It goes without saying, however, that the more formalized structure of a corporate joint venture removes much of the flexibility of the partnership or consortium arrangement and, in some circumstances, makes it more difficult to provide suitable escape routes in the event that the parties have a falling out. Because of this, the corporate-structure joint venture is, perhaps, more suitable for the longer-term or more permanent ventures than for the single-project undertaking. It is also an easier vehicle to use if the joint venture is to own a major capital asset, such as real estate.

As mentioned above, there are various forms the corporate entity may take. It may be a private company limited by shares or more unusually, a public company limited by shares; it may be an unlimited company having a share capital, or a company not having a share capital but limited by guarantee; or it may be a limited partnership where the liability of one or more partners is limited but the liability of the other or others is not. Corporate entities of this type may be found, under one guise or another, in most European countries, although, for joint-venture purposes, the private company limited by shares is by far the most common.

In the United Kingdom the formalities for incorporating a private company are comparatively simple. The company must have at least two shareholders and there are no mandatory requirements as to the size of the paid-up-share capital. The company must have a board of directors, who have ostensible authority to act on behalf of the company; a company secretary; and a registered office. The registration documents giving details of the shareholders and officers of the company must be filed at the Companies Registry and this information is available for public inspection. The constitution and bylaws of the company are contained in a document known as the Memorandum and Articles of Association, which must describe the objects of the company, give details of its share capital, and contain regulations for the management and administration of the entity.

In the majority of cases, the corporate joint venture will be established by a joint-venture or shareholders agreement which will provide for the formation of the company and for the proportions in which the joint-venture participants are to be interested in the share capital of the company. The agreement will normally also provide a mechanism for the participants to appoint their nominees to the board of directors and contain provisions as to the management of the company, which restrict or preclude the opportunities for directors appointed by one party to act in a manner prejudicial to the interests of the other. It should be remembered, however, that the agreement is a private matter between the contracting parties and any act or omission on the part of one party, which might be in breach of the agreement, will not normally invalidate any commitment entered into by the company with a third party acting in good faith. To a limited extent, it is possible for a participant to build in safeguards by including them in the Memorandum and Articles of Association, of which, since it is a public document, third parties are deemed to have been given notice.

It is not uncommon in corporate-entity joint ventures to find that the share capital of the company is divided into different classes of shares, which carry with them special rights as to voting, payment of dividends, or repayment of capital. One of the most frequently encountered special rights is that which entitles the holder of one class of shares to appoint or remove his nominated directors without interference or obstruction from the other shareholders. This is an important requirement which needs to be built in to the shareholders agreement or, preferably, the Articles of Association; for, without it, as a matter of law, directors can be appointed or removed only by a majority resolution passed at a shareholder meeting. In a fifty-fifty joint venture it is also important to consider the question of casting votes. If nothing is said, the person who is appointed as chairman of either a shareholders' meeting or a meeting of the board of directors, will have a second or casting vote, which may well defeat the objectives of the parties.

As in the case of the consortium or partnership joint venture, the fifty-fifty corporate joint venture presents its own special problems if a deadlock or impasse arises in the management of the company. Innumerable formulae and schemes have been devised to cope with this situation but none of them is simple or without pitfalls. Some of the solutions proposed involve third-party arbitration or quasi-arbitration, some an enforced buy-out or liquidation, and some merely leave the ultimate resolution of the problem to the courts, who have jurisdiction to resolve a deadlock in management by ordering a buy-out of a liquidation. It is, of course, preferable for the joint-venture agreement to address the possibility of a breakdown or major default, and to provide some mechanism for the dissolution of the joint venture in as orderly a manner as possible, if all other remedies fail.

If, in the corporate joint venture, it has been agreed that one party should have a majority interest, quite apart from any protective safeguards which may be written into the joint-venture agreement, the law itself provides minority shareholders with a certain degree of protection which cannot be overridden by agreement. The objects and constitution of the company, for example, as embodied in the Memorandum and Articles of Association of the company, cannot be changed except with the approval of a 75 percent majority of the shareholders; the special rights attached to any particular class of shares cannot be altered unless the holders of that class of shares approve the change; the company cannot be liquidated voluntarily unless 75 percent of the shareholders agree. These safeguards, clearly, do not provide a minority member with complete protection against an abuse of power, but in many respects they are an improvement on the position of a minority partner in a partnership-type joint venture.

Another difficulty which can sometimes arise in a corporate-entity joint venture is the manner in which profits are distributed. Unless the corporate entity is expressly acting as a pure nominee of its participants, which is occasionally the case, profits arising from the venture belong to the company as an independent entity, and not to the shareholders. Consequently, profits become taxable in the hands of the joint-venture company. In most cases, the only means of distributing profits to the participants is by way of a dividend declaration, a distribution on liquidation, or a whole or partial purchase or redemption of the participants' shares. In any of these cases, there is a danger that the distribution will become taxable again in the hands of the recipient.

Certainly, in the United Kingdom, there exist various statutory exemptions to avoid such double taxation, but appropriate planning is needed at the outset to ensure that the joint-venture structure will qualify for the tax relief available. Similar problems exist in relation to losses incurred by the joint-venture company, and it is necessary to make specific provision in the arrangements to permit losses to be made available for off set against other income of the participating members.

It is sometimes the case that the interests of the joint-venture participants in relation to profit-distribution policy may differ, often due to taxation considerations. One party, for example, may not wish to receive a distribution at all but may prefer to take over the other party's share and operate the joint-venture company as a wholly-owned subsidiary, utilizing the funds locked into the company for other projects. With a properly structured venture which provides specifically for a buy out or redemption of one party's shares, there is no reason why this should not be achieved without any adverse consequence for the parties involved. Obviously, the tax rules differ from country to country and suitable professional advice will be needed to ensure that the joint-venture structure selected meets the individual taxation requirements of the parties.

As mentioned earlier, the formation of a joint-venture company in the United Kingdom and, indeed, in most other European countries requires the filing of certain documents with the appropriate company's registry. These documents become matters of public record and are available for inspection. The public record is, however, not limited to the incorporation documents. There is a requirement to file annually a return giving details of the officers, the shareholders, and the share capital, and also to file a copy of the company's annual accounts or financial statements. This requirement does not generally exist for partnership or consortium joint ventures or for unlimited companies; and sometimes, for reasons of confidentiality, the disclosure requirements for companies can cause problems for the parties involved. If confidentiality of financial information is an important factor, the parties should either opt for some other form of joint-venture vehicle or consider the incorporation of a joint-venture company in a jurisdiction such as the Channel Islands, where the disclosure requirements are less exacting.

Insofar as employment and insurance matters are concerned, the joint venture obviously provides an entity to act as employer or insured independent of its participants. Whether or not the company employs its own workforce or makes use of personnel seconded from its shareholders will, of course, depend upon the nature of the joint venture and the requirements of the parties; but the facility is there if needed. Similarly, the company may be separately registered for value-added tax, which may well be of assistance to a foreign partner in the venture who is not himself registered. Finally, the existence of the corporate veil may mean that a foreign partner does not need to become a deemed resident of the country of the joint venture, for tax purposes. These factors are not necessarily advantageous but there are cases in which they will be and they certainly warrant due consideration in the formative stages of the venture.

OTHER CONSIDERATIONS

One of the most important factors to be considered by parties proposing to joint venture in Europe is the question of the antitrust laws and the effect or likely effect of the joint venture on competition. Each of the countries in Europe has its own domestic rules on restrictive practices, monopolies, and the abuse of dominant positions. These rules may well apply to joint ventures, and the arrangement between the parties may need to be registered or even worse, the arrangement may be found to be void or illegal and involve the parties in legal proceedings. These antitrust rules differ in form, nature, and severity from state to state, but for those countries who have become members of the European Community, there is another set of antitrust rules, having the force of law contained in the Treaty of Rome to which each member state has acceded. These rules are, in general, more far reaching and of wider application than any of those contained in domestic legislation.

The principal provisions of the European Community rules on competition are contained in Articles 85 and 86 of the Treaty of Rome.

Article 85

1. The following shall be prohibited as incompatible with the common market: all agreements between undertakings, decisions by associations of undertakings, and concerted practices which may affect trade between member states and which have as their object or effect the prevention, restriction or distortion of competition within the common market, and in particular those which:

- Directly or indirectly fix purchase or selling prices or any other trading conditions.
- Limit or control production, markets, technical development, or investment.
- Share markets or sources of supply.
- Apply dissimilar conditions to equivalent transactions with other trading parties, thereby placing them at a competitive disadvantage.
- Make the conclusion of contracts subject to acceptance by the other parties of supplementary obligations which, by their nature or according to commercial usage, have no connection with the subject of such contracts.

2. Any agreements or decisions prohibited pursuant to this article shall be automatically void.

3. The provisions of Paragraph 1 may, however, be declared inapplicable in the case of:

- Any agreement or category of agreements between undertakings.
- Any decision or category of decisions by associations of undertakings.
- Any concerted practice or category of concerted practices.

which contributes to improving the production or distribution of goods or to promoting technical or economic progress, while allowing consumers a fair share of the resulting benefit, and which does not:

- Impose on the undertakings concerned restrictions which are not indispensable to the attainment of these objectives.
- Afford such undertakings the possibility of eliminating competition in respect to a substantial part of the products in question.

Article 86

Any abuse by one or more undertakings of a dominant position within the common market or in a substantial part of it shall be prohibited as incompatible with the common market insofar as it may affect trade between member states. Such abuse may, in particular, consist in:

- Directly or indirectly imposing unfair purchase or selling prices or other unfair trading conditions.
- Limiting production, markets, or technical development to the prejudice of consumers.

- Applying dissimilar conditions to equivalent transactions with other trading parties, thereby placing them at a competitive disadvantage.
- Making the conclusion of contracts subject to acceptance by the other parties of supplementary obligations which, by their nature or according to commercial usage, have no connection with the subject of such contracts.

As can be seen, the wording of these rules is capable of a wide interpretation and potential joint ventures in Europe will ignore them at their peril. The sanctions for breach of Articles 85 or 86 are that, first, the agreement between the parties is void and, secondly, the participants can be made liable to massive fines, amounting to many millions of dollars. The commission has power to impose fines of 10 percent of a party's turnover and breaches of the treaty are actively investigated and prosecuted.

If there is any question that a particular joint venture might infringe on the antitrust provisions of the Treaty of Rome, the proper procedure is for the parties to notify the European Commission, based in Brussels, Belgium, of the agreement. After an investigation, the commission may, in appropriate cases, confirm that the agreement is not in breach, grant a specific exemption, which may be subject to certain conditions, or merely issue a comfort letter. Alternatively, the commission may confirm that the agreement falls within one of the Block Exemptions which it has made. Such Block Exemptions include patent licensing agreements, distributorship and purchasing agreements, specialization agreements, and research and development agreements. The nature of the Block Exemptions and the type of specific exemptions which have been granted in individual cases, suggest that, in general terms, the European Commission looks favorably upon joint ventures, particularly those which involve a pooling of different, but nevertheless compatible, resources and result in the creation of a new competitive enterprise. Although the formation of a joint venture may mean that the participants themselves are unlikely to compete with the venture or, perhaps, with each other, the commission is not particularly concerned with the effect on competition if the market in which the joint venture is carrying on its undertaking has no barriers to entry or is already well serviced by numerous competing suppliers. They have, however, recently issued a set of guidelines indicating the type and structure of joint venture which will be most likely to find favor with them.

In many cases, particularly in respect of research and development joint ventures, the commission will find that, although in its opinion the enterprise infringes on Article 85, it nevertheless merits a specific exemption on the grounds that it encourages technological or economic development and progress. Exemptions of this type have been granted in many cases, but the parties receiving such a derogation must realize that it may well not be the end of the matter. The commission takes upon itself a continuing role of monitoring the venture. If at a later date it concludes that competition is being effected by the activities of the joint venture, by virtue of some change in the venture, it has the authority to intervene again and introduce new requirements. This "moving target" approach is frequently, at the least, a source of irritation and, at the worst, a cause of abandonment by parties who, for good and sound commercial reasons, wish to join forces to develop new technology for their mutual benefit, which they would be either unable or unwilling to develop on their own. The difficulty arises out of the retrospective nature of the commission's powers. Joint-venture parties may find that after a considerable period of careful and detailed negotiation, they agree upon terms which are notified to the European Commission who then sanctions the arrangement but only subject to certain conditions which go to the root of the underlying commercial objectives of the parties involved, and result in a reappraisal of the project and a further period of renegotiation.

One of the most frequently encountered conditions is that relating to the exploitation of technology after it has been developed by the joint venture. While the commission looks favorably upon research and development ventures, it takes a much stricter view if the joint-venture arrangements extend to sales as well as development and manufacture. The intention is, of course, to enable the technology to be made available to others and to stimulate competition. The commission's Block Exemption on research and development arrangements exemplifies this point. The regulations exempt joint research and development as well as joint production, but subject them to certain conditions; for example, joint exploitation is not permitted unless the product is particularly innovative or is protected by some form of intellectual property right. Furthermore, the regulations contain restrictions on market shares and on joint-marketing operations and provisions relating to arrangements for the joint-venture participants to obtain supplies of the product. The scope of the Block Exemption is unlikely to have wide application for joint ventures, and the majority of cases will have to be dealt with on an individual basis with the parties taking a view as to whether or not Article 85 applies and, where appropriate, seeking a specific exemption or a letter of comfort to the effect that the agreement merits exemption.

If a comfort letter is issued the parties can proceed on the basis that the commission will not take any action; but it must be borne in mind that the very issue of such a letter implies that the arrangement infringes on Article 85. If, therefore, the parties have a falling out and the agreement has to be litigated in the local courts, a party may well be faced with the argument that since the article applies, the agreement is void; and in the light of the commission's letter, the local courts may have difficulty in avoiding such a finding.

The various legal, tax, and other considerations referred to above are, of course, by no means exhaustive but the would-be joint venturer in Europe should not find the systems any more onerous than those existing in other jurisdictions. Indeed, with its advanced legal systems, free-trade policies, and extensive accessions to international conventions and agreements, Europe provides the parties with a stable and yet flexible base for their undertaking. Unless the objects of the joint venture require the entity to be based in a particular country, the laws of the different countries within Europe provide the parties with the ability to select the country of operations or registration which is best suited to their needs. The suggested use of the Channel Islands as a jurisdiction in which disclosure requirements are limited, has already been made. There are other countries within Europe where the same principles apply; and mention should also be made of the tax havens which exist. The use of a tax haven must, of course, be treated with care and may not prove to be the panacea for all the tax ills that the parties wish to cure, but in appropriate circumstances, their use can prove to be remarkably beneficial and is certainly worthy of consideration.

CHAPTER 15

JOINT VENTURING IN CANADA

R. H. Teskey
Edmonton, Alberta law firm of Field & Field

As business people bring themselves together to undertake a new business activity, one of the many questions to be answered is what organizational structure the new activity is to adopt. Until recently, often without a lot of serious thought, the decision has usually been made to use a corporation.

The corporation has a separate and distinct personality and is viewed as a separate person in the eyes of the law and the tax gatherer. Thus the traditional corporation can sue and be sued in its own name, hold property, and, for the most part do anything else a person can do. Through its board of directors and its management, it makes decisions and takes on an identity of its own. It even has the capacity to commit crimes and to be convicted of offenses which require a specific personal intention.

Although the modern corporations' legislation of the Canadian federal government and of provinces like Ontario and Alberta does permit a blurring of the separation that traditionally has existed, the typical corporation draws a clear distinction between the owners as shareholders and the heart and soul of the corporation—in the form of the directors. The shareholders are passive and rely upon their nominees in the form of the directors to guide the fortunes of the corporation and its business.

That traditional corporate model, which is essentially similar to structures available to business in most of the western world, continues to be a vehicle of choice for most businesses in Canada. However, as businesses have become more complicated and as the parties involved have become more sophisticated in defining the objectives to be achieved from their

organizational structure, they have looked for alternatives. As a result
the joint venture in one of its various forms is more and more being
chosen as a preferred alternative when two or more existing business
organizations, often quite different in personality, embark upon a new
enterprise.

In Canada there is no clear legal or other technical meaning for the
term *joint venture*. It is a term of art used by business people to describe
business relationships in which the participants are pursuing a defined,
specific, and limited objective; usually their separate personalities are not
merged into a new personality in the new venture. Rather than the new
enterprise having a unique corporate identity, with the freedom of action
and initiative which that implies, it will be a creature of precise contract.
While its facade appears to be that of a distinct and separate entity; beneath
that facade will be the separate identities of the owners. As will be seen,
a joint venture in Canada can be achieved through a variety of available
legal and accounting vehicles.

WHY A JOINT VENTURE?

If there is a universal definition of business or entrepreneurship, it is
probably this—the process by which capital and expertise are joined to
achieve a commercial objective. Both of these key ingredients are rare
commodities.

Capital is scarce and risk (or the commitment of capital) must be
carefully managed; therefore, many enterprises are too large to be undertaken individually. Real estate development provides a useful example
of this type of enterprise. While there are a variety of reasons why the
joint venture is widely used in real estate, one of the key reasons is that
the joint venture preserves scarce capital and allows a developer to spread
its risks. Rather than having 100 percent of one development which will
be subject to the fortunes of a single market, a single group of tenants,
particular design elements, or obsolescence, the developer or investor
can have 50 percent of two projects or 25 percent of four.

Similarly expertise in a number of different areas may be required
by a new enterprise. A successful real estate development will require
skills in municipal politics, construction, financing, leasing and property
management. Moreover it may require these skills in quite different types
of development. Thus a joint venture may, in one case, bring together

skills of financing from one joint venturer and development and construction from another. In another case one joint venturer may have skills in residential development; while another joint venturer would have the required skills for commercial development.

The joint venture may also be mandated by the nature of the underlying asset. Resource development, particularly the oil and gas industry in western Canada, is dominated by joint ventures. This reflects the fact that companies and individuals have historically been able, under land law, to acquire interests in land for exploitation of resources in what is known in law as a "tenancy-in-common." In a tenancy-in-common, two or more parties may own an individual interest in the same resource asset. In order for that asset to be exploited there must be either cooperation or an accounting among the owners. The rights of owners have developed from the common law, imported to Canada from Great Britain (which provides the foundation of the Canadian legal system) and from U.S. jurisdictions such as Oklahoma and Texas, which have dealt with similar issues and to which Canadian industry regulators and the courts have looked for guidance in establishing the rules which prevail in Canada. The result is a body of convention which has grown into the foundation for the separate agreements regarding individual properties. Thus there is an efficient and well-understood system, which not only makes the system of tenancy-in-common of resource properties workable but allows small investments in properties to be acquired and exploited efficiently.

In a somewhat similar way, the real estate development industry sometimes must use a joint venture to permit the most effective joint development of adjoining parcels of land or concurrent interests. Often the planning process will place a premium on cooperation between or among adjoining landowners. For example, the maximum density for a major development may only be available if all of the land in a particular block is included. Perhaps none of the owners is prepared to sell to another or to an outsider, or perhaps the resulting development would simply be too large to handle for either of the parties. A joint venture for the development is the obvious answer.

Sometimes a critical element of the new undertaking can only be obtained by sharing the benefits of ownership. Obvious examples are the marriage of distinct but necessary assets or other elements of a successful venture. Thus in the real estate industry there may be joint ventures between a developer and a major tenant or a supplier of capital. Often the joint venture could involve all three of these or even other parties.

The developer contributes the development skill and drive, the tenant the preleasing commitment (and thus an assured base of cash flow and leasing momentum for the project), and the lender provides the debt or perhaps even some necessary capital. Each shares in the long-term benefits which accrue to the project.

In other cases the joint venture may be less an agreeable option and more an absolute necessity. The Trans-Canada Telephone System was set up in 1976 between Telesat Canada, a corporation set up by the Canadian Parliament to operate satellite telecommunication systems, and the nine separate corporations which are the major providers of public telephone services in the various regions of Canada. The joint venture which they created was an extension of a much earlier agreement among the telephone companies permitting interconnections between the various systems. What is characterized as the Trans-Canada Telephone System might be thought to be a separate and distinct entity, but it is really just the creature of a complex contractual agreement among the parties to provide for the equitable and efficient joint use of their facilities for their greater mutual benefit. It is just a more complex version of the cooperation which exists between a cabdriver who pays the doorman of a hotel when he picks up a trip, or the charge back of the cost of warranty repairs by a car or appliance dealer to a distributor or manufacturer.

Often tax-related considerations are a major factor in choosing a joint venture as the vehicle for a particular undertaking. In its purest form, the joint venture attempts to direct all of the benefits and discretion related to the tax treatment of each party's interest in the undertaking to that party. Because of the particular approach reflected in the Income Tax Act of Canada which establishes unique rules for partnerships, and because corporations are treated as separate entities for tax purposes, the goals of tax planning for the joint venture are to avoid both partnership and corporate treatment. By being able to make the various selections available to taxpayers under the Income Tax Act without regard to the tax objectives of the other owners, and by being able to "flow through" the tax implications to the owner itself, a joint venturer can often achieve real advantages that would not otherwise be available. Thus in real estate, a co-owner who needs the tax shelter provided by capital cost allowance (depreciation) can take up to the maximum deduction allowed by the tax rules; while another co-owner, such as a developer who may not need such shelter on a current basis, need not take the deduction.

Sometimes a joint venture is appropriate simply because of the narrow purposes of the undertaking. Some otherwise competing business may enter into an arrangement to pool purchasing power or to engage in a joint-advertising campaign.

In summary, the complex nature of the modern business environment coupled with the broad range of various advantages to be realized from being able to tailor-make by contract a relationship between ongoing distinct entities, often makes the option of using a joint venture attractive.

WHAT IS A JOINT VENTURE?

As we have noted, the term *joint venture* is a term of art. Like so many other terms of art it has whatever meaning we choose to give it. If we accept that for our purposes "a joint venture includes any vehicle which preserves, to some extent at least, the unique personalities of the participants," then there are a variety of legal structures which may be used. The key in all cases is the imposition on the vehicle of a structure which permits the participants to continue to pull the strings; to directly, and typically separately, influence the direction of undertaking.

Although not usually the case, the most common business structure, the corporation, can be used as the vehicle for a joint venture. Under normal circumstances the shareholders of a corporation delegate most of the responsibility for direction of the corporation's affairs to the board of directors. Under Canadian law directors are supposed to act in the best interests of the corporation, which may, but not necessarily must, be what the shareholders would have them do. The problem is pointed up in the case where there are distinct groups of shareholders with different interests. A director who has been elected as the nominee of a controlling shareholder must still, in making his or her decisions as a director, consider the interests of all shareholders. In an incorporated joint venture the investors or shareholders maintain a much firmer control. In many early incorporated joint ventures the control was achieved by an understanding, sometimes reflected in contract sometimes not, that all owners would have director nominees who would be torchbearers at the board level for the owners they represented. New corporate legislation, such as that found at the federal level and in provinces such as Ontario and Alberta, now permits the shareholders of a corporation to enter into what is called a "unanimous shareholders' agreement." By this method the shareholders can displace the directors to the extent set out in the agreement and specifically determine by contract how the corporation is to operate. However, the corporation retains its separate personality in law. The shareholders continue to have the traditional insulation from liabilities that is provided by a corporation, and except in special circumstances (such as where the corporation has issued so-called flow-through shares under the Income Tax Act) the tax benefits and burdens are trapped in the corporation and cannot be directly passed along to the shareholders. If direct control by the investors is the objective to be achieved by the joint venture, the corporation may be used without difficulty. The corporation can also flow-through some of the tax or accounting effects of its operation to the investors either by specialized debt instruments or by acting simply as the nominee or trustee of the investor.

Another traditional vehicle which might be available for a joint venture is a partnership. In simplest terms *partnership* is defined in the Partnership Acts found in various Canadian provinces as "the relation that subsists between persons carrying on a business in common with a view to profit." A general partnership provides no protection to investors against partnership liabilities. Each partner is jointly and severally liable for any shortfall of the partnership assets in meeting partnership liabilities. Also troublesome is the concept found in partnership law that, unless a third party has notice to the contrary, ". . . each partner is an agent of the firm and of his other partners for the purpose of the business of the partnership." The major advantage which the partnership model provides for joint venturing is the ability to flow-through tax benefits and burdens to the partners. However, the significant disadvantages of general partnerships mean that they are not usually a good choice as a joint-venture vehicle.

On the other hand limited partnerships are often used in Canada for one form of specialized joint venture. That is a situation in which investors are prepared to delegate management and decision making to a manager, the general partner, but wish to retain the flow-through of tax benefits. In return for giving up its say in management the limited partner has his liability for obligations of the partnership limited to his actual investment.

Most joint ventures in Canada are simply creatures of contract. They may utilize corporations, trusts, or partnerships for particular aspects of the overall arrangement but the core of the relationship is a private contract. This is consistent with each of the parties retaining its own personality and character and with the undertaking itself not taking on a unique character of its own. However, the primary advantage of the relationship being a creature of contract is that the parties are given a free hand in settling the form and terms of the joint venture. The free hand of the parties is subject only to their insuring that they do not run into any technical problems and do not break any laws of general application. For example, as we will see, the parties may not want to risk being characterized as a partnership.

DISTINCTION BETWEEN PARTNERSHIP AND THE TYPICAL JOINT VENTURE

There is often confusion as to the difference between partnership and joint venture. Both are creatures of contract, and both have some similar qualities; however, the differences are very important. Thus, in the creation of most joint ventures one of the most important issues to be faced is how to ensure that whatever else the relationship is, it is not really a partnership. There are a number of reasons for this concern. A partnership, by law, makes each of the partners an agent for the partnership in the conduct of partnership business, unless the third party with whom the partner is dealing has notice of a limitation in the partner's authority. Each of the partners (and where the partners are corporations, those corporations' officers) has the ability to enter into contracts and to assume liabilities on behalf of the partnership. It is one thing to be pursuing a common business objective with another party; it is quite another to have to live with the possibility that that party can bind the partnership (and thus the other partners) in all manner of issues related to the business of the partnership, without having received specific authority from the partners to do so. In a joint venture there is usually no agency between the parties.

One of the fundamental elements of a general partnership is the unlimited liability of the partners. Inasmuch as the liability relates to the liabilities of the partnership business, the effect is that each partner becomes *jointly and severally* liable for all of the unsatisfied obligations of the partnership and not just severally liable for that partner's share. However, it should be noted that tax liability arising from partnership activities is not a partnership liability, so the joint liability of partners for partnership obligations does not extend to the tax bills of the individual partners arising from the partnership profits.

The effects of unlimited liability can be contained by a partner having its partnership interest held through a separate corporation, set up for this purpose alone. In such a case the unlimited liability in the partnership is backstopped by the limited liability of the single-purpose corporation holding the partnership interest. However, the shield which the corporation provides against liability is also a barrier to the flow-through of tax benefits from the partnership to the benefitting owner of the partnership interest. In a joint venture there should be no liability for the other party's share of the obligations of the venture.

If the activities of the venture are such that there is no harm to be suffered by ''trapping'' the tax consequences in a separate entity, then the single-purpose corporation acting as the nominee partner for a party can be tolerated. However, even in these circumstances the rigidity which the Income Tax Act imposes upon partners makes partnership an unattractive choice. That rigidity arises from the characterization, for income tax purposes, of a partnership as a separate and distinct entity in terms of calculation of income and various elections.

In a partnership the tax treatment to be elected by the partnership must be negotiated and settled among the partners. This is because the tax gatherer, while not looking to the partnership as a taxpayer, will look to the partnership as an entity for purposes of how taxable income has been calculated. The partnership itself will have its own year-end for tax purposes, and it will have its own financial statements for the tax purposes of the partners. The year-end will establish the point in time at which the partnership income (and the various decisions which are reflected in how that income was calculated) will be taken into the income of the partners themselves.[1] Those statements will reflect the various decisions and elections that the partners have made with respect to the tax treatment of the partnership income. The decisions are then necessarily adopted by each partner in how the partnership affairs are molded into the partners' overall taxation picture.

Freedom of choice should remain available if a joint venture is used. Depending on the type of business that it is in, or other business trans-

---

[1] A tax-planning technique frequently used by partnerships to take advantage of this rule is to establish the partnership year-end early in the taxation years of the partners, thus achieving a deferral in the reporting of that income.

actions which will have an impact on a taxpayer's overall tax position, a taxpayer may choose to treat income or available tax elections from a particular business activity in a way which is most beneficial to the taxpayer overall. If that activity is one which is carried on jointly with some other party, the taxpayer may not wish to be restricted in the tax treatment which it elects simply because the joint enterprise itself has made a decision to proceed in a particular manner.

There is one other significant difficulty in the area of income tax which makes partnership as a structure unattractive. Entities which look to the public markets as sources of their capital or which have fiduciary or quasi-fiduciary (*i.e.*, similar to trustees) responsibilities with respect to the funds they administer are often concerned about having their investments and income qualify as "legal for life." The term *legal for life* is really a nontechnical description of standards and tests contained in various federal and provincial statutes (such as the Income Tax Act) as to what qualifies for investing funds which qualify for tax-exempt treatment and which must be met in order for the investments to be permitted to be made by the organization which is subject to the test. For our purposes the difficulty arises because investments in partnerships are characterized as "foreign property" for various tax-exempt vehicles such as pension funds. Those vehicles in turn are restricted to having a total of 10 percent of their assets (based on book value) in foreign property. If it exceeds that limit, the vehicle is subject to a penalty tax. Since "foreign property" is so restricted and also includes a variety of desirable investments (such as U.S. stocks or property), most investors who are subject to such rules are anxious to insure that, wherever possible, investments be structured so that they are not characterized as partnerships and thus "foreign property."

Like any other issue which must be the subject of negotiation the resolution of accounting and tax issues by partners almost always involves compromise and a final position which is less than optimal for individual partners. In an era in which tax planning is a significant activity for most major businesses and in which the options with respect to the tax questions are many and varied, it is not surprising that few businesses find that they have or are likely to have objectives in this area which are precisely aligned with other parties with whom they are proposing a joint enterprise. The only significant advantage that a partnership structure provides for joint venturers is that it does permit the flow-through of the tax treatment adopted by the partnership to the partners.

When all of the disadvantages and uncertainties found in a partnership structure are considered, it is not surprising that partnership is not the vehicle of choice in most joint undertakings of two or more distinct businesses. While there are exceptions, most partnerships in Canada are found in limited areas. Professions like law and accounting continue to embrace the structure, perhaps because of a need to provide the perception of unlimited liability on the part of partners for their professional activities and because they are, in fact, businesses in which the objectives of the partners, both in tax and other areas, tend to be common ones. There is probably also some justification for the sometimes cynical observation that those professions are particularly resistant to change of any kind.

The other major exception is in the area of limited partnerships. These are now a widely used, if still somewhat mysterious, structures, which permit flow-through of tax advantages while providing limited liability. Because the structure requires a limited partner to be passive, if he is to avoid being characterized as a general partner and thus lose his limited liability, the structure is best suited and is most often used for market investments where the primary objectives for investors are tax benefits with limited or no management responsibilities.

As we have noted, there are many areas where the rules which apply to partnership are also applicable to other forms of joint venture. A recent high profile lawsuit which is presently making its way through the Canadian courts has important implications for parties proposing to engage in a joint venture. The plaintiff, International Corona Resources Ltd., owned certain mining rights in northern Ontario. The defendant, Lac Minerals Ltd. approached Corona with a view to establishing a possible joint venture or partnership to develop the rights. In the course of negotiation Corona revealed to Lac the results of Corona's test drilling, which indicated value in adjacent property. Corona attempted to acquire the property but was outbid by Lac. The property turned out to be one of the most successful gold claims in Canadian history. Corona sued.

At trial, the court applied partnership rules to the relationship between the parties, even though neither a partnership or any other form of joint venture was ever entered into by them. The court found that the disclosure of confidential information by Corona to Lac in the course of negotiation was passed only for the purpose of establishing the joint venture. Thus Lac had a trustee relationship in favour of Corona to hold and use that information for Corona's benefit.

The case clearly established two important standards for joint ventures. First, the highest standard of fairness and good faith will be expected by the courts to be found between joint venturers. Second, and perhaps even more important, this standard will not be confined to the period after the joint venture contract has been concluded, but will govern the conduct of the parties in the course of their negotiations and even if they are not successful in coming to an agreement.

The trial judgment in the *Corona* v. *Lac* case was confirmed on appeal. It is presently being further appealed to the Supreme Court of Canada. That appeal is expected to be heard in the fall of 1988.

CREATING A JOINT VENTURE WHICH IS NOT A PARTNERSHIP

Once we recognize that partnership is not the vehicle of choice for most joint undertakings by two or more businesses, then the question is how we create an acceptable vehicle. The key is really found in the last word. To avoid the possibility of being characterized as a partnership it is important to avoid having the joint activity characterized as a separate and distinct business or a separate vehicle. Most Partnership Acts in Canada define *partnership* as "the relationship that subsists between persons carrying on *a business* in common with a view to profit." The reference to *business* in the singular is critical. If the activity is separately characterizable as one business and not two or more businesses being carried on parallel, a key element of partnership will have been provided.

For this reason there is an understandable concern with the term *joint venture* itself. It has not taken on a technically understood meaning in Canada as being the antithesis of a single business. Thus the term is used gingerly for fear that it might imply a joint business, and thereby strike at the heart of the distinction between joint venture as we understand it for purposes of this discussion, and partnership. Thus joint ventures in real estate are typically called "co-ownerships" or "co-tenancies." This avoids use of the term *joint venture*. As well the term is useful because Partnership Acts give some help in distinguishing such relationships from a partnership by saying that such a relationship does not "of itself" create a partnership even if the "tenants or owners do . . . share profits made by the use of . . ." the subject property. The opposite analysis is even more important. If the activity in question cannot be characterized as a business then one of the required elements of the definition of a partnership will not have been provided.

In many agreements there is a bold declaration by the parties that their relationship is not a partnership. Unfortunately the question is not one which can be established by the declaration of the parties. Rather the question will be answered by the actual nature of the relationship which the parties have with one another in carrying on the activity. The well-crafted agreement will try to create a relationship in which the activities of the parties, in the day-to-day conduct of their affairs, is as much as possible inconsistent with them running a single common business. It is then extremely important for the parties to follow that structure in the day to day conduct of their affairs.

To see the type of structure which is created for a joint venture it is helpful to look at a typical real estate co-tenancy. The parties may have come together at a very early stage in the evolution of the project. Land may not have been assembled, the features of the project may not have been settled. Typically the parties enter into a variety of agreements. The most basic will be the Co-Tenancy Agreement itself. In addition there would usually be a "Development Agreement," a "Management Agreement," and an agreement or agreements providing a separate structure for day-to-day decision making—a means of making "business decisions" with the smallest practical risk of the whole venture being characterized as "a business."

The Co-Tenancy Agreement is the master document. It will contain the declaration against partnership. However, it will also put some meat on the bones of that declaration by declaring that the parties are not agents for one another. Since the Co-Tenancy Agreement is almost always a private document, and since for such a provision to be binding on outsiders if the relationship is a partnership, the declaration must be known by the outsiders, it may be of limited assistance in determining whether or not there is a partnership. However, these provisions are at least evidence of the intention of the parties.

If the parties are acquiring the subject real estate at this stage (whether from each other or from outsiders) every effort is made to avoid the appearance of a new and distinct business. Each party acquires a fractional interest in the whole and this is done as the first transaction. While it is recognized that the property conveyances will not have taken place without the conclusion of the Co-Tenancy Agreement, they are at least first in the sequence of events. Each party stands at the starting line of the new relationship holding an interest which in law is separate and distinct from that of the other parties. It is subject to certain rules as to how issues will be dealt with but the property interests themselves are each separate and distinct.

In effect the parties then say to one another: "We find ourselves as co-owners (or tenants-in-common); how can we order our affairs so each of us can most effectively develop our separate interests?" Clearly the answer to that question could be to contribute the property to a corporation or partnership. However, in effect the parties respond by saying: "Each of us wants to make the most profitable use of our property; each of us has objectives which we want to achieve; some of those objectives are common ones; others are not, what is more, neither of us wants to hold our interest indirectly through a share certificate or partnership interest." Each party simply wants to order its affairs to continue the tenancy-in-common, while at the same time maximizing the value of the investment of that party as an owner. Again the last point is critical. The parties are not committing to create a new vehicle and to maximize the value of the property of that new vehicle. Neither are they committing, except incidentally, to increase the value of the property of the other co-owner or co-owners. They are simply saying that each wants to pursue its own objectives and maintain as much control as possible over its own fate. However, they recognize that their best interests are served by cooperating in certain aspects of the development and operation of their property with other parties which have an interest in the same piece of real estate. Analogies are helpful here. The approach of the parties is not dissimilar to ownership of separate condominium units in the same project or the separate halves of a side-by-side duplex. There is significant freedom of action available to each owner, but in certain areas cooperation is necessary. In the case of a condominium, cooperation is necessary with respect to maintenance of common areas, the setting of rules, and the like. In a commercial development held in a co-tenancy, cooperation is necessary with respect to development and major new directions for the project.

On the other hand, the co-tenants in a commercial real estate joint venture may, and often do, retain individual control over rights of disposition, financing, tax treatment, and other similar areas. Obviously, the most sensitive and difficult areas relate to day-to-day management of the commonly owned property. The issue is relatively easily dealt with when there is little need for the exercise of discretion or for subjective decision making. For example, in joint-operating agreements typically found in the Canadian oil and gas industry, the operator is effectively vested with the responsibility of operation of the jointly owned property, and the other owners are relatively passive. In the case of the Trans-Canada Telephone System the court, which was deciding whether or not the relationship was a partnership, concluded that it was not a partnership at least partly because there was a need for unanimity on all decisions. While unanimity of all of the owners for all decisions technically is not itself inconsistent with the management of a single business, obviously such an arrangement for the operation of a business would be an exception to the norm.

Again the commercial real estate joint venture is instructive as a model of how the issue of day-to-day management may be dealt with. Typically, in this type of situation there are a large number of day-to-day details which must be tended to and a significant number of important but relatively routine decisions to be made. At the level of day-to-day details, there may be a need to deal with tenant disputes, perhaps to promote the property to improve its leasing activity, to acquire supplies, and to mandate minor repairs. At the second level, leases must be negotiated and settled, ongoing contracts with suppliers must be settled, and significant repairs and renovations must be considered and dealt with. Obviously at both levels such issues and decisions give a distinct impression of being activities related to "a business." Among more sophisticated projects where the consequences of being found not to be a co-tenancy could be devastating, a variety of structures have evolved to deal with the issue.

One obvious approach is for the owners to delegate all of the decision making in such areas to one of their number or to a third-party manager. The obvious difficulty is that such an arrangement may simply be a version of a partnership. A somewhat similar and more attractive approach is to enter into a head lease[2] with a manager and to build into the lease the right on the part of the lessee to make such decisions in its capacity as the holder of the long-term leasehold interest. The control mechanisms on the head lease will vary. At one extreme the head lease simply agrees to lease the premises at an agreed upon rent, to operate the property, and

---

[2]A *head lease* is a lease between an owner of a property as lessor and another party as lessee which permits the lessee to enter into subleases of the premises with various subtenants which will actually occupy the premises.

to enter into tenant subleases for its own account. It takes the risk and gets the reward of the actual management and leasing of the property. At the other extreme the head lessee makes the decisions but doesn't bear the risk or get the reward—the rent under the head lease simply amounts to a flow-through of the net "income" from the property. Obviously none of these arrangements is attractive to an owner who wants not only to have ownership but who also wants to be able to exercise some of the prerogatives of that ownership such as the right to actively participate in decision making.

Anxiety among lawyers about the possibility that an arrangement in which an owner or owners has too much direct "hands-on" control will be characterized as a partnership has resulted in the widespread use in Canada of what is called a "two-tiered" joint venture for major real estate projects. While very widely used and now generally accepted by many lawyers and other professional advisors as the model for real estate joint ventures, the structure itself has never been effectively reviewed or ruled upon by a superior court. Indeed this is true of virtually all of the structures crafted to avoid characterization as partnerships. Thus there is no judicial checklist of what is necessary to avoid being viewed by the courts as partnership. Widespread and continued use has given the two-tiered structure a formidable legitimacy, and it is now the accepted model for major real estate joint ventures.

Essentially the two-tier structure creates a formal break between the ownership and management of the property. In its purest form the structure sees the owners cooperate to acquire or develop a project. Then a new corporation is created which may (or may not) be beneficially owned by the co-owners. In the purest form there is at least an attempt to create some distinction between the ownership of the shares of the corporation and the ownership of the common property. For example, there might be some small difference in the sizes of the ownership proportions of each of the parties, or the interests may be held by different arms of the same parent. The co-owners as owners of the property then enter into a head lease for the entire project with the corporation as lessee. The essential terms of the lease are that there is a net flow-through of all but a small portion of the income generated by the corporation through its activities in subleasing and operating the property. Typically debt service and items like casualty insurance are the responsibility of the co-owners to be paid from the cash flow generated under the head lease, or where that cash flow is not sufficient, from the co-owner's other resources.

As has been noted, the flow-through from the corporation to the co-owners of cash generated in the hands of the corporation is not entirely complete. Typically the corporation is a small profit center in its own right. Thus 1 or 2 percent of cash flow to some maximum annual amount is retained by the corporation to be made subject to taxation and is either accumulated in the corporation or distributed from time to time in the form of normal corporate dividends. The theory is that this accumulation will distinguish the corporation from being characterized as a mere nominee of the co-owners and give it legitimacy as a separate business entity in its own right. In effect the relatively small accumulation and the recognition that this sum is subject to tax in the hands of the corporation, even if there was shelter available to shield the accumulation from tax in the hands of the co-owners, is a sort of "license fee" for the greater possibility that the structure of ownership of the property will be acknowledged to be a co-tenancy in the eyes of the tax gatherers (and to some minor extent in the eyes of others such as creditors who might otherwise benefit from a characterization of the ownership as being a partnership).

Although there has been no full-blown examination and review of the structure by a senior court, the structure does seem to be accepted by Revenue Canada, perhaps because it does not ultimately avoid tax liability arising from the operation of the property, but rather just shifts the point at which the liability might otherwise be calculated.

The general acceptance of the structure notwithstanding, the difficulties and risks associated with it must nonetheless be recognized. The structure itself is complicated and in order for it to work properly there must be care exercised to ensure that decisions are made at the appropriate level. The role of the corporation is typically not well understood by tenants and other third parties, or indeed by the owners themselves. They tend to forget that the corporation must be operated and its decisions made separately from the ownership. For example tenants' leases must be approved and entered into at the corporation level and decisions on such issues must be made by the corporation's board of directors. On the other hand, decisions about capital expenditures would normally be in the hands of the owners themselves. The participants regularly find themselves wearing the wrong hats. The accumulation of income and payment of tax by the corporation may be inefficient. The administration generally is complicated. Moreover, in the final analysis the accumulation of income and payment of tax, which is usually minor in comparison to the overall project, is certainly open to possible characterization as a sham without sufficient commercial justification or significance to be justified on its own merits. However, the two-tier structure is firmly entrenched and accepted in Canada as the most likely approach to be used for sophisticated real estate joint ventures.

ONGOING JOINT-VENTURE ISSUES

While the issues of the creation of the joint-venture structure consume much of the time and energy of the parties and their professional advisors, there is the usual spectrum of ongoing problems which must be addressed in the final structure. In most instances these are not unlike the issues addressed in any partnership or corporate structure—they are issues common to any relationship between two or more parties.

Management

Because, at least on the surface, the joint venture is not a separate entity it should not have to have its own management structure. Since it is not a business, it doesn't need one of the essential elements of a business— its own distinct management. However, the commonly held assets must be operated, revenues distributed, and decision making facilitated.

In some cases pure theory is abandoned and a separate administration set up. However, usually in such cases that separate administration is a separate entity, also owned by the co-owners but separate from the joint-venture assets, as in the case of the corporation in the two-tier real estate structure discussed above. It is contracted by the co-owners to manage the enterprise. The fee structure is likely to be structured to ensure that only a minimum "profit" is retained and that the corporation's assets are limited only to those directly related to its administration activities. Such an arrangement may deliver the benefits of a separate corporate identity at relatively little cost. The ambiguity of the joint-venture structure to the casual outside observer is avoided. The third party believes that a corporation with which he deals is not only the operator but also the owner of the assets. The owners may be sheltered from certain unattractive contractual obligations. In the most obvious example, the corporation may be the employer for the project with the result that it, and not the joint venturers in their own rights, is to collective agreements and other labor contracts and obligations.

In other cases the theory is abandoned altogether and the management is simply regarded as a necessary element of the co-ownership of the joint-venture assets. In such cases it is not a separate profit center but rather is simply lost in the confusion of other larger issues. Not surprisingly the joint venturers' professional advisors typically are not impressed by such an arrangement.

Often management is undertaken by one of the co-owners (either directly or through an affiliate) or by an outsider under a management or operating agreement. Such an appointment may reflect the reality that the appointee has in effect put the joint venture together, and simply brought in the other parties as a form of fully participating financing. The benefits to the manager include the right to the fee income generated under the contract. However, perhaps even more important in many cases, the manager continues to be perceived as the "owner" of the joint-venture property. Its corporate identity continues to have a high profile, and all but the most sophisticated outsiders are unaware that the manager may have a small or even nonexistent ownership interest. This is particularly the case in the real estate and oil and gas industries. Most major real estate developments undertaken by developers are joint ventures, yet the developer is usually perceived as being a sole owner. In the oil and gas industry the operator of a well is usually perceived as the owner. Often the other joint-venture partners are also happy with this result since it allows them a continuing low profile with respect to their investments.

Decision Making

Decision making in any situation where there are competing interests is always a difficult issue. Not surprisingly, there is no rule of thumb as to how the issue is dealt with. Where there are several co-owners it is most likely that some form of majority vote mechanism will be used. Often the fear of a tyranny of the majority is tempered by separating out issues of major importance for higher or different tests or even veto rights. Usually there are special restrictions on a party voting on issues where it has a conflict of interest—for example the renewal of a management agreement in which the owner is to be appointed the manager.

Where there is a smaller number of parties, and particularly where they are relatively evenly matched as to size, the issue is more difficult. One possibility, although rarer than might be expected, is a 49 to 51 percent type of voting relationship. More likely there will be a recognition of the practical difficulties that arise when a major owner has no voting strength. Thus it is not unusual to find a requirement for unanimity on all or at least most decisions. Such an arrangement obviously necessitates machinery to deal with the real possibility of a deadlock.

Liquidity and Breaking a Deadlock

Upon reflection it will be clear that the need for liquidity and the need to be able to break a deadlock are really just the opposite sides of the same coin. A properly structured investment must provide a means for the parties to individually turn their investment to account. In a like manner the joint venture must be assured of a means of dealing with a situation in which the parties simply can't agree on an issue. The obvious solution in such a case is for one or more of the parties to leave.

Many joint-venture agreements tie the liquidity provisions to a fundamental disagreement among the parties. Obviously that approach puts a premium on creating a disagreement by a party who simply wants to turn its investment to account.

The area of liquidity provisions is fertile ground for creative structures and solutions. Where the identity of individual parties is not terribly important, the easiest solution to the liquidity issue is to simply give each party a right to sell its interest to any other party, whether already a participant in the joint venture or not, subject only to that party entering into the necessary joint-venture agreements. A variation often found is to permit such a conveyance but only after the operation of a mechanism giving existing parties a right of first refusal. Similar provisions may also apply with respect to the rights of a party to mortgage its interest in the joint-venture assets. The mortgagee must agree to be bound by the joint-venture agreement and to bind any purchaser of a foreclosed interest from it, while usually also giving the other parties a first right to acquire any foreclosed interest in the hands of the mortgagee.

Sometimes a "right of first offer" is viewed as being more practical than a "right of first refusal." In a first refusal there is always a difficulty in finding an outside purchaser who is prepared to make a binding offer which can then be used as the basis for soliciting other competing offers. In a first offer the party wishing to sell sets his offering price and terms which he offers to the other parties. If they pass, he is then free to sell to outsiders on the same (or better to him) terms for a given period of time.

Where the joint venturers are disproportionate in interest or where one of them has brought some unique quality to the project (*i.e.*, financing) a party may have the right to "put" its interest to the other party or parties who are obligated to buy. Obviously the biggest problem is pricing. Where pricing issues are likely to be relatively objective a formula may work. Otherwise arbitration or appraisal (usually based on agreed-upon standards) may have to be resorted to.

Where there are only two (or at most three) parties or interested groups involved in a joint venture, the agreements may provide for what is graphically known as a "shotgun buy sell." This approach provides a means of dealing with the two most bothersome issues which arise when one or both of the parties who have been partners in a venture conclude that they must go their separate ways—setting a price and settling which of the parties will remain in the venture and which will leave. While there are a variety of refinements to the basic approach, the "shotgun" in its simplest form is straightforward. At any time, either of the parties can give a notice to the other commencing the process. The notice is in effect an offer to sell the interest in the joint venture to the other party at a given price. In the joint-venture agreement, the parties have agreed that, in the event such an offer is made and the party which receives the offer rejects it (in other words, says that it is not prepared to buy the other's interest at the offered price), that party is deemed to have agreed to sell its interest in the venture to the party which made the original offer *at the same price and on the same terms.*

The process is a variation on the old solution offered by wise parents to two children fighting over how to divide up a treat: one child divides it and the other chooses which part it wants to take. Because in the shotgun the party which initiates the process can't be sure whether it will be the buyer or the seller it must be scrupulously careful in setting the price. Because by the joint-venture agreement the parties have agreed that the process, once started, will result in one party ultimately selling to the other, it is not a process which can be started lightly. On the other hand it provides a guarantee that in the event the parties (or either of them) come to the conclusion that their joint venture can no longer work, there is a way of bringing if efficiently to an end.

There are a number of points which must be remembered in structuring a shotgun buy sell if it is to work effectively. Obviously the parties must have relatively well-matched financial strength. Otherwise the process can be used as a means by which a weaker party can be taken advantage of by a stronger party. In the same way the procedure works best if the parties are of approximately equivalent size. There must be clear limitations on the way in which the offer is structured—in other words, the process works best where it is required to be a cash offer without any unique terms. If there are elements of the joint venture which are separate from ownership, but which reflect part of the contribution being made by one side or the other, there must be a means of dealing with these. For example if one party has provided financing to the venture on nonmarket terms, then there must be a means of valuing that financing or any valuation of the ownership interest of the party if the financing were to be unfairly weighted against the party. There must be a sufficiently long response time, so that a party which receives the first offer can make reasoned efforts to evaluate the offer and see whether it can arrange financing for a purchase. Finally, the process obviously works best where there are only two parties. Where there are more than two parties, the mechanism must provide a way of involving all of them or provide an alternative way for the excluded parties to gain their own liquidity. Sometimes where there are several parties the shotgun machinery essentially has the effect of placing all nonofferors in one camp and requires a consensus to develop in that group before it can respond to the initial offer. The consensus building may require the triggering of a separate shotgun within that group before it can respond. Alternatively in some situations a small participant will be excluded from the shotgun but will have a right to ''put'' its interest to the others, or perhaps be subject to requirement to sell its interest if the number of other parties is reduced to one.

The great advantage of a shotgun is that it is simple, straightforward, and imposes a fundamental honesty on the parties as they deal with one another. The honesty is not only in the question of pricing but also in the relationship which must exist among the parties during the life of the joint venture. If the parties all know that an efficient mechanism exists to effect a divorce, so that no party can be given an unfair tactical advantage in the relationship, it is more likely than not that reasonableness will prevail.

The beauty of the joint venture approach to new business relationships is not found in any particular advantage which precedent may suggest is available. Rather the joint venture should be viewed as a wide-open opportunity for the parties to create precisely the relationship which best suits their purposes. The limitations on the joint venture are virtually all of a nature which can be resolved by creativity on the part of the parties and their advisors. This being the case, it is almost certain that joint ventures, in all of their various forms, will become more and more common.

CHAPTER 16

JOINT VENTURING IN MEXICO

Gilbert Alvarez
Banco Cafetero International Corp.

INTRODUCTION

The United Mexican States, or Mexico, includes an area of 1,958,201 sq. kms. and occupies the major part of the region between the United States and South America, bordered on the south by Central America. Mexico's total population of approximately 80 million people is grouped together in three major industrial urban centers. Almost 60 percent of the total population is represented by urban dwellers.

Census figures indicate that the capital of Mexico, the Federal District (D.F.), now contains over 20 million people. The three major cities in which the population is concentrated are the Federal District, Guadalajara, and Monterrey. Other cities and towns which are beginning to emerge as industrial, urban, and economic motor centers are Querétaro, Tamaulipas, State of Mexico, Chiapas, Veracruz, and the peninsula of Yucatan.

According to the Political Constitution of the United Mexican States, adopted in 1917, the political regime of the country is defined as a democratic and representative federal republic. It is constituted of 31 free and sovereign states united in one federation, and the Federal District, where the capitol, Mexico City, is located. The constitutional structure of Mexico is the same as that of the United States, with the supreme power of the federation divided by its functions into legislative, executive, and judiciary branches. Unlike the President of the United States, however, the President of Mexico is elected to one life-term of six years, after which there is no reelection. This allows for the administration's policies to be carried out in a more stable and continuous environment, so that development and modernization plans can be fulfilled within the same term.

Direct foreign investment, meaning the entry of any foreign capital into Mexico, has always been prominent. In fact, it has been the foundation of Mexico's development and industrialization. Foreign investment policies have always been flexible in one way or another, and have provided many opportunities to the prospective foreign investor.

Mexico has always been an eager recipient of foreign capital. To this day, authorities continue to give incentive and help to investors who wish to initiate financial transactions in Mexico. The National Commission on Foreign Investment was devised to guard the country's political, social, and economic interests as well as to aid, guide, and protect the foreign investor. This commission, based upon the 1973 Law to Promote Mexican Investment and to Regulate Foreign Investment, serves as the vehicle by which foreign investment in the country is regulated, and establishes limits on the amount of foreign participation allowed in certain sectors of the economy, according to the type of industry.

The general rule for the mix of foreign investment capital in a corporation located in Mexico is 51 percent national capital and 49 percent foreign capital. This allocation of investment capital is the most widely accepted, and the one that provides the greatest ease for the foreign incorporator to follow when filing with the authorities for authorization to enter into a joint venture. If a foreign individual or corporation wishes to invest in a proportion not exceeding 49 percent of the firm's capital, it may do so simply by registering with the National Commission on Foreign Investment. (Ninety percent of the applications submitted within the last three years have been approved by the Commission.)

Partnership with a Mexican entrepreneur can facilitate access to the domestic market, as well as good treatment from Mexican banks. In addition, when Mexican participation in a joint venture is more than 50 percent, favorable financial conditions and fiscal treatment can be obtained from the Mexican government. In cases where foreign capital provides majority ownership, authorization by the National Commission on Foreign Investment is required.[1]

---

[1]A legal exception expressly authorizes foreign investments of up to 100 percent in the capital stock of in-bond companies, or for those wishing to operate in the textile or automotive industries. An in-bond company or a *maquiladora* is a company formed with 100 percent foreign consumption. Traditionally, these have been companies formed along the U.S.-Mexican border to complement or

PRECEDENCE, TRENDS, AND CONSIDERATIONS
WHICH PROMPT A JOINT VENTURE IN MEXICO

History of Foreign Investment in Mexico

Foreign investment has always been present in Mexico. In its early years, Mexico was viewed as a gold mine in every sense. Foreign entrepreneurs originally installed companies to extract natural resources. As time passed, a great number of extracting and manufacturing companies were in foreign hands. But profits were always repatriated back to their countries, leaving Mexico with a very low national income.

American entrepreneurs, attracted by huge profits, the close proximity to the United States, and the ability to supply their own national demand, installed operations in Mexico. The accessibility of local markets and low labor costs, along with the availability of natural resources and primary factors of production, were fundamental reasons for the attractiveness of Mexico as a market for U.S. companies.

As a consequence, Mexico's economic and industrial infrastructure did not develop at the same pace as did the foreign companies. Nevertheless, the exports Mexico generated and inflow of foreign capital proved to be beneficial to the nation's balance of payments.

The founding of the first national government after the Independence Movement of 1910 not only allowed Mexico to take advantage of foreign investment, but also encouraged U.S. firms to invest in Mexico. Such foreign capital was used by the government along with Mexican capital. During this time, foreign investment was concentrated mainly in the extractive sector of the economy. Mexico, being abundant in natural resources, was not concerned with their depletion, and U.S. firms engaged in exploitive mining. Mexico saw the opportunity to receive the capital needed to develop the country, the opportunity to create industrial centers to supply the people of those regions with jobs, and the opportunity of allowing the industrial centers to interact with the national economy.

During World War I and afterwards, presidents gave "open door" policies to foreign investment. They granted attractive fiscal arrangements to foreign corporations and adapted the country's national goals to meet

---

finish the production of foreign goods (usually American) and to provide development and employment in this region. The government is now promoting industrial parks located outside the border belt for in-bond companies to install. One such park is in the city of Merida in the Yucatan peninsula.

the needs of the corporations. This unlimited treatment was very instrumental in attracting foreign capital.

In 1938, Mexico's economic liberalism was made manifest with the nationalization of the oil industry. At this time, the National Petroleum Company of Mexico (PEMEX) was founded. Other energy-related activities were also nationalized as well as public transportation, communications, and the production and distribution of gas and electricity. This was known as the Mexicanization Process, and was focused on protecting key industries that were vital to Mexico's strategic economic plans for growth and development.

During the period between the 40s and mid-50s, little attention was paid to the conflict between Mexican nationalism and foreign interests. It was a period marked by conservatism in this respect. However, it was not until the mid-1940s, when manufactured imports were scarce, that the industrialization process in Mexico escalated. On June 29, 1944 an "Emergency Decree" was enacted, as an effort by the Mexican government to control the entry of foreign capital into Mexico's booming economy. Priority was given to capital investment that would help Mexico's war effort and contribute permanently to the development of the country. This decree vested authority in the Secretariat of Foreign Affairs and authorized it to grant priority approval to every corporation as part of the incorporation process. The Secretariat became the effective government agency determining whether the mix of foreign and Mexican capital in joint ventures was consistent with government policy and had the final say on the establishments of trusts in the prohibited zones.[2]

After World War II, Mexico curtailed its imports by establishing an import substitution policy. American companies entered the newly created manufacturing industry with the same force they had entered the extractive one. Consequently, the manufacturing industry began to contribute to Mexico's economic development by lowering unemployment and boosting the nation's GNP. With the Lopez Mateos Administration (1958–

---

[2]The "Calvo Clause," included in Article 27 of the Mexican Constitution, Paragraph 7, Fraction 1, states that "only Mexicans by birth or naturalization and Mexican associations have a right to acquire dominion over lands, waters and their access or to obtain concessions to exploit mines and waters. The State may grant the same right to foreigners as long as they register with the Secretariat of Foreign Affairs as nationals in relation to such wants and rights and not invoke the protection of their governments in relation to these wants and rights. In case that they go against the convention they will lose the rights they could have acquired."

1964), the country entered a more conservative era, brought about by a major nationalist policy. It was during 1959 and 1962, respectively, when precedents of the Mexicanization Process were activated with the "Mining Laws" and the "Decree of Automotive Integration." Both the mining laws and the automotive decree were measures taken on behalf of the government to protect the nation's strategic industries for economic development.

The Diaz Ordaz Administration (1964–1970) continued the same policy and took it one step further with the "Mexicanization Decree of 1970." This decree gave the government the constitutional power to Mexicanize foreign firms at any time it deemed necessary to further the nation's economic development.

Of all the Mexican administrations, the most extreme in its treatment of foreign investment has been the Echeverria Administration (1970–1976). Prior to this administration, the absence of restrictions with respect to areas of manufacturing where investments were allowed, the fiscal incentives, and lack of technological limitations, combined with the existence of a captive market and the ease with which profits and royalties were repatriated through a free foreign exchange system, made Mexico a very desirable and attractive arena for foreign investment.

In the mid-70s, however, a wave of nationalism led to new rules and guidelines to regulate and protect direct foreign investment. Two separate documents evolved: the "Law of the Register of Transfer of Technology and the Use and Exploitation of Trademarks and Patents" (1972), and the "Law to Promote Mexican Investment and Regulate Foreign Investment" (1973).[3]

It was during this period that all joint ventures of foreign and Mexican companies were forced to become Mexican corporations and had to be stated as such in their articles of incorporation.

During the Lopez Portillo Administration (1976–1982), the policies basically remained the same with variations in flexibility. The United States has always been the largest investor in Mexico. During the De

---

[3]The law of transfer of technology and trademarks and patents has as its primary objective the regulation of the transfer of technology, reducing its costs, strengthening the negotiating position of the firms and the avoidance of the use of restrictive practices. The law to promote Mexican investment and regulate foreign investment defines the activities in which direct foreign investments are allowed and establishes the limits of its participation in new firms and in preestablished firms.

LaMadrid administration in 1986, the United States held 63 percent of the total foreign investment in Mexico, followed next by West Germany with 8.5 percent, Japan with 5.5 percent, Switzerland with 7 percent and 16 percent held by other countries combined. (Exhibit 16.1) It is estimated that for 1987 the total U.S. foreign investment in Mexico will amount to $1.5 billion, an increase of 698 percent over 10 years.

EXHIBIT 16–1
Foreign Investment

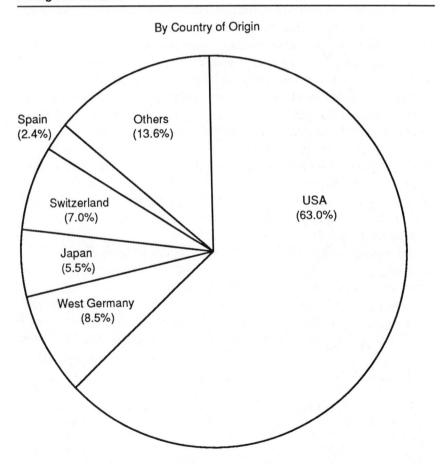

By Country of Origin

Spain (2.4%)

Others (13.6%)

Switzerland (7.0%)

USA (63.0%)

Japan (5.5%)

West Germany (8.5%)

ECONOMIC TRENDS AND POLITICAL CURRENTS INFLUENCING JOINT VENTURES IN MEXICO

Economic Policy 1982–1988

In accordance with The National Program for Industrial Development and Promotion for Foreign Commerce, initiated by the De LaMadrid Administration, this policy for foreign investment is a plan to oversee the development of national technology, substitute selectively as many imports as possible, and generate exports through the competitive production of international goods. The central consideration of this policy is to selectively promote foreign investment so it does not displace the national capital or dominate any one area, production line, or priority consumer goods that the national industry may produce. Its goal is to facilitate the entry of foreign capital and guide it toward areas where its contribution will be beneficial to the development objectives of the country.[4] To meet the country's economic objectives the national program takes on a supervisory role to assure the fulfillment of such.

Foreign capital investments are preselected by the government to insure the industrial and technical development of the country. The logic behind this is to ensure Mexico's overall economic development strategy. Activities which the government defines as suitable to accomplish its goals receive priority.

The process of selectively promoting joint ventures effectively guides foreign capital toward activities that ensure the inflow of foreign exchange. This inflow should be capable of incorporating and adopting adequate technologies for contributing to the scientific and technological development of the country and to complex ventures that require a high marginal investment. The purpose behind this is to contribute in a positive manner to the development objectives of the national program without displacing the Mexican entrepreneur.

Joint ventures, besides being channeled toward activities which are complex and require a high marginal investment, are also encouraged in

---

[4]"Foreign Investment Regulation Policies." *Programa Nacional de Fomento Industrial y Comercio Exterior 1984–1988.* (National Program for the Promotion of Industry and Foreign Commerce.) (Federal Government of Mexico: 1984).

high technology and export products. In cases where the joint venture is deemed beneficial to Mexico, the policy to promote foreign investment is applied by means of specific projects. In these cases, competing technologies are put up for a tender offer in order to select the most suitable.

Preferential treatment is given to joint ventures as a mechanism to guarantee real transfers of technology in areas where the technological factor is a decisive one in reaching high levels of international competitiveness. These foreign/national ventures are encouraged in order to further the country's import-substitution policy and to integrate the national chains of production that receive governmental priority. Projects that are principally destined for export are considered priority as long as they are not subject to specific regulations. A principal objective of the current national policy is to diversify the sources of origin of investment capital in order to expand the spectrum of international growth inside Mexico.

Joint ventures are also regulated in regard to the percentage of company ownership. Regulation thus assures that the Mexican partner exercises a real control over the decision-making process of the firm. Joint ventures are authorized by the Mexican government for the capitalization of passive assets in firms where the passive-active ratio is deemed high, for expansion of already installed firms, or for firms which hold prior commitments. Examples of such commitments could be those that increase national integration, subcontract to Mexican firms, firms that better the foreign exchange budget or achieve a surplus, and those that open markets for nonpriority sectors. Special consideration is given to those that hold a foreign exchange deficit or those that expand sectors that could contribute to the country's strategic economic policies.

In relation to Mexico's balance of payments and industrial structure, joint ventures are regulated in order to ensure equilibrium in the balance of payments and to achieve a greater integration with national production. In addition, mechanisms and instruments have been established through the National Commission on Foreign Investment (NCFI). Joint-ventured firms are required to present an annual foreign exchange budget and keep the national commission abreast of all of the importing that they do.

In relation to financing, joint ventures are regulated through a central plan that rations the access of joint-ventured firms to local credit depending upon the availability of required resources. This is done to avoid distortions in the national financial and credit system.

In relation to the transfer of technology, joint ventures are regulated by selecting the most convenient technologies appropriate for Mexico's development objectives and industrialization strategy. Through the adaptation and assimilation of foreign technology, the process of effective transfer of technology is met. To guarantee this, predetermined volumes of production are subcontracted out to small and medium-sized firms. Additionally, the training of technicians must be completed at the firm's world headquarters. Payments for foreign technology are authorized by function according to the continuous transferability of new technology, training, and access to new developments.

Mexico's economic policy is linked directly to the National Development Plan, the highest ranking document for national planning. It constitutes the general framework for the integration of sectorial programs. Its goal is to upgrade the economy through the utilization of the social, sectorial, and regional policies. The rationale behind the national plan is summed up in the economic reordering and structural change strategy, which states two primary objectives. The first is to lower inflation, stabilize foreign exchange, and protect employment and basic consumption. The second is to concentrate on the social and redistributive aspects of Mexico's growth. Ideally, its effect will be to reorient and modernize the productive and distributive sector of the economy, to decentralize the areas of production, to adopt new financing modes for development priorities, to fortify the rectorship of the State, and to stimulate growth in social and private sectors.

BEHAVIOR OF FOREIGN INVESTMENT THROUGH JOINT VENTURE

Joint venture is viewed as a positive step toward achieving Mexico's national goals for economic development. It complements internal savings, increases the flow of currency, and leads to technological development. From 1970 to 1976, the total accumulated foreign investment in Mexico increased from $3.7 billion to $5.3 billion, representing a 43 percent increase. From 1977 to 1982, new foreign investment rose steadily, reaching a record level of $1.7 billion for that year. In 1982, as a result of the economic crisis and the shortage of domestic resources for joint ventures, foreign investment fell by 36 percent from 1981 to $626

million. Thus, in 1982, total accumulated foreign investment reached
$10.7 billion, showing an increase of $5.1 billion in the 1977–1982
period. In this period, total accumulated foreign investment nearly dou-
bled, representing nearly 50 percent of all foreign investment in Mexico's
foreign investment history.[5]

Authorities claim that, as a result of the policy carried out during
the last three years, the inflow of foreign investment in Mexico has
surpassed that of 1982; the foreign investment authorized by the NCFI
in 1984 was 110 percent more than in 1983. For 1985, the value of foreign
investment authorized by the NCFI rose to $1.8 billion, an increase of
nearly 77 percent. As of December 31, 1985, total accumulated authorized
foreign investment was $14.6 billion; 27 percent was approved during
the present administration.[6] (See Exhibit 16.2.)

The joint ventures approved by the commission in 1985 were allocated in the following way. The transformation industry received the bulk
of the total investment with 65 percent, followed second by the trade and
services sector with 34 percent. These figures show the importance of

EXHIBIT 16–2
Direct Foreign Investment

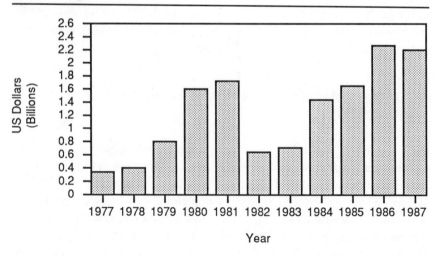

[5]Bank of Mexico. (Statistical Information 1987)
[6]*Ibid.*

Mexico's foreign investment policy in the strengthening of its industrial infrastructure and its economy.[7]

Examining the participation of joint ventures in the economy, the commission lists 6,895 firms which have ventured in this manner. Of these, 2,820 reported a majority share of foreign capital, and 4,075 firms reported a foreign investment of 49 percent or less of their capital stock. Based on the 6,895 firms, an analysis was carried out by the commission to determine their location by state, as well as the number of firms by economic sector. With respect to the distribution of foreign investment, it was concluded that Mexico City is the most highly concentrated area with 66 percent of the total; second is the State of Mexico with 12 percent. Eighty percent of the total foreign investment is concentrated in the metropolitan and surrounding areas.[8]

MEASURES AND CONDITIONS IN JOINT VENTURES

The Mexican government has effected four major ways to invest jointly with national firms in Mexico.[9]

The first is by way of the Export Bank. The Export Bank (BAN-COMEXT) provides, through its representative offices abroad, a link between firms interested in joint venturing and Mexican firms willing to receive foreign investment. Promotional activities of the commercial advisory offices of the bank publicize the opportunities. Once the bank has generated interest from prospective investors, it relays the information to the Secretariat of Foreign Commerce and Industrial Development (SECOFI).

The second is by way of international development corporations. BANCOMEXT supervises through authorization from the National Commission on Foreign Investment the contribution of ''venture capital'' by seven international development financing corporations. These institu-

---

[7]*Ibid.*

[8]''General Direction on Foreign Investment Promotion.'' *An Investment Guide to Mexico.* (Federal Government of Mexico: 1985).

[9]Ministry of Commerce and Industrial Promotion. ''General Direction on Foreign Investment Promotion.'' *Overview of Foreign Investment in Mexico.* (Mexico: 1986).

tions often help finance joint ventures by acquiring shares and participating in the resulting company and/or grant loans, channel funds for research, provide collateral and finance the cost of industrial studies.[10]

The third is by way of installing manufacturing plants. Small and medium-sized companies can joint venture in Mexico with a foreign capital ratio in excess of 50 percent as long as they comply with the requisites stated in the 1973 law.[11]

The fourth is by way of debt-equity swaps. In order to cut back on Mexico's foreign public debt and to increase the productivity of joint-venture investments, the government has developed a means by which to convert its foreign debt into opportunities for joint ventures. The "Operating Manual for the Capitalization of Liabilities and Substitution of Public Debt by Investment" contains the legal, regulatory and economic policy arrangements established in the 1973 law. This mechanism came about through the Restructure Agreement on Mexico's foreign debt

---

[10]National Commission of Foreign Investment. *Law to Promote Mexican Investment and to Regulate Foreign Investment*. General Resolution No. 14, (Federal Government of Mexico: 1986).

1. Neutral capital is defined as that which is invested by international financial development corporations, where the main objective consists in fostering the economic and social growth of developing countries, through temporary risk capital. The National Commission on Foreign Investment can authorize the rule of neutral capital to international financial development corporations such as the International Financial Corporation (ICF) of the World Bank, The Japanese International Fund for Economic Cooperation (OECF), The Finnish Fund on Industrial Cooperation for Developing Countries (FINNFUND), The Swedish Fund of Industrial Cooperation for Developing Countries (SWEDFUND), and the Interamerican Investment Corporation (IIC) of the Interamerican Development Bank.

2. Authorizations granted by the National Commission will be subject to compliance with the conditions set forth in Articles 5, 13, and 14 of the 1973 law.

[11]National Commission on Foreign Investment. *Law to Promote Mexican Investment and to Regulate Foreign Investment*. Federal Government of Mexico: General Resolution No. 15, (1973).

1. When constituting small and medium-sized companies with majority of foreign capital, no authorization from the National Commission is required as long as they comply with the following conditions:

A) In relation to the capital's origin: The main office at the international level should not exceed net sales of $8 million U.S. dollars and should not employ more than 500 persons.

B) In relation to the capital's destiny: The company joint ventured must be a manufacturing firm exclusively with at least 250 employees. Net sales in Mexico should not exceed 1.1 billion Mexican pesos/year at 1985 prices. It must export 35 percent of its annual production and maintain equilibrium in its trade balance of payments. The firm must be established within the geographical zones destined for economic development and industrial decentralization as stated in the "Official Gazette of January 22, 1986."

EXHIBIT 16–3
Public Foreign Debt

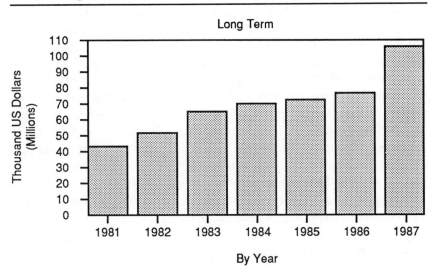

at the Euromoney Conference in 1985. Through these swaps, the Mexican government seeks to sell between $680 and $700 million U.S. dollars of its foreign debt (which now amounts to $105 billion U.S. dollars) for shares in Mexican private or public companies. Foreign investors may acquire these debt rights at a discount (now on the secondary market at approximately a 47 percent discount) and exchange them for shares in Mexican companies. This is a new and viable method of joint venturing in Mexico and allows a prospective investor to participate in an established firm.[12]

Treatment of Foreign Investment

All direct foreign investment in Mexico is regulated and supervised by the National Commission of Foreign Investment and the Underministry of Foreign Investment and Technology Transfer through the 1973 law on

---

[12]National Commission of Foreign Investment. *Manual Operativo para la Capitalizacion de Pasivos y Subtitucion de Deuda Publica por Inversion.* (Operating Manual to Capitalize and Substitute Foreign Debt for Investment). (Federal Government (Passive Assets) To-Liabilities of Mexico: 1986).

Foreign Investment.[13] This statute establishes limits on the quantity of foreign participation allowed in identifiable sectors of the economy according to the type of industry destined. For example, the government reserves exclusive operational jurisdiction in the oil industry, in the petrochemical industry, in radioactive mineral exploitation, in nuclear energy, and in certain mining operations. In addition, no direct foreign investment is permitted in electric utilities, railroads, or telegraphic or wireless communication. The government reserves for 100 percent-owned Mexican companies involvement in radio and television broadcasting, all forms of urban and interurban transportation, gas distribution, and forest exploitation. Generally, if a foreign firm desires to own a percentage of a Mexican company which is less than 49 percent, it may do so by registering with the National Registry of Foreign Investment. If it wishes to joint venture as a majority-owning partner, it must seek approval from the National Commission of Foreign Investment.

Establishing a Corporation

Foreigners are permitted to incorporate in Mexico as Mexican Corporations. This widely used method enables foreigners to limit their liability to the invested equity. Many corporations are federally chartered and consequently carry no state franchise tax. All corporations formed in Mexico, whether owned by nationals or foreigners, are subject to Mexican corporate law.

Size, venture objective, capital requirements, liability of exposure of each partner, organization and management requirements, and profit repatriation desires play an important role in choosing the corporate organization best suited for the venture. In general, there are two types of business entities which are similar to U.S. corporations, the limited liability company (S. de R.L.) similar to a closely held corporation in the

---

13National Commission an Foreign Investment. *Law to Promote Mexican Investment and to Regulate Foreign Investment. Legal Framework and its Application.* (Federal Government of Mexico: 1986).

As stated in Article 1 of the Foreign Investment Law, "the purpose is to promote Mexican investment and regulate foreign investment in order to stimulate a just and balanced development and consolidate the country's economic independence." The law consists of 31 articles, 5 transitory articles, and 15 general resolutions.

United States, and the stock company (Sociedad Anonima, S.A.) which is in fact a better vehicle in most cases than a joint venture.[14]

Two types of stock companies are authorized, the pure S.A. where the authorized capital may be increased at a later date in accordance with the company's articles of incorporation, without the requirement of an extra meeting of shareholders and without the need for charter amendment.

A foreign investor may invest in a firm through the stock market by purchasing stock in an amount of no more than 5 percent of the total shares outstanding. Within the past year the Mexican stock market has climbed 105 percent, claiming an unprecedented boom in the history of the market. There are currently approximately 30 brokerage houses through which an investor may buy or sell securities.

In order to establish a Mexican corporation, the following prerequisites must be met:

1. There must be at least five shareholders. Four shareholders may own a nominal amount of shares which must be registered with the National Commission.
2. A permit from the Ministry of Foreign Affairs is required. This permit specifies the name of the company, corporate purposes, address, duration, capital stock, and nationality of the incorporators.
3. The articles of incorporation, bylaws, minutes of the first shareholders' meeting, and other pertinent documents must be signed in the presence of a Notary Public. Foreign shareholders may be represented through proxies.
4. A shareholders' meeting must be held to adopt the articles of incorporation and bylaws, appoint board members, and managers.
5. The application for registration together with the corporate documents must be filed at the Public Registry of Commerce.
6. Registration is required with the Statistics Bureau and with Federal and Local Tax Authorities.
7. Registration in the National Registry of Foreign Investments is also required in case foreign capital participates in the company

---

[14]Ricardo Mendez Silva. *El Regimen Juridico de las Inversiones Extranjeras en Mexico.* Universidad Autonoma de Mexico, Instituto de Investigaciones Juridicas, (Mexico: 1969).

in a minority position, or, in case of majority participation, authorization is required from the National Commission on Foreign Investment.

8. Appropriate bylaws for the joint venture must be prepared, and the bylaws should provide adequate minority shareholder protection.

Management of a Mexican stock company may be entrusted either to a Board of Directors or to a "sole administrator" who is equivalent to a "sole director." The responsibilities and obligations of the officers and directors in Mexico are similar to those of the U.S. corporation. If the nature of the activity of the corporation requires the participation of Mexican investors, the directors appointed by foreigners cannot exceed the proportion of foreign investment.

The Financial System

The Mexican financial system is coordinated and supervised through the Secretariat of Public Finance and Credit. The Under-Secretariat of the National Bank (Banco de Mexico), which is a division of the secretariat, formulates all general policies, financial programs, technical outlines, and criteria with respect to data processing and statistics of the banking, insurance, and bonding agencies. It regulates investment societies, auxiliary credit organizations, and stock brokers.

Foreign Exchange

Mexico has two exchange rates which must be taken into account by those seeking to joint venture. The "controlled market" represents 80 percent of the total amount of all trade and financial transactions abroad, including imports and exports of goods. The exchange rate for the "controlled market" is set by Banco de Mexico and is used exclusively for official payments of imports and authorized official transactions.

This rate is known as the "Preferential Rate" and is currently at 1,070 Mexican pesos to the U.S. dollar. The free rate is set by the forces of supply and demand and is presently oscillating between 2,400 and 3,000 pesos to the dollar. Having two exchange rates can have a beneficial effect on both future capital needs and, more importantly, the profit of a firm in foreign currency.

The Mexican peso in 1987 was devalued 150 percent. The reason for continually letting the currency slide is that it is generally believed that it is not beneficial to the country to continue to artificially support the peso. Consequently, it has become customary at the end of each administration to allow the currency to suffer a drastic devaluation in order for the currency to reach its natural equilibrium level.

Areas in Which to Joint Venture

Foreign investment in areas which can incorporate new technology and contribute to Mexico's scientific development are actively, but selectively, promoted. Foreign participation is favored most in activities that are especially complex and require a high investment-to-labor ratio. This way, foreign investment can contribute in a positive manner to the development objectives of the nation without displacing or competing with Mexican investment. The 1984–1988 National Industrial and Foreign Trade Development Program (PRONAFICE) sets forth with specificity the areas of investment the government encourages.[15]

The Mexican government has also prepared a list of high-priority industrial activities where special incentives are granted to joint ventures with Mexican partners who have majority control of the venture. The high priority industries are those that complement the population's basic consumption needs and those necessary to consolidate the industrial structure of the economy.

Special Incentives

At present, a fiscal incentive plan is being applied with an objective toward increasing employment, promoting the development of medium and small industrial firms, and encouraging the production of capital goods. It also aims to promote a balanced regional development and an increase in exports.

These special incentives are granted, in most cases, only to companies with a majority of Mexican capital who perform needed services or locate in maximum priority geographic zones. The support is emphasized when it deals with small or microindustries. These fiscal incentives

---

[15]See footnote 4.

are granted through certificates of fiscal promotion (CEPROFI) which are credits against certain federal taxes. These certificates have a life of five years commencing with the date of issuance.

The new governmental strategy for industrial location aid has decentralization of industrial growth as its main objective. Medium-sized cities have been selected for development, thus increasing their potential for service business or for motor centers.

There are three locations in which investments are geographically encouraged that range from maximum national priority to minimum national priority. Each zone has a specific percentage of investment requirements which must be met in order to receive fiscal incentives. These fiscal incentives range from 20 percent to 30 percent of the initial investment.

CONCLUDING REMARKS

Foreign investment has grown since the promulgation of the law which regulates it. While there was a decrease in 1982 and 1983, it was a temporary phenomenon. This was due to the grave economic problems Mexico faced during that time as a result of the devaluation of its currency which, in turn, brought about a diminished confidence of foreign investors. The present administration's policies, incentives, and plans should enhance the growth of foreign investment in Mexico. The introduction of highly sophisticated technology to Mexico will also lead to increases in foreign investment through joint venture.

CHAPTER 17

JOINT VENTURING IN THE MIDDLE EAST

James R. Bridges
Thelen, Marrin, Johnson, & Bridges

WHY A JOINT VENTURE MAY BE NECESSARY OR APPROPRIATE

The exact geographical extent of the "Middle East" may be in some doubt. Nonetheless, most would agree that the term at least comprises Saudi Arabia and the other states of the Arabian Gulf and the Arabian peninsula, Iraq, Syria, Jordan, Lebanon and Egypt. These states are diverse in many ways. Their forms of government range from monarchies through forms of democracy to the equivalent of dictatorships. They comprise the oil rich, such as Saudi Arabia and Kuwait, and the oil poor, such as Egypt and Jordan. Some, such as Egypt, have large indigenous populations. Others, such as Saudi Arabia and Oman, are sparsely populated. The most striking common feature of the states of the Middle East, in addition to their language and religion, is their relative lack of economic development.

Although great strides have been taken, the industrial and manufacturing bases of the states of the region remain in a developing mode. Much also is yet to be achieved in terms of the mechanization and modernization of agriculture. The various states have adopted laws, regulations, and practices designed to channel foreign investment and participation in the local economy toward those areas in which a need for an infusion of know-how and technology is perceived, and, often, to discourage foreign investment in those areas perceived to be sufficiently developed.

The general goal of these restrictions is to create a lasting change in the local economy. The prevailing view in the region is that the accomplishment of this goal requires the "transfer of technology." Quite naturally, if technology is to be transferred, it must be transferred to someone. That someone is a local participant.

In some Middle Eastern countries it is literally impossible for a foreign concern to do business without associating itself in some form or fashion with a national of the country involved. In Kuwait, for example, not even a branch of a foreign company can be established except through the use of a Kuwaiti agent.

In those countries which do not mandate a local partner, joint venturing with a national is encouraged in various ways. In some countries, such as Saudi Arabia and the United Arab Emirates (UAE), a price preference is given to local firms on government tenders. Generally, such a preference is effected by discounting the bid of a local firm by a percentage, such as 10 percent, in comparing that firm's bid to the bid of a foreign firm for purposes of contract award. A firm will constitute a "local" firm for these purposes if it has the requisite percentage of local capital. Although the private sectors of many Middle Eastern countries are growing in importance, the governments and their various entities, agencies, and instrumentalities remain far and away the most important customers of the vast majority of foreign firms, whose goal is to sell their products or services locally, rather than to use a Middle Eastern country as a base for export. Thus, such governmental price preferences are an effective inducement to joint venturing.

Similar inducements can be provided by "buy local" and "contract local" requirements. In Saudi Arabia, for example, non-Saudi prime contractors are required to subcontract a minimum of 30 percent of the work on certain government contracts to Saudi subcontractors. The current interpretation of this rule treats joint venture prime contractors (but not subcontractors) which are majority Saudi owned as Saudi companies for purposes of the rule.

Most Middle Eastern countries now have income tax laws on their books which are applicable to business entities, if not also to individuals. Such laws may apply only to foreign interests, as is the case in Saudi Arabia and Kuwait, or may apply across the board. To the extent such laws are not applied in practice only to oil producing companies, as, at least in the past, was the case in Kuwait and certain of the Emirates, but are applied to the whole spectrum of business income, the availability of tax holidays to joint venture companies, or foreign participants in such companies, provides a powerful incentive to joint venturing. Whether by law or as a matter of practice, such tax holidays usually are available only in the case of joint venture companies in which local participation is not less than a given minimum. In addition to tax holidays, Oman provides tax incentives in the form of reduced rates, with the maximum reduction available to companies which are majority Omani owned.

In some circumstances joint venturing becomes the only practical alternative available to a foreign firm because the ability to register a branch of a foreign company is limited to certain business purposes and, either by law or practice, it is impossible to form a local company which is 100 percent foreign owned.

In addition to tax incentives available only to joint venture companies, often import tariff exemptions can only be taken advantage of by local companies, as in the case of activities conducted in the so-called "new communities" in Egypt.

Even in those circumstances in which a foreign firm might be able to do business without a local partner while avoiding significant tax disadvantages, there may be special considerations which dictate the use of a joint venture company. If ownership of real property is important to the foreign firm, those Middle Eastern countries which permit any degree of foreign ownership of real property generally do so only in the case of foreign participation in a local company which is majority owned by nationals.

As a purely practical matter, all other considerations aside, the foreign firm contemplating entry into a Middle Eastern market is likely to find that its prospects for success will be greatly enhanced by association with an appropriate national or nationals of the target country.

SELECTING A JOINT-VENTURE PARTNER

Selection of the local partner is an extremely important decision. Once an association has been formed with one national, it may be difficult for the foreign firm to add other nationals to the association or to form an additional association with another national. Such difficulties can arise as a result of the inability to obtain requisite approvals of the relevant foreign investment licensing authority or other governmental authorities, unless the consent of the first local partner is given. In some instances, the business ethics or sensibilities of potential additional local partners may dictate that the consent of the first partner be obtained even though no legal requirement for such consent exists.

The foreign businessman seeking to form an association with a local partner in a Middle Eastern country must be aware that such an association, once formed, is not easily unilaterally dissolved. Quite apart from the legal complexities involved in liquidating a joint venture company or enforcing a buy-out agreement, the foreign participant is likely to find that, however unhelpful the local participant may have been as a joint venturer, he has the ability to cause the foreign participant significant damage should he choose to do so. That often being the case, divorcing a local partner may involve considerable expense to the foreign participant, whether as a matter of law or contract, or as a purely practical matter. Thus, there is a premium on initial selection of an appropriate local partner.

In approaching the selection process, a foreign firm should be aware that, with some exceptions, it will not be able to locate a local individual or firm who will bring to the venture the kinds of skills and abilities which would normally be expected of a joint venture partner in a fully developed economy. In most cases, a prospective local partner will have no substantial experience in the foreign firm's field of activity, and, therefore, will not be able to contribute experienced personnel, whether executives, professionals, or technicians, or sophisticated market analysis to the venture. In large part, this is in the nature of things. Generally speaking, the very reason the particular Middle Eastern market is attractive to the foreign firm, as well as the reason the local government permits or encourages foreign investment and presence, is a lack of local capacity in the relevant field. For example, there is now a reasonably high level of local capability in most of the Middle East in the contracting area. As a result, competition in this area has greatly increased and many licensing authorities are either discouraging or refusing to license the formation of new joint venture contracting companies.

Rather than searching vainly for a local partner able to make traditional contributions to the joint venture, a foreign firm would be well advised to seek partners with other attributes. First among these is a reputation for scrupulous honesty in business dealings. A foreign firm which fails to pay adequate attention to the honesty of its prospective partner runs a risk of being gravely embarrassed at some point by its association, if not subjected to local fines or penalties. U.S. firms, of course, also must be mindful of potential violations of the Foreign Corrupt Practices Act, whether real or imagined.

In addition to business honesty, the ideal local partner should have an administrative staff conversant with local rules and regulations governing licensing of foreign investment, commercial registration, issuance of work permits for expatriate personnel, import restrictions, and the like, and which is capable of assisting the foreign partner's compliance with those rules and regulations.

Above all, a local partner must be well connected. When opportunities arise or can be created, the well connected local partner will be among the first to be aware of them. When unexpected problems arise, as they almost surely will, the well connected local partner will be able to assist the foreign partner in quickly and effectively resolving them. Virtually by definition, a well connected local partner will be able to introduce the foreign partner to appropriate officials in ministries and governmental agencies, and to useful local banking and other commercial relationships.

Lastly, most foreign participants will find their lives much easier if they are able to locate a local partner experienced in the ways in which international business transactions are conducted by Western businessmen, and fluent in the native language of the executives of the foreign firm. No matter how honest or how well connected a local partner may be, problems in the relationship are apt to develop for the foreign partner if the two do not speak the same literal and figurative language. Given the different cultures and backgrounds of the parties, the potential for misunderstandings will exist in any event. A common language and a common business experience tend to minimize that potential.

Commercial attachés of embassies and consulates may be useful in identifying the universe of potential local partners. Word of mouth, however, is usually a far more reliable source of information. Other foreign firms already doing business in the particular Middle Eastern jurisdiction can be especially helpful, as can major accounting firms and law firms and their respective local correspondents.

THE FORM OF THE JOINT VENTURE

Having selected a local partner, the foreign firm next must decide on the form which the joint venture will take.

The classic joint venture, in the Western sense of the term, is a partnership for a limited and specific purpose. Such joint ventures, however, are not legal creatures in the states of the Middle East. Rather, they are matters of private contract between the venturers, the existence of which is not a matter of public knowledge, much less of registration. Indeed, if in his dealing with third parties the local joint venturer makes known to the third party the existence of the joint venture, the result can be the unlimited liability of the foreign joint venturer to the third party. Since the classic joint venture lacks legal identity, the foreign venturer for most purposes will be viewed as if operating through a branch, and will be unable to obtain tax holidays, price preferences, and other inducements which require some minimum level of local participation. Not surprisingly, few foreign investors in the Middle East choose to structure their relationships with their local partners as classic joint ventures.

In some countries and in some fields of activity it is possible for a foreign firm to have no more than a principal-agent relationship with a local participant. Generally, however, the incentives and inducements available to a joint venture company will not be available to a foreign company operating, in essence, through a local branch, regardless of the presence of a local agent.

The great preponderance of joint ventures in the Middle East take the form of joint entities—either stock companies or partnerships. These entities have separate legal existence under the companies laws of the various Middle Eastern states. Formation of such an entity generally requires a permit, approval, or license from the relevant foreign investment authority, and compliance with applicable commercial registration formalities.

In most Middle Eastern countries, provision is made for a limited liability company, similar in attributes to a French S.A.R.L. Limited liability companies normally can be formed by only two participants. Corporations or joint stock companies, corresponding to a French S.A., also are permitted in most jurisdictions. Corporations usually cannot be formed by less than three (or a number greater than three) shareholders; generally must offer their stock to the public in some form and for some period, however limited; and are subject to much more rigid and inflexible provisions regarding management than are limited liability companies. In the case of either a corporation or a limited liability company, the exposure of a participant to the liabilities of the company is limited to the participant's share of capital.

The partnership form, both general and limited, is available in most Middle Eastern countries. As would be expected, the general partners in a limited partnership and all partners in a general partnership are unlimitedly liable for the obligations of the partnership. In some jurisdictions, at least one general partner of a limited partnership must be a national.

Despite general provision for various forms of organizations in the relevant companies law, on occasion one or another form will be limited to local participants by law, absent governmental decree, or will be unavailable to foreigners in practice. In Kuwait, for example, absent a special determination, foreigners cannot be shareholders in a corporation. In Saudi Arabia, the Foreign Capital Investment Committee in recent years has evidenced an unwillingness to approve foreign investments through the vehicle of a partnership.

In general, where limited liability companies are permitted and are available to foreigners, they are the preferred vehicle for foreigners joint venturing in the Middle East. The preference for limited liability companies is attributable primarily to the limited liability of the participants and the relatively high degree of flexibility generally allowed with respect to management arrangements and other matters that are the subject of agreement between the participants.

In the UAE, unless and until the new federal commercial companies law becomes effective, there is no provision in the laws of the various Emirates permitting limited liability companies. Failing a special decree by the ruler of the relevant Emirate, in effect granting limited liability to all partners in a partnership, the partnership with unlimited liability of the general partners remains the only joint venture entity available in the UAE. The foreign partner in a partnership formed in one of the Emirates can, of course, participate through a low net worth subsidiary. However, a parent company guarantee of the subsidiary's obligations may be required as a condition of licensing in some cases.

In Kuwait, limited liability companies are permitted by law, but participation in them is limited to natural persons. Thus, unless the Kuwaiti partner is an individual and the foreign firm is prepared to participate in the joint venture through a Kuwaiti nominee, the use of a limited liability company in Kuwait is not a real option for the foreign investor. A possible alternative may be the use of a private joint stock company, for which provision is made under the Kuwaiti companies law. If the know-how or technology to be transferred to Kuwait is viewed by Kuwaiti authorities as sufficiently important to the economy, the foreign firm may be granted permission to hold shares in a private joint stock company. Absent such permission, the only form of joint venture entity available to a foreign investor in Kuwait is a partnership form.

THE JOINT-VENTURE AGREEMENT

Given the fact that formation of a joint venture entity necessarily involves local participation, and the requirement that such participation be at a given minimum level, often, especially in the case of the more important inducements, above 50 percent, the foreign participant is faced with two critical questions—how to ensure its control of management, and how to ensure that the local participant's share of profits is commensurate with his actual contributions to the venture's success.

Control should not present an insuperable problem. Under most companies laws of states in the region, a great deal of flexibility is allowed the participants in a limited liability company in determining how the company's directors or managers are selected. Generally speaking, especially in the normal case of a company with only two or three participants, the participants are free to agree that there will be only one manager, and that he will be appointed or nominated by the foreign participant, or that there will be three directors, two of whom will be appointed by the foreign participant and one of whom will be appointed by the local participant. In those situations in which such freedom does not exist, resort is generally had to a formation agreement or a shareholders' agreement, or to some other contractual agreement between the participants regarding the manner in which directors or managers will be chosen. This agreement is not made a part of the Articles or Memorandum of Association of the limited liability company. Typically, such a side agreement provides that the company is to be governed by and interpreted under the laws of some foreign country, and provides for disputes to be resolved outside the country of formation, under, for example, International Chamber of Commerce rules. Such agreements are generally considered enforceable, subject to the effect of any local law which may purport to merge side agreements into the Articles of Association. In any event, even if there is an element of uncertainty as to enforceability, such a side agreement provides the foreign participant a significant level of comfort.

Often the foreign participant does not have a great deal of difficulty negotiating control rights over operating decisions. The local partner is usually prepared to recognize that he has little expertise in the operation of the particular business. The local partner is more prone to insist on veto rights in areas such as the declaration of dividends, borrowings, major capital expenditures, mergers, sales of substantial assets, and the like. In short, the local partner will be likely to seek at least negative control over exactly those decisions which would be expected to concern an essentially passive investor.

Profit sharing presents greater problems than does the issue of control. Quite apart from legal and tax considerations, it is not unusual for the partners to have difficulty agreeing on the level of the local partner's share in the profits of the joint company. Agreement on this point also will have to encompass agreement on the manner in which the foreign partner will charge the joint company for such things as know-how, technical support and services, home office general and administrative costs, and similar items. It may be, particularly in noncapital intensive activities such as consulting or technical or professional services, that the local partner will wish to receive a share of profits equal to a percentage of the gross revenues of the joint company. Such an arrangement is sometimes referred to as "disguised agency." Since, in such an arrangement, the local partner cannot be assured that the joint company will have profits sufficient to cover his agreed percentage of gross revenues, or, indeed, any profits at all, he can be expected to request some form of offshore guarantee by the foreign participant or an entity related to the foreign participant. Foreign investors in the Middle East should take into account the possibility that any payment made under such an offshore guarantee might cause tax problems in the foreign investor's home country.

Happily, the foreign investor will find that, virtually without exception, the minimum local participation requirements which apply for various purposes all relate solely to capital. Thus, while in order to obtain a tax holiday, or perhaps even to obtain a foreign investment license, it may be necessary to allocate 51 percent of the capital of the joint company to the local participant, it usually will not be necessary to also allocate 51 percent of the profits to the local participant. Moreover, most companies laws specifically permit the participants in a limited liability company to agree that its profits will be split in some manner other than in accord with capital shares. Practices, however, vary from country to country and, within a country, from time to time. For instance, contrary to their past practices, it appears that the Saudi authorities are becoming less willing to approve Articles of Association which either flatly provide for a profit sharing ratio different from the capital sharing ratio, or which provide that profits will be shared as the participants agree, annually or from time to time. Where the latter form of provision is accepted, the participants, by private contract, may agree at the outset on a profit sharing ratio or formula which will apply thereafter until altered by mutual agreement.

In those instances in which the parties are forced to include in the Articles of Association a profit sharing provision other than the one they have agreed upon, the result usually will be Articles which provide for a lesser share of profits for the foreign participant than the parties have privately agreed. Recourse then can be had to a management services or technical services agreement, under which the joint company pays a fee to the foreign participant for various services. Care must be taken in the use of such agreements. Tax holidays, even if initially available, do not last forever. The tax authorities of Middle Eastern countries are becoming increasingly sophisticated. The deductibility of fees paid under such arrangements may be limited or denied outright. In circumstances in which a profit sharing imbalance cannot be safely redressed through the use of such a service agreement, a last resort is a private agreement between the participants, involving offshore payments from the local participant to the foreign participant. The enforceability of such a private agreement may be doubtful.

INCOME TAX ASPECTS OF JOINT VENTURING

The foreign investor in a Middle Eastern joint venture usually will have two levels of concern regarding income taxes. The first level is the local income tax. The second is the ability to credit the local tax against home-country income tax.

Most Middle Eastern states impose an income tax on foreign companies, although in some cases not on individuals or on firms owned by nationals. There are some exceptions. Five of the seven Emirates comprising the UAE have no income tax law at present. These are Ajman, Fujairah, Ras al Khaimah, Sharjah and Umm al Qaiwain. Both Abu Dhabi and Dubai, the Emirates with the most highly developed economies, have income tax laws, providing for tax at graduated rates up to 50 percent or 55 percent. However, in practice, both Abu Dhabi and Dubai have yet to generally apply their respective tax laws to nonoil producing companies.

The nominal effective rates under the various tax laws of general application to foreign investors range, for example, from 40 percent in Egypt and Jordan, to 45 percent in Saudi Arabia and 55 percent in Kuwait. Although a 50 percent rate applies in Oman in the case of a joint venture company with less than 35 percent Omani participation, that rate is reduced to 20 percent with at least 35 percent Omani participation, and to 15 percent with majority Omani participation. Taxes on oil producing companies may vary significantly from taxes of general applicability. Taxes on the oil producing sector aside, the income taxes of the states of the region generally should qualify as creditable foreign taxes for U.S. income tax purposes.

Prior to the adoption of the Internal Revenue Code of 1986 (the 1986 Code), the maximum U.S. federal income tax rate applicable to corporations was 46 percent, a rate which appeared to allow sufficient room in most instances for full credit for income taxes paid to Middle Eastern states. In a number of instances, this appearance was deceiving. Local tax authorities in the region tend to be suspicious that home office and other offshore charges to local joint companies are disguised dividends. Disallowances of deductions for such payments may raise the real effective incremental tax rate in a Middle Eastern country, on a U.S. tax base, to as much as 70 percent or more. This concern has been heightened by the reduction of top U.S. corporate rates and a lessening of some flexibility as regards foreign tax credits in the 1986 Code. Foreign investors in the Middle East are now even more well advised than in the past to structure intercompany arrangements with a clear eye on the treatment those arrangements are likely to receive at the hands of the local tax authorities.

For the same reasons, the ability of the foreign participant to obtain a local tax holiday has become more important. Tax holidays, however, do not provide complete solutions for tax problems. Tax holidays, after all, are of limited duration, generally five or six years. Intercompany arrangements should be structured during the continuance of a tax holiday with a view to the ultimate expiration of the holiday. Even during the period of a tax holiday, there may be local tax exposure. It is generally accepted, for example, that profits from contracts entered into prior to

314 International Joint Ventures

the licensing of a joint-venture company in Saudi Arabia do not receive the benefits of the tax holiday granted the new company. In countries, such as Saudi Arabia, in which the income tax applies only to the interest of the foreign participant in the profits of a joint venture company, it is at least possible that the tax authorities may seek to tax the foreign participant's share of profits, even during the period of the tax holiday, if and to the extent that that share exceeds an amount proportionate to the foreign participant's share of capital.

After the expiration of a tax holiday, differences in the ratios of capital sharing and profit sharing may cause other problems in jurisdictions in which only the foreign participant's share of profits is subject to income tax. The Saudi Arabian Department of Zakat and Income Taxation has been known to assert an income tax liability on a share of profits of a limited liability company equal to the foreign participant's share in capital, even though the foreign participant actually has a lesser share in profits in the particular year. Such a lesser share of profits can result, for example, from an arrangement under which the Saudi participant's share of profits is determined by reference to a percentage of gross revenue.

Egypt is the only Middle Eastern country which has a tax treaty with the United States. The presence or absence of a tax treaty, however, is not a particularly important factor in a U.S. corporation's ability to credit local income taxes against U.S. tax. As mentioned, at least as applied to nonoil producing businesses, the income taxes of the various Middle Eastern jurisdictions generally should qualify as creditable taxes. Therefore, local income tax imposed on the U.S. participant in a local general or limited partnership normally should be fully available for credit against U.S. tax. The situation with respect to U.S. participants in limited liability companies is less clear.

Limited liability companies share features in common with partnerships as well as with corporations. A question has always existed whether, for U.S. tax purposes, a Middle Eastern limited liability company will be treated as a partnership or a corporation. If the limited liability company is treated as a partnership, the local tax burden borne by the foreign participant is treated, for U.S. tax purposes, as, in effect, a tax levied on and paid directly by the foreign participant. In that case, no untoward tax-credit problems arise. If, on the other hand, the limited liability company is treated as a corporation, the result may be a serious erosion of the U.S. participant's ability to obtain a U.S. tax credit for the full local tax burden it has borne.

Under U.S. tax laws, an "indirect" credit is available to a U.S. corporate shareholder in a foreign corporation for income taxes paid by the foreign corporation abroad so long as the U.S. corporation directly owns at least 10 percent of the voting stock of the foreign corporation or, through not more than two tiers of foreign corporations, indirectly owns not less than 5 percent of the voting stock of the foreign corporation in question. The indirect credit is available in any year in which the U.S. corporation receives dividends paid from accumulated earnings of the foreign corporation on which foreign taxes were paid. The indirect credit is limited to the same proportion of the foreign taxes which the dividends paid to the U.S. shareholder bear to the after-tax earnings from which the dividends were paid.

In the past it had been hoped that, in a case in which the local tax applied only to the foreign (U.S.) participant's share of profits, only those after-tax profits would be taken into account in determining the indirect credit for taxes paid by a limited liability company treated as a corporation for U.S. tax purposes. Rev. Rul. 87-14, 1987-6 I.R.B. 14, issued in early 1987, dashed that hope. Rev. Rul. 87-14 makes it quite clear that, in such circumstances, the position of the Internal Revenue Service is that the entire accumulated earnings of the limited liability company will be taken into account.

Rev. Rul. 87-14 deals with a Saudi limited liability company in which profits are shared 50-50 by the U.S. corporate participant and the Saudi participant. From its pre-tax earnings of 200X, the limited liability company pays a tax of 45X (45 percent of the U.S. participant's 100X share of profits). The after-tax balance of the U.S. participant's share of profits, 55X, is distributed to it as a dividend. The ruling concludes that the U.S. participant is entitled to an indirect credit for only 16X of the 45X Saudi tax it has borne (determined by multiplying 45X by the fraction 55X over 155X). This result, of course, is disasterous for the U.S. participant.

Rev. Rul. 87-14 has placed a premium on classification of limited liability companies as partnerships for U.S. tax purposes, at least in those countries, specifically including Saudi Arabia, which either do not apply the income tax to the profit shares of local participants or which subject local participants' profit shares to a significantly lower rate of income tax.

For U.S. tax purposes, a limited liability company will be treated as a corporation under current regulations only if it has a preponderance of the four so-called corporate characteristics of (1) limited liability, (2) centralization of management, (3) continuity of life, and (4) free transferability of interests. For practical purposes, this means that if an entity clearly lacks at least two of these characteristics, it will be treated as a partnership. The presence or absence of certain characteristics will be a question of local law, and of other characteristics will be a question of fact. When the IRS was prepared to issue private letter rulings on the classification of an entity for tax purposes, it ruled, in appropriate-fact circumstances, that Saudi Arabian limited liability companies would be treated as partnerships for U.S. tax purposes. The Internal Revenue Service then changed its policy. Until quite recently, it would not normally issue rulings on such issues. U.S. participants in limited liability companies in Saudi Arabia, and other Middle Eastern states which do not tax nationals as they do foreigners, had to find comfort in the advice of tax counsel and other tax advisers. Fortunately, the Internal Revenue Service is again willing to rule on the characterization of a limited liability company.

Generally speaking, the classification issue is a fairly straight-forward matter. All limited liability companies, by their very nature, have the corporate characteristic of limited liability. This is one of the features which makes them attractive vehicles to foreign investors. It will usually be the case that the foreign participant will insist upon operating control, if not policy control, of the limited liability company. As a consequence, it will seldom be possible for a U.S. participant to safely rely on the absence of the corporate characteristic of centralization of management. Of necessity, the U.S. participant will have to be satisfied that the limited liability company lacks continuity of life and lacks even a modified or attentuated form of free transferability of interests.

The Saudi Arabian companies law does not provide any help on either continuity of life or free transferability of interests. Absent specific provisions in the Articles of Association of the limited liability company negating the existence of these corporate characteristics, they will be present, at least in modified form. In the normal course of events, it should be possible for the U.S. participant to negotiate provisions of the Articles of Association, acceptable to both it and its local partner, which will adequately prevent the existence of these characteristics. For example, the Articles can provide that the bankruptcy of either participant will cause a dissolution of the limited liability company, and, for good measure, can provide that either participant can cause the dissolution of the company at will. As to free transferability, the Articles can simply provide that neither participant may transfer its interest without the consent of the other—which consent the second party may withhold at its absolute discretion. Such a provision would not represent a great concession on the part of either participant since, as a practical matter, any transfer of interests will require the approval of the licensing authority, an approval unlikely to be granted over the objections of the other participant. Such provisions as these are permissible under Saudi Arabian and similar companies' laws.

CHAPTER 18

JOINT VENTURING IN THE SOVIET UNION

William E. Butler
University College London

INTRODUCTION

In August 1986, the Soviet Union commenced a fundamental restructuring, the first in more than 50 years, of its system for conducting foreign economic relations. This structuring is integrally linked with sweeping domestic reforms in the national economy. As regards trade relations with "capitalist and developing countries," the restructuring is of the utmost significance in two respects: (1) a new State Foreign Economic Commission has been established and more than 100 ministries and state enterprises have been given the right to transact business directly with foreign parties, eliminating the specialized foreign trade organizations of the USSR Ministry of Foreign Trade as intermediaries; and (2) for the first time in the Soviet Union the concept of the joint enterprise (JE) and "other production entities" has been extended to firms of Western and developing countries; i.e., foreign parties may, on Soviet territory, jointly own and operate such entities with Soviet partners.

Hundreds of companies began to explore the potential for joint enterprises in the Soviet Union, and by autumn of 1988 more than eighty joint enterprises with American, Italian, Japanese, English, Finnish, French, and German participation already had been registered and had commenced operations. For some who are already established in the

Soviet market, the joint-enterprise form of cooperation has made it possible to develop commercial links in new directions; for others who are new to this field of trade, the access to a market of nearly 300 million people has proved to be attractive. Soviet foreign-trade partners have a history of loyalty to firms they find to be reliable and competitive; once in the market, Western companies who meet that standard are likely to maintain an edge over their competitors and will be difficult to dislodge.

Terminology

It is widely, but *wrongly,* accepted, even in Soviet legal materials published in the English language, to speak of the "joint venture." That term is a general expression for diverse levels or degrees of industrial and commercial cooperation in the West, and it is a term which Soviet legislation has deliberately avoided. Soviet legislation governing foreign economic relations with Western and developing countries originally referred only to the "joint enterprise." If that expression were translated as "joint venture" it would be impossible to account for other corporate forms of cooperation if Soviet legislation introduced them, which indeed it did in 1987 by adding the words "and other production entities," meaning additional corporate models besides the joint enterprise itself. Moreover, within the framework of the Council of Mutual Economic Assistance (COMECON)—the organization dedicated to achieving socialist economic integration in the Soviet Union, Eastern Europe, Mongolia, Cuba, and Vietnam—parallel Soviet legislation on joint enterprises also authorized the formation of international economic associations and joint societies, both forms of corporate organization which are quite distinct from the joint enterprise. Consequently, the expression "joint venture" can be highly misleading when applied to what is a specific form of corporate organization—the joint enterprise.

VIRTUES OF JOINT ENTERPRISES AND OTHER PRODUCTION ENTITIES

For the Soviet Union

While the Soviet authorities are in principle willing to entertain any suggestion for a joint enterprise, Soviet law requires that priority be given to schemes which will bring advanced technology, know-how, or management experience to the Soviet Union; increase Soviet exports and hard-currency earnings; provide the Soviet domestic market with higher-quality products; and reduce irrational or uneconomic imports to the USSR. All things being equal, the Soviet authorities are required to give precedence to proposals for joint enterprises from COMECON members rather than from Western and developing countries. These are, it must be stressed, not abstract objectives. Feasibility proposals for joint enterprises must make a case in detail on the basis of specific criteria.

For the Western Partner

Considerable interest has been created among Western companies in participating in joint enterprises in the Soviet Union, particularly those seeking to maintain or secure a preferential position in the Soviet market. Technological, labor, and raw-material resources are available in the Soviet Union, often at advantageous rates, and the Soviet domestic market has simply not been directly available to foreign goods for more than half a century. Some Western companies are utilizing Soviet manufacturing, processing, or assembly expertise, and exporting all or a substantial percentage of the goods produced; others hope to develop the Soviet domestic market as the principal outlet for their products. Tax concessions are offered for the early years of joint-enterprise operations. In selected areas the combination of Western and Soviet skills and resources may enable companies to become, or maintain their positions as, world leaders in technology and development.

A Warning

Just as that of other countries introducing equity joint ventures, Soviet legislation on the subject has been extensively evaluated by the international business community. On 17 September 1987 numerous alterations and clarifications were introduced into law, many of them responsive to Western reactions and criticisms. More doubtless will follow as experience accumulates. Much detailed regulation, moreover, is being left to subordinate legislation issued by various ministries and departments. Any company proceeding with a joint-enterprise proposal must ensure that its advice on Soviet law is as thorough and up-to-date as possible.

Efforts are underway through the International Chamber of Commerce to develop, in collaboration with specialists from the Soviet Union, a model joint-enterprise charter and to secure modifications or clarification of legislation where appropriate.

JOINT ENTERPRISES AND THE
SOVIET DOMESTIC ECONOMY

Since 1928 the Soviet Union has been a centrally planned economy in which the principal instruments and means of production have, since 1917, been owned by the State. As the economy has become more complex and sophisticated, it has been increasingly difficult for planning agencies and ministries to respond adequately and promptly to the requirements of decision making at intermediate and enterprise levels. Since 1965, with some reversals, the trend in economic reform has stressed enterprise autonomy and initiative, relaxation of central planning control, and the disciplining of enterprise discretion through law and contract. Partial reforms along these lines proved to be promising but insufficient. In 1986-87 a massive restructuring of the Soviet economy was begun with a view to overcoming the stagnation and inertia endemic to the late 1970s and early 1980s. Production enterprises, accorded even further autonomy, are expected to pay their own way to a far greater extent than before under the principles of ''self-financing'' and ''nonsubsidy.'' Greater freedom to contract and some price flexibility is being introduced. Hundreds of design and research organizations, traditionally financed from the State budget, are being transferred to the system of ''economic accountability.'' Higher quality standards and inspections have been imposed. Wage differentials are being increased and payment refused for substandard work. Managers are being elected directly by the labor collectives, often in contested elections. Brigades are utilized in many industrial units to integrate individual effort with specialist skills. Dozens of other measures have been introduced, sometimes experimentally, with a view to enhancing productivity, quality, and quantity.

The foreign trade reforms are an integral part of this strategy. Under the 1987 USSR Law on the State Enterprise, foreign economic links are to be a constituent part of the operations of all enterprises. For those granted direct access to foreign markets, the bureaucracy of foreign trade has been greatly simplified. Where joint enterprises are created, they too are to function on the basis of economic accountability, self-financing, and nonsubsidy. Their links with national economic planning are confined principally to reporting the indices of their operations. Those joint enterprises formed within the COMECON framework are to be approved because they further the notion of socialist economic integration. In short, foreign economic relations are no longer to be regarded as purely an appendage to the domestic national economy, and this, in the long term, should reinforce the stability of foreign relationships within the Soviet economic and legal systems.

DEVELOPING A JOINT-ENTERPRISE PROPOSAL

Although there is no prescribed pattern for developing a proposal to create a joint enterprise, in practice the following steps are likely to be essential.

Protocol of Intent

If preliminary discussions disclose that there is a sound basis for proceeding to negotiate a joint enterprise in detail, the parties may conclude a nonbinding Protocol of Intent. Such a protocol might name the parties to the proposed arrangement, any relevant intergovernmental agreements, the articles or services to be jointly produced, and the general area of cooperation. Although technical specifications may be included, they are subject to readjustment by the parties involved. The protocol also may specify the amount of capital to be contributed by the parties, the equity share of each party, and, for the Soviet party, the forms in which capital contributions may be made. Those forms include the value of a site lease, technological equipment, available infrastructure (including social amenities), raw materials and other materials, and other services or supplies made available by the Soviet party.

The Protocol of Intent may also make reference to the technical documentation required to operate the joint enterprise, and whether it is to be of either foreign or Soviet origin or is to be developed jointly. As a rule, there will be an indication as to who is to supply the documentation, and a requirement that the object(s) being jointly produced meet "world standards" and the demand of future markets. Eventually the technical documentation will be reduced to a list. Once the technical documentation is received, the Protocol may lay down the procedure and time limit for preparing a trial sample of the items to be jointly produced. The protocol should further project the annual planned volume of production for at least a five-year period.

Commonly a Protocol of Intent states basic principles for organizing a joint enterprise which are drawn from Soviet legislation. These include a stipulation that joint-enterprise property is to be valued in a particular currency with regard to world market prices; that the partners to the joint enterprise may reinvest their shares of profit into production development; that the joint enterprise is to plan its operations on the basis of projected consumer demand and foreign-exchange receipts; that the joint enterprise use a certain procedure for conducting foreign trade operations and obtaining supplies from or making sales to the Soviet domestic market; and that joint-enterprise personnel shall comprise principally Soviet citizens.

Reference commonly is made to the basic methods of structuring and managing the enterprise, setting out the general functions of the board and of the management. It is further specified that the remuneration and work schedule of Soviet citizens and their social security and social insurance are to be governed by Soviet labor legislation and paid for by the joint enterprise. Foreign employees of the joint enterprise likewise are subject to Soviet labor law except with respect to remuneration, leave, and pensions. As a rule those posts to be held by foreign specialists will be determined later in the negotiations and included on a list.

The protocol may state that the liabilities of the joint enterprise for its obligations are limited to the extent of its assets; that the enterprise is to be created and is to operate on the basis of Soviet legislation, the constitutive agreement, and the charter of the joint enterprise; that operations may commence once registration with competent Soviet agencies has been effected; and that the joint enterprise is a legal person under Soviet law. When necessary, a joint enterprise may open a branch in the country of the foreign partner(s).

Drawing upon existing patterns of joint-enterprise structure, the Protocol of Intent may lay down the model structure of the joint-enterprise charter. The charter would, *inter alia,* include the name and registered address of the joint enterprise; its legal status; the objects of its activities; capital contributions; the rights of the founding partners; the frequency of board meetings and procedures for making decisions; the scheme of management and procedure for making its decisions; the officials of the joint enterprise; finance and audit; creation of enterprise funds; principles for profit distribution; the procedure for dissolution of the joint enterprise; and the period for which the joint enterprise is created.

A Protocol of Intent, it must be stressed, is neither a mandatory step nor binding upon the parties, though in the early days of negotiating joint enterprises it was widely used. As a device for recording the preliminary results of negotiations and reminding especially the Western party about the basic principles of a joint enterprise under Soviet law however, the protocol has much to recommend it.

Feasibility Study for Joint Enterprise

Although any Western company exploring the formation of a joint enterprise with a Soviet partner should have worked out its own notions about the potential of the venture, as the Protocol of Intent is negotiated or immediately after concluding the protocol the two sides must develop a "technical and economic substantiation" for their contemplated joint enterprise. This document will constitute the substantive case for the project when the higher authorities consider, review, and approve it. While there is no prescribed model, as a rule such a document would include the following data:

- The production program of the joint enterprise over a five-year period, specifying production volume for each year or a list of products and services for each year.
- The quantities of products or services to be produced for the Soviet market and for export, with projected receipts in rubles or foreign currencies.
- A comparative evaluation of the technical quality of joint-enterprise products against the best world examples, and the prospects for improving the quality and technical standard of the product.
- The costs of production for each product, converted into internal and foreign currencies.
- Annual production costs, including depreciation for capital repairs and renovation.
- Quantities and costs of raw materials and semifinished products imported or acquired on the Soviet market.
- Projected annual profits of the joint enterprise and the distribution of profit to the Soviet and foreign partners.
- The value and amounts of production resources in the USSR to be transferred to the joint enterprise.
- Estimated costs of equipment and other material resources needed to create the joint enterprise.
- Requirements for labor resources, including foreign personnel.

- Estimated value of land plot and minerals provided by the Soviet partner.
- Total value of basic and circulating funds of the joint enterprise (charter capital).
- The shares of Soviet and foreign partners in the charter capital.
- The periods for beginning and completing construction of the joint enterprise, for mastering production techniques, and for the enterprise to commence operations.
- The conditions for export and import deliveries; credit terms (including types of currency, repayment periods, and interest rate), and the conditions for the return of shares invested in the charter capital.
- The indicators to be employed in measuring the economic efficiency of the joint enterprise and individual product types; the profitability of the enterprise; and the net profit for Soviet and foreign partners.
- For the Soviet partner, a comparison of production indicators for joint-enterprise products with those for analogous or substitute products in Soviet enterprises.
- The economic effects in the national economy to be obtained from the use of joint-enterprise products.
- Any economies to be obtained from a reduction of purchases in capitalist countries by reason of the joint-enterprise operations.
- The relationship of hard-currency revenues from exports to hard-currency expenditures, including the payment of dividends.

All of these calculations and projections, together with others deemed to be relevant, are to be made for a five-year period and broken down annually. Feasibility studies that fail to show that a joint enterprise will be both profitable and able to generate sufficient foreign-currency earnings to cover the transfer of the Western partner's share of the profits are unlikely to be approved. Although the Soviet side has formal responsibility for preparing the feasibility study in collaboration with its superior ministry, the full collaboration of the Western side is essential in providing the requisite information.

Once completed, the feasibility study will be verified by the USSR Ministry of Foreign Economic Relations, which will especially pay attention to the effect of the future product on the Soviet market, implications for other products exported from the USSR, how prices in the feasibility study compare with world market prices and with the prices in the country of each joint-enterprise participant, and the overall accuracy of the study.

Draft Joint-Enterprise Agreement and Charter

If the parties are confident of their feasibility study, they may prepare the draft of the final agreement to create the joint enterprise. In form, the agreement will encompass those points embodied in the Protocol of Intent, but in greater detail and reflecting the feasibility study and further negotiations. It is in the agreement that any special concerns of the Western partner should be addressed, especially where the relevant legislation seems to be ambiguous or silent.

The charter of the joint enterprise is treated as an annex to and integral part of the agreement. Model charters are available for guidance; in general they contain provisions common to most Western corporate charters and recite the basic provisions of Soviet joint-enterprise legislation. The charter will specify the name of the joint-enterprise, the agreement to which it is annexed, the object of joint-enterprise activities, its status as a legal person under Soviet law and concomitant right to conclude contracts, acquire property and have personal nonproperty rights, bear duties, and be a plaintiff or defendant in a court or arbitration tribunal. The model charter that is available states that the joint enterprise has the right to contract and agree on prices for its products when engaging in exporting and importing.

The rights of the joint enterprise as a legal person are effective from the moment of registration with the USSR Ministry of Finances. The joint enterprise has its own seal and the charter specifies the city and country of location. It is wise to designate the official and working languages of the joint enterprise. Other structural aspects are best dealt with under the general account of the joint enterprise discussed below.

Approval of Joint Enterprise

Once the agreement and charter are agreed upon by the parties and the feasibility study has been verified, the Soviet side will submit these to its higher ministries and departments. In turn, the higher agencies are to obtain the agreement of the USSR State Planning Committee, the USSR Ministry of Finances, and "other interested ministries and departments." The Ministry of Foreign Economic Relations is among those in the last category, though on this occasion its concern is not commercial but rather the conformity of the constitutive documents to Soviet law. The needed approvals can be obtained simultaneously. Originally all agreed-to proposals to create joint enterprises were then submitted to the USSR Council of Ministers for approval, but in September 1987 the procedure was simplified to allow ministries and departments of the USSR and union republic councils of ministers to independently make decisions on the creation of a joint enterprise.

THE FORMATION OF A JOINT ENTERPRISE

Definition

Soviet legislation does not define a "joint enterprise" as such but merely provides that a "joint enterprise with the participation of Soviet organizations and firms of capitalist and developing countries" may be created in the territory of the Soviet Union on the basis of contracts concluded between or among the participants in such enterprises. In the absence of a generic definition, presumably a corporate entity formed under Soviet law in accordance with the principles and procedures laid down in Soviet decrees appertaining to joint enterprises is, ipso facto, a joint enterprise. The issue is important because Soviet legislation leaves open the possibility of other "production entities" being created in the USSR with foreign participants, but their appellations and legal nature have not been elaborated.

Relevant Legislation

Joint enterprises are to be guided in their activities by laws, edicts, decrees, regulations, and other normative acts adopted by Soviet legislative, governmental, judicial, administrative, and social agencies or organizations except insofar as international treaties may establish exceptions. Double taxation treaties, for example, will be relevant for many Western countries and one may expect to see investment-protection treaties negotiated in the near future. Western companies need to understand what the "sources of law" are in the Soviet Union, for there are material differences that will baffle the uninitiated.

Aims of Joint Enterprise

Reference already has been made to the reasons for introducing joint enterprises and the criteria applicable when approving applications. The preamble to the Decree of the USSR Council of Ministers adopted January 13, 1987 on the procedure for creating joint enterprises lays down the general objective of "the further development of trade, economic, scientific, and technical cooperation with capitalist and developing countries on a stable and mutually advantageous basis. . . ." Those creating joint enterprises in the USSR are to have as their purpose the "fuller satisfaction" of domestic requirements for specific types of industrial products, raw materials, and foodstuffs; the attraction to the Soviet economy of progressive foreign technology, management experience, and additional material and financial resources; the development of the export base of the USSR; and the reduction of "irrational" imports. Broadly conceived as these aims were, early experience with joint enterprise ideas found them to be too constricting. The Decree of 17 September 1987 on additional measures to improve foreign economic activities, adopted jointly by the Central Committee of the Communist Party of the Soviet Union and the USSR Council of Ministers, provided that cooperation with Western firms also would embrace science and technology, trade, finance, services, tourism, and advertising, and that, to this end, joint scientific research and design organizations, engineering, marketing and advertising firms, and joint service and repair firms for export technology and goods be created.

It is worthy of note that priority of place is given to the satisfaction of domestic requirements. This means that access to the vast Soviet market is available; joint enterprises will be able to help meet that demand and also set standards of quality and competitiveness as a challenge for Soviet industry. Under changes introduced in September 1987, the joint enterprise may market its products and services through Soviet foreign-trade organizations or directly through Soviet domestic marketing networks.

Participants

The participants in a joint enterprise may be one or several Soviet enterprises, associations, cooperative, or other organizations which are legal persons and one or several foreign firms, companies, corporations, and other organizations which are legal persons. The foreign firms may be from the same country or several countries and, it would seem, could also include economic entities formed within the COMECON framework.

Legal Personality

A joint enterprise is a legal person under Soviet law and possesses the full attributes of legal personality, that is, it operates on the basis of "full economic accountability, nonsubsidy, and self-financing." The joint enterprise has an independent balance sheet, is expected to operate as a profit-generating entity, may conclude contracts in its own name, may acquire property and personal nonproperty rights, and may be a plaintiff or defendant in a court or arbitration tribunal.

As a legal person, the joint enterprise may possess, use, and dispose of its property in accordance with the purposes of its activities, the purpose of the property, and the provisions of Soviet legislation. Its property may not be requisitioned or confiscated in an administrative proceeding; on the contrary, such property is entitled to protection in accordance with those Soviet legislative provisions established for Soviet State organizations. Execution may be levied against joint-enterprise property only by decision of agencies that, under Soviet law, have the right to consider disputes involving joint enterprises.

A joint enterprise is liable for its obligations with all the property that belongs to it. In accordance with the standard prescription in Soviet law with regard to legal persons, the Soviet State and the participants in a joint enterprise are not liable for its obligations, nor is the joint enterprise liable for the obligations of the Soviet State or of its participants. If branches of the joint enterprise are created as separate legal persons on Soviet territory, they too are not liable for obligations of the joint enterprise, and vice versa.

Charter

The preparation of a draft charter has been discussed above. Soviet joint-enterprise legislation requires that there be a charter and that it contain the following: the object and purpose of enterprise activities, its location, the participants, the amount of the Charter Fund, the share held by each participant, the procedure for forming the Charter Fund (including equivalent value in foreign currency), the structure, composition, and competence of the agencies managing the enterprise, the procedure for adopting decisions and the range of issues whose decision requires unanimity, and the procedure for dissolving the enterprise. Any other provisions may be included in the charter which are not contrary to Soviet legislation provided they appertain to distinctive aspects of joint-enterprise activities.

Term

Unlike certain other socialist legal systems, the Soviet Union has not prescribed any minimum or maximum time limits for the existence of the joint enterprise. This is a matter to be agreed upon by the parties involved and recorded in the agreement creating the joint enterprise or in the Charter.

Registration

Employing the procedure normally used in the Soviet legal system for the creation of legal persons, Soviet law attaches the status of legal person to a joint enterprise not when approval has been secured from the duly authorized confirming agency but thereafter upon registration with the USSR Ministry of Finances.

Until registration is effected, Soviet State, cooperative, and other social enterprises and economic organizations are prohibited from concluding any legal transactions or contracts whatever with the joint enterprise; nor may Soviet banks open accounts, issue cash assets, or engage in credit operations with them. The registration is performed by the State Revenues Administration of the USSR Ministry of Finances on the basis of an application in writing, notarially certified copies of an extract of the decision of the State agency creating the joint enterprise, and copies of the constitutive documents. At the request of the State Revenues Administration, other documents confirming information to be entered in the register must be submitted.

Any changes in the constitutive documents or other changes and additions subject to registration must be submitted to the USSR Ministry of Finances.

A joint enterprise is issued a registration certificate, on the basis of which notice is published of the creation of the joint enterprise. The information entered in the register and published is considered to be known to third parties; disputes arising in this respect are not subject to consideration by the USSR Ministry of Finances.

The Charter Fund

The initial capital of a joint enterprise, called the Charter Fund, is made up of contributions from the participants. By law the minimum share of the Soviet side in the joint-enterprise Charter Fund must comprise not less than 51 percent. The Charter Fund may be increased by contributions from the profits arising out of the economic activities of the enterprise or by additional contributions from the participants.

Contributions may be in cash or in kind and may include buildings, installations, equipment, other "material valuables," the right to use land, water, and other natural resources, buildings, installations, or equipment, and also other property rights (including the use of inventions or know-how). Cash contributions may be in the currency of the participants' countries or in another freely convertible currency.

The contribution of a Soviet participant to the Charter Fund of a joint enterprise is to be valued in rubles at prices fixed in the constitutive agreement, taking into account world prices. The contribution of a foreign participant is to be valued in the same procedure, the value of the contribution then being converted into rubles at the official exchange rate of the USSR State Bank on the date of signing the constitutive agreements or another date agreed on by the participants. Under changes introduced in September 1987, by arrangement between the participants in a joint enterprise their respective contributions to the Charter Fund may be valued either in Soviet or in foreign currency.

In the absence of world market prices, the value of contributed property is to be determined by agreement between the participants. Western companies should expect, however, to encounter on the Soviet side detailed calculations showing, for example, the comparative values of property sites in the foreign participant's country of origin as a basis for valuing the Soviet contribution of a land site, or equivalent comparisons for construction costs, building values, and the like. These are a basis for negotiation and are not binding.

Equipment, materials, and other property imported into the USSR by foreign participants in a joint enterprise, as their contributions to the Charter Fund, are exempt from customs duty.

Loans

Capital may be made available on loan to the joint enterprise by the participants or outside sources, but would not constitute part of the Charter

Fund. There are several sources within the USSR to whom the joint enterprise might apply, as well as the usual foreign sources. The former include the Bank for Foreign Economic Activity of the USSR (Vneshekonombank SSSR), the State Bank of the USSR, or the appropriate sector bank, such as the Industrial-Construction Bank of the USSR or the Agro-Industrial Bank of the USSR. If foreign banks or firms are used, the consent of Vneshekonombank must be obtained first.

MANAGEMENT OF A JOINT ENTERPRISE

The Board

The highest agency of a joint enterprise is the board, consisting of persons appointed by the participants. The respective numbers of Soviet and foreign board members are not stipulated by legislation nor is it required that the minimum 51 percent share of the Soviet participant be reflected in the composition of the board. In practice, parity in board membership may be quite acceptable.

More important is the procedure by which the board makes decisions. It is left entirely up to the parties to agree on a procedure in the constitutive documents, and on vital matters the participants may require that decisions of the board be unanimous.

The Directorate

The day-to-day activities of a joint enterprise are to be managed by a directorate composed of Soviet and foreign citizens. There is no legislative stipulation as to the size of the directorate or of minimum Soviet participation, although obviously the Director General of the joint enterprise must be a member. In practice the directorate is likely to include the Director General, his deputies, and perhaps the Chief Bookkeeper and Legal Adviser.

Chief Executives

Soviet legislation requires that the Chairman of the Board and the Director General of the joint enterprise be citizens of the USSR. Their powers and functions, as those of other executive personnel, are left to be negotiated by the parties and then incorporated in the charter or other appropriate document. By analogy with charters adopted for joint enterprises within COMECON, the Director General would be accountable to the board and bear responsibility for carrying on enterprise activities and performing the tasks and functions entrusted to him. He would, in particular, ensure that the enterprise plans are fulfilled, arrange for board decisions to be executed and report thereon, dispose of joint-enterprise property, including cash assets, within the limits determined by the board, conclude contracts without a power of attorney in the name of the enterprise and ensure they are performed, perform other functions arising from the charter, and represent the joint enterprise in relations with other organizations, enterprises, institutions, or State agencies—domestic and foreign—with regard to enterprise activities within his competence. Further he would expect to make all decisions relating to other enterprise activities not relegated exclusively to the board.

The Western partner should give careful thought to appropriate means for protecting the rights of all concerned in relation to appointment and removal of executive personnel and board members, voting rights, and the duties and powers of management.

PERSONNEL OF A JOINT ENTERPRISE

Nationality

Although there are no numerical quotas or limitations, the personnel of a joint enterprise principally comprises Soviet citizens. Foreign nationals represent a foreign currency burden to the joint enterprise and, while they must be utilized where essential, will otherwise be kept to a minimum.

Labor Conditions

Soviet citizens employed by the joint enterprise will, with respect to their wages, working conditions, holidays, social security, and social insurance, be governed by Soviet legislation and incorporated either explicitly or by reference in the collective contract concluded annually between management and the trade union organization in the joint enterprise. State social insurance and State pension contributions for Soviet citizens are to be made to the State budget by the joint enterprise at the rates fixed for Soviet State organizations.

Labor discipline, safety regulations, hiring, dismissal, and the like are regulated in detail by the Fundamental Principles on Labor Legislation of the USSR and Union Republics, by the labor codes of the union republics, and other labor legislation. Labor discipline is normally governed by a set of rules adopted for each enterprise or branch of industry. The grounds for dismissal are laid down in the labor codes, but for a dismissal to be valid the prescribed procedural rules must have been punctiliously observed. There are no formal restrictions on recruitment from localities other than that where the joint enterprise is situated, but accommodation may be a problem. If the joint enterprise can provide housing to workers, its ability to recruit will be greatly enhanced.

Foreign Personnel

Accurate calculations will need to have been made at the feasibility-study stage as to how many foreign personnel will be required by the joint enterprise, with what expertise or specialization, how much time they will be required to spend in the Soviet Union, their job specifications, and whether their families will accompany them. Soviet labor legislation will extend to foreign personnel with the exception of wages, holidays, and pensions. The latter issues are to be regulated by contract individually with each foreign citizen. The appropriate Soviet State organs and trade-union bodies will develop special legislation for the application of social insurance regulations to foreigners.

The joint enterprise must pay contributions to the State budget for the social insurance of foreign personnel. Pension contributions may be paid into appropriate pension funds at the permanent place of residence of the foreign personnel, in the currency of those countries.

The earnings of foreign personnel are subject to income tax pursuant to the Edict of the Presidium of the USSR Supreme Soviet adopted May 12, 1978. The unspent portion of those earnings may be transferred abroad in foreign currency.

Western companies will need to carefully consider the amount of time foreign personnel should spend in the Soviet Union, their living conditions, travel arrangements, medical services, schools, family amenities, and the like. While these are not to be underestimated, there is considerable relevant experience in analogous arrangements made by

Western firms to service long-term cooperation agreements. The joint enterprise may be able to more readily accommodate a foreign presence as an integral part of a collaborative venture than can a purely contractual relationship.

THE JOINT ENTERPRISE IN THE SOVIET ECONOMIC AND ADMINISTRATIVE SYSTEM

Relations with Planning Bodies

A joint enterprise independently works out and confirms its own program of economic activities. While this information is reported to the planning authorities, Soviet State agencies may not establish obligatory planning tasks for a joint enterprise. It follows of course that, being outside the planning system, neither is the sale of joint enterprise products guaranteed. However, under the legislation of September 1987 a joint enterprise is free to determine by agreement with Soviet enterprises and organizations the procedure for the realization of its products on the Soviet market, and the procedure for the delivery of goods to that market. This would appear to include an agreement to distribute products through the planning system, if appropriate.

Relations with Agencies of State Administration

Under Soviet legislation the joint enterprise is to enter into relations with central agencies of State administration of the USSR and union republics through the agencies superior to the Soviet participant in the joint enterprise, that is, the joint enterprise may not circumvent the agencies to which its Soviet partner is subordinate. Local organizations of State administration (defined presumably with reference to the stature of the Soviet partner) and other Soviet organizations may be approached directly.

Communications

A joint enterprise has the right to carry on correspondence, telegraph, teletype, and telephone communications with foreign organizations; although telex and fax are not mentioned, they are being used in Moscow.

Export and Import Operations

A joint enterprise has the right to independently conduct export and import operations which are necessary for its economic activities, including operations in the markets of COMECON countries. If, however, the joint enterprise wishes, those operations may be effected through Soviet foreign-trade organizations or the sales network of the foreign participants on the basis of respective contracts. Presumably this would include the foreign-trade sections of Soviet participants, if such exist. All goods and property exported from or imported into the USSR by a joint enterprise must be pursuant to permits issued in the procedure established by Soviet legislation.

Capital Construction Projects

The designing and capital construction of joint-enterprise installations, including social amenities, must be performed under contract and financed from joint-enterprise funds or by borrowing. Before final approval the designs must be agreed upon in the procedure laid down by the State Construction Committee of the USSR. Joint enterprises are granted a right of priority under Soviet legislation to construction work quotas and assembly work and to material resources required for construction.

The Soviet construction industry is notoriously overburdened. These rights of priority may require elaboration in the constitutive documents of the joint enterprise.

Transport

No special provisions are made for the transport of joint-enterprise goods. Whether by air, river, sea, rail, or motor vehicle transport, the carriage of goods is to be effected in the procedure established for Soviet organizations.

Insurance

The property of a joint enterprise is subject to compulsory insurance under policies issued by Soviet insurance agencies.

FINANCIAL ASPECTS OF JOINT-ENTERPRISE OPERATIONS

Banking

The cash assets of a joint enterprise must be deposited in a ruble or currency account respectively at the State Bank of the USSR or the Vneshekonombank SSSR and must be spent for purposes connected with the activities of the enterprise. Interest is to be credited to these accounts based on world money-market rates for foreign-currency accounts and for ruble accounts, on terms to be designated by the State Bank of the USSR.

Exchange-Rate Differences

All exchange-rate differences relative to currency accounts of joint enterprises, as well as with regard to their operations in a foreign currency, are to be relegated to the profit-and-loss account of the joint enterprise.

Foreign Currency Expenditure from Export Earnings

All currency expenditures of a joint enterprise, including payments of profit and amounts due to foreign participants and specialists, must be covered from receipts obtained by the joint enterprise from realizing its products on the foreign market. Vneshekonombank SSSR will be responsible, among others, for seeing that this stricture is observed.

There may be occasions, however, when sales to the Soviet market generate foreign currency. Under the legislation of September 1987, a joint enterprise determines, by agreement with Soviet enterprises and organizations, the type of currency for settlements with respect to products realized and goods purchased.

Commercial Credits

When necessary, a joint enterprise may obtain credits in foreign currency on commercial terms from the Vneshekonombank SSSR or, with its consent, from foreign banks or firms, or credits in Soviet currency from the State Bank of the USSR, Vneshekonombank SSSR, or sector banks.

These banks have the right to watch over the designated use, provision, and timely repayment of credits issued to a joint enterprise.

INDUSTRIAL PROPERTY

The rights to industrial property which belong to a joint enterprise are protected by Soviet law, including patents. It is left to the constitutive documents to determine the procedure for transferring industrial-property rights from participants to the joint enterprise and the basis on which those rights are to be used and protected. There is already considerable experience with such transfers in East-West trade, but careful attention needs to be given to confidentiality and the protection and ownership of improvements, should such emerge.

CALCULATION AND SHARING OF PROFIT

The profits of a joint enterprise are subject to certain statutory deductions before being shared among the participants.

Reserve and Other Funds

In common with normal Soviet practice, a joint enterprise is required to create a reserve fund equal to 25 percent of the value of its Charter Fund. The reserve fund is formed from annual transfers from profits in amounts to be agreed upon in the constitutive documents.

Other funds may include a social development fund, a housing fund, or a technological development fund. These are evidently at the discretion of the joint-enterprise participants and, if formed, are to be enumerated in the constitutive documents, which should also lay down the procedure for spending them.

Depreciation

A joint enterprise is required to make depreciation deductions in accordance with the standards in force for Soviet State organizations unless the constitutive documents provide otherwise. The amounts set aside will remain at the disposal of the joint enterprise. This formulation makes it possible to forego depreciation deductions or to alter the usual standard. Western companies would be well advised to consider whether the normal Soviet practice is suitable, for Soviet practices may differ sharply from depreciation policies in other countries.

Sharing of Profits

After deducting transfers to the reserve, depreciation, and other funds and payment of the tax on profits (see below), the joint-enterprise profits are to be distributed to the participants in proportion to their respective share in the Charter Fund.

Transfer of Profits Abroad

Foreign participants are guaranteed the transfer abroad in foreign currency of amounts due them from the profit distribution of the joint-enterprise activities. Presumably this is subject to the requirement that export sales have generated the requisite foreign currency.

JOINT-ENTERPRISE ACCOUNTING

Accounting data is collected by a joint enterprise for two reasons. First, to inform the participants about joint-enterprise operations and the state of its assets, profits, or losses. This data should be provided for in the constitutive documents. Western firms may wish to have such data gathered and presented pursuant to Western accounting practices, in which event an appropriate provision should be agreed upon with the Soviet side. Second, to meet Soviet requirements for reporting on economic performance.

Soviet legislation requires that operational, bookkeeping, and statistical records are to be kept in the procedure applicable to Soviet State enterprises. In a document issued on February 27, 1987 by the USSR Ministry of Finances and the USSR Central Statistical Administration, those agencies gave notice that the model forms of primary documentation confirmed for Soviet State organizations should be used for joint enterprises; that inventory should be taken according to the forms and methods used by Soviet State organizations; that bookkeeping records and reports should be prepared by bookkeepers whose activities are governed by the

1980 Statute on Chief Bookkeepers; and that other types of accounting operations should follow standard Soviet practices, subject to certain modifications elaborated upon in the document. Export and import operations are accounted for in the procedure established for foreign-trade associations of ministries and departments.

The joint enterprise bears responsibility in accordance with Soviet legislation for observing the procedure for keeping records and for the reliability of the records and reports.

Access to Information

The participants in a joint enterprise have the right to information on joint-enterprise activities in the procedure laid down in the constitutive documents, especially with a view to supervising joint-enterprise operations. However, Soviet legislation expressly prohibits the joint enterprise from providing any reports or information to State or other agencies of foreign governments.

Audit Commission

It is customary in the Soviet Union for every corporate entity to appoint an Audit Commission to supervise the financial and economic activities of the enterprise. The commission reports to the enterprise management and is usually composed of individuals from within the enterprise itself. Useful as it may be, the Audit Commission is no substitute for the kinds of audits regularly performed by Western, especially Anglo-American, accounting firms. Soviet joint-enterprise legislation recognizes this in two respects. First, it makes the creation of an Audit Commission discretionary and leaves the matter to be resolved by the participants in the constitutive documents. Second, provision is made for the mandatory verification of the financial, economic, and commercial activities of a joint enterprise by an independent Soviet auditing organization. Such an independent organization, "Inaudit," was founded on September 30, 1987, in Moscow. It charges a fee for its services and has formed relationships with Western firms of accountants.

Soviet accounting methods will certainly be used, so that additional measures will need to be provided in order to ensure that data is compiled and verified to meet reporting practices in the foreign participant's country and firm.

The early involvement of accountants and lawyers, including those conversant with Soviet law, is highly desirable.

TAXATION

The taxation of joint enterprises on Soviet territory is regulated by the Edict of the Presidium of the USSR Supreme Soviet adopted January 13, 1987, "On Questions Connected with the Creation on the Territory of the USSR and the Activity of Joint Enterprises, International Associations, and Organizations with the Participation of Soviet and Foreign Organizations, Firms and Agencies of Administration;" decrees of the USSR Council of Ministers of January 13, and September 17, 1987 governing joint enterprises, and an Instruction of the USSR Ministry of Finances issued on May 4, 1987, as amended on November 30, 1987.

Taxation of Profits

Joint enterprises are subject to tax at the rate of 30 percent on profits remaining after deductions for the Reserve Fund and other joint-enterprise funds earmarked for the development of production, science, and technology. Revenues are taxed if they have been received by joint enterprises or their branches which have been created and are located on Soviet territory and have emanated from activities on Soviet territory, the continental shelf and economic zone of the USSR, or the territory of other countries. The joint enterprise must be operating on the principle of economic accountability, have an independent balance sheet, and have its own bank account.

The amount of deductions for the Reserve fund and other funds are for the participants in the joint enterprise to determine; however, the Reserve Fund may not exceed 25 percent of the value of the Capital Fund. The tax is due in rubles and paid into the State budget.

Exemptions from Tax

Under the legislation of September 1987, joint enterprises are exempt from tax on profits during their first two years of operations at a declared profit. Furthermore the Ministry of Finances has the right to reduce the tax on profits or wholly exempt the joint enterprise from such tax upon application by the taxpayer with supporting accounting data. The application for exemption with reasons is submitted to the local financial agency where the joint enterprise is located and, after verification, referred to the USSR Ministry of Finances with a recommendation. The ministry is to make a decision within one month after receiving all the materials.

It may be possible to negotiate tax reductions or exemptions when the feasibility study or constitutive documents are being prepared.

Losses

No reference is made in Soviet legislation or ministry instructions to the possibility of losses being carried forward to offset future profits. While this may be clarified subsequently, such losses would certainly be considered as a possible grounds for continued tax exemptions.

Assessment and Payment of Tax

A joint enterprise is required to estimate its profit tax liability for the forthcoming year, taking into account its financial plan, and making quarterly payments on account. A return for the final amount of tax on profits is due by March 15 of the year following and final payment of any balance owing is due on April 1. For each day of delay there is a penalty of .005 percent. Arrears of tax are recovered in a procedure established for foreign juridical persons by a statute confirmed on January 26, 1981. Excess payments of tax may be credited to the current year or refunded upon application. Financial agencies at the place where the joint enterprise is located have responsibility for verifying that tax returns are correct and payments are made in a timely way.

Appeals

A joint enterprise has the right to appeal the actions of financial agencies connected with the recovery of tax. The application of appeal is filed with the financial agency which verified the amount of tax within one month after the enterprise received the results of the verification. The failure to appeal within the month means the amount of tax due is regarded as final and is no longer subject to appeal. If an appeal is filed, the financial organ must render its decision within one month of receiving the appeal, and its decision on the appeal may in turn be appealed to the next higher agency. The filing of an appeal does not suspend payment of the tax.

Tax on Share of Profit Transferred Abroad

Unless provided for otherwise by a treaty between the USSR and the state where the foreign participant is located, the share of profit due to a foreign participant in a joint enterprise is subject to a tax of 20 percent when it is transferred abroad. Only the amount actually transferred is taxed.

If the foreign participant is exempt from that tax or entitled to a reduced tax rate, he must pay the tax when the profit is transferred and apply to the State Revenues Administration of the USSR Ministry of Finances for a refund within one year from the date that the tax was withheld.

Indirect and Local Taxes

It will be important when regulating the joint-enterprise documents to ascertain what other taxes and charges will be payable. Customs duties and social insurance contributions are expressly mentioned in joint-enterprise legislation, but consideration also needs to be given to any liability for turnover tax, local charges for land, utilities, and the like, and any other form of taxation.

Taxation of Foreign Personnel

Under Soviet legislation dating from May 12, 1978, foreigners are subject to income tax in the procedure and amounts applicable to Soviet citizens on monies received from activity carried out on Soviet territory and authorized in the established procedure. Many countries, including the United States and the United Kingdom, have double-taxation treaties with the Soviet Union.

ASSIGNMENTS

Transfers and Preferential Rights

The legislation originally authorizing joint enterprises, that of January 13, 1987, provides that, subject to mutual consent, the participants of a joint enterprise have the right to transfer their share in the joint enterprise wholly or partially to third persons on condition of securing, in each individual instance, the authorization of the State Foreign Economic Commission of the USSR Council of Ministers. The Soviet participants have a preferential right to acquire the shares of foreign participants.

In September 1987 it was further stipulated in the decree on additional measures for improving foreign economic activity that the practice should be introduced of "purchasing shares, bonds, and other securities, and of issuing and placing them." Whether a market is contemplated for such shares is unclear, and in any event there is no indication as to what price a Soviet participant would pay when exercising its preferential right.

So long as it remains a requirement that the Soviet party own 51 percent of a joint enterprise, there can be no preferential right for the foreign participant to acquire the Soviet share.

Reorganization

When a joint enterprise is reorganized, its rights and obligations pass to the legal successors.

LIQUIDATION

Grounds and Procedure

A joint enterprise may be dissolved in the instances and procedure provided for in the constitutive documents or by decision of the USSR Council of Ministers, if joint-enterprise activities do not correspond to the purposes and tasks laid down in the constitutive documents.

Notice of the liquidation must be published in the press and the liquidation registered at the USSR Ministry of Finances.

If domestic practices are followed, a liquidation commission will be appointed under the aegis of the ministry or department superior to the Soviet participant.

Return of Contributions and Property

In the event of liquidation, a foreign participant has the right to the return of his contribution in cash or in kind in accordance with the remaining value of the contribution at the moment of liquidation and after the payment of his obligations to Soviet participants and third persons. The same right exists if the foreign participant withdraws from the joint enterprise.

SETTLEMENT OF DISPUTES

The following types of dispute may, by arrangement of the parties, be considered in an arbitration tribunal or, in the absence of such an arrangement, in the courts of the USSR:

- Disputes of joint enterprises with Soviet State, cooperative, and other social organizations.
- Disputes between joint enterprises.
- Disputes between participants of a joint enterprise regarding issues connected with its activities.

There is no stipulation that arbitration necessarily be in the Soviet Union, although the Arbitration Court attached to the USSR Chamber of Commerce and Industry is empowered to accept such disputes for consideration at the behest of the parties. Western firms may wish to consider the inclusion of an arbitration clause in the constitutive agreements, in which case they should bear in mind that Soviet arbitration practice accepts the doctrine of the separability of an arbitration clause.

Suits by individual citizens against a joint enterprise, and vice versa, would fall within the jurisdiction of the ordinary Soviet courts.

FURTHER READING

For general background on the Soviet legal system, see W. E. Butler, *Soviet Law* (London, Butterworths, 2d ed., 1988). Translations of Soviet legislation on foreign economic relations are available in Butler (ed. & transl.), *Commercial, Business and Trade Laws: Soviet Union and Mongolia* (Dobbs Ferry, N.Y.: Oceana Publications, 1988), a looseleaf service supplemented as appropriate.

Particular care should be taken in working with the English translations of Soviet legislation. Many of those available are less than adequate. The early involvement of Russian-speaking specialists with a knowledge of the Soviet legal system to work with the lawyers and accountants on the Western side is highly desirable.

CHAPTER 19

JOINT VENTURING IN SOUTH AMERICA

David M. Bridges, Esq.
Eric T. Laity, Esq.
James E. Miller, Esq.
Beverly J. Kimmitt, Esq.

South America has long been host to foreign investment. Early investment in South America was generally limited to exploiting the continent's wealth of mineral resources. Foreign investment today is widespread, and may be found in particular in the areas of light and heavy industry, agriculture, forestry, hydroelectric power, and mineral exploration and processing. While the size, wealth, population, and types of government of the South American nations differ greatly, these countries do share the problems and opportunities of possessing developing economies.

REGULATION OF FOREIGN INVESTMENT

South American countries have taken two divergent paths in their pursuit of economic growth. The paths diverge in the treatment they accord to foreign investment. One group of nations provides for the equal treatment of all business enterprise, whether foreign or domestic, or a mixture of both. The other countries, all members of the Andean Pact (also known as the Andean Common Market), heavily regulate foreign investment. Both approaches have advantages and disadvantages.

The Free-Access Nations

The free-access nations are Argentina, Brazil, Chile, Paraguay, and Uruguay. Their economic policies are characterized by the relative absence of restrictions on foreign investment. In those countries, foreign investors are free from mandatory associations with local concerns and stipulated ceilings on foreign industrial holdings.

This general rule of nondiscrimination against foreign investment is not without exception. Practically every South American nation, whether or not a free-access country, bars, in some way inhibits, or requires official approval of foreign participation in designated industries. Those industries most commonly include domestic airlines, newspapers, radio and television, utilities, and petroleum and mining.

Mandatory local affiliation requirements occasionally appear in free-access countries. Paraguay, for example, specifies that before a foreign consulting or engineering firm is authorized to do business there it must be represented by or associate with a local consulting or engineering firm, or open a local branch office. The same rule applies to successful bidders on Paraguayan public works projects, with the additional limitation that the local share of the project be at least 20 percent.

In a similar vein, some free-access countries impose labor requirements on the foreign investor. For instance, many enterprises in Brazil and Chile must have a work force with a composition of at least 66 percent and 85 percent local workers, respectively, though technical jobs that cannot be filled by nationals are generally excluded from the calculation. While Brazil now has no other express participation laws, in practice the Brazilian government does not hesitate to intervene to force local involvement.

Other legal limitations on the foreign investor's ability to conduct business are scattered throughout the free-access countries. In Argentina, transfers in company ownership from domestic shareholders to foreign investors typically require Executive Branch approval. Transfers of capital between foreign entities doing business in Argentina and their related entities ordinarily require Argentine Executive Branch approval as well. The laws of certain countries, Brazil and Chile in particular, can make the acquisition of local real estate very difficult, if not impossible. Some countries, like Chile, specify that any vessel on which a foreign-based entity imports or exports goods have a certain minimum percentage of local ownership. Capital assets of foreign entities doing business in Paraguay may not be sold, traded, or transferred until five years have lapsed since the date of customs clearance. Finally, outsiders are normally obliged to register their investment and capital with, and often obtain the approval of, a national government agency.

The Andean Pact Nations

Quite apart from the free-access countries are the countries who presently belong to the Andean Pact (Bolivia, Colombia, Ecuador, Peru, and Venezuela). The Andean Pact is an international organization created to spur economic growth in its member nations. Policies toward that end are implemented by the Cartagena Agreement Commission in the form of decrees called decisions. In the field of foreign investment, the commission has created a complex matrix of rules codified in Decision 220, formerly known as Decision 24.

The rules promulgated thus far by the commission generally discourage the inflow of investment from abroad. To illustrate, Decision 220 prohibits ''direct foreign investment,'' which is expansively defined, in any activity that the various national foreign investment ministries have determined is adequately covered by existing enterprises. Of pact members, Bolivia and Ecuador generally are the most liberal in concluding that existing enterprises do not adequately cover a specific activity.

Other commission rules tending to inhibit foreign investment in Andean Pact countries include:

1. Goods subject to certain industrial programs of the Andean Group may be produced only in those countries to which such goods have been allocated.
2. Direct foreign investment for the production of goods reserved or allocated exclusively to Bolivia or Ecuador cannot be authorized by other Pact countries.
3. The benefits provided under the trade liberalization program sponsored by the pact are unavailable to a foreign enterprise unless it agrees to bring local investors into the enterprise over time under the Andean Pact's Transformation Program. (The trade liberalization program eliminates the conditions and restrictions on the transfer within the Andean Pact of products originating in the territory of one of the member countries.)

4. Intellectual property rights cannot be used as capital contributions.
5. Income remittances and the reinvestment of profits are limited.

Andean Pact Nations: The Transformation Program

The Transformation Program promotes local participation in business enterprise within the Andean Pact, and should be thoroughly understood before a joint venture is undertaken in any Andean Pact country.

Central to an understanding of the Transformation Program are the definitions of foreign enterprise, mixed enterprise, and national enterprise. A foreign enterprise is one established in an Andean Pact country with local ownership of not more than 51 percent of total capital. Even if local ownership exceeds 51 percent, the proper national authority has the discretion to classify the enterprise as foreign under specified conditions. A mixed enterprise is one in which local ownership ranges from 51 to 80 percent of capital or in which the State, State-controlled entities, or State-owned enterprises have at least a 30 percent ownership interest, provided the State controls those positions which are fundamental to the enterprise's operation. A national enterprise is simply an enterprise with more than 80 percent local ownership.

The Cartagena Agreement Commission calls for the transformation of foreign enterprises to mixed and then national enterprises in accordance with the laws of member countries. Under the programs implemented by Andean Group members, transformation generally is compulsory in Venezuela (regardless of whether the foreign enterprise seeks the benefits of the Andean Pact's trade liberalization program), but is generally optional in the rest of the Andean Pact countries. Bolivia, for instance, permits 100 percent foreign ownership for unlimited duration. However, Decision 220 stipulates that in order to benefit from trade liberalization within the Andean Group, foreign investors generally must enter into, and subsequently follow, a transformation agreement with the pertinent authority.

In the event that a foreign enterprise concludes an agreement under the Andean Pact's Transformation Program, its owners must sell, on a gradual and progressive basis, a percentage of their ownership to local investors in accordance with the time requirements of local transformation law. The term of transformation varies from country to country.

Colombia's transformation schedule is typical. Local ownership of Colombian enterprises must represent:

1. At least 15 percent of the enterprise's capital once three years have elapsed from the date of signing of the enterprise's transformation agreement.
2. At least 30 percent, once one-third of the period for transformation has elapsed.
3. At least 45 percent, once two-thirds of the period for transformation has elapsed.
4. At least 51 percent of the capital before the transformation period terminates.

Exemptions from the Transformation Program are available. Foreign enterprises that export 80 percent or more of their output to non-Andean Pact countries and enterprises in some economic sectors (e.g., agriculture, tourism, and construction of immovable property) are not subject to transformation restrictions. Venezuela may provide for a suspension of the transformation process for a given foreign enterprise when there is sufficient economic justification. Some Andean Pact nations are quite lax in their enforcement of the transformation rules.

Andean Pact Nations: Other International Requirements

The Cartegena Agreement Commission's decisions dealing with intellectual property rights affect foreign investment in the Andean pact nations. For instance, the life of a patent, new industrial design, model, or trademark is five years in member countries; one five-year extension is available. Contracts for the transfer of technology must conform in content to the requirements of Decision 220 and the pertinent national government ministry. A number of restrictive covenants, such as clauses giving the sellers of technology the right to fix the sale or resale prices of products manufactured on the basis of their technology or the right to restrict the value and method of production, are prohibited.

Andean Pact Nations: National Requirements

While the Cartagena Agreement Commission is responsible for issuing Andean Group rules on foreign investment, the responsibility for implementing those rules and the power to regulate foreign investment further within each member country is vested in a specific national bureau. In Bolivia, the ministry vested with control of foreign investment is the

National Institute of Investments; in Colombia it is the National Planning Department; and in Ecuador it is the Ministry of Industry, Commerce, and Immigration. The relevant ministries of Peru and Venezuela are CONITE (Comision Nacional de Inversiones y Tecnologia Extranjeras) and the Superintendency of Foreign Investment (SIEX), respectively. These agencies are empowered to vary, within specified limits, the rules of Decision 220 and further to formulate policy and promulgate rules in the area of foreign investment. These foreign investment agencies, with the exception of those of Bolivia and perhaps Ecuador, have been fairly assiduous regulators. The agencies have been particularly active in the field of mineral extraction.

Individual Andean Pact nations have established foreign investment requirements over and above those imposed by the Andean Pact as a whole. For example, Colombian labor law requires that at least 90 percent of all unskilled workers employed by a foreign venture, and a minimum of 80 percent of all skilled workers, be Colombian nationals. (Colombia places no limit on the number of foreign nationals in managerial and technical positions, unless the venture is subject to a transformation agreement.) In addition to compulsory allocation of work to local labor, some countries, like Peru, have a compulsory allocation of profits to local labor. Every business enterprise turning a pretax profit in Peru must distribute 25 percent of that profit to its employees and laborers. Most of the other limitations on investment in the Andean Pact countries are not easily categorized.

Currency Exchange and Repatriation of Profits

Most of South America experienced trying economic times during the 1980s. Almost every country has been squeezed by the twin pressures of heavy external debt and rampant inflation (witness Bolivia's 30,000 percent rate of inflation in 1986). Stung by this experience, most countries have imposed rigorous foreign exchange controls and limitations on income remittances and the repatriation of earnings.

As a result, capital transactions and the exchange of currency can be difficult for the foreign investor. Typically this means that the foreign investor must obtain Central Bank approval of any remittances of earnings or other foreign transfers. Even such perfunctory tasks as determining the conversion rate can prove difficult; the majority of countries adjust the official rates of exchange daily. To complicate matters further, some countries such as Paraguay have created a multitiered exchange schedule in which more than one exchange rate is available.

Aside from the difficulty of converting local currency, there are usually restrictions on to the amount of investment capital and profits that can be repatriated by the foreign investor. The non-Andean Pact countries, while usually allowing the foreign investor to remit profits without limitation, provided all necessary taxes and surcharges have been paid, generally forbid the repatriation of capital within three years from the date the capital entered the country. Andean Pact countries, on the other hand, do not provide for moratoriums on capital repatriation. The Andean Pact countries instead limit repatriation of earnings, and limit the repatriation of earnings in any year to 20 percent of the foreign investor's profit in Andean Pact countries for that year. In addition, in any given year the typical foreign investor may reinvest his profits in Andean Pact nations only to the extent of 7 percent of his invested capital. A greater rate of reinvestment requires governmental approval. The Andean Pact also restricts foreign investors' access to local credit.

Perhaps more worrisome to international investors is the possibility that a South American country might suspend, as Peru did in 1986, all financial outflows in times of serious disequilibrium in its balance of payments. The measures taken by Peru include a two-year suspension of (1) remittances of dividends, profits, royalties, and similar payments (but specifically excluding fees under technical assistance agreements); (2) payments of principal and interest on foreign medium- and long-term loans to the private sector; and (3) the repatriation of the proceeds from the disposition of an investment in Peru. In addition, most resident entities were forced to surrender to the Central Bank foreign currency accounts and deposits held at site. The two-year ban is scheduled to be lifted on August 7, 1988. Other countries have given their governments emergency suspension rights similar to those invoked by Peru.

INCENTIVES FOR FOREIGN INVESTMENT

South America's unhappy fiscal experience in the 1980s, while resulting in generally strict foreign exchange controls, has benefited the foreign investor in one sense. Determined to restore economic stability and investor confidence, most South American governments have implemented policies specifically designed to attract foreign investment. It should be noted at the outset that some countries are more aggressive than others in the pursuit of foreign investment. Argentina, for example, is less inclined to provide the foreign investor with investment incentives than, say, Uruguay or Paraguay.

On the whole, current incentives tend to be specific to an industry; most incentives are designed to channel foreign investment into the particular economic sectors deemed by a government to be inadequately developed and away from those sectors where development is deemed sufficient or is not a priority.

The foreign investor's right to receive favorable treatment often depends upon the classification that the supervising government agency assigns to the proposed investment. For example, under Paraguay's Industrial and Social Development Law No. 550, which gives special benefits and tax exemptions to foreign investors and offers guarantees against expropriation, the Paraguayan government classifies the qualifying investment as either necessary or advantageous. As the terms suggest, as investment classified as necessary (that which uses native materials and increases exports) entitles the foreign investor to more generous benefits than does an investment classified as advantageous.

One widely offered incentive in South America is the governmental guarantee against future changes in tax rates and customs and export regulations. Positive guarantees, like assurances of convertibility of domestic funds into the currency of the foreign investor, are also offered in some countries. Chile offers to guarantee to a foreign investor the right to petition the Chilean government for redress in the event that the government introduces any regulation discriminating against the foreign investor. The effectiveness of these guarantees as incentives turns upon foreign investors' confidence that a government will be in a position to honor these commitments in the future.

Another common incentive available in South America relates to machinery and raw materials. In sectors where these items are needed, the foreign investor is often exempted from paying custom duties and taxes on these items. If these items are used to produce goods primarily for export, some countries allow for exportation of the goods without the usual export tariffs, surcharges, and taxes. If the goods (whether or not for export) are produced as a result of a joint venture in which a South American governmental agency is a partner, the goods themselves, and the foreign partner, will benefit from a number of concessions.

Favorable tax and regulatory treatment also is available to foreign investors who locate their operations in free trade zones. Such zones have been established by virtually every nation on the continent, and are intended to facilitate the industrial processing of goods destined for export. Ecuador does not yet offer free trade zones.

SELECTING A JOINT-VENTURE PARTICIPANT

In choosing a local participant for a South American joint venture, a foreign investor should consider a number of factors. The financial history and strength of the prospective partner should be reviewed, particularly if the joint venture is to be located in a country that has a history of economic instability. The foreign investor should confirm the experience of other foreign investors in conducting a joint venture with the prospective participant. The compatibility of the respective organizations should be explored, including the structure of the entities, their attitudes toward labor relations, their technical capabilities, and their available personnel. The foreign investor should verify the reputation in the marketplace of the prospective partner, in order to gain the access to information and markets that an impeccable reputation can bring. The efficiency of the prospective partner's operations, including its quality control procedures and relationships with suppliers, merits investigation. A potential partner should have adequate governmental and financial contacts to aid the foreign investor with local regulations, commercial registration and licensing, and financing options. This handbook's chapter on joint ventures in the Middle East contains a fuller discussion of the factors pertinent to the selection of a local joint-venture partner.

Possible resources for finding suitable partners are consulting firms who specialize in identifying prospective joint-venture participants, banks with overseas offices, national or prominent local law firms and accounting firms, trade associations, U.S. companies engaged in exporting, the U.S. government, and the relevant South American government.

CHOICE OF ENTITY

The foreign investor who wishes to form a joint venture with a local investor in South America may choose from several entities. Although not all choices are available in every South American country, the choices include the *sociedad accidental* (an informal arrangement by private agreement), the *sociedad anonima* (roughly equivalent to a U.S. corporation), the *limitada* (or limited liability company, with no common equivalent in the United States), and general and limited partnerships. The Andean Pact also offers two forms of companies known as Andean Multinational Enterprises.

The foreign investor who will be operating in South America without local participation generally may take advantage of any of these entities other than the Andean Multinational Enterprises. The use by such a foreign investor of a local branch, however, may be ill-advised. The restrictions placed on local branches of foreign corporations can be severe. One example of such a restriction is the tax rate applicable to the taxable income of foreign corporations, which can range as high as 50 percent in some countries. (The lowering of the U.S. corporate tax rate to 34 percent provides a smaller U.S. foreign tax credit to foreign investors.) Furthermore, the registration and authorization of the local branch can be a lengthy and expensive process, since most countries require government approval of the branch operation. Local branches of foreign corporations may also be confronted with discriminatory legislation that allows preferential treatment for local companies. Local statutes often impose on local branches of foreign corporations the same minimum capital requirements imposed on local subsidiaries. Lastly, the foreign corporation can be liable for the debts incurred by the local branch in its operations.

Sociedad Accidental

Several South American nations recognize the *sociedad accidental,* although the arrangement bears a number of different names. The *sociedad accidental* is created by private agreement among investors and is not a formal entity at all. In this type of arrangement, one party's identity is revealed to those with whom the venture is conducting business and the other parties' identities remain confidential. Foreign investors are permitted to serve in the role of silent participant. Management of the *sociedad accidental* can be shared or vested solely in the party known to the public. The party who deals with the public is, in some countries, liable to a greater degree for the debts incurred by the group than the other participants. There are few restrictions on the division of profits among the parties to a *sociedad accidental.*

Sociedad Anonima

The *sociedad anonima,* or corporation limited by stock, is a frequent choice for conducting business in South America. While the requirements for this type of entity will vary from country to country, the similarities are sufficient to produce a general description.

There is no minimum capital contribution required upon the incorporation of a *sociedad anonima* in a majority of the South American countries. A few countries do require a stipulated amount of capital, foreign or local, to be available to the *sociedad anomina* before its incorporation will be approved by the local governing authority. After incorporation, the failure to maintain a required level of capital in some South American jurisdictions can cause the involuntary dissolution of the *sociedad anonima.* One such country is Colombia, whose laws require the dissolution of the corporation in the event that its capital is reduced by 50 percent. Uruguary is the least restrictive country of this group in that its laws allow a corporation's stated capital to be impaired by two-thirds before dissolution is mandatory.

The number of shareholders required prior to the approval of the *sociedad anonima*'s incorporation varies among South American countries, but requirements for a minimum of either two or three shareholders are not unusual. A minimum number of shareholders for ongoing operations is also sometimes required, with dissolution required for corporations whose number of shareholders falls below the minimum. The registration requirements for a *sociedad anonima* with foreign shareholders can be expensive and time-consuming.

Generally, the management and control of the *sociedad anonima* is vested in a board of directors. There may, however, be restrictions imposed on the composition of the board of directors. Some countries, such as Peru, mandate labor representation on the company's board of directors. Along these lines, control of corporations located in foreign trade zones will be limited by some governments, thus minimizing foreign ownership benefits in these areas.

There are restrictions in South America on a *sociedad anonima*'s ability to distribute profits to its shareholders. For instance, most South American countries limit the amount of profits that can be paid to shareholders as dividends by requiring the corporation to set aside a percentage of its net profits as a reserve. This percentage ranges anywhere from 5 percent to 50 percent. The governments also may levy windfall profits taxes upon profits deemed by legislation to be excessive. Peru, for example, allows the distribution of only a small percentage of profits without government approval and taxes the excess over this amount at a higher rate.

The Limitada

The limited liability company, or *limitada,* also is a possible vehicle for the foreign investor interested in conducting operations jointly with local investors. The primary advantage of the *limitada* is the limited liability of the partners who establish the company. The partners' liability generally is limited to the amount of their individual capital contributions.

Typically, the *limitada* is a commercial company formed by two to three owners. A number of South American jurisdictions impose a limit on the maximum number of persons allowed to participate in the *limitada.* Several countries do not allow foreign corporations to participate in these limited liability companies; however, foreign individuals may be partners and have an ownership interest in the *limitada.* Ecuador is an example of such a country.

Each country differs in its registration and formation requirements for the *limitada,* including whether there must be a minimum capital investment. Generally, the initial capital investment requirements for *limitadas* mirror the requirements for *sociedad anonimas.* Furthermore, most of the South American countries require a stipulated percentage of the capital to be subscribed and paid into the *limitada* within a certain time after formation or even, in some jurisdictions, prior to formation. As with a *sociedad anonima,* a *limitada* may be restricted by government decree from participating in certain economic sectors such as banking or insurance.

The management of the *limitada* differs from that of the *sociedad anonima,* which delegates the management of the organization to a board of directors. Management of a *limitada* can either rest with the partner or partners appointed as manager in the formation documents or be shared by all the partners. Other ways in which a *limitada* differs from a *sociedad anonima* include relaxed financial recordkeeping requirements, the impossibility of public offerings of shares, and fewer formalities necessary for formation. In Brazil, a *limitada* is not subject to the same requirement of a *sociedad anonima, i.e.* that it distribute at least 25 percent of its net profits for the year to its shareholders as a dividend.

Partnerships

Of all the forms of business enterprise in South America, partnerships are most similar to their U.S. counterparts. Most South American countries recognize both limited partnerships and general partnerships. As in the United States, the limited partnership comprises both limited and general partners and provides limited liability for the limited partners. General partnerships have the same traits as their U.S. counterparts, including joint and several liability by all partners for all debts incurred by the partnership and the management and control of the business by all partners. Several countries recognize other forms of partnership. These include commercial partnerships with limited liability or partnerships limited with shares.

Other Entities for Conducting Joint Enterprise

A few South American nations recognize a temporary association of two or more persons for the conduct of joint operations. Depending upon the particular jurisdiction, there can be registration requirements and formalities for such a temporary association. For example, the laws of Argentina provide for the temporary union of companies to undertake a specific project. The duration of the association is limited to the duration of the project. The laws of Bolivia recognize a temporary association of two or more persons having a direct interest in one or more operations that will be transitory and completed from a common fund. Parties to this Bolivian type of temporary association conduct the operations in their own names, and third parties can acquire rights against the association.

Andean Multinational Enterprises

For those foreign investors contemplating operations in one of the Andean Pact nations, a possible business entity is the Andean Multinational Enterprise (or EMA from its Spanish acronym). An Andean Multinational Enterprise is a *sociedad anonima* organized under the laws of one of the Andean Pact nations, that qualifies for its special status as an EMA under either Decision 46 or Decision 169 of the Cartagena Agreement Commission. A *sociedad anonima* cannot qualify as an EMA under both Decision 46 and Decision 169. The benefits of the two decisions are mutually exclusive.

In order to qualify as a Decision 46 EMA, the *sociedad anonima* must have received capital contributions from investors from two or more member countries and such investors must hold at least 15 percent of the enterprise's capital. Foreign investors may hold no more than 40 percent of the capital of the enterprise. The management and control of a Decision 46 EMA must reflect the Andean capital contributed to the enterprise. A Decision 46 EMA qualifies for the benefits of the trade liberalization program of the Andean Pact and is entitled to any economic support otherwise reserved for national enterprises. A Decision 46 EMA may reinvest its profits without prior authorization.

The other form of Andean Multinational Enterprise is a *sociedad anonima* qualifying under the more recently adopted Decision 169. At least 80 percent of the capital of a Decision 169 EMA must be held by local investors from two or more member countries (until 1992 the percentage is 60 percent for Bolivia and Ecuador). In addition, investors from the country in which the EMA is domiciled must hold at least 15 percent of the capital. As with the Decision 49 EMA, the Andean capital must be reflected in the control and management of the enterprise. The benefits accorded to Decision 169 EMAs include exemption from authorization requirements for investment and reinvestment in the country of the EMA's domicile. The Decision 169 EMA has the right to transfer abroad, with proper authorization, the profits of the EMA allocable to foreign investors. In addition, the EMA has the right to establish branches in member countries and to transfer the profits of those branches to the EMA's principal office.

[Editor's Note: After this article was prepared for publication, Brazil ratified and adopted a new constitution imposing significant restrictions on foreign business operations in Brazil.]

CHAPTER 20

JOINT VENTURING IN JAPAN

Richard V.L. Cooper
Coopers & Lybrand
With the assistance of Elana Ben-Haim and Hayato Ono

The joint-venture era in Japan is ending. But a new one is beginning. Western companies once established joint ventures in Japan because they thought that was the only way they could do business there. They established these joint ventures for largely tactical reasons—to sell in Japan, to obtain lower-cost sources of production, and to gain access to Japanese personnel for local operations. As Japan has changed—and indeed it has over the past two decades—the reasons for establishing joint ventures with Japanese companies have likewise changed. Western companies are increasingly establishing joint ventures with Japanese companies for strategic reasons. In this chapter, we explore, first, the reasons for establishing joint ventures with Japanese companies and how these reasons have changed over time; second, selecting a joint venture partner; third, the commercial and legal form of the joint venture; and, finally, the tax implications of establishing a joint venture in Japan.

CONSIDERATIONS IN DECIDING TO JOINT VENTURE IN JAPAN

There are many reasons companies decide to establish joint ventures with Japanese companies and these reasons are going through a period of substantial change. But before we deal with these, let us first explore some of the reasons companies enter into joint ventures in general, irrespective of the site of the venture or the domiciles of the contracting parties. This will provide some perspective for the past and future motivations for entering into joint ventures with Japanese companies.

In thinking about joint ventures and the reasons companies enter into them, consider the following eight general categories.

- *Access to Products.* A company may seek to gain access to or sell a product that it itself does not produce. Sometimes, a company desires to sell its product in conjunction with a product that it itself does not produce, such as a manufacturer of computer hardware entering into a joint venture with a manufacturer of computer software. A company may also enter into a joint venture with the purpose of developing a new product.
- *Access to Markets.* A company wants to sell in a market in which it has little presence or access to the local distribution system. This is particularly common in countries where the local market is legally protected and where the distribution system is seen as especially hard to penetrate. A company may want to reduce the risk of entering a new market on its own. Or it may seek to consolidate its market with that of a competitor to reduce ruinous price competition and protect its market share.
- *Access to Technology.* A company may want to gain access to new product technology or to new manufacturing and production technology. In industries requiring large R&D expenditures, companies sometimes enter into joint ventures to reduce risk and share the cost of R&D. Sometimes companies enter into joint ventures not so much to gain access to a specific technology, but rather to gain a ''window'' on promising new technologies.
- *Management.* Companies often desire access to management know-how or specific expertise. When a mature product line begins to lose its strategic interest, the company may enter into a joint venture to reduce the management burden, in essence handing off the management burden to the joint venture. Companies also often use joint ventures as a way of gaining access to local personnel.
- *Operations.* Companies enter into joint ventures for a variety of operational or tactical reasons such as ensuring access to local suppliers, utilizing excess capacity, or obtaining additional capacity. Another reason is to gain access to low-cost sources of production, whether for parts and components, subassemblies, or the finished product.

- *Financial.* Sometimes companies enter into joint ventures simply to reduce costs: including production costs, marketing costs, management costs, or even real estate costs. A company with a mature product line may enter into a joint venture to clean up its balance sheet—that is, transferring the assets and liabilities of the product line to the joint venture. Companies also enter into joint ventures for investment or portfolio purposes.
- *Legal.* In some countries, particularly developing countries, local laws preclude or make wholly owned foreign investment very difficult. Even if such laws do not preclude wholly owned foreign investment, they may give preferential treatment to local entities and entities with significant local ownership. If a company wants to set up operations there, a joint venture thus becomes a legal or at least a practical necessity.
- *Strategy.* Although many of the above reasons often can and will be strategic in nature, strategy itself can be a primary motivation. For example, a company may enter into a joint venture as a prelude to acquisition, as a first step toward diversification, or as a means of divestiture. It may also serve the tactical purpose of buying time while the company changes strategy.

Past Motivations for Joint Venturing in Japan

We began this chapter by saying that joint ventures in Japan were at the end of an era, but that a new era was beginning. Before considering why companies will want to joint venture in the future, it is therefore useful to consider first why they joint ventured in the past, if for no other reason than to dispel some common myths. Of all the different reasons cited above, it is probably fair to say that four motivations dominated with regard to why Western companies established Japanese joint ventures in the past. For the most part, these reasons were tactical, or operational, in nature.

First, and probably most important, Western companies saw the establishment of a joint venture in Japan with a Japanese company as the only practical way to gain market access. The Japanese distribution system is legendary for its perceived impenetrability. In some industries, for example, companies had to be listed as approved vendors to even be allowed to compete. Thus, setting up a joint venture with a Japanese company that had ready access to that distribution system was seen as the only practical alternative. As is the case with most legends, this one is part fact and part fiction. The success of Coca Cola's wholly owned subsidiary, which was established in Japan in the late 1950s, testifies that a company can be successful in Japan without resorting to a joint venture. The success of Coca Cola and a few other companies such as IBM and Nestle notwithstanding, it still remains true that gaining market access in Japan was more difficult without a joint-venture partner well connected into the Japanese distribution system. It is thus not surprising that the large majority of companies deciding to enter Japan decided to do so through joint ventures with Japanese companies.

A second major reason leading to joint ventures in Japan was legal in nature. Indeed, it is surprising how many usually knowledgable businessmen still think that a joint venture is legally necessary to do business in Japan. Although this is not true, the legal system clearly encouraged joint ventures in the past as the preferred way of establishing operations in Japan. Prior to the convertibility of the yen in 1964, setting up a wholly owned subsidiary required the establishment of a "yen company," which could not repatriate profits to the foreign-owned parent. Although a few farsighted—at that time many would have said foolish—companies chose to follow this route, most chose the alternative form of direct investment in Japan. Under this alternative approach, companies could apply to the Japanese government for approval, which, if obtained, would allow them to repatriate their profits and capital. Not only was the Japanese government somewhat restrictive in its approval, but more important, it typically did not allow the foreign company to own more than 50 percent of the enterprise—hence, the need for joint venture.

Following the convertibility of the yen in 1964, the "yen company" route was abolished for new ventures, so that all new foreign direct investment had to receive government approval. Again, the Japanese government limited foreign companies' investment to no more than 50 percent of the venture, so that joint ventures became further ingrained as the only real way to have a presence in Japan.

This was changed in 1973, when the Japanese government approved new foreign investment regulations to allow 100 percent ownership of Japanese enterprises, both new and existing. The government, of course, retained the authority to deny certain foreign investments, as is the case in most Western countries. From a legal viewpoint, then, foreign investment regulations in Japan today are no more restrictive than those found in most Western countries and are actually more favorable than those in some. Yet, the myth that joint ventures are required in Japan persists, showing once again that it takes time for perception to catch up with reality.

A third factor that led to the predominance of joint ventures as the preferred way of doing business in Japan was personnel. A combination of culture, nationalism, the university system, the "old boy" network, and the nature of the Japanese labor market all conspired to reduce foreign companies' access to top-notch Japanese managers. As a result, the Japanese joint-venture partner became the source of much-needed personnel, particularly managerial talent. The other side of this coin, however, is that unless the joint venture was of strategic significance to the Japanese partner, it usually did not assign "the best and the brightest" to the joint venture. Nevertheless, irrespective of whether the joint venture got the best and the brightest, the foreign company typically fared better under the joint-venture umbrella than it would have on its own.

The fourth reason underlying many joint ventures in the past was that Japan was seen as a source of low-cost supply. Combined with the high productivity of the Japanese workforce and the concern for quality, the artificially low value of the yen made Japan an attractive place from which to source parts and components, subassemblies, and finished products. This led to the establishment of many joint ventures and other forms of collaborative efforts between Japanese and Western companies.

Much of this has changed. Beginning with market access, the Japanese distribution system is much more open now than it was even 10 years ago. To be sure, it is still not easy. But, neither is the U.S. market easy to penetrate for the foreign company, once geographic and cultural diversity within the United States are taken into account. Granted, penetrating the Japanese market is still more difficult for a foreign company than most foreign companies find the United States. It is possible, however, and Western companies are increasingly finding that they can get in if they are willing to devote the necessary time, effort, and resources.

The legal system, too, has changed. Foreign companies can now easily operate in Japan with 100 percent-owned subsidiaries. Although few Japanese companies are put up for sale, foreign companies can even acquire Japanese companies.

As the Japanese economy has opened up, so have its society and labor force. Gaining access to qualified personnel is also no longer the obstacle it once was for Western companies operating in Japan. Personnel turnover rates are still considerably less in Japan than in the West—

particularly the United States—but young, bright Japanese are increasingly turning to job change as a way of progressing "up the ladder." Also, foreign companies operating in Japan, once taboo for most mainstream Japanese, have become an increasingly attractive opportunity for the best Japanese managers.

Finally, Japan is no longer necessarily a low-cost source of supply. Whether or not the yen retreats from the lofty levels reached in 1988, it is doubtful it will retreat to the levels found in the early 1980s. The Japanese economy is simply too strong to see such a retreat, so the yen will probably remain strong in the future. Moreover, Japanese wages are on the rise. Thus, while high quality still makes many goods a good "buy for the buck," or yen, fewer Western companies will be rushing to Japan to establish joint ventures simply because of cost.

Thus, the situation has changed. Many of the tactical reasons that led to joint ventures in the past are no longer valid. Furthermore, companies that entered into such ventures often found to their later regret that they paid a much larger price than they originally bargained for in order to gain the short term tactical advantage. Japanese joint venture partners became at first low cost imitators and suppliers, then low cost competitors, and finally industry leaders. The result has typically been a loss of market share for the Western company and then a loss of strategic advantage.

Joint Ventures in Japan: Looking Ahead

If we are witnessing the end of one era regarding joint ventures in Japan, as we have argued, and the beginning of another, then the driving force for this change lies in the motivations for establishing these joint ventures. Whereas the motivations for establishing joint ventures in Japan were once largely tactical in nature, they have become increasingly strategic.

As noted by Abegglen and Stalk:[1]

All too often, by the time Japanese products begin to appear in volume in Western markets, the competitive advantage has already shifted away from the Western competitor. The strategic battleground is the Japanese economy; it has been yielded by too many Western competitors without a fight.

---

[1]James C. Abegglen and George Stalk, Jr., *Kaisha: The Japanese Corporation*, (New York: Basic Books, 1985).

The case of Eastman Kodak illustrates this point. Once the undisputed leader in photographic equipment and film, Kodak now faces serious competition from Fuji Photo Film. Kodak did not confront the threat from Fuji when it was still only a potential one, even though Kodak had been doing business in Japan for 65 years. Kodak did not devote adequate resources to keeping up with Fuji in terms of R&D for manufacturing technology. The result has been loss of market share and some of its strategic advantage in its mainstay product.

The opposite point is illustrated by Olin Corporation of the United States, which used its joint venture in Japan to thwart Japanese competition in the market for urethane polyols before a serious competitive advantage was developed in Japan.[2] Olin formed a strategic joint venture with Asahi Glass in 1970, while most Western companies were still pursuing joint ventures for tactical reasons. The venture was carefully conceived with benefits and payoffs for both sides: Olin was able to establish close working relationships with users in Japan and was able to receive the financing for a new state-of-the-art manufacturing complex through the joint venture. Asahi benefited from initial technology transfers, but Olin carefully structured the venture so that any new technologies developed through joint R&D efforts were shared by both partners.

The Asahi-Olin venture also enabled both partners to fulfill their strategic aims to diversify into related areas that neither partner had the resources to pursue independently. For example, the partners integrated forward into the urethane systems business and established a new joint venture in the United States to produce thick film substrates for the electronics market.

Looking beyond these two immediate examples, it seems clear to us that most successful, future joint ventures in Japan, at least among large Western companies, will be strategically based, not tactically based. Even smaller Western companies, which still seem inclined to follow the tactical route, ought to pursue more strategically based ventures, lest they pay the same price in the future that their larger brethren paid in the past when they failed to heed the importance of viewing Japanese joint ventures in more strategic terms.

---

[2]Nathaniel Gilbert, "Asahi-Olin: An International Joint Venture Can Be a Many-Splendored Thing," *Management Review*, (February 1987).

Just as three or four principal motivations dominated the formation of Japanese joint ventures in the past, the same is likely to be true in the future. What are they?

Again the first is market presence. Only this time, the underlying motivation will be different. In the past, companies often viewed Japan as simply one more country in which to sell their products. This time, the concerns about the Japanese market will be more strategic. To begin with, the Japanese market itself is now much more important than it was in the past. Indeed, as a single-country market, it ranks second only to the United States in size. More important, though, companies have come to realize that they need to be successful in the three major markets of the world—the United States, Japan, and Europe—to have the scale to compete successfully with their peers. Japan is thus an integral part of what has come to be called the Triad Strategy.

When Western companies enter into joint ventures for this reason, they will not simply trade technology to their Japanese partners in exchange for the rights to sell a few more products in Japan. In many cases, in fact, the Japanese partner will have superior technology of its own. Rather, the terms of the trade in the future are more likely to involve two-sided sharing of technology, two-sided sharing of market access, and a joint effort to gain market presence in the uncovered market—Europe for joint ventures with U.S. companies and the United States for joint ventures with European markets. In essence, the target will be to develop global products or global-like products with the distribution systems and market presence to back it up.

A second reason for forming joint ventures in Japan concerns access to technology. This includes both new-product technology and, particularly for the Western partner, manufacturing-process technology. The importance of access to technology as a motivation for forming joint ventures in the future is well illustrated by this statement from William Wray of Honeywell, who has been active in his company's joint-venture efforts:[3]

> Originally, we used the joint-venture approach more frequently in the international arena from a marketing point of view. But, in recent times,

---

[3]Interview conducted by Coopers & Lybrand and Yankelovich, Skelly & White in March 1984 in preparation for the jointly authored study, "Collaborative Ventures: A Pragmatic Approach to Business Expansion in the Eighties."

with the tremendous growth of technology, it has become increasingly necessary to gain expertise and market products in a more timely way—it is important that we reduce the product planning and development cycle. In some instances, the only way we have found to do so is to work with a company that is already advanced in an area we are interested in. In that case, the joint venture becomes the most rapid way to respond to our needs.

As product life cycles continue to shorten, the joint venture becomes an increasingly important tool for retaining competitive advantage, since no one company can stay on top of all new technologies. Moreover, Japanese companies have become a more important source of that technology, particularly in the area of manufacturing-process technology.

A third motivation that is likely to lead to many joint ventures with Japanese companies in the future is the desire to link with related products and technologies. Whether it is computer systems that can talk to one another or consumer products that can be marketed jointly, companies are searching for ways of linking their products with those of other companies. In a sense, this motivation is related to both market access and access to technology previously discussed. The desire to link with other products is driven in part by the desire to increase market penetration; it is also driven in part by the desire to gain access to related technologies.

Thus, in contrast to past joint ventures, which were driven largely by such tactical concerns as gaining a licensing fee on products sold in Japan or obtaining lower-cost sources of production, future joint ventures in Japan are likely to be driven more by strategic considerations.

The above should not be taken to mean that tactical joint ventures are all in the past. There will still be a place for tactical joint ventures, but they are likely to differ from their earlier counterparts. First, tactical joint ventures are unlikely to predominate the way they did in the past. Second, even when tactical ventures are used, there will be more strategic undertones to the ventures. For example, the GM-Toyota auto manufacturing joint venture in Fremont, California is a tactical joint venture in most respects. From GM's point of view, though, the joint venture has helped to keep GM in the small car business while it develops its own follow-on effort in small car manufacturing and it exposes GM to Japanese-style management on the plant floor. At the same time, companies entering into Japanese joint ventures for tactical reasons need to be careful not to give away their strategic advantage, as many of their predecessors did.

Joint Ventures with Japanese Companies Outside of Japan

The venue of the joint venture with a Japanese company has become much less important today than it was in the past. When the motivations for the joint venture largely concerned gaining access to the Japanese economy, the logical site was Japan. Now that Japanese companies are world class competitors in their own right, and the reasons for joint ventures are more strategic in nature, it is less important for the joint venture itself to be located in Japan.

The above is not to deny the importance of Abegglen and Stalk's argument noted earlier that the Japanese economy itself has become the key battleground. Quite the contrary, the Japanese economy has become so important that companies should not leave it to their joint ventures alone, but instead need their own independent presence in Japan.

When considering a joint venture with a Japanese company, the Western company thus has an additional factor to consider—namely, where it should be located. To be sure, many ventures will continue to be located in Japan. But many already are and will continue to be located elsewhere. The recent joint venture between the Japanese advertising giant Dentsu and the U.S. advertising agency of Young & Rubicam is a case in point.[4] In Japan, the venture provides Young & Rubicam with expertise in targeting Japanese clients, as well as access to clients through Dentsu's considerable network of complex business relationships. For its part, Dentsu seeks to improve its ability to service first hand the accounts of Japanese companies outside of Japan. The Asahi Glass-Olin joint ventures cited earlier provide another illustration. The two companies set up one joint venture in Japan and then subsequently set up another in the United States.

CHOOSING A JOINT-VENTURE PARTNER

Choosing a joint-venture partner in Japan is both easier and more difficult than choosing one in most other countries of the Far East. It is easier in Japan with regard to such factors as reputation and ability to deliver what

---

[4]Bernard Krishner, "Biggest Ad Agency," *Fortune*, (November 1, 1982).

is promised, since sources of information in a developed economy such as Japan are generally quite good. This is particularly true when the Japanese company is large and maintains a high profile. For smaller Japanese companies—as with smaller companies anywhere—one needs to be a bit more careful. But even in this instance, information sources are still usually available.

Where Japan is more difficult is from the strategic viewpoint. Western companies should take greater care than they often do to answer such questions as "Is there a strategic fit?" and "Are there strategic pitfalls or dangers?" These same two questions are equally appropriate, whether it is the Western company that is seeking a Japanese partner or whether a prospective Japanese partner has approached the Western company.

Beginning with the question of fit, it is useful to think of the joint venture and the potential joint-venture partners in two different respects. First is whether the underlying motivation for the joint venture is strategic, tactical, or portfolio (i.e., investment). Second is the type of competitive relationship between the companies:

- Direct competitors. Examples would be GM and Toyota or Kodak and Fuji Film.
- Producers in the same industry, but not typically competing in the same markets. An example would be Young & Rubicam and Dentsu.
- Producers of similar or related products, but not usually direct competitors. Examples would be Olin and Asahi Chemical or Fujitsu and Microsoft.
- Vertically related companies—that is, in an industry somewhere up or down the production or distribution chain. An example would be Sara Lee and Seiyu supermarkets.

With this framework in mind, Table 20.1 illustrates how a company may use its underlying motivation to assess the type of Japanese company it should consider as a joint-venture partner. For example, if a company is looking to link its product with those of another company, then it would most likely look to a vertically related company.

More broadly, it is clear from Table 20.1 that the strategic opportunities lie mainly with producers of similar or related products that are not typically direct competitors. To a lesser extent, strategic opportunities may also lie with vertically related producers and producers of the same products that sell in different markets. Direct competitors, on the other hand, are generally much less viable as partners for strategic ventures,

TABLE 20.1
A Guide to Choosing a Joint-Venture Partner in Japan*

If your specific objectives are listed in the table, then look for a joint-venture partner that is a:

If your broad objectives are:	Direct Competitor	Producer of Same Products Selling to Different Markets	Producer of Similar Products	Vertically Related Producer
Strategic	Develop new product Divestiture	Develop new product Strategic marketing Access to mfg. technology	Develop new product Strategic marketing Access to product technology Access to mfg. technology Management know-how Diversification Acquisition	Access to product technology Divestiture Acquisition
Tactical	Consolidate markets Protect markets Access to mfg. technology Reduce technology risk Management know-how Obtain capacity Low-cost production Reduce costs Buy time	Sell more into Japan Access to product technology Reduce technology risk Obtain capacity Utilize excess capacity Low-cost production Reduce costs Buy time	Sell more into Japan Access to products Reduce technology risk Utilize excess capacity Reduce cost	Access to related products Ensure suppliers
Portfolio	Reduce mgmt. burden Clean up balance sheet		Reduce mgmt. burden Clean up balance sheet	

*To use this table, begin with the broad objective on the left. Then look across the row. Then look for the specific objective(s) in the main body of the table. Then look up to the top of the table to see the type of joint-venture partner to choose.

except when the two want to develop a new product together. The reason for this, of course, is that the success of one partner is more likely to come at the expense of the other when the two are direct competitors. Direct competitors thus find it more difficult to use the joint venture as a tool for meeting their strategic objectives. For producers of different but related products or services, the joint venture can help to satisfy a common strategic need without generating the kind of conflict that direct competitors face.

By way of contrast, direct competitors will often be the most attractive choice for tactical joint ventures, although other kinds of companies can be worthwhile partners as well. To understand why, consider first that tactical joint ventures are typically intended to realize nearer-term, less-strategic opportunities or to solve nearer-term, less-critical problems. In this instance, the direct competitor typically brings more to the joint venture than a company not in the same industry or market. The key, however, lies in structuring the joint venture such that the joint-venture partner cannot use it to gain a larger strategic advantage.

This brings us to the second issue raised earlier—namely, the pitfalls and dangers of joint ventures with Japanese companies. Unlike the past and unlike the joint-venture situation in many other Asian countries, where the concern may have been or may be about piracy of technology, the principal danger today in Japan is much more likely to center on whether the Japanese partner will be able to use the joint venture to seize a strategic advantage on its own. Japanese companies have shown themselves to be particularly adept at taking and combining various ideas, recognizing the market opportunities, and focusing on quality and manufacturing cost to achieve strategic advantage. To avoid this danger, the Western company needs to keep two things in mind, particularly when joint venturing with a direct competitor. It must be sure to structure the joint venture in a way to minimize the chances of its partner using the joint venture to successfully gain strategic advantage. It must also not be content with its existing product and manufacturing technology, as too many Western companies have been in the past. It must instead continually work toward improved quality and reduced cost, for it is clear that its Japanese partner will be doing so.

Beyond these broader issues of strategic fit and the pitfalls and dangers, the Western company needs to be aware of two additional aspects of Japan's industrial structure in order to identify specific partner candidates. The first, which is particularly important if the joint venture intends to sell in Japan, is that distribution channels in Japan are very specific and often narrower than in the West. It is therefore important to be sure that the prospective joint-venture partner has access to the necessary distribution channels. Second, just as Japanese society is structured much more according to rank and status than is the case in the West especially in the United States, so Japanese industry is much more structured along these lines. Thus, if it is the Western company that is seeking the joint venture, it should begin by approaching companies of its approximate status. Fortune 100 companies can feel comfortable in approaching Japan's industrial giants. Smaller- and medium-sized Western companies will usually have greater success in approaching second- or third-tier Japanese companies, or second- or third-tier subsidiaries of larger Japanese companies.

Once the type of potential joint-venture partner has been selected, then the company should identify the specific candidates. In general, the Japanese company should be approached at a high level by a high-ranking member of the Western company, lest the joint venture get lost in the bureaucracies of the two companies.

One final consideration bears mentioning. As noted in the next section, Japanese companies often operate as part of a group of companies, the so-called *Keiretsu* or *Shudan*. The issue then becomes the extent to which joint venturing with a member of one of these groups can be used to gain better access to other members of the group. The Western company should thus first compile a list of the group's member companies, examine the extent to which other members of the group might have something to contribute, and then explore the extent to which they are willing to do so.

COMMERCIAL AND LEGAL STRUCTURE

Up until now we have used the term *joint venture,* when in fact a better term for much of the discussion up to now would probably be *collaborative venture.* The term *joint venture* often carries the connotation of a specific legal entity. Yet, many of the most successful joint ventures, particularly looking ahead, may have no formal legal status at all. The term *collaborative venture,* which does not carry a legal connotation, may therefore be more descriptive. Collaborative ventures embrace a variety of specific constructs, including strategic alliances, joint-marketing agreements, cross-licensing, and, of course, legal joint ventures.

To understand why we prefer the concept of collaborative ventures, it is important to have some understanding of Japan's industrial structure. Unlike most Western countries, where economic enterprises and relationships among them tend to be transparent and well defined, Japan's industrial structure is more complicated, more subtle, and less transparent. For example, Japan's industrial structure includes companies, called *Kaisha*.

It also includes groups of companies with vertical ties known as *Keiretsu*. The *Keiretsu*, which have legal status, generally revolve around a related set of activities, such as vehicle manufacturing. There is usually a head company and other companies in the group refer to themselves as affiliates. An example is the Toyota group, with Toyota Motor Corporation as the head company. Other companies in the group are involved in a wide range of activities generally related to manufacturing of vehicles, parts for vehicles, and financing of vehicles. In one sense, *Keiretsu* are like Western-style conglomerates, with the *Keiretsu*'s affiliates comparing somewhat to a conglomerate's subsidiaries. In another sense, the two are very different. Unlike the conglomerate, in which its subsidiaries are usually wholly owned, the *Keiretsu*'s affiliates are not usually wholly owned. Moreover, they do not have the same centralized management as the Western conglomerate, but instead work together in informal ways.

Another group of interrelated companies known as corporate *Shudan* are in many ways even more interesting. They are descendents of the famed prewar, family-controlled *Zaibatsu*, which controlled much of Japan's prewar industrial structure. Unlike the *Keiretsu*, in which there is some degree of formal or legal relationship, the *Shudan* have no legal status or structure. Instead, the *Shudan* consist of groups of very informally related companies that span virtually the entire economic spectrum in their activities, including trading, heavy industry, finance, real estate, and so forth. The names of these groups have come to be well known in the West: Mitsui, Mitsubishi, Sumitomo, Fuyo, Daiichi-Kangin, and Sanwa. The informality of the groups is reflected in the names that they often go by in Japan. For example, Mitsui is referred to as the "Second Thursday of the month luncheon conference." There is also no formal head of the group.[5] These groups instead coordinate policy and strategy informally.

---

[5]However, the trading companies, or *Sugoshosha*, are at the center of activities for the Mitsui, Mitsubishi, and Sumitomo groups, while the Fuyo, Daiichi-Kangin, and Sanwa groups center on their lead banks.

There are other types of relationships as well, such as interlocking ownership among different companies. Moreover, even seemingly well-defined relationships among the *Keiretsu* and *Shudan* are actually less well defined than they are often portrayed as in the Western press.[6] For example, some Japanese companies belong to more than one *Shudan*; others occasionally change their group, while still others float in and out of groups.

The point is that Japan's industrial structure embraces a wide variety of networks and forms of relationships, some of which have a formal legal structure as in the West, but many which do not. As a result, the Western company that insists on a specific legal structure may miss some of the most interesting and potentially fruitful collaborative opportunities. Of course, there will be many formal joint ventures in Japan and with Japanese companies, but there will be other types of collaborative efforts as well. In general, collaborative ventures with Japanese companies fall into three broad categories:

• Informal Collaboration: Under this approach the collaborating companies agree on some specific goals and methods, but do not form a legal entity. Methods can include joint marketing, cross-selling of each others' products, and personnel exchanges, among others.

• Informal Collaboration with Cross-Ownership: This approach is similar to the above, except that in addition to the agreement, the companies each purchase some of the others' shares, sometimes as little as 1 percent of each others' outstanding shares. This cross-ownership of shares typifies the corporate *Shudan*. Occasionally, each company will take someone from the other on its board of directors. The purpose of such an exchange of shares is simply to demonstrate a greater commitment to the common goals of the collaborative effort.

• Formal Joint Venture: This is still the most common form of collaboration, both because it is the form most common to Western companies and because Japanese companies are beginning to think more along these lines as they gain greater experience with Western companies, their ways of doing business, and the legal structures of their countries.

For all our discussion about relationships and the various types of informal collaboration that are both likely and worthwhile, let the Western

---

[6]It is more typical in Japan to refer to the *Keiretsu* and *Shudan* members by their names—e.g., the Toyota group or the Mitsui group—rather than the formal names *Keiretsu* and *Shudan*. Note further that the *Shudan* and *Keiretsu* described here are sometimes both labeled *Keiretsu* in common usage, particularly in The Western press. *Shudan* is the more recent term for an old concept.

company be forewarned. Its Japanese partner, though faithful to the agreed-upon goals of the joint venture, can easily be its fiercest competitor in other areas. A warm and cozy relationship in one area thus does not necessarily translate into a warm and cozy relationship in other areas. This is not unique to the relationship between Japanese and Western companies, but rather is even more characteristic of the relationships between Japanese companies themselves. They will cooperate on one project and be tough competitors on others. Thus, as a Western company considers a collaborative effort with a Japanese company, it needs to think about what type of relationship will be most suitable. There is generally considerable latitude in this choice.

If the companies elect to establish a formal joint venture—that is, a legal entity—the choice is much more circumscribed. To begin with, Japan does not have a joint-venture law per se, but rather relies on its standard commercial structures. Therefore, we need to first consider the primary company forms used in Japan:

- *Kabushiki Kaisha (KK)*. Roughly translated, a KK is a limited-liability company with perpetual life, although termination provisions can be specified in the articles of incorporation. As such, it is the most common form of corporate entity, particularly for larger companies, Japanese or foreign-owned.
- *Yugen Gaisha*. A limited-liability company that is usually family owned. The *Yugen Gaisha*'s directors, however, have greater liability than is the case for either a KK or a U.S. corporation. Foreign ownership is possible, but not frequent.
- *Gomei Gaisha*. An entity, part corporation and part partnership in nature, that must be family owned and has unlimited liability. Again, foreign ownership is possible, but very unlikely.
- *Goshi Gaisha*. Like the above, it is part corporation and part partnership, but with limited liability and is usually family owned. Again, foreign ownership is possible but unlikely.
- *Kumiai*. It is the closest Japanese counterpart to a partnership in the United States, which thus has unlimited liability. It is generally not-for-profit, except for certain special cases such as farmers' cooperatives. Therefore, although foreign ownership is possible, it generally occurs in only specialized circumstances.

In most cases, the joint-venture partners will therefore establish the joint venture as a *Kabushiki Kaisha* (KK) or limited-liability company.

It is the most similar to a corporation in the United States, with its limited liability, perpetual life (unless otherwise defined), and shareholder structure. (Note: the other *Gaisha* company forms do not really have a Western counterpart.) The KK is also the form used by most major Japanese corporations.

Since the KK was originally intended primarily for publicly listed companies with many shareholders, the incorporation procedures tend to favor such enterprises. Although the KK format can be used for closely held companies and is in fact the form used by most formal joint ventures in Japan, the approval process is somewhat longer and more cumbersome if the KK has fewer than seven shareholders.[7] Thus, one sometimes finds joint-venture KKs set up with the Japanese and foreign companies joined by five Japanese individuals, who hold only one share each. This is usually done only for organizational purposes; the individual Japanese shareholders usually return their shares to the Japanese partner after a short period of time.

In rare circumstances, other legal forms may be used such as the *Kumiai*. Because *Kumiai* are generally nonprofit, the *Kumiai* has limited usefulness for joint ventures. An exception would be if two or more companies wish to set up an R&D partnership, where the joint-venture partnership is not expected to earn a profit, but rather the shareholders "profit" through access to the jointly funded R&D.

TAX CONSIDERATIONS

In this section, we review briefly the tax consequences of establishing a joint venture in Japan. It should be noted at the outset that there are many subtleties to the Japanese tax system, many more than can be adequately explained in a short section such as this. We will therefore merely provide a brief overview of the tax structure in Japan. Companies seriously considering a joint venture in Japan should use the discussion here as a general guide and should then consult their tax advisors for specific guidance.

---

[7]For a discussion of some of the legal issues involved in establishing a KK, see James A. Dobkin, *et. al.*, *International Joint Ventures*, Federal Publications Inc., A Longman Group Company, Washington, D.C., 1985.

Recall from the last section that most joint ventures in Japan will use the *Kabushiki Kaisha* (KK) format for their corporate structure. Since Japan does not treat joint ventures differently from other corporations, the joint-venture KK is taxed according to the rules of other KKs. Briefly, a KK is subject to three principal taxes:

• *Income Tax.* A corporation established in Japan (domestic corporation) is, as a rule, subject to corporate national income tax at the rate of 42 percent and corporate local income taxes at rates discussed below on its worldwide net income. For income earmarked for dividends, the 42 percent rate is dropped to 32 percent. Further, for a domestic corporation with a capital of ¥100 million or less, the 42 percent and 32 percent tax rates are reduced to 30 percent and 24 percent, respectively, for the first ¥8 million of income. Note: for local branches of foreign corporations, the tax rate on income earmarked for repatriation does not drop to 32 percent, but instead remains at 42 percent.

• *Corporate Enterprise Tax.* A domestic corporation is subject to corporate enterprise tax mainly at the rate of 13.2 percent on its net income. The tax is payable to each prefecture in which a domestic corporation has its business offices or factories. The aggregate amount is distributed among the prefectures according to a formula that takes into account such factors as the number of employees in each prefecture. The 13.2 percent rate is reduced somewhat for corporations that do not have a presence in at least three prefectures, are capitalized at less than ¥10 million, or that are located exclusively in smaller prefectures. Enterprise tax is not imposed on foreign branches of domestic corporations (*e.g.,* foreign branch offices of a joint-venture KK are not subject to the enterprise tax). Enterprise tax is deductible from income in the accounting period in which it is paid for purposes of determining corporate national income tax.

• *Corporate Inhabitants Taxes.* The corporate inhabitants taxes are payable to prefectures and municipalities at the rates of 6 percent and 14.7 percent, respectively, of the national corporate income tax liability where a domestic corporation locates its business offices, etc. For Tokyo, the rates are combined to yield an aggregate rate of 20.7 percent of the corporate national income tax. For certain other localities and smaller businesses, the 6 percent and 14.7 percent rates are lowered to 5 percent and 12.3 percent, respectively. In addition to these rates, inhabitants per capita taxes are payable regardless of net income or national tax liabilities.

In Tokyo, for example, the combined prefectural and municipal tax ranges from ¥50,000 to ¥3,750,000, depending on the size of the corporation.

Combining the above yields an effective tax rate of 56.44 percent on income not earmarked for dividend distribution and 44.37 percent for income earmarked for dividend distribution, exclusive of per capita corporate inhabitants taxes. These rates will be somewhat lower for smaller companies and for companies located outside the large prefectures or municipalities.

For the most part, the computation of taxable income follows rules similar to those found in most Western countries. Key exceptions are as follows. Dividend income received from domestic corporations is excluded from taxable income, except that if dividends received exceed dividends paid, then 25 percent of the excess is added to taxable income. Enterprise taxes, as noted earlier, are deductible from income. Depreciation and depletion are not deductible unless recorded in the company's books. A provision for doubtful accounts may be deductible to an extent specified in the tax code. There are also certain tax credits or incentives available, such as the tax credit for incremental R&D and export incentives for companies capitalized at less than ¥500 million.

Looking beyond the tax liability of the joint-venture KK itself, the Western partner's ultimate tax liability will depend on how its KK participation is structured. In this regard, the Western company faces three principal alternatives regarding its participation in the joint-venture KK.

Investment Through a Japanese Subsidiary

The foreign corporation can establish a subsidiary in Japan, usually in the form of a KK, which is a domestic corporation. The foreign company's subsidiary KK then makes the investment in the joint-venture KK. Under this format, a 20 percent withholding tax is imposed on the payment of dividends from the joint-venture KK to the subsidiary KK, as well as to the Japanese investor. When the subsidiary KK pays a dividend to the foreign parent, another 20 percent withholding tax is imposed for companies from non-tax-treaty countries. Companies from tax-treaty countries pay a smaller withholding tax on the repatriation of dividends from the subsidiary in Japan to the foreign parent (for the United States, the withholding tax rates are 10 percent if the U.S. investor holds more than

10 percent of the joint-venture KK and 15 percent if the U.S. investor holds less than 10 percent—*i.e.*, so-called portfolio investors).

Investment Through a Japanese Branch

Alternatively, the foreign company can establish a branch in Japan, which in turn invests in the joint-venture KK. The tax treatment for the joint-venture KK is the same as described above. Regarding the tax treatment for the branch, the branch is still liable for the 20 percent withholding tax on dividends paid from the joint-venture KK to the branch, as is the case for the subsidiary. But, there is no withholding tax on moneys paid from the Japanese branch to its foreign parent since, technically, this is not viewed as a dividend payment. Note, however, that if the branch has other income-producing activities beyond its investment in the joint-venture KK, this income is not eligible for the reduced tax rate on amounts earmarked for repatriation since, again, these are not technically viewed as dividend payments. The reduction of national tax rates from 42 percent to 32 percent for income earmarked for dividends only applies to domestic corporations, which include subsidiaries incorporated in Japan and owned by foreign companies, but not Japanese branches of foreign corporations.

Direct Investment from Abroad

As a third alternative, the foreign company can invest in the joint-venture KK directly from abroad, thus bypassing any local presence. Again, the tax treatment of the joint-venture KK has already been discussed. However, the withholding tax is imposed directly on the payment of dividends from the joint-venture KK to the foreign investor, since there is no intermediate entity such as a branch or subsidiary. The amount of this withholding tax is again governed by the relevant tax treaty. For foreign investors from countries without a tax treaty, the rate is 20 percent. In the case of a U.S. investor, for example, the rate will be 10 percent or 15 percent, depending on whether the U.S. investor holds more than 10 percent of the joint-venture KK or less, respectively.

Thus, the overall tax burden for the foreign investor, including both the taxes paid directly by the KK and the withholding taxes paid on dividends, is greatest if the foreign company invests in the joint-venture KK through its own wholly owned Japanese subsidiary. But, its freedom of permissable activities in Japan is also the greatest. By way of contrast, the total tax burden is the least if the foreign company invests directly from abroad, but its range of activities in Japan is also the most circumscribed. Investing in the joint-venture KK through a Japanese branch represents a middle ground in terms of both taxes and range of business activities that can be conducted in Japan. Alternatively, some companies follow the two-pronged approach of investing in the joint-venture KK from the foreign parent while operating an unrelated subsidiary for their other operations in Japan.

In closing, it should again be emphasized that companies seeking to establish operations in Japan, whether through a joint venture or on their own, should obtain tax advice based on their own unique circumstances. The Japanese tax system is not simple and is full of subtleties.

CONCLUSION

The proliferation of various types of collaborative ventures throughout virtually all sectors of the world economy attests to the increased importance of the collaborative venture as a tool for enhancing a firm's competitive position. And nowhere have collaborative ventures sparked more interest, concern, and controversy than in Japan.

The interest stems from the allure and mystique of the Japanese market, which continues to draw Western companies into collaborative ventures with Japanese companies. The concern and controversy, of course, come from watching Japanese companies change from low-cost imitators and marketers of Western technology to world-class competitors and innovators in their own right, with the result being a loss of Western competitive advantage. As noted by Reich and Mankin,[8] "America's engineers risk losing the opportunity to innovate and thereby learn how to improve existing product designs or production processes . . . Unless U.S. workers constantly gain experience in improving a plant's efficiency or designing a new product, they inevitably fall behind the competition."

Much of the problem stems from the fact that too many have viewed the collaborative venture as an end in itself, when in fact the collaborative joint venture should be viewed as a means to an end. Accordingly, before

---

[8]Robert B. Reich and Eric D. Mankin, "Joint Ventures with Japanese Give Away Our Future," *Harvard Business Review*, (March-April 1986).

a company begins the arduous task of searching for an appropriate venture partner, it must first examine carefully what its basic business objectives are. As part of this process, the company must assess the major external forces that create new demands on an industry and on the company. Among these are the degree of present and projected globalization in the given arena, technology requirements and the pace of technological change, availability of resources needed, and the nature of competition in the industry.

Increasingly, vital changes in these areas such as rising capital costs, escalating business risks and R&D costs, increasing scarcity of resources, rapid rates of technological change, and deregulation of previously protected industries are making collaborative ventures more attractive, particularly collaborative ventures with Japanese companies. But, unlike the past when joint ventures in Japan were pursued for largely tactical or operational reasons, they are now generally being pursued with more strategic concerns in mind.

Looking ahead, we can envision three main types of collaborative ventures with Japanese companies that will result from these concerns. First are collaborative ventures undertaken by large companies that are truly strategic in character. Second are collaborative ventures undertaken by large companies that are more tactical in nature, but which are established in a strategic context. Examples would be filling a particular market niche or managing the final years of a mature technology. Third are the old-style "gain access to the Japanese market" tactical joint venture that many smaller companies just entering Japan are likely to pursue. Unfortunately, many of these companies will learn the hard way the lessons that their larger counterparts have already learned. For although Japan remains a difficult and time-consuming market to penetrate, the Japanese commercial and legal system has opened sufficiently that joint ventures of this sort are no longer a necessity.

PART 3

JOINT VENTURING WITH FOREIGN COMPANIES IN THE UNITED STATES

James A. Dobkin
Arnold & Porter

AN OVERVIEW

In increasing numbers, foreign businesses have been reaching beyond their national boundaries to the United States in an effort to locate new opportunities for growth, new markets, new technology and/or new venture capital.These business activities have taken a wide variety of forms, including licensing and technology transfer agreements, export transactions, establishment of U.S branches and subsidiaries, and joint ventures with U.S. companies. The joint-venture form of association, in particular, has proven to be a conducive and flexible vehicle for such activities, especially in fields requiring high initial cost outlays.

Consider, hypothetically, a foreign corporation that has long been involved in the research and development of certain fuel-cell technology. It has made significant advances towards developing a prototype system capable of generating large quantities of electrical energy. However, in so doing, it has expended very considerable sums, and foresees that substantial additional risk capital will be required to bring the system to a point of commercial application sufficient to interest the electrical utility industry. The management of the foreign corporation is reluctant to invest the amounts still required and has decided to seek outside financing arrangements. Additionally, the company has not been involved in marketing activities for the type of system involved, particularly in the United States, has no contacts or influence with U.S. utilities, and is, therefore, interested in locating a U.S. firm with marketing expertise and utility industry experience to participate in a cooperative effort. Thus, the foreign company is considering an arrangement pursuant to which such a U.S. firm would contribute to a joint venture consideration—in various forms—roughly comparable to the sum already expended by the foreign company in the development of its fuel-cell technology. The foreign company would be willing to contribute its technology and know-how, but, at least initially, is unwilling to contribute any additional capital.

The foreign company has had preliminary discussions with an established U.S. corporation, that has in place a marketing network for systems similar to the one in point and that has useful business contacts with U.S. electrical utilities. The U.S. corporation has also been engaged in some research and development work for the same type of system, but its work has not progressed to the same stage as that of the foreign company. The U.S. corporation, therefore, has a natural interest in combining forces with the foreign company and, if a joint enterprise does not work out, in obtaining the technology and know-how developed as a result of the collaborative effort and as much of the foreign company's background technology as may be necessary to effectively utilize the joint-venture technology.

The parties' initial discussions indicate that their objectives and goals appear to be complementary to a significant degree. It is contemplated that a joint venture could complete the development and engineering efforts of the foreign company, which efforts would culminate in the production of several prototype systems. Full-scale production and marketing activities would follow. The joint venture would be owned equally by the joint-venture partners (JVPs), who would also participate equally in management decisions.

The parties determine that the foreign company will contribute its existing technology, which the parties have agreed should be valued at an amount roughly equivalent to the developmental costs already expended by the foreign JVP. In essence, the foreign company will be contributing an ongoing business, including contracts, patents, and technology (*i.e.*, trade secrets, technical data, and know-how). The U.S. corporation, although contributing all of its interest in the field, will also be required to contribute cash as consideration for the development costs already expended by the foreign company. Cash contributions in equal installments covering five years will be made in a total amount equivalent to the past R&D expenditures of the foreign company. This cash will be used to complete the development and engineering of the prototype systems. Thereafter, systems would be produced and marketed in the United States by the joint-venture company. To the extent additional capital is needed, the JVPs would be equally responsible for the funds.

THE NATURE OF A JOINT VENTURE

A joint venture is a distinctive form of business association created by co-owners for the purpose of engaging in a joint enterprise or undertaking. The attributes of a joint venture include co-ownership and co-management in a partnership-type relationship characterized by close interaction and cooperation. In the United States, the courts have defined a joint venture as an association of two or more persons (whether corporate, individual, or otherwise) combining property and expertise to carry out a single business enterprise and having a joint proprietary interest, a joint right to control, and a sharing of profits and losses.

Although joint ventures are normally governed in the United States and many other countries by the substantive law of partnerships, they differ from partnerships in that partnerships contemplate operation of a more general business. The joint venture need not be formally organized as a corporation, but in more substantial undertakings it is customary to do so in the United States. What form the association takes—partnership, general business corporation, close corporation (or its equivalent in other countries)—depends on several factors, including the objectives of the parties involved.

The motivations of foreign companies forming a joint venture in the United States are several and often overlapping. The foreign company may not have sufficient resources to undertake a particular project, and may need the financial resources of a U.S. partner with similar needs or interests to share the business risks and reduce the burden of investment costs. Research and development or applied engineering activities which require a substantial initial cost outlay may best be carried out through such a joint-venture operation. Or, both parties may wish to pool their respective technology and expertise, thereby expanding the capabilities and business opportunities available to each other. Or, a foreign company may desire to enlarge its market power or to expand into the U.S. market, with which it may have little or no familiarity. All of these factors characterized the interests of the foreign company in our hypothetical example. As in the example, a U.S. joint-venture partner, which is well established, knowledgeable in U.S. business customs, and equally at risk, may provide the most satisfactory mechanism for completing the technological development and establishing a viable presence in the United States for the foreign firm.

Regardless of the motivating force, the joint venture provides a means of achieving business and economic objectives potentially beyond the capabilities of either joint-venture partner acting alone. This is the primary advantage and hallmark of this form of association—the ability to combine the strengths, expertise, technology, and know-how of separate businesses with the concomitant benefit of sharing investment costs and risks.

The primary advantages of the joint venture are that:

• A joint venture can allow the participants to undertake potentially speculative and high-risk endeavors without exposing assets to unlimited liability. Accordingly, a company can experiment with larger projects or enter into new areas without making a permanent commitment or risking capital beyond its means. In addition, the JVPs can define at the outset the extent to which each shall be liable for costs and shall share the risks associated with the endeavor.
• A joint venture provides a substantial degree of flexibility in distributing operational responsibilities and authority between the JVPs, allowing the parties to utilize effectively the particular strengths of each.

The primary disadvantages of the joint venture are that:

• A joint venture usually involves co-ownership and co-management, creating a risk that problems will develop in the decision-making process. This is particularly true in the case of 50/50 ventures where there is an increased probability of management deadlocks that can effectively stalemate all activities.
• A joint venture may have its effectiveness undermined by negotiated compromises between JVPs replacing the certainty of a more autocratic form of management. Although recognition of this problem at the outset allows the JVPs to provide for dispute-resolution mechanisms, the disruptive potential remains.

Given the close cooperation necessary for effective operation of the joint venture, a substantial unity of interest between JVPs is a prerequisite for success. Unlike merger or acquisition transactions which necessitate agreement of the parties only for a short period of time and after which only one of the parties will control the enterprise, a joint venture requires continuing agreement between the JVPs as to the nature and scope of the enterprise. If the basic objectives of the individual JVPs are incompatible at the outset or if they change over time, these differences can create significant problems and bring about the premature termination of the venture.

OVERVIEW OF RELEVANT CONSIDERATIONS

The formation of an international technology joint venture located in the United States can be a complex process. The goals of the enterprise must be defined, the structure must be negotiated, numerous legal issues must be recognized and resolved, and potential areas of conflict between the JVPs must be identified and reconciled. Careful planning is required at all stages.

At the outset of every proposed joint venture, it is necessary to have an understanding of the basic objectives of the proposed enterprise. This includes identification of the nature and scope of the undertaking, as well as the parties' expectations and goals. For example, if a foreign company is seeking a short-term arrangement to measure the potential market for a product in the United States, a licensing or straightforward contractual arrangement might be preferable to a joint venture, which generally contemplates a relationship of greater duration and more substantial commitment.

If a joint venture in the United States is deemed desirable, one of the first major considerations is the selection of a compatible U.S. joint-venture partner. Generally, a foreign concern will seek a co-venturer of equal business stature and with comparable corporate policies, philosophies, and financial resources; although achieving this objective obviously is not always possible. There is an understandable fear on the part of many smaller foreign companies that a U.S. megacorporation could easily swallow up its foreign partner, especially if the foreign JVP holds a less-than-equal equity interest in the joint-venture entity.

Through the process of active negotiation, involving business people as well as lawyers, the JVPs should determine whether their objectives are compatible. This process would commonly be employed for any transaction, but it may be substantially more difficult, although even more important, in the context of multinational joint ventures, given the cultural, linguistic, political, and social differences between the parties. Similarly, there may be legal, accounting, and tax differences between the countries of the JVPs. All of these differences may give rise to misunderstandings that must be reconciled before the joint venture is consummated.

The next step is to establish the basic structure of the business venture. A variety of complex legal and practical considerations are involved at this stage. It is necessary to identify the respective contributions of the parties and the proposed financing arrangements, in order to measure the compatibility of the potential JVPs, to establish their respective equity interests, and to determine the appropriate organizational form. Frequently, as in the example, the foreign JVP looks for a capital infusion and, in return therefor, shares its technology, expertise, and know-how. The evaluation of that technological contribution must balance the capital contribution of the U.S. JVP in order to justify equal equity interests in the venture, assuming no other material contributions by either side.

Next, counsel must identify and resolve major U.S. and foreign legal issues and potential problem areas, including governmental regulatory matters. For example, U.S. national security interests could serve to preclude any type of release or "export" of information to a foreign JVP. Similarly, a significant U.S. antitrust problem could preclude certain close business associations. The antitrust problem might or might not be curable by the manner in which the relationship is structured (*e.g.*, by a licensing or other nonassociational form of arrangement, as opposed to a joint venture). To the extent reporting requirements may be applicable (such as filing with the U.S. Department of Justice and Federal Trade Commission under the Hart-Scott-Rodino Antitrust Improvements Act), the foreign JVP should be alerted to such requirements at an early stage of negotiations. The disclosure system of U.S. law is often unknown in other countries and may be problematical to a foreign JVP, which may be reluctant to disclose its financial and business arrangements. Foreign laws and regulations may also have an impact on the proposed joint venture, in which case it may prove necessary to consult foreign professional advisors in connection with particular problem areas.

It is also important to identify potential areas of conflict between the JVPs so that they can be reconciled prior to making an irrevocable commitment. For example, the parties may have to deal with differing tax goals resulting from fundamentally different business goals, or more commonly, different constraints of the tax laws and accounting practices of the United States and the home country of the foreign partner. Early recognition of such issues allows the parties sufficient flexibility to structure the joint venture to minimize or avoid these problems.

STEPS COMMONLY FOLLOWED IN NEGOTIATING AN INTERNATIONAL TECHNOLOGY JOINT VENTURE BASED IN THE UNITED STATES

The Information-Exchange Agreement

One of the first steps in the selection of a U.S. joint-venture partner should be an information-exchange agreement by which the parties agree to exchange certain limited technological and business information. The exchange of information at this stage allows each party to evaluate its prospective partner to determine, at least preliminarily, their potential compatibility, the stage of technological development of each, their respective financial strengths (or weaknesses), their respective management structures and ideologies, and whether these various factors are or can be made to be complementary. In sum, this exchange of preliminary information allows the parties to assess the feasibility of the joint venture and sets the stage for the subsequent negotiations.

In the case of our hypothetical example, the technological disclosure by the foreign company should be sufficiently explicit to demonstrate the current state of the fuel-cell development and the anticipated developmental goal. A preliminary business plan prepared by the foreign company might also be provided for analysis by the financial personnel of the U.S. company. The plan would demonstrate to the U.S. corporation the economic feasibility and attractiveness of the proposed venture. The U.S. corporation would probably prepare its own business plan. Sometimes the plans prepared by the parties do not agree in all respects because of different business or accounting philosophies, such as the extent to which revenues would be retained or profits distributed. Ultimately, of course, such differences must be resolved.

The Letter of Intent or Memorandum of Understanding

If, after the exchange of information, both parties are still interested in pursuing the venture, the next step usually is the negotiation of a letter of intent, memorandum of understanding, or "heads of agreement." Although there is no legal or other requirement for such a document, it serves to memorialize the fundamental understandings and intentions of the parties. It can also be used to obtain any necessary corporate authority to pursue further the joint venture, and it is the first step towards a definitive Joint-Venture Agreement. In other words, it is an important interim measure to "keep the ball rolling." This can be more important than might be readily apparent, since joint-venture negotiations can take many months, even years, to conclude and anything that keeps up the interest of the parties is helpful.

Generally, the letter of intent or memorandum of understanding sets forth the skeleton of the proposed venture. However, it can describe the contemplated venture in as much detail as the parties feel is appropriate. In some cases, such a document can be almost as detailed and as vigorously negotiated as the Joint-Venture Agreement itself, and in such instances it will, hopefully, reduce the effort to arrive at the Joint-Venture Agreement. The letter of intent or memorandum of understanding should not purport to bind either party and should stipulate that any obligations are subject to a number of contingencies, including the consummation of a mutually acceptable definitive agreement; receipt of any governmental approvals, consents or authorizations that may be necessary; acquisition of outside funding if that is contemplated; and any required board of director or shareholder approvals.

The main purpose of the letter of intent is to provide assurance that both parties are serious. In this regard, it should require a commitment that neither party will pursue any efforts to locate an alternate joint-venture partner, pending consummation of a definitive agreement.

The Joint-Venture Agreement

The Joint-Venture Agreement, sometimes called a "Stockholders Agreement" if the joint venture will be embodied in a corporate form, is the heart and soul of the joint venture and, as such, must be comprehensive and unambiguous in its terms and conditions. In addition to a number of relatively standard provisions, the Joint-Venture Agreement should seek to anticipate all of the material contingencies that might occur during the life of the joint venture and prescribe means for dealing with each of them. This is particularly important in an international arrangement if the foreign JVP is not accustomed to doing business in the United States.

Many foreign JVPs are understandably confused by the complications of U.S. regulatory activities, the reputed litigiousness of U.S. corporations, and other real or imaginary concerns, all of which may be compounded by the need to provide for the future disposition of rights in technological assets upon termination of the joint venture. The result, more often than not, is a far more complicated and comprehensive Joint-Venture Agreement than either party might customarily employ in its own domestic affairs.

Each Joint-Venture Agreement is unique and should take into account the particular relationship, including equity interests, contemplated by the JVPs, as well as local and foreign law considerations. There are, however, certain generic provisions which should appear in all such agreements, but which unfortunately, sometimes do not. Indeed, while the inclusion of these provisions often is to the advantage of the foreign JVP, it is the foreign partner who most likely has done business in the past without such formality and comprehensive documentation.

Management of the Joint Venture

Provisions defining the structure and responsibilities of the management of the joint venture are particularly important. In the rare case, a foreign JVP may abdicate its management prerogatives and permit the U.S. partner to run the show. This may not be a bad idea where the U.S. operations of the joint venture are better left to the partner most familiar with, and geographically closest to, the operations of the joint venture and the marketplace. In most ventures, however, both partners participate actively in the management of the joint-venture entity. In a 50/50 joint venture, the JVPs normally desire equal voice in and control over operations of the joint venture and will exercise these rights through their management designees.

The mechanism for appointment and/or election of the executive officers and other management personnel of the joint venture should be spelled out in the Joint-Venture Agreement. Moreover, their respective responsibilities and duties should also be set forth in the agreement in order to avoid future misunderstandings concerning the scope or any divisions of authority.

Procedures for Resolving Disputes

Inherent in joint ventures, particularly 50/50 ventures, is the potential for stalemate or deadlock between the JVPs' representatives. A major goal of the parties, to the extent reasonably possible, is to anticipate areas of conflict and to build into the agreement acceptable dispute-resolution mechanisms in order to avoid premature termination of the joint venture or protracted and costly litigation.

Termination of the Joint Venture

Termination of the joint venture may occur for many reasons, including fulfillment of the purposes for which it was formed, a fundamental disagreement of the parties that precludes continuation of the relationship, or a change in the law that is of such nature as to render continuation impractical. Those events which the parties agree will trigger termination should be specified in the agreement, and the consequences of such a termination should be set forth in detail.

The Patents and Technology to be Transferred

The technology, including know-how, which is commonly referred to as intellectual or industrial property, may be one of a company's most important assets. A company normally would have difficulty justifying substantial expenditures on research and development without some assurance that it will have exclusive control over the results. Accordingly, the laws of most countries provide incentives to undertake research and development efforts that protect against infringement and misappropriation of the fruits of the effort.

In international joint ventures, such as in the hypothetical example, the transfer of technology, whether by way of separate assignment or license agreements or as part of the Joint-Venture Agreement itself, is often the essence of the deal. Even though the transfers of technology are usually made to the joint-venture entity (in which the owner of the technology will have an interest), the transfers must nonetheless be made with the same care and deliberation as transfers to unrelated entities.

CONCLUSION

It is apparent that the international joint venture located in the United States is a popular and efficient means of conducting international business relations. However, it can be a complex and difficult undertaking when different cultural, technical, legal, and entrepreneurial values are involved. Because the stakes in this field are often so high and the distances so great, considerable care must be taken to assure that goals can be achieved and, if they are not, that one party does not suffer disproportionately. The joint venture can often be the best means for penetrating new U.S. markets, but there is a degree of risk that must be assumed as in any venture which presents the opportunity for substantial reward. Advance planning and the anticipation of problems that could frustrate the efforts of the parties can reduce that risk to an acceptable level.

CHAPTER 21

JOINT VENTURING IN THE UNITED STATES WITH EUROPEAN COMPANIES

Reinhard Augustin
Price Waterhouse

European companies with multinational interests are currently facing a crossroad. Rapidly changing markets in the United States and elsewhere may require changing or abandoning strategies which have been successful in the past.

While focusing on German companies as a European example, this article outlines some aspects of the U.S. market and how the U.S. market will be effected by global market developments. Adjusting to these trends, companies may be required to take risks and to provide human and financial resources beyond their capability. A joint venture might be the solution, if it is planned and executed with care.

THE U.S. MARKET

Traditionally, German businesses have been heavily export-oriented. Recent figures indicate that industrial companies such as machinery and automotive manufacturers export more than 50 percent of their total production.

Among the foreign markets, the United States is viewed as one of the most attractive for German businesses for many reasons including:

the size of its market, a highly industrialized economy which appreciates the full range of German products, affluent buyers, relatively unrestricted access to the markets, and no currency restrictions. In 1986 exports to the United States totaled 53 billion deutsche marks; direct industrial investments represented over 8 billion deutsche marks. While 1986 exports to the United States represent only 10 percent of all German exports, German direct investments in the United States are about 50 percent of all German direct investments abroad.

One weakness in the German-American export situation is the volatility of the U.S. dollar. The recent decline of the U.S. dollar has clearly demonstrated how dependent German export companies are on currency fluctuations. The dependency is best reflected by a statistic published in 1987 by the Bureau of Labor Statistics. Expressed in percent of the U.S. labor costs, the German labor costs have developed as follows:

Date	% Labor Cost
1985	75
1986	103
Jan 1987	120

While the dramatic percentage increase in labor costs does not reflect any changes in productivity, it nonetheless has a clear message—German production costs expressed in U.S. dollars exceed U.S. production costs. This trend will continue in the near future because of the continuing volatility of the dollar and because of Germany's extremely inflexible system of labor costs which—contrary to that of the United States—makes it almost impossible to lower labor costs. In addition, the U.S. Congress is discussing a trade bill, which is likely to impose certain trade restrictions, such as quotas and/or stiffer tariffs on imported foreign goods.

These developments make it more attractive to consider the establishment of German production facilities in the United States.

EFFECT OF GLOBAL MARKET TRENDS ON THE U.S. MARKET

International market developments also have an impact on U.S. markets; and the following factors should be considered by German companies in planning future U.S. strategies.

1. *Market Globalization.* For many industries it is not enough to be a leader in one or two geographic regions. A competitor with a strategy for global leadership will ultimately surpass regional market leaders.
2. *Technological Advances.* The increased pace of technological change has resulted in shorter product lives. The company that can initiate and quickly adapt to technological advances will be the most successful.
3. *Increasing Capital Needs.* Future growth will hinge on a company's ability to raise necessary capital.
4. *Increased Competition.* Nearly every market continues to see new competitors. For instance, South Korean companies, unknown only a few years ago, have become successful market players worldwide. Sound business planning will account for potential new players in the market.
5. *Industrial and Economic Saturation.* The most recent forecast for the German economy indicates a growth rate of 1.5 percent to 2 percent. With few exceptions similar forecasts have been made for other industrialized countries.

MARKET STRATEGY

These developments mandate critical review and alteration of once-successful strategies. Only after reviewing the existing U.S. market, current German and U.S. political and economic positions, and future challenges can a company choose between a go-it-alone strategy or a corporation with partners.

The go-it-alone strategy simply means exporting directly/distributing abroad through a wholly owned subsidiary. It has the clear advantage of allowing the parent company complete control of the activities in the foreign market. A significant disadvantage is that complete control requires the assumption of the full risk of the venture and the burden of providing all the necessary human, technical, and financial resources. In a cooperation, control is shared among the partners while the risk and commitment of resources is greatly reduced.

Cooperations can be undertaken in nonequity form *e.g.* licensing-, trademark-, distribution-, or production-agreements, or in equity form such as joint ventures or majority/minority investments. Among cooperatives, a joint venture is the most flexible. Partners can tailor-make the three components of every business venture: control, risk, and resources. Since flexibility will become a very important issue in developing future strategies, the joint venture is expected to play a more important role for future German companies in the United States than it does today.

ESTABLISHING A JOINT VENTURE

What steps should a German firm take to establish a joint venture in the United States?

The Planning Phase

The most important decision in a joint venture is selecting the appropriate U.S. partner. Initially, a list of criteria for, or profile of, the ideal partner in the joint venture should be developed. The profile should be designed to complement the German firm in such areas as similarity in culture and strategic thinking, supplementing strengths, and covering weaknesses. A joint venture requires a high degree of accord among the partners at the outset and requires continuing agreement between the participants. The desired partner may be identified through individual efforts or with the help of outside sources, such as investment banks, accounting, or law firms. If assistance is desired, the German firm must describe as precisely as possible the desired profile. This will help to reduce the time and costs of the search.

When a suitable and interested partner is identified, the next step is to get a better understanding of each others's intentions. This often requires exchanging general as well as proprietary information. Care should be taken that the candidate is serious about the joint venture and has no hidden agenda. Also, an agreement should be reached that, in case the negotiations fail, all shared materials will be returned and all proprietory information will remain confidential.

Certain general, legal, and tax implications should be discussed to identify the following: any potential antitrust problems in the United States or in Germany; the filing requirements with both U.S. and German agencies; and, the different tax exposures or accounting regulations in the two countries.

To complete the planning phase, potential partners should sign a letter of intent or memorandum of understanding to:

- Document that the parties are serious.
- Clarify the initial mutual understanding and the goals to be accomplished.

The letter of intent is not meant to legally bind the partners, and any obligations should be subject to contingencies such as obtaining sufficient financing or governmental approval. Also, the parties may agree to commit themselves to a time schedule and not to pursue alternative strategies as long as the negotiations continue.

Implementation

The most important issue to resolve in the implementation phase is the issue of control. *Control* is a somewhat ambiguous term that usually means two things: (1) Authority to make decisions, and (2) the ability to obtain timely and complete information which is necessary to make sound and rational decisions. The joint-venture partners and the proposed joint-venture management must agree on the segregation of controls with the following objectives:

1. To provide the joint-venture management with the flexibility to run the day-to-day operations, *e.g.*, delegation of responsibilities by the partners to the joint-venture management.
2. To approve actions which may be in conflict with each partner's own business, or the joint-venture's intentions, *e.g.*, the joint-venture management is planning to compete in markets retained by each of the partners.
3. To monitor the decision-making process among the partners to avoid both unfriendly disputes and deadlock situations.
4. To provide the partners and the joint venture with complete and timely information which is required to make sound and meaningful decisions, *e.g.*, monthly, quarterly, and annual reporting on the results of the joint-venture operations, or external and internal audits.

In order to accomplish these objectives the following methods may be used:

1. Voting rights may differ from the equity interests and/or profit participation, *e.g.*, a partner with a minority equity interest may have a veto right on certain decisions.

2. To avoid deadlock situations it may be appropriate to arrange for a 49/49 venture with 2 percent in the hands of a third party. On the other hand, a planned deadlock resolution may force the partners to settle on disputed issues out of court, on a friendly basis.
3. Different contractual agreements may be used. The many different objectives and interested parties involved may create a complex network of contractual relationships. The following are some possible alternatives:

- Joint-venture agreement among the partners.
- Bylaws or partnership agreement of the joint venture.
- Management contract between joint-venture management and joint-venture partners.
- Supply contracts between the joint venture and its partners for the delivery of goods, services, or know-how.

There are no specific regulations for joint ventures in the United States or in Germany; therefore, the legal form of the entity can adopt several structures. Although industrial joint ventures usually are organized as corporations, a general/limited partnership should also be considered. The following issues should be reviewed:

1. Liability risks for obligations of the joint venture.
2. Management structure.
3. Terms of the joint venture.
4. Transferability of interest.

All four issues can be resolved to the same degree of the partners' satisfaction under the corporate or the partnership concepts. However, the partnership concept may require extra steps. Most ventures favor a corporate structure since this vehicle is readily available, more structured, and—for industrial companies—a customary format.

TAX ASPECTS OF THE JOINT VENTURE

The tax aspects between German and U.S. partners do not represent a separate issue but follow the tax regulations for corporations or partnerships, respectively. For example, if the joint venture is organized as a corporation, its U.S. income is protected from German taxation; only dividends paid to the German partner will ultimately be subject to German taxation. Dividends, paid by a U.S. corporation to a German shareholder are subject to 15 percent U.S. Withholding tax which can be credited against the shareholders German tax liability.

The tax treaty between the United States and Germany allows the transfer of royalties free of U.S. income or withholding taxes. Considering the difference between the corporate income tax rates of the two countries, transfer of fees from the United States to Germany may not be an attractive alternative. For instance, currently the U.S. corporate income tax rate is 34 percent compared to the German rate of 56 percent for retained income. Even with a projected tax decrease, Germany's rate will remain at 50 percent.

Under a partnership agreement, the transfer of income to Germany is attractive, assuming the German joint-venture partner is an individual subject to German personal income taxes. If the German partner has to pay 28 percent in federal income tax in the United States, he is exempted from the German income tax of up to 56 percent. The U.S. partnership income will be taken into account only in determining the overall tax rate to be applied to the taxable income (Progressionsvorbehalt), still leaving the German partner a relatively low tax rate. Unfortunately, this structure may expose the German partner to a considerably high liability risk because there is no corporate entity to provide legal protection.

FINANCING THE JOINT VENTURE

Typically, a German investor will finance the U.S. corporation with equity and debt, at an acceptable ratio under tax and legal guidelines. Frequently the debt financing is arranged through a U.S. holding company in order to fully utilize the interest expenses in consolidating the U.S. results. In the case of a joint venture, the major condition for the consolidation—ownership of at least 80 percent—may not be met. The U.S. holding company may have to arrange for other income sources from the joint venture or from other investments of the German partner in order to service its debt. As an alternative, the German partner may decide to provide the financing directly through his German corporation. However, under certain circumstances in Germany, the tax deductibility of the interest expenses related to the financing of an U.S. investment may be restricted.

The financing of a joint-venture partnership allows more flexibility since related interest expenses of a partner can be deducted from his taxable income irrespective of his percentage of ownership.

Terminating the Joint Venture

The joint venture is a business entity requiring day-to-day decisions by its management and guidance by its partners. A well-run joint venture can be disrupted by the following situations:

- A deadlock preventing the joint venture from operating.
- An issue or act that contradicts the joint-venture agreement.
- Failure of the joint venture to meet expectations, or to comply with the changed strategies of one of the partners.

A lasting dispute among partners will negatively affect the joint venture; therefore, the agreement must provide for resolution procedures, such as these.

Dispute Resolution

There are two options in dispute resolution: arbitration and litigation. Arbitration and litigation can be very costly. It is advisable to obtain from an arbitrator a conciliation plan which represents only a recommendation, that the parties may feel free to accept or reject.

In joint ventures with U.S. and German partners, arbitration might be the best solution since both countries are signatories to the 1958 United Nations Convention on Recognition and Enforcement of Foreign Arbitrated Awards. If the joint venture has operations in different countries with different laws, an arbitrator may be selected from a "neutral" country. If the joint venture has only U.S. operations, it may be more practical to select an arbitrator acquainted with U.S. laws and regulations. On the contrary, litigation may be required to settle a case in the U.S. and the German courts.

Dissolution

In a joint venture engaged in industrial operations, a dissolution of the joint venture would be the least desirable solution. The liquidation values are usually low and do not reflect any recognition of goodwill.

Buy-out Agreement

Under such an agreement one partner will be required to buy out the other partner. A most complicated provision is to determine in the initial agreement a formula/method for the transfer price before a dispute arises. Such formula can be based on values, capitalized earnings, or a combination of both. Also the parties may agree to determine periodically adjusted prices for the joint-venture interests. Frequently the above arrangements are supported by a clause that, in case of disputes among the partners, an outside appraisal should be requested.

An elegant way to resolve a buy-out problem is a so-called "buy-sell options," often referred to as "Russian Roulette" or a "Texas Draw." The mechanics are relatively simple. The partner who initiates the termination "draws first" by offering to buy the other partner's interest at a specific price. The other partner then—after a given period of time— has the choice to accept the offer or to buy at the same price the interest of the initiating partner. Similar to western movies, the partner who draws first is not always the winner.

TIPS TO AVOID VENTURING FAILURES

1. Choose compatible partners with a high degree of long-term homogenous priorities and expectations.
2. Don't expect the joint venture to be a solution to every problem. The joint venture may help the partners to set the stage under more favorable conditions than under a stand-it-alone strategy would have; but the market does not necessarily have to buy it.
3. Control the joint venture. Delegation of authority does not mean giving away the right to information—the one element of control. Also, any changes of business stragtegies, *e.g.*, expanding by crossing into the other partner's territories should be monitored by the partners.
4. Delegate authority. The management by the partners shall be prepared to delegate authority to enable the joint-venture management to react flexibly to market changes.
5. Don't use the joint venture as dumping ground for undesired personnel. Their previous failures are often self-fulfilling prophesies.

OUTLOOK

Changes in world markets, including the United States, will require many German companies to revise their negative attitude towards joint venturing and to consider the joint venture in many situations as the only viable alternative to exploit the market. These market changes have already had an effect in the United States—German automotive part producers have recently formed several joint ventures, and these major joint ventures were recently publicly announced:

- Siemens-Allied Signal combined their automotive parts division.
- AEG-Westinghouse combined major portions of their transportation businesses.
- Henkel-Hercules joined to produce the market water-soluble polymers.

The three above-mentioned joint ventures all have one aspect in common. None of the partners has bet a major part or even all its business on a single joint venture.

CHAPTER 22

JOINT VENTURING IN THE UNITED STATES WITH ASIAN COMPANIES

Thomas T. Yamakawa
Price Waterhouse

AN OVERVIEW

Introduction

While the title of this chapter is joint venturing in the United States with Asian companies, most of the chapter will be devoted to joint venturing with the Japanese. The Japanese are primarily the Asians doing the most investing in the United States. Discussions of Japanese-American joint ventures in the United States will delineate many of the basic considerations, problems, and helpful suggestions applicable to joint ventures between U.S. and other Asian businesses. Direct investments in the United States from other Asian nations are much less frequent and smaller in size, and not much information about them has been compiled or made public. Consequently, very brief references will be made later in this chapter to some of the other Asian entities expected to increase their U.S. direct investments—such as Korea, Taiwan, and Hong Kong.

The most important aspects of joint venturing with Japanese and other Asian businesses are these: first, effective communication—mutually understanding the other partner's needs, desires, and background, and moving in harmony in all aspects of organizing and managing a joint venture. This sounds so simple and self-evident, but is very difficult in practice. It becomes more difficult when the two partners are from entirely different cultural, social, and business backgrounds as they are in American-Asian joint ventures. The differences can be the sources of synergy and strength or the obstacles to good communication and the cause for ultimate, irreconcilable disaster. Many ventures could thrive, but some may fail; no one general formula works for all joint ventures, and generalization is often very dangerous. Homework, commitment, and efforts to understand the other partner are critical factors in a successful joint venture with an Asian company.

The second most important aspect of joint venturing is to bridge the differences in legal, regulatory, tax, accounting, management/corporate cultures, and practices so that the Asian partner understands, and is not bewildered by, the U.S. practices to which the joint venture must adapt in order to succeed. The U.S. partner must also study and understand the differences in order to do this.

The U.S. partner's role will be (1) to understand and anticipate the Asian partner's needs, desires, and constraints, (2) to help the Asian partner understand the whys of the environment, rules, and practices under which the joint venture in the United States must operate, and (3) to help the joint venture achieve its goal in the most optimum, efficient, cost-effective manner from the viewpoints of all—the joint-venture management and partners—shareholders.

"Adventures" in Joint Ventures (in Japan)

A booklet entitled *Adventures in Joint Ventures* was published by the American Chamber of Commerce in Japan in the heyday of U.S. and Japanese joint ventures in Japan in 1960s and 1970s. With humor, it told Americans of horror stories and what could happen if certain basic do's and don'ts are not observed. The Japanese were too polite to bring out their version, but how to joint venture with a U.S. company was a topic intensively studied in Japan.

Adventurous or not, many Japanese and Asian businesses are "old hands" at joint ventures with U.S. multinational companies in their home countries—many were, and still are, very successful; some have been dissolved; others taken over by one of the partners. For more than 30 years since the end of the World War II, it was mostly U.S. companies that invested in Asia and formed joint ventures whenever local restrictions precluded complete ownership control by foreign companies or whenever joint ventures made sense for business reasons.

Also, it was in Japan that joint ventures as a form of doing business and a business strategy literally flourished. In the days of the more restrictive foreign-exchange control environment of 1950s and 1960s, while Japan needed foreign technology, resources, and capital, joint ventures were generally the only way that foreign companies could enter Japan. The Japanese over the years have become used to the idea of joint ventures, their problems and rewards.

Most Japanese-American joint ventures have been successful in Japan. A number of well-known Japanese companies are joint ventures born in 1950–1970 period. Some are public companies and many are well-recognized names in Japan such as Tonen (Exxon and Mobil - Public), Fuji-Xerox, Nippon Light Metals (Alcan - Public), SECOM (started as a joint venture, now public), Mitsubishi Motors (Chrysler-Mitsubishi), Mitsubishi-Caterpillar, 3-M Japan, Nippon UNIVAC, and many others.

Joint Ventures in the United States

Beginning in the mid-1970s, particularly in 1980s, and into 1990s, a reverse trend has been in motion. With rapidly increasing Japanese and Asian direct investments in the United States—in new businesses, plants, real estate, acquisitions or R&D, some are bound to take on U.S. partners as joint ventures. Unlike the situation in Asia, since there are no foreign-investment controls that would limit the percentage of ownership in the United States, except in isolated cases (*i.e.*, regulated industry), joint ventures are formed based strictly on business and strategic considerations and necessities. The trend for joint venturing with Japanese and other Asian businesses will accelerate along with the general acceleration of Asian investments in the United States through 100 percent ownership. A brief look at the following factors would strengthen this view:

1. Manufacturing in the United States is a way of overcoming the rising protectionism in the United States.
2. As auto and other end-products manufacturers from Asia (Japan) move their production to the United States, so must suppliers for the same reasons—overcoming protectionism—move (due to local contents requirements) and more importantly, to keep and develop their market position vis-a-vis the home-country customer expanding overseas markets.
3. Asian productivity and technology have achieved progress over the years through local competition and customer demands. This

includes improvements on what was originally U.S. licensed technology.

4. Financial resources backed by Japanese and Asian financial institutions, in turn, are supported by trade and capital surpluses and a high savings rate.

5. Joint ventures are a way of complementing each partner's market, manpower, facility, infrastructure, and of achieving economy of scale.

6. High-tech and venture businesses (*e.g.*, advanced materials, electronics, biotechnology, food) are increasingly becoming global in sourcing, marketing, and product development. These strategic goals often require working with Asian companies.

What is so unique about joint venturing with Japanese or other Asian partners in the United States? Basically, joint venturing with an Asian company involves the same strategic considerations as joint ventures with any U.S. or foreign company. Equally, many fundamental legal, tax, management, and operational considerations in joint venturing with any third party would apply to joint ventures with Asian businesses. However, there is much more. An Asian partner and an U.S. partner come from almost completely opposite cultural, language, business, management, statutory, and regulatory environments. Each side must understand the other reasonably well and work out a joint-management routine satisfactory to both. Good communication is the key, but it is difficult to communicate without constant special effort. This is more easily said than done. A book such as *Adventures in Joint Ventures* and the myriad other books about Japanese culture, society, business customs, and plain how-to's would not be on the market if it were simple to communicate with, work with, or sell products, services, and ideas to the Japanese and vice versa.

During the negotiations necessary in forming a joint venture and throughout the life of the joint venture, there will be situations in which both Americans and Japanese are bewildered by each other's requests, reactions, and behaviors. The following are some examples of this:

1. A simple, often-heard misunderstanding of the Japanese response to a question—*Yes* alone may mean "I hear you" and not "I agree."

2. *Very difficult,* or *It's a problem* could almost mean "No." Japanese are generally reluctant to use the word *No,* which they regard as too negative and final.

3. The key person in a Japanese company may be a middle-level staff member and not the CEO, someone who tends to lead the people and not necessarily the business. A good understanding of the general pattern of the Japanese corporate decision-making process (both top-down and bottom-up) and an insight into the internal workings of a specific company on a specific project will be necessary. How to identify the key people with regard to a project is almost an art by itself.
4. Consolidated tax filing does not exist in Japan, although most corporations operate with subsidiaries. Primary financial statements are unconsolidated statements. Even published price earnings ratios are based on unconsolidated numbers.
5. Despite a high tax burden, Japanese businessmen generally take more pride in being a good corporate taxpayer. This is partially a by-product of tax rules that require most tax deductions to be booked, creating a dilemma between tax saving and reporting more profits to shareholders and bankers.

Simply stated, the most important message in this chapter boils down to the points discussed below:

1. There are a minimum of three distinct parties involved in a joint venture—the two partners and the joint-venture management. It is important to bear in mind that each has different background, perspectives, motivations, and at times interests, depending on the situation. The parties must constantly work toward maximizing and optimizing synergy, benefits, and economy to all parties involved, and avoid duplication, waste, loss of cohesive direction, and conflicts. A joint venture can range from a mere shell to pool and account for joint venture and expenses to an independent, free-standing organization with its own strategic goals which are in large measure consistent with those of the shareholders. Where a particular joint venture is within this wide range of the varying "joint arrangement" does not matter. What matters is how effective the venture is as one business managed by three or more heads. With Asian companies, these principles become far more important because the process requires mutual understanding and good communication regarding the cultural, language, and "technical" (legal, tax, accounting, business practice) differences.

2. "Technical" differences are more often based on the deeper cultural, social, and business backgrounds. Even though the joint venture is to operate in the U.S. environment and things are to be run the American way for the most part, good communication with the Asian partner is still the key to a successful joint venture. Therefore, those who deal with an Asian partner should gain an appropriate level of understanding of the culture, language, social customs, and business practices of the partner's home country. Each country in Asia should be regarded as different from other Asian countries, although there may be some similarities among some of them. The "orientation" process (so to speak) can include hiring the services of someone who can provide this understanding.

3. It is advisable initially to utilize outside advisors and experts who can bridge the technical diversities in legal, tax, accounting, and many other areas between the two countries. Then, over time, the internal people of the joint venture and the partner companies could develop the ability to bridge the gap on their own. The outside advisors should always be available. One does not learn and develop skills in such complex and deep-rooted diversities overnight or even in a couple of years. This expertise usually comes from working in each of the countries for many years. These outside people could include lawyers, accountants, and other consultants who are intimately familiar with both U.S. and the Asian (*e.g.*, Japanese) practices. Normally, one should deal with specific individuals known to have the expertise with these organizations, preferably those with offices in both countries.

4. The joint-venture partners, particularly the key individuals, need to develop relationships and get to know each other. They should meet regularly both while conducting business and socially. Repeated confirmations of their intentions, progress, and discussion of any problems they may have will help the partners avoid any unpleasant surprises. The distance and time differences between the United States and Asia make communication more difficult. Facsimile machines, home telephones, and face-to-face meetings are valuable in doing business with countries in Asia.

5. In the context of capital flow into the United States in the foreseeable future, an Asian company might be from Japan, Korea, Taiwan, Singapore, Hong Kong, the Philippines, Malaysia, Indonesia, India, Burma, Sri Lanka, Bangladesh, Pakistan, and possibly Mainland China.

Each national background must be dealt with differently, with a fairly good understanding of the specific industry in the home country of the partner, the background of the individual executives one is dealing with, and last but not least, a reasonably in-depth understanding of the culture, the political and economic history of the country, and the environment in which the Asian company has been operating. The influences of an Anglo-Chinese background need to be understood to do business with Hong Kong-and Singapore-based companies. The Spanish and U.S. influences on the Philippines, and other multicultural influences in Indonesia and Malaysia are examples of the diversities one must understand.

AMERICAN-JAPANESE JOINT VENTURES IN THE UNITED STATES

Japanese Investments in the United States

Japanese investments increasing annually at the $5 to $10 billion level in the last two years probably set at least one common pattern for direct investments by other Asian countries. In a large majority of cases, they would prefer to have complete control of their U.S. operation through a 100 percent direct or indirect ownership. However, a trend has emerged more prominently in recent years towards more joint ventures. We are seeing this in automotive, chemical, and financial-service industries as well as R&D projects. Specific reasons and expectations vary from industry to industry and from case to case.

Today, roughly, 2,000 wholly or partially Japanese-owned businesses operate in the United States. There are altogether some 6,000 establishments and premises in separate locations throughout the country, including branches and sales offices. A number of directories and statistics are available on Japanese investments in the United States, facilitating surveys and studies.

A review of a published data—the "Japanese Multinationals," a comprehensive listing of Japanese businesses overseas—indicates that about 80 percent of Japanese operations in the United States are wholly owned by Japanese, including some joint ventures among related and unrelated Japanese entities. Japanese direct investments cover sales, import, distribution and manufacturing operations, financial-service industry, real estate, mining and extractive industry, R&D, and service industry.

The seventh JETRO (Japan External Trade Recovery Organization— so called after the World War II, now with different focuses—encouraging imports to Japan, Japanese overseas investments, and foreign investments in Japan) survey of Japanese-owned manufacturing plants in the United States conducted in May 1987 indicated, among other things, that there are some 640 manufacturing plants and that slightly less than 18 percent of those responding indicated that they were joint ventures. Geographically, they are spread out from the Pacific Coast to the Eastern seaboard, and in the manufacturing corridors in middle America from Michigan and Illinois to Georgia and Texas. Electronics, food, chemicals, automobiles, and machine tools were among the more prominent product lines, according to the JETRO data.

The survey also reported that Japanese executives in the United States listed the following as their concerns—Yen-dollar fluctuations, quality control, competition from NICs (the newly industrialized countries), U.S.-Japan cultural differences, changing demands and markets, product liability, home office relations, environmental controls, and employee relations.

Factors, Trends, and Considerations Prompting Japanese-American Joint Ventures in the United States

The Japanese Perspective

The JETRO survey mentioned above states that joint ventures will be likely to increase. From the Japanese viewpoint, many combinations of strategic considerations point to joint ventures rather than to going it alone. Japanese may share the financial and business risks with a U.S. business which knows its way around.

Joint ventures will give the Japanese partner an access to additional market brought in by the American partner and the benefit of economy of scale. In the auto parts industry, this was the main reason that prompted many Japanese parts manufacturers to seek a U.S. partner.

Japanese companies in the United States generally have spent years studying the market, developing a core of U.S. salespeople, and building a network of dealers and distributors. New Japanese investors who understand this often seek a joint venture route.

In some cases, access to technology held by the American partner motivates Japanese to seek a joint venture. In the high-technology and venture businesses, Japanese are interested in joint venturing or taking active or even passive equity participation in order to have a window on new technology.

In the financial services industry, Japanese have invested significant amounts in passive equity positions, primarily in order to be able to send in one or two directors and a number of young staff members to learn about or jointly handle new financial products, asset-management techniques, etc. In these cases, most of the U.S. partners wanted the access to investor markets and the capital and financial strength of the Japanese partner. There have also been majority acquisitions of banks, primary dealers in government securities, and finance and leasing businesses.

For Japanese to learn management know-how in nonfinancial-service sectors is still an attractive end result, although in the past few years, learning has been mutual in many situations.

Other reasons for joint ventures may include: (1) access to ready production or support facilities which may be owned by the U.S. partner but may be sitting idle, and (2) access to talents, management, industry specialists, and other people essential to the business which might be better attained by joint ventures than by employment contracts under a 100 percent buy-out.

The U.S. Perspective
Generally, motives and rationale for U.S. companies to organize a joint venture with Japanese are pretty much the other side of the same coin—a similar set of strategic considerations to those that prompt the Japanese to go the way of the joint venture. However, joint ventures sometimes can be used innovatively.

A U.S. company may need to modernize its manufacturing process, but further borrowing or debt issue may be difficult due to existing financial positions and restrictions by lenders. A joint venture might be formed with a Japanese manufacturer who would otherwise sell the new process and plant to the U.S. company. The Japanese would contribute the new process and the core plant, while the U.S. company provides other facilities. This would enable the U.S. company to effectively have an off-balance-sheet project financing for the needed process and plant and to utilize otherwise idle utility and support plant and equipment. This assumes that the joint venture can sell the output and generate cash flow not only to compensate for the investment-in-kind by partners but also to provide adequate returns on their investments.

In some cases, joint venturing may be a way of strengthening the company's domestic and global competitive position. As the market becomes global, so must the manufacturers and their suppliers. We are seeing this development in many industries, including auto parts, machinery, chemicals, and services such as financial services and advertising. You go wherever customers are; customers now do business globally and so does your competitor.

Some examples of Japanese-American joint ventures in the United States include:

New United Motor Manufacturing (GM-Toyota)—Automobiles.

Diamond Star (Chrysler-Mitsubishi Motors)—Automobiles.

ALUMAX (AMAX-Mitsui, Nippon Steel)—Aluminium. Japanese partner withdrew recently.

Chino Mines (Phelps Dodge-Mitsubishi)—Copper ore.

Amdahl (Amdahl-Fujitsu)—Computers.

Bull-Honeywell (Bull-Honeywell-NEC)—Computers.

Toshiba Westinghouse (Westinghouse-Toshiba)—TV tubes.

TAP Pharmaceuticals (Abbott-Takeda)—Pharmaceuticals.

GM-Fanuc (GM-Fanuc)—Robots.

DYR (Y&R-Dentsu)—Advertising.

Orient-U.S. Leasing (Orient Lease-U.S. Leasing)—Leasing.

Eastdil (Eastdil shareholders-Nomura)—Real estate investment banking.

More Advantages to a U.S. Partner

Joint ventures usually allow two or more parties to pool their strengths and complement whatever is needed but lacking in the individual partner. In addition to what has already been discussed in this chapter, *i.e.*, a U.S. company seeking a joint venture with a Japanese company, the following are further advantages.

Access to New and Potential Future Markets. As more Japanese companies manufacture products in the United States, as in the case of automobile manufacturers, a joint venture between a U.S. parts manufacturer and a Japanese manufacturer of corresponding parts would provide an expanded market access to Japanese automobile makers establishing their plants in the United States.

Although at present, most of the output may be for U.S. domestic consumption, it is conceivable that in the future, certain car models and parts may be exported to Japan and elsewhere. Thus, the possibility of expanded market access may bring about far more than just one or two

Japanese auto plants in the United States. Some markets will always be captive to specific manufacturers, often on a global basis, and a joint venture can be a vehicle to capitalize on that situation.

The market access advantage is also sought in service industries, such as financial service and advertising. Access to Japanese institutional and individual investors has prompted a number of investment bankers, dealer/brokers, and others to accept significant capital participation or to form joint ventures. Deals such as Sumitomo Bank-Goldman Sachs, Nippon Life-Shearson Lehman Brothers and Nomura-Eastdil were prompted by strategic considerations which included the access to the Japanese financial and investors market as well as the financial strength of the individual Japanese institution. In the advertising field, a joint venture might similarly provide market access to Japanese advertisers from the U.S. partner's perspective.

Access to Financial Resources.   Increasingly, U.S. companies in joint ventures with the Japanese look to the latter's financial strength—backed by their Japanese banks. High liquidity and availability of financial assets have reached a point where some occasional corrections may be due, but the underlying strengths, such as the high savings rate, the stronger trade and capital account position, the increased collateral value of land, and equity securities in Japan still have not changed much, except for a modest correction in the stock market.

With the decline in the manufacturing sector and the continued restructuring of U.S. industries, the Japanese are becoming the providers of capital to businesses that might not have continued otherwise.

Access to Technology.   In current U.S. and Japanese joint ventures technology benefits are often mutual. Each side may have something to contribute. Many Japanese companies were licensees of technology and production processes during the period of capital and technology infusion from the United States to Japan from 1950 to 1970.

In chemical, industrial products, and auto parts industries, what we see now are Japanese licensing U.S. joint ventures with improved technology, production processes, and know-how. Apparently, the improvements and changes made are significant enough in the market place in terms of quality, performance, and cost to warrant introduction in the United States. In many cases, it is the Japanese customers' demands that prompted many changes and adaptations to the technology once imported from the United States. They are now the key to selling products in the United States, to both Japanese and U.S. customers. Of course, brand new technologies are also developed in Japan as seen in chemical, pharmaceutical, and electronics fields.

The above tendency will probably increase in the future, as seen from the U.S. government's efforts to have a technology listening post vis-à-vis Japan. Other Asian countries such as Korea and Taiwan may also become sources of some technology and production know-how.

Related to technology and production are the production-management, quality-control methods, the just-in-time (JIT) inventory, and production management. Manufacturing consultants are actively incorporating the Japanese JIT systems. Joint ventures such as GM-Toyota's NUUMI in California and Chrysler-Mitsubishi's Diamond Star are examples of ventures in which Japanese production management techniques are playing an important role.

Sharing People.   For joint ventures in Japan, being able to avoid the difficulties of finding people willing to change jobs or companies at mid-career is one of the most important advantages of a joint venture. While this may not be exactly the case in the United States, still the advantages are there. Often it is not one or two executives but a whole team of people working together for many years that makes the difference in business success. A joint venture or an acquisition is an easier way to acquire the services of such groups of experienced people. To Americans, a joint venture may be a strategic move to retain good people in the shifting business environment.

Sharing the Facility.   Again, in Japan this is an important factor because of scarcity of real estate and high prices. In the United States, more land is available and various local industrial development efforts make it easy for Japanese companies to acquire land to build new plants. However, extensive time to find and improve land, obtain necessary permits, check any environmental control problems, and build the basic structure, support facilities, etc. may be cut short and money can possibly be saved by utilizing facilities already available from a U.S. partner. In addition, from the U.S. company's perspective, this may result in better utilization of its facility, especially if it happens to be idle.

Indeed, in many joint ventures in recent years, this basic approach wherein a part of capital contribution by a U.S. partner is represented by facility and equipment is increasing. Usually, the equipment used for the core production and process is contributed by the Japanese.

Since the facility thus offered to the joint venture is usually adjacent to or inside the same compound in which the U.S. company has a larger operation and facility, it is possible for the joint venture to use various support facilities on a cost-sharing or cost-plus basis. This brings additional economy and efficiency to the joint venture and to both partners.

In addition, common services can be shared by the joint venture and the U.S. partner company. Examples include payroll, legal, pension, insurance, personnel, and a host of support functions where appropriate.

Japanese and other Asian partners in a joint venture generally are happy with, and probably used to, the sharing and mutually consultative approach to running a business. Except in direct manufacturing functions and other areas where they may feel they can do a better job and thus contribute to the venture's success, Asian partners generally will trust and rely on the support given by the U.S. partner.

Disadvantages, Problems and Pitfalls

Once a strategic decision leans towards a joint venture, efforts need to be made minimize any disadvantages, and avoid problems and pitfalls. Japanese experience may be a guide to Asian experience in future.

Management Control.   While ownership percentage is generally the key element of control, experience in American-Japanese joint ventures indicates that in day-to-day management, relative strength and leverage relate directly to what each partner brings to the joint venture. Having a 51 percent interest does not always mean smooth majority decisions and conversely, with less than 50 percent interest, sometimes, one of the partners could be running the show. The important thing is that each side feel comfortable about the way initiatives are taken by each shareholder and their designates regarding various management functions. Assignment of various functional initiatives are usually agreed upon at the outset, often with key persons being seconded from each shareholder, to handle specific functions.

Strategic Conflicts.   At the outset, strategic goals of the joint ventures are usually clearly understood and agreed upon by the three parties— the two shareholders and the joint-venture management. As the shareholders' own strategies, the competitive environment, or the products change, irreconcilable conflicts often develop, causing conflicts and confusion. Conflicts may also arise from the joint-venture management becoming very independent of the shareholders and appearing to go its own way, or the management leaning more toward one shareholder than another.

In some cases, a joint venture should be entered into with a general understanding that it is to focus on specific market, product, or service only as long as the strategy makes sense for all parties. In other cases, a joint venture can be a truly independent company unlimited in its scope and duration, but always bridging the strategic voids of the two shareholders so that everyone benefits from the arrangement for years to come. Continuing and full dialogue among the shareholders and joint-venture management is very important in this regard. With a Japanese joint-venture partner, a U.S. company must remember that there may be different viewpoints with regard to how long the joint venture should wait for payback, the level of profitability, and the timing and the extent of profit repatriation and reinvestments. Generally, Japanese businessmen are not pressured as much as their U.S. counterparts to show quick profits, high returns on investments or a rapid growth in earnings, by their shareholders and institutional investors. The Japanese are long term oriented and look to an orderly growth in market share. Special attention and effort is necessary to synchronize these expectations and goals.

Japanese Expatriate Personnel.   An American-Japanese joint venture in the United States is usually staffed by Americans—some transferred from the U.S. parent company and others hired from outside. Generally, only a small percentage of people are from Japan. Key officer spots should be discussed in joint-venture agreements, articles of incorporation, and bylaws. There may be additional people from the Japanese partner, where applicable, to provide support in manufacturing, engineering, marketing/customer relations (for Japanese customers in the United States), and Japanese banking relationships.

The integration, and some special handling, of Japanese assignees is an area that requires special attention, just as with American expatriates overseas. The following are areas of concern:

- Compensation arrangements—Integrate in the joint venture or separate? Gross or net of tax?
- Housing and other allowances—Gross-up when taxable.
- Japan source salary, if any—Mechanism to ensure U.S. tax compliance, while maximizing treaty and domestic credits and benefits.

- Local employee benefits plan—Exclude? Include? Which benefits?
- Who bears any "excess" cost—Joint venture or the Japanese shareholder?

One answer might be for the Japanese shareholder to administer a part of or the whole Japanese payroll and benefits through a U.S. holding or service company and to charge the joint venture for personal services rendered. Another solution might be for the joint venture to administer and charge any "excess" to the Japanese shareholder. There are many alternatives in between.

From visa and social security applications to payroll witholding taxes and individual tax filings, there are many planning and administrative details with regard to Japanese expatriates, in both the United States and Japan. These matters should be reviewed during the intitial stages of negotiation and start-up, particularly by the Japanese partner. Professional advisors such as law firms and accounting firms serving either partner can help the joint venture address these routine, but cumbersome details.

Typical Japanese partners in a joint venture in the United States place greatest importance on strengthening their competitive position in the U.S. market, *i.e.*, ensuring that quality products are punctually and economically delivered to U.S.-based customers. In addition, they do not expect an immediate payback and are willing to sustain and invest in losses for several years. They also prefer to use the familiar corporate form for the joint venture unless convinced by their U.S. partner and outside advisors that a partnership, for example, would be more efficient. They seek the U.S. partner's contribution with regard to any U.S. (as opposed to Japanese customers in the United States) market, personnel, labor relations, facilities, management, regulatory interface, and legal matters, yet they expect to actively participate in production, engineering, and quality control as well as sales to Japanese customers in the United States. Furthermore, typical Japanese partners have access to lower-cost funds from financial and capital markets in Japan and offshore, arranged by Japanese financial institutions, often with tax deductions or benefits taken in Japan or offshore.

Several Japanese foreign-exchange controls effect international joint ventures. First, Japanese companies must submit to the Bank of Japan or the Ministry of Finance (MOF) a "report" of the pending overseas investment, the "acceptance" of which makes it official. Secondly, Japanese residents (for foreign-exchange purposes) must generally follow the foreign-exchange control characterization concerning the movement of funds in and out of Japan—*i.e.* capital contribution/withdrawals, loans, imports, service fees, royalties, dividends, interest, etc. Finally, Japanese (foreign exchange) residents, with minor exceptions, are still not allowed to offset intercompany charges and credits, these companies and their affiliates overseas remit gross amounts of cash to each other rather than settling net amounts.

A number of Japanese corporate statutory rules and practices also affect international joint ventures. Dividends, for example, are declared by shareholders (except a mid-year interim by the board of directors) at the annual general meeting of shareholders within three months after the end of a fiscal year and are often expressed as a percentage of the par value of capital stocks. In addition, Japanese would understandably discuss and deal with most of the capital transactions (dividends, recapitalization, contribution/withdrawals, etc.) through their own experience. Though capital contribution in kind within Japan involves cumbersome formalities, an alternative is to contribute cash which is used to purchase the assets to be contributed. Capital is usually identified with the shares and the capital stock account of the balance sheet; the paid-in or capital-surplus account is used less frequently in Japan. Often explanations are necessary when capital contributions and distributions are directly credited or debited to a paid-in surplus account. Also, distributions to shareholders—whether in the form of dividends or the return of capital—could be treated differently for statutory, accounting, and tax purposes by the United States and Japan. However, it often takes an outside advisor to sort out the confusion which often develops between partners.

A Japanese accounting-related background is important in pursuing an international joint venture with Japan. For example, primary financial statements are still unconsolidated, as consolidated financial statements are a supplementary disclosure reserved for public companies. Futhermore, price earnings ratios are based on unconsolidated statements. Also, the equity method of accounting for investment is adopted only as a part of consolidated statements, not for books or for unconsolidated primary financial statements. On the books and unconsolidated financial statements, investments are generally carried at cost—subject to write-down—in case of significant impairment; and marketable securities are adjusted to market price only by investment companies and in other limited cases. Real estate and marketable securities, carried essentially at historical cost net of depreciation and other allowances, are two frequent items with a significantly higher value not reflected in the historical-basis financial statements. Deferred-tax accounting is generally not used in Japanese accounting. Financial statements may reflect provisions and reserves under tax rules, yet the impact of this, except in certain regulated industries (*e.g.* insurance), is rarely significant. Interim disclosure for public companies is on a semi-annual basis. Japanese accounting practices represent the statutes comprising the Commercial Code (all corporations), MOF regulations (public companies), tax law, and other prevailing guidelines and practices. U.S. and Japanese GAAP differences narrow as slowly as Japanese standard-setting bodies deliberately adopt international practices (such as the consolidation in 1976); and widen as fast as the U.S. standard setting bodies such as the SEC and the Financial Accounting Standards Board (FASB) come out with new pronouncements. Thus, a considerable gap exists between the accounting rule-setting bodies of the United States and Japan.

The pursuit of an international joint-venture with Japan also requires the Japanese partner to understand U.S. accounting rules. "Pushdown accounting" which often occurs in the United States after the ownership change of a business, does not occur in Japan; likewise "Fair market value" and amortization of any goodwill is reflected only in consolidated tatements. One Japanese CFO could not believe that the management of the acquired unit can "accept" the substantial amortization charges in post-acquisition income statements. The reason for this is that in Japan acquisitions do not occur daily (as they do in the United States) and that the acquired unit will continue the financial statements on the same basis as before without reflecting the price paid for the acquisition. Since partnerships are not common in Japan, partnership accounting must be explained to the Japanese partner if that form is used. And because Japanese tax law requires most tax-deductible items to be booked (although some items booked may not be currently deductible until actually paid), Japanese are not used to the degree of book-tax differences that exist in the United States. Often a confusion arises over this point unless both sides understand whether they are discussing book basis or tax basis.

Several Japanese tax aspects should also be considered. Tax burdens in Japan are higher than in the United States; the effective rate (combining national and local taxes) is 56.44 percent for earnings retained in the business and 44.37 percent for earnings distributed. Pending tax law changes will lower the former rate and eliminate the use of the latter, preferential rate. In addition, deductions to arrive at taxable income are not liberal; prescribed depreciation lives are longer than they are in the

United States and deductions for accruals are often limited. Special-incentive deductions and credits are limited to specific transactions such as pollution control. Individual, gift, and inheritance taxes are progressively applied, and upper ends are considerably higher than in the United States, although a move toward lowering the rates is now underway. Branch and partnership operations outside of Japan need to be recomputed based on Japanese tax rules and included in the tax filing of the Japanese entity. Japan has an equivalent of sub Part F provision (*i.e.*, earnings of certain tax-haven subsidiaries are currently taxed in Japan at the parent's level) and limits deemed-paid foreign tax credits to dividends from the first-tier subsidiaries. Though Japan has no group or consolidated tax filing, many businesses are owned and run through a group of subsidiaries; the advantages of a consolidated return often need to be explained. While Japanese businessmen are generally interested in saving taxes, they often focus more on reported earnings when charges, if booked to obtain tax deductions, would depress the company's earnings because of a required degree of tax compliance accounting. Many corporate managements take pride in being good corporate citizens, as taxable income of corporations and individuals above a certain threshold is published by the tax offices for public information. Moreover, local income taxes in Japan are generally uniform under the Local Tax Law (a national statute), but the variance of tax codes among the different states must be explained to the Japanese. Finally, the ability to reorganize a group of related companies or transfer assets on a tax-free basis is considerably limited in Japan; therefore, Japanese tax implications need reviewing in any U.S. reorganization which involves shares or other assets owned by Japanese entities.

OTHER ASIAN INVESTMENTS AND JOINT VENTURES IN THE UNITED STATES

In comparison to the Japanese, the volume of investments from other Asian countries is considerably small and the availability of information is limited. With that premise, a very brief summary of observations follows.

Korea

Today, Korea in economic terms is often referred to as the Japan of tomorrow. The same impetus behind Japan's overseas investment will soon influence Korea's global business strategy. The protectionist trend in the United States is one. Korea, like Japan, lacks many essential natural resources. Shifting comparative advantages in cost, market, product, etc. as well as technology-transfer prospects provides additional impetus to investing overseas, especially in the United States. However, due to the past shortage of its dollar reserve, it is only in recent years that Korea's own restrictions over Korean companies investing abroad have partially loosened. Korea's overseas investment in 1987 probably resulted in a triple increase over 1986 to a level close to a half-way mark to $1 billion. Of this, about 40 percent represents investment in North America.

At present, only a few of Korean investments in the United States are joint ventures. Most representative of these is the joint venture between Korea's Pohang Iron and Steel Co. and U.S. Steel with its California plant and the Western market. Another is a proposed textile plant in South Carolina involving the Korean Federation of Textile Industries (KFOTI), Daewoo, and local interests. The Koreans are trying to establish a local presence in the U.S. market to avoid head-to-head price competition with countries with lower wage rates. For the U.S. partners, such joint ventures help create new jobs and reclaim lost ground in a declining domestic industry. In 1990s, Korea will seek joint-venture partners in the United States in automotive, textile, and many other industries in which Korean companies will increase their international competitiveness.

American partners in joint venture with a Korean business should understand the possible areas of constraints stemming from Korea's exchange control, tax system, legal, and other practices; and they should work together to minimize any negative impact.

Hong Kong

While a significant amount of "Hong Kong" money has been invested in this country, particularly in real estate and more passive investments, not much information is available except for such cases as Hong Kong & Shanghai Bank's holding in Marine Midland Bank and activities conducted or owned by Jardine Matheson. For tax reasons, many of Hong Kong's investments in the United States might have been made through traditionally tax-advantaged jurisdictions such as the Netherlands Antilles. For other reasons, the initial capital flow go through Canada to the United States. The motive for many Hong Kong businessmen in investing overseas is the 1997 factor—the reversion, to China. Several Hong Kong garment and electronics manufacturers have established factories in the

United States and joint-venture operations may also exist in the textile and apparel industries. In some cases, such joint ventures are structured to give incentives to U.S.-based salesmen. With Hong Kong businesses, much of search and negotiation for joint ventures must be through word-of-mouth and personal contacts. Understanding the other party's need—which may be more personal than business-oriented—is important at the outset. While Hong Kong is literally a free-trade, exchange-control-free jurisdiction, a U.S. businessman must remember that there is no tax treaty between the United States and Hong Kong; and tax advisors should be consulted to minimize the impact of this on the Hong Kong partner and the U.S. company. Withholding tax rate, where applicable, would not be reduced by treaty rates.

Taiwan

With the shifting of comparative advantages among the Asian NICs (newly industrialized countries) and Taiwan's rapidly growing strength, it is likely that some Taiwan companies will invest in the United States for one reason or another, and some might opt for joint ventures. Furthermore, the relationship with China may from time to time cause a flight of capital to North America similar to that of Hong Kong. However, Taiwan's restrictions on overseas investments may delay capital flow to the United States from happening in any appreciable volume. Taiwan's exchange control, tax, and legal implications should be reviewed and understood by the U.S. partner joint venturing with a Taiwan-based company.

Singapore

Not much public information is available with regard to Singapore-based companies investing abroad. However, some of the Singapore-based major players in southeast Asia are probably interested in North America and could very well become a partner with an U.S. company in joint venture. Singapore does not have the uncertainty of the Hong Kong Treaty or the regimen of foreign-exchange controls of Korea or Taiwan. One can expect considerably more Occidental attitudes and manners in business dealings since many Singapore businessmen have been educated in the United Kingdom, Australia or the United States. However, tax and legal requirements applying to the Singapore partner should be reviewed.

Ethnic Asians in the United States

A few words should be included about joint venturing with Asian businessmen already in the United States. Some of the traditions, management styles, and business philosophies unique to the partner's home or ancestor country might remain a part of such businesses not matter how Americanized they may be. In these situations, it would be helpful, and certainly not harmful to have some understanding of the particular national origin of each partner and how they came to be in business in the United States. The U.S. businessmen joint venturing with Asians in the United States will be more effective and reap more benefits by understanding the pride, aspirations, and commitments of the individual Asian businessmen.

CHAPTER 23

JOINT VENTURING BY FOREIGN AND U.S. COMPANIES FOR U.S. DEFENSE DEPARTMENT PROCUREMENT

James A. Dobkin
Arnold and Porter

INTRODUCTION

There is a general resistance in U.S. law to the participation of foreign businesses in the procurement of supplies and services by agencies of the U.S. government. Policies that favor domestic contractors are deeply entrenched in the Buy American Act and, in the case of the Department of Defense (DOD), the Balance of Payments program, both of which apply a substantial differential to the bids of non-U.S. firms bidding on government contracts.

In the case of companies located in certain foreign countries, however, the burdensome nature of these laws has been relieved to some extent, particularly with respect to DOD procurements. As a result of Memoranda of Understanding (MOUs) executed by the United States and our NATO and some non-NATO allies and, to a lesser degree, of the GATT Agreement on Government Procurement, numerous items commonly purchased by DOD are excepted from the buy-national requirements that would otherwise apply to such purchases. At least with respect to those items covered either by an MOU or by the Agreement on Government Procurement, foreign businesses can compete on an equal footing with U.S. companies. Thus, DOD represents a major potential market for many foreign firms engaged in the business of selling military equipment and services.

While the MOUs and the Agreement on Government Procurement have permitted foreign companies to penetrate the sectors of the U.S. defense market concerned with the procurement of commodities, the international agreements have not been effective, as a practical matter, in connection with the procurement of major weapons systems. The U.S. competition is simply too fierce. Accordingly, collaborative efforts with U.S. firms in such instances have proven more advantageous for the foreign firm that wishes to participate in the U.S. defense market. Additionally, foreign military contractors from the same allied countries and U.S. corporations involved in common technological fields have been afforded opportunities to cooperate in the research and development of new weapons systems for DOD.

An international joint venture—in the form of either a "teaming arrangement" or a more permanent "equity" joint venture—can be an excellent form of business relationship to promote these ends. Many foreign businesses, generally lacking capital, can still offer a significant contribution to a joint-venture partner as a consideration for the cooperative effort. For example, as a result of the disproportionately large number of scientists and engineers conducting research and development in some countries, like Israel, a substantial inventory of battle-tested technology has been accumulated and an impressive capability to solve difficult and sophisticated military problems has been developed overseas. Thus, a joint venture between a foreign firm with such technology and a U.S. company with capital and contacts within DOD can achieve objectives that would be exceedingly difficult, if not impossible, for one joint-venture partner (JVP) acting alone.

BACKGROUND: OPPORTUNITIES FOR FOREIGN FIRMS IN THE U.S. DEPARTMENT OF DEFENSE MARKET

The Buy American Act and Balance of Payments Program

A number of restrictions in U.S. law overtly discriminate against foreign firms. As a result, foreign contractors until recently received only a few pennies of the annual U.S. procurement dollar.

The best known impediment to foreign contractors is the Buy American Act, 41 U.S.C. §§ 10(a)-10(d), Federal Acquisition Regulation (FAR) 25.100, *et seq.,* which operates to increase the bids of non-U.S. firms competing for government contracts by certain specified percentages.[1] Pursuant to the Buy American Act, a firm bidding a foreign product— *i.e.,* one having the cost of U.S. components less than 50 percent of the cost of all components or final assembly occur outside the United States— must bid 6 percent less than its U.S. competitor to win award of non-defense procurements and 12 percent less to win procurements in which small businesses or labor surplus area concerns are bidding U.S. products. (*See* DOD FAR Supp. 25.102, *et seq.*) Import duties must be added to the foreign bid, or the differential, which must be overcome, increased to *50 percent.*

In the case of Department of Defense procurements for supplies, services, or construction outside the United States, these already disabling percentages are automatically increased to an effectively disqualifying *50 percent* under the Balance of Payments program. (FAR 25.105.) Thus, absent some relief from such provisions, a firm offering a foreign product competing for DOD procurements having the worst of these characteristics would have to underbid a competitor offering a U.S. product by more than 50 percent to win award of the contract.

Certain concepts play an important role in the implementation of the Buy American Act. For example, since the act does not apply to U.S. products, the manner of calculating the percentage of "foreign content" can be significant. Similarly, since the act is concerned only with end products, the definition of an "end product" also can be significant. And finally, the operations that do or do not constitute "manufacture" are significant under the act and have generated much controversy. Although these concepts have been the subject of many judicial and administrative rulings, the law on the subject is far from a model of pristine clarity. The cases are all too often fact-specific and the decisions too result-oriented for many meaningful guidelines to be drawn from them. The only way to approach the subject is on a case-by-case basis with a careful eye on subjective factors that may influence a final determination.

---

[1]Other regulatory and legislative restrictions eliminate foreign competition entirely. Examples of these are procurements of textiles and specialty metals, procurements from U.S. companies that comprise the domestic mobilization base, procurements limited to U.S. small businesses, and naval vessel construction and conversion.

NATO Memoranda of Understanding

In the mid-1970s, Senator Sam Nunn and others endorsed a policy of increased standardization of NATO armaments and argued that the United States should rescind its buy-American policies. Standardization was alluring for military, as well as economic reasons. The NATO alliance, some argued, paraded an inventory of weaponry that was not compatible. Moreover, cooperation and economies of scale held out the promise of great economic savings at a time when inflation and unemployment were ravaging Western economies. The central feature of the standardization effort was the so-called "two-way street," which was to be implemented through bilateral Memoranda of Understanding.

At present, the United States has MOUs with thirteen NATO allies, Israel and Egypt. The agreement with France is classified; only a synopsis of its provisions has been published. The other 12 NATO agreements are included in the FAR. In the case of each of these MOUs, the Secretary of Defense has exercised his discretion under the Buy American Act to waive its restrictions for offers of defense equipment as "inconsistent with the public interest." As a practical matter, the heads of departments may exercise considerable discretion in determining what is "inconsistent with the public interest."

Each bilateral MOU embodies four fundamental conditions with respect to DOD procurement:

1. Offers are to be evaluated without applying price differentials such as those mandated by the Buy American Act or the Balance of Payments Program.
2. Offers will be evaluated without the cost of import duties and provision for duty-free entry certificates will be made.
3. Defense equipment will be solicited from qualified sources in the foreign country in accordance with the policies and criteria of the DOD purchasing officer.
4. Offers from sources located in the foreign country will have to satisfy the solicitation requirements.

The GATT Agreement on Government Procurement

The Tokyo Round of trade negotiations under the General Agreement on Tariffs and Trade (GATT) produced several important international codes, including the GATT Agreement on Government Procurement (Government Procurement Code). The Government Procurement Code, which became effective on January 1, 1981, imposes on signatory countries uniform rules regarding solicitations, bids, and contract awards. The code also restricts the applicability of buy-national requirements or practices by the signatory countries.[2]

There are, however, a number of limitations on the scope of the code. For example, the code only restricts the applicability of buy-national requirements or practices for procurements with a value of 150,000 special drawing rights (approximately U.S. $160,000) or more. Commencing January 1988, however, the code's threshold coverage will be 130,000 special drawing rights (approximately U.S. $148,000) which represents a 13 percent reduction from the current amount.[3] In addition, the code expressly exempts a significant portion of each country's defense procurements from its coverage. Nonetheless, DOD procurement regulations which implement the Government Procurement Code still list a number of defense-related products that are eligible for nondiscriminatory treatment.[4] This list of "eligible products" thus provides an additional avenue for foreign defense contractors to compete on an equal basis with U.S. companies.

MEANS OF INDUSTRIAL COLLABORATION FOR U.S. DEFENSE BUSINESS

While the MOUs and the Agreement on Government Procurement have permitted a number of foreign companies to penetrate certain sectors of the U.S. defense market by removing the legal impediments to meaningful foreign participation, they have not been effective as a practical matter

---

[2]The Trade Agreements Act of 1979 is the U.S. legislation which implements the Government Procurement Code by authorizing the President to waive application of "any law, regulation, procedure, or practice in government procurement" that would result in more favorable treatment of U.S. contractors than contractors from eligible foreign countries. *See* 19 U.S.C. § 2155, *et seq.*

[3]The Free Trade Area Agreement (FTA) between the United States and Israel, which went into effect on September 1, 1985, lowered to $50,000 the threshold figure for waiver of buy-national requirements in the case of Israel.

[4]*See* FAR 25.4; DOD FAR Supp. 25.4.

in the case of major weapons systems where the U.S. competition is simply too fierce. The key to foreign participation in these monumental transactions, at least for the time being, would seem to be some kind of cooperative arrangement with the megacontractors of the Department of Defense. Similarly, it appears that the only way that foreign firms with technological expertise can get in on the ground floor of a developing DOD weapons system is through some form of R&D industrial cooperation.

In terms of U.S. defense market penetration, a technology-licensing arrangement begs the essential question of foreign participation in the procurement itself. Licensing a U.S. contractor under foreign-developed technology or even licensing DOD for purposes of competitive procurement may give a foreign firm income in the form of a running royalty and/or lump-sum payment, but it denies that firm the major profits and organizational advantages of first-hand participation in the procurement process. That is not to suggest that licensing, and particularly cross-licensing, does not play a significant role in joint ventures. It almost always does, but as an integral part of a much larger arrangement.

Direct investments potentially provide technology owners with full control over their overseas marketing programs, a way of overcoming international trade restrictions, lowering transport costs, and often lowering labor costs. As compared to licensing and exports, however, investments require substantially greater commitments of resources, and pose much higher risks. In addition, investments often require a substantial waiting period before any profits are realized. Direct foreign investments have the further disadvantage of subjecting the firm's activities to an unfamiliar body of law.

An investment alternative available to a domestic firm is to acquire a foreign firm. Such an acquisition can instantly provide the acquirer with new technology, equipment, and managerial resources; but, in addition to the obvious drawbacks, the acquired firm may also lose its status as a small business which might have been essential to its participation in defense procurement. Also, if the acquired firm dealt in classified contracts, foreign ownership, control, or influence (FOCI) will disqualify it from further participation without a waiver of applicable law.

An international joint venture represents an excellent form of business relationship to promote these ends. It would contemplate a pooling of resources, a sharing of risks, and a blending of expertise for the achievement of objectives that would be exceedingly difficult, if not impossible, for one party acting alone. Generally, U.S. courts have defined a joint venture as an association of two or more persons (whether corporate, individual, or otherwise) combining property and expertise to carry out a single business enterprise and having a joint proprietary interest, a joint right to control, and a sharing of profits and losses.

What form the association takes—partnership, general business corporation, or close corporation—depends on several factors, including the objectives of the parties involved. Sometimes a combination of forms might be most advantageous. For example, a partnership might be most suitable for an R&D cooperative effort or for the development phase of a joint venture contemplating subsequent production, while a corporation might be best for the production phase when exposure to product liability is greater.

The joint venture is quickly becoming one of the most popular means for conducting international business and its applicability to the defense market is obvious.

A HYPOTHETICAL JOINT VENTURE

Consider, hypothetically, an Israeli corporation that has long been involved in the research and development of a certain airborne electronic warfare system. The system, when fully developed, would have significant military applications. The Israeli firm has made substantial progress towards developing a prototype system. However, in so doing, it has expended very considerable sums, and foresees that substantial additional risk capital will be required to bring the product to the point of practical application. Moreover, it is clear that the barriers that exist to the procurement of the system by the largest potential customer—the U.S. Department of Defense—are formidable, even though DOD has indicated an interest in acquiring a system of this type.

The management of the Israeli company is reluctant to invest the amounts still required to complete the development and has decided to seek outside financing arrangements. Additionally, the company has not been involved in marketing activities for the type of system involved, particularly outside of Israel, and is, therefore, interested in locating a U.S. firm with DOD marketing expertise to participate in a cooperative effort. For these reasons, the company is considering a formal joint venture, or a less formal "teaming" arrangement, with a large U.S.

government contractor. The Israeli company is willing to contribute its technology, know-how, and ongoing business in the relevant field but, at least initially, is unwilling to contribute any additional capital.

The U.S. corporation has also been engaged in research and development work for the same type of system, but its work has not progressed to quite the same stage as that of the Israeli company. The U.S. corporation, therefore, has an interest in combining forces with the Israeli company and, if a joint enterprise does not work out, in obtaining the technology and know-how developed as a result of the joint undertaking and as much of the Israeli company's background technology as may be necessary to effectively utilize the joint-venture technology.

The parties' initial discussions indicate that their objectives and goals appear to be complementary to a significant degree. It is contemplated that a joint venture could complete the development and engineering efforts and produce several prototype systems. Full-scale production would follow, if a requirement for the proprietary system can be established at DOD.

CREATING AN INTERNATIONAL JOINT VENTURE

Contributions of the Joint-Venture Partners

In our hypothetical case, the parties have determined that the Israeli JVP's contribution should be valued at an amount roughly equivalent to the amount already expended by the Israeli JVP for R&D. In essence, the Israeli JVP will be contributing an ongoing business, including ongoing R&D contracts, patents, and technology (*i.e.,* trade secrets, technical data, and know-how). The U.S. JVP, although contributing all of its interest in the field, will also be required to contribute cash as consideration for the more substantial development costs already expended by the Israeli JVP. To the extent additional capital is needed, the JVPs would be equally responsible for the funds.

Steps Toward the Joint Venture

The Information-Exchange Agreement
One of the first steps to be taken by our hypothetical Israeli company following its identification of a potential joint-venture partner would be

to agree with the U.S. company to exchange certain limited technological and business information. This would allow each party to consider with respect to the other the chances of compatibility, the electronic warfare system in question and the technological capabilities that a joint venture would have available to it, the financial resources that could be contributed to the venture, the stage of development of respective management structures and ideologies, and whether these various factors are or can be made to be complementary. This exchange of preliminary information permits the parties to better evaluate the feasibility of the joint venture. It also sets the stage for subsequent negotiations.

Of course, the technological and business information to be exchanged at this point is necessarily limited. The Israeli company must reveal enough of its proprietary system to demonstrate its feasibility and innovativeness, but not so much as to compromise its proprietary rights. The disclosures by each party must be sufficiently substantive to demonstrate that each party can make a meaningful contribution to the venture. The agreement pursuant to which the disclosures occur should make them subject to appropriate confidentiality measures and the return of all information in the event discussions are terminated. Promises of confidentiality in such circumstances are, of course, no panacea in the event of deliberate or inadvertent unauthorized disclosure. Where, however, the disclosures are made in countries that recognize proprietary rights and afford judicial enforcement of such rights, the disclosure becomes less risky. Israel and the United States are good examples of countries in which there is a healthy regard for and appreciation of proprietary rights in technology and of the need to protect them.

If the selection of a potential U.S. partner by the Israeli company was based on the involvement of the U.S. company in the electronic warfare field—as well it might, since that would promote the access of the joint venture to the appropriate offices of the defense establishment—then the Israeli company must be wary of any concealed design on the part of the U.S. company to secure as much technical information as possible, essentially at no cost, without intending to enter a joint venture.

In some instances, the prospective partner may be interested in manufacturing or marketing a competing product abroad or in the United States, and requires certain additional information to commence that effort. Moreover, some companies would consider entering a joint venture purely to impede the development of a system that would compete with one of its own. Accordingly, a careful assessment of intentions is required, and information, even of a nonconfidential nature, should not be freely given if there is any reason to suspect improper motivation on the part of the inquiring prospective partner.

A preliminary business plan should also be provided for analysis by the financial personnel of the prospective JVP. Such a business plan would normally demonstrate the economic feasibility and attractiveness of the proposed venture. Of course, where the market is controlled by a simple entity—namely, the U.S. Department of Defense—and is a function of a military requirement that has yet to be established, the ability to meaningfully project revenues becomes quite attenuated.

The Memorandum of Understanding

Assuming, in our hypothetical case, that after the preliminary exchange of information the parties are still interested in pursuing the venture, the next step would usually be the negotiation of a Memorandum of Understanding (MOU), or letter of intent, as it is sometimes called, or "heads of agreement." Such a document would serve to record the fundamental principles of the joint venture envisaged by the parties involved.

An MOU is generally employed when the parties are preparing for a long-term relationship, or what is often referred to as an "equity" joint venture. As discussed in greater detail below, an equity joint venture can take a corporate form or be conducted as a partnership. In either case, however, a new legal entity is created and the conduct of an ongoing business is contemplated. If a less formal relationship, designed to compete for one or more discrete defense contracts, is intended, then a "contractual" joint venture or "teaming" arrangement may be utilized. In that case, the parties may embody the transaction solely in a contractual instrument, skipping the MOU stage. It should be noted, however, that some teaming arrangements for multiple defense projects can get quite complicated and may benefit from an MOU which permits the parties to focus on the salient points of the intended relationship at an early point in time.

The more common practice in the defense area, particularly where the sale of commodities is contemplated, is to use a teaming arrangement. The parties agree in such a case to combine their resources and capabilities to prepare a proposal responsive to a defense agency solicitation and then, if they are successful in obtaining an award of the contract, to perform the contract in a more traditional prime-subcontract relationship—*i.e.*, by one party assuming the role of prime contractor to the government and the other performing as a subcontractor under the prime contract. To the extent that additional products or services may be required in support of contract performance, they can be secured by either party, as appropriate, from third-party suppliers, and subcontractors.

It would not be unusual, however, in instances such as that posed by our hypothetical case, to enter into an "equity" joint venture. This would be justified by the several purposes that the venture must serve, not the least of which is to complete the development of the airborne electronic warfare system. An equity joint venture, which would involve the creation of a new legal entity as an embodiment of the joint venture, and which would have its own management structure, would be justified by the longer-term and less well-defined business objectives of the parties involved. Thus, when the joint venture is ready to bid on a defense contract, it could do so either in its own name—assuming it could demonstrate the requisite responsibility to be a government contractor—or in the prime-subcontract arrangement described above.

The Joint-Venture Agreement

If negotiations continue beyond the MOU stage, the next major step would be to negotiate and draft the Joint-Venture Agreement, which will formalize the joint venture and define the relationship of the JVPs. The Joint-Venture Agreement is the heart and soul of the joint venture and, as such, must be comprehensive and unambiguous in its terms and conditions. In addition to a number of relatively standard provisions, the Joint-Venture Agreement should seek to anticipate all of the material contingencies that might occur during the life of the joint venture and prescribe means for dealing with each of them. This would be particularly important in our hypothetical case if the Israeli JVP were unaccustomed to doing business in the United States. Many foreign JVPs are understandably confused by the complications of U.S. regulatory activities, the reputed litigiousness of U.S. corporations, and other real or imaginary concerns. These concerns would be vastly compounded in cases such as the hypothetical one by the need to provide for the future disposition of rights in technological assets upon termination of the joint venture. The result would probably be a more complicated and comprehensive agreement than either party might customarily employ in its own domestic affairs.

Although each Joint-Venture Agreement is unique and takes into account the particular relationship contemplated by the JVPs, as well as local and foreign law considerations, there are certain provisions that should appear in such agreements. This would be true whether an equity joint venture is created or a teaming arrangement is employed.

Management and Control of the Joint Venture.   Control and management issues may vary depending upon the circumstances and objectives of the JVPs. However, certain topics are normally covered by the agreement, including:

1. JVP representation on a board of directors and/or management committee and how interests will be voted to ensure equal representation;
2. Designation of who will be the officers or managers and their respective responsibilities;
3. Veto powers;
4. Methods for resolving disputes and deadlocks among the shareholders, directors, or JVPs; and
5. Reservation of specified matters and powers to the JVPs.

Procedures for Resolving Disputes.   Inherent in joint ventures, particularly relationships involving equal voting power, is the potential for stalemate or deadlock between the JVPs' representatives. Premature termination of the joint venture or protracted and costly litigation can result from a deadlock unless the drafter anticipates major areas of conflict and builds into the agreement acceptable dispute-resolution mechanisms. These mechanisms may include the presence of a tie-breaking party (the "swing vote"), elected every other year by each JVP or filled by an unaffiliated third party; a delegation of ultimate authority with respect to prearranged issues; put-call or buy-sell options; informal dispute-resolution procedures; arbitration; or a combination of one or more of the foregoing.

Certain additional provisions in the dispute-resolution clause may be useful. For example, the parties should consider including a mandatory informal dispute-resolution procedure or a "cool down" period prior to institution of formal proceedings. The idea is to provide all means necessary to permit amicable resolution of controversies before forcing the parties to resort to an adversarial proceeding.

Termination of the Joint Venture.   Termination of the joint venture may occur for many reasons, including fulfillment of, or failure to achieve, the purposes for which it was formed, a fundamental disagreement of the parties that precludes continuation of the relationship, or a change in the law that is of such nature as to render continuation impractical. Those events which the parties agree will trigger termination should be specified in the agreement, and the consequences of such a termination should be set forth in detail.

Several options are available, depending upon the context and the parties' intentions and objectives. For example, the JVPs could provide for termination at will by either party or only after the party seeking termination has first offered to sell his shares to the other (at a set price or a price to be fixed by formula) and the other JVP has refused to purchase the shares. Or, the parties could provide for termination only upon unanimous agreement of the parties or only upon the occurrence of specified events or contingencies. Of course, the termination provisions should set forth clearly and unambiguously the rights and obligations of the JVPs and, if applicable, the joint-venture company, upon a termination. A termination may contemplate a liquidation and dissolution of the joint-venture entity or its continuation by one of the JVPs.

In a joint venture such as the hypothetical one, the rights and obligations arising on termination should be described for termination occurring at different stages of operations. For example, the U.S. JVP may contribute capital over the course of the developmental stage of the joint venture, whereas the Israeli JVP will be making its contribution of patents, technology, and other assets at the outset. Accordingly, the rights of the JVPs at any given time should not be equal, but in proportion to their respective contributions to that date. The JVPs should also discuss at the outset, and incorporate in their agreement, provisions effective on termination as to:

1. The return of all confidential material coupled with continuing confidentiality requirements;
2. Any appropriate licensing or assignment-of-technology rights;
3. Payment of outstanding loans that may have been guaranteed by the JVPs;
4. Any appropriate releases;
5. Division of the assets and liabilities of the joint-venture company (including contingent or unknown liabilities arising from such matters as product liabilities or tax audit issues);
6. Indemnifications, and
7. Discharges

THE FORM OF THE JOINT VENTURE

When considered in connection with an undertaking as substantial and complex as a technology joint venture, the corporate form, and in particular what is known under U.S. law as the "close" corporate form, has certain advantages over the partnership structure; including a broader limitation on the liability of the JVPs, a better-defined and somewhat more conventional organizational structure, and more readily enforceable rights and obligations. In addition, there may be certain business advantages to operating as a corporation rather than a partnership. As many commentators point out, when a joint venture involves a long-range, large-scale operation, the corporate structure is generally employed. Indeed, there is an expectation in the United States that businesses involving large-scale operations will be conducted in the conventional corporate form.

The joint venture proposed in our hypothetical case is to be a multimillion-dollar, high-technology enterprise. If it is ultimately successful in capturing the DOD business for which it was created, it may need major production facilities, significant financing, substantial sourcing and supply contracts, and international operations. There may be certain circumstances, therefore, under which the joint venture could be subject to the risk of substantial claims and liabilities, perhaps well in excess of its net worth. The corporate form would more effectively protect the joint venturers from such claims and liabilities than would a partnership.

Thus, even if the joint venture breaches its major contracts, becomes subject to substantial product liability claims, or goes bankrupt, absent special circumstances the JV-shareholders would have no direct liability. They would risk losing merely the capital they had invested in the corporation. Moreover, the close corporation statutes explicitly or implicitly affirm the limited-liability rule with respect to close corporations operating under shareholders agreements.

On the other hand, if the joint venture were formed as a general partnership, a different set of principles would apply to the question of the potential liability of the JVPs. As indicated, for purposes of liability, a general partnership is viewed not as a separate entity but rather as an aggregation of persons governed by agency principles. Accordingly, each JVP is fully accountable for the liabilities of the partnership. In addition, a party with a claim against a partnership generally may proceed directly against any partner and recover his full damages from that partner, and there is no limit on the amount of liability to which a partner may be exposed.

Thus, unlike a corporation, the liabilities of a partnership are not limited to the assets of the business enterprise but rather are passed through to the partners and are limited only by the assets of the partners themselves. Although partnership agreements generally provide for indemnification or contribution by the other partner or partners in the event that liabilities from partnership operations are satisfied out of the assets of one partner, it may be difficult to recover under indemnification provisions and such provisions do not limit the amount of the claims that may be brought against a partner.

As previously noted, the Joint-Venture Agreement should provide a framework within which the co-venturers' rights and obligations with respect to ownership, management, operations, finances, and other matters are clearly defined and can be readily enforced. In this regard, the corporate form also appears to have some advantages over the partnership form. This is particularly true under the close-corporation statutes, which in general combine the greater certainty of the corporate structure with a significant degree of latitude and specific powers for shareholders, and also provide for enforcement of the shareholders' agreement by specific performance.

If the corporate form is chosen (whether the general-business or close-corporation form), many of the basic structural elements of the joint venture will be predetermined by the corporation statute of the state of incorporation. For example, pursuant to statute, the JVPs' ownership interests will be represented by shares of stock with statutorily defined characteristics. As required by statute, the business and affairs of the joint-venture corporation may be managed by a board of directors, subject to the shareholders' agreement. The JVPs, in the corporate charter and by the shareholders' agreement, can define the decision-making authority of the board of directors with respect to selected matters, or reserve to themselves ultimate authority as to particular areas. Pursuant to statute, the charter and bylaws of the corporation will set forth the titles, responsibilities, and means of selection of the corporate officers. Corporate decisions made with the required statutory formalities will ordinarily take effect. In short, by using the corporate form, the JVPs will have a well-defined set of basic rules with relatively certain operation that can be further refined by their shareholders' agreement to meet the needs of the joint venture.

This may not be quite as readily accomplished under a partnership. Although a partnership can be given virtually all of the powers of a corporation and the partners can be given essentially the same rights and duties as shareholders (with the major exception being the unlimited liability of general partners), almost all aspects of the partners' relationship must be determined by contract rather than by statute. For example, the JVPs' ownership interests in the joint venture would not take the familiar form of stock; instead, if interests with the characteristics of stock were desired, those interests would have to be specially provided for in the Joint-Venture Agreement. Similarly, the general powers of a corporation and the functions and duties of directors and officers are for the most part well defined by statute and interpreted by relevant case law; unless modified by agreement of the shareholders, they need not be specifically enumerated. Under the partnership form, such powers, functions and duties must be specified in detail in the Joint-Venture Agreement.

Of course, in either case, careful draftsmanship can accomplish the desires of the parties. However, the same level of certainty may be more difficult and more time-consuming to achieve under the partnership form. Additionally, if the joint venture is structured as a corporation, it may be easier for the JVPs to enforce their specific rights and obligations under the Joint-Venture Agreement. Certain of the close corporation statutes have important procedural provisions that facilitate the specific enforcement of co-venturer rights and obligations.

In contrast, under common-law partnership doctrines, the enforcement of specific co-venturer rights and obligations may be more difficult. Generally, as a matter of partnership law, questions relating to the obligations of a partner to the partnership or to the other partners cannot be litigated without first having a complete "accounting" of the partnership affairs. The Joint-Venture Agreement could, of course, spell out specific rights and obligations of the JVPs and their related remedies in the event of a breach, including their intention that the terms of the Joint-Venture Agreement be specifically enforced without the usual accounting. However, the extent to which a court would give effect to such provisions in light of the common-law accounting requirement is not clear. Even if a court did permit the litigations and specific enforcement of such rights and obligations, the important remedies of injunction and specific performance might be available only in the event the court first determined that money damages were not adequate compensation.

On balance, the close corporation form of doing business appears to be the most suitable organizational vehicle for the joint-venture enterprise contemplated by our hypothetical case. This conclusion does not, however, account in any way for the possible need to do, or advantage in doing, business with DOD in the name of the U.S. partner which has an existing reputation and established capability in DOD procurement matters. Nor does the conclusion apply where the R&D to be performed or the procurements sought involve classified information and, absent special provisions, a contractor that is owned, controlled, or influenced by a foreign entity might be disqualified. Finally, as previously noted, it is possible that some sort of combination of forms might be most advantageous. For example, a partnership for an R&D cooperative effort or for the developmental phase of a joint venture contemplating subsequent production, and then a close corporation for the production phase when exposure to liability is greater.

CONCLUSION

A company's individual goals will significantly affect the selection of the most appropriate format for any business transaction. Though sometimes complex, a joint venture can be a highly satisfactory business relationship and the best way to become meaningfully involved in U.S. defense work. The form of the venture, the management structure, the termination circumstances, and a host of other considerations must be worked out in advance to maximize the chances of success. And, of course, a suitable partner must be located and must agree to the relationship.

Nonetheless, the joint venture is quickly becoming one of the most popular means for conducting international business. Its applicability to U.S. defense business seems apparent. It may seem complicated but the process will yield to persistence and the results can be quite gratifying.

APPENDIX

JOINT VENTURES AND U.S. ANTITRUST LAW

David M. Bridges, Esq.,
with assistance from
Eric T. Laity, Esq., and
Christopher A. Jiongo, Esq.

INTRODUCTION

The formation of a joint venture creates an entity which is stronger and more potent than its members acting alone; this is the basic business reason for joint venturing. The formation of the venture necessarily means that the venturers will not compete among themselves with respect to the subject of the venture. Therefore, the laws concerning reduction of competition should be considered at the time of formation.

This is not an exclusively American concern. The European Economic Community and many countries besides the United States have laws which regulate anticompetitive conduct.

This chapter deals with the legal exposure of joint venturers to U.S. antitrust laws. The formation of a joint venture may violate the law, and the government may seek an injunction requiring the dissolution of the venture. The government also may recover damages caused by the joint venture's operations, but it is not necessary that damages be shown in order for it to obtain an injunction-forcing dissolution. Equally or more important, competitors of the venture can recover three times their damages plus reasonable attorneys' fees in a civil suit if the formation of the venture can be proven to have violated the antitrust laws. In addition, criminal penalties may be imposed on the venturers and their officers and directors under some circumstances. These are serious risks, and are the reason for this discussion.

U.S. antitrust law does not distinguish between domestic and foreign companies with respect to activities which affect interstate or foreign commerce of the United States. However, the reach of U.S. law does not extend to activities which have impact solely on commerce in foreign countries. Activities in the United States which affect only U.S. export trade are subject to somewhat less stringent rules. It should be noted that projects in other countries which are funded by the U.S. government will be considered to be within U.S. antitrust jurisdiction.

DOMESTIC JOINT VENTURES

This section will discuss the legal rules applicable to joint ventures dealing in the interstate or import-export markets of the United States.

Principal Antitrust Statutes

The Sherman Act of 1890 and Clayton Act of 1914 are the most important federal antitrust statutes affecting joint ventures. The Sherman Act is directed toward existing monopoly power and prohibits all contracts, business combinations, or conspiracies in restraint of trade in the United States or with foreign countries. The Clayton Act prohibits entities from mergers and acquisitions that would be likely to cause a substantial reduction in competition or which tend to create a monopoly.

Other federal antitrust legislation that may affect the operations of a joint venture are the Federal Trade Commission Act, which created the Federal Trade Commission, and the Robinson-Patman Act, enacted to prevent discriminatory pricing practices.

Industry exemptions from antitrust laws exist, as do specialized antitrust laws applicable only to particular industries. The Webb-Pomerene Act grants an antitrust exemption for associations formed to engage in collective export sales. The Export Trading Company Act of 1982 was enacted to grant immunity from suit under federal and state antitrust laws to export associations, provided they first obtain a "certificate of review" from the Secretary of Commerce. The energy, agriculture, insurance, and newspaper industries enjoy special antitrust exemptions while the banking, export association, meat-packing, and securities industries benefit from antitrust laws unique to each respective industry. These industries receive special treatment because they are subject to the jurisdiction of federal regulatory agencies which are able to closely control their commercial conduct.

The antitrust guidelines published from time to time by the Justice Department are essential reading. The FTC also issues regulations in the antitrust area. The Justice Department offers a "Business Review Procedure" in which it will opine as to the antitrust implications of the proposed transaction or association. Although the guidelines issued by the Justice Department and the FTC are useful tools for analyzing potential antitrust problems, they are not binding upon a court when deciding a lawsuit brought by a private party, rather than the government.

Several foreign countries and the European Economic Community also have adopted antitrust laws regulating the formation and operation of business organizations affecting important markets inside their borders. Virtually all of the 50 states within the United States have enacted antitrust legislation.

Formation Analysis

There are three anticompetitive risks normally associated with joint ventures; market entry barriers, collusion in other business lines, and loss of competition between the venturers.

The U.S. Supreme Court decision in *United States v. Penn-Olin Chemical Company,* 378 U.S. 158 (1964), remains the leading judicial authority on the evaluation of loss of competition due to joint-venture formation. The Court likened a joint venture to a merger in that, in both cases, two or more previously independent entities are pooling all or a portion of their individual talent and resources to create a separate entity. The Court ruled that joint ventures should therefore be evaluated under §7 of the Clayton Act, as are corporate mergers.

The litigation commenced because Pennsalt Chemical Company and Olin Mathison Corporation had formed the Penn-Olin joint venture to manufacture and distribute sodium chlorate products in the southeastern United States. The government claimed that the formation and existence of Penn-Olin violated both §7 of the Clayton Act and §1 of the Sherman Act and sought a court order for the immediate dissolution of the venture.

The trial court found no violation of the Sherman Act since there was no division of the market among the venturers. The court further ruled that the government had failed to prove that both of the venturers would have entered the southeastern market on their own, in the absence of the joint venture. As to the possible entry into the market of one of the venturers, the court found that Penn-Olin was a stronger competitor than either venturer would have been individually, so that formation of the venture did not create a substantial likelihood of lessened competition, in violation of §7 of the Clayton Act.

The Supreme Court upheld the trial court's ruling that there had been no violation of §1 of the Sherman Act, but ruled that the trial court should have considered the possibility that either venturer would have entered the market in the absence of the venture, while the other waited on the sidelines as a "potential competitor." The case was sent back to the trial court for this analysis.

On retrial, the trial court stated that it would address two issues: (1) whether either venturer would have entered the southeastern market alone, and (2) if so, whether the other would have retained such an interest in the market as to be a significant potential competitor. If the answers to the first two questions were affirmative, the trial court said it would address the defendants' contention that a third issue must be considered: whether the entry of one venturer into the market, together with the potential competitor status of the other, would have created significantly more competition than was in fact caused by the entry of Penn-Olin into the market. The court found insufficient proof that either venturer would have entered the market alone, and thus did not address the defendants' third issue.

A business with a substantial market share must consider whether a contemplated joint venture would be likely to substantially reduce competition in the affected market. If so, its formation may violate §7 of the Clayton Act. If no material lessening of competition is likely to follow the formation of the venture, because of, *e.g.*, the large number of other competitors, the formation of the joint venture will not run afoul of the loss of competition test.

As an example, in one recent case, a foreign manufacturer of outboard motors sought to joint venture in the United States with a major U.S. manufacturer of outboard motors. The court found that the foreign company could have entered the U.S. market on its own, and ordered the dissolution of the venture.

The review of a joint venture's other anticompetitive effects will focus on market entry barriers and the possibility of collusion in other business lines. If entry into the market will be either controlled outright by the venture or will be so dominated by the venture that entry can only be accomplished by joining the venture, formation of the venture may violate both the Clayton Act and the Sherman Act. If the joint venture develops into a bottleneck monopoly, the antitrust problem can be alleviated by allowing U.S. competitors to join the venture. Second, there may be a likelihood of collusion, *i.e.*, the sharing of information, such as market, industry, technical, and pricing data regarding "nonventure" products or services, so great as to substantially lessen competition. This problem can be reduced by having the venture operate independently from the business organizations of the members.

Not all joint ventures are anticompetitive. Some may actually promote competition in the marketplace, such as a situation in which none of the venturers could have entered the market alone. As a general rule, minor anticompetitive effects, *e.g.*, the sharing of test marketing program results, will be legal if (1) reasonably tailored to the purpose of the joint venture; (2) instituted to achieve greater efficiencies of scale in the joint venture's operations; and (3) there is no less-restrictive method for achieving the anticipated benefits of the joint venture.

Post Formation Constraints on Doing Business

Domestic joint ventures are subject to the same restrictions on anticompetitive behavior as other businesses operating in the United States. Analysis of these rules, however, is beyond the scope of this chapter.

Research and Development Joint Ventures

The National Cooperative Research Act of 1984 (NCRA) liberalized the antitrust laws as they apply to research and development (R&D) joint ventures. The most important modifications include: (1) a broader definition of the market for R&D activities; (2) the elimination of treble damages in civil suits, but only if the joint venture has previously notified the FTC and the Justice Department of its membership and the nature of its activities; and (3) a partial exemption from antitrust restraints for the transfer or licensing of any intellectual property developed by the joint venture.

Because of the nature of R&D activities and the importance of sharing confidential product or service information to facilitate the venture's efforts, the adequacy of the safeguards instituted to prevent the anticompetitive use of this sensitive information for purposes not reasonably related to the successful operation of the joint venture will be examined. One safeguard suggested by the Justice Department in its guidelines is the establishment of the R&D joint venture as an independent entity staffed by individuals free from the direct control of the venture participants.

The joint venture's agreements for the transfer and licensing of the intellectual property developed by the venture will also be scrutinized. These agreements usually take the form of exclusive licenses to the joint venture's participants for specific territories for as long as the patents or know-how are protected by law. Generally, these exclusive licensing arrangements do not raise antitrust problems if the joint venture is free to license the use of the patent or know-how to other parties outside the previously designated territories and the members of the joint venture are free to acquire or develop competing technology.

Hart-Scott-Rodino Premerger Notification

The Hart-Scott-Rodino Antitrust Improvements Act requires potential joint venturers who plan to use a corporation as the vehicle for their joint venture, and who meet stipulated threshold tests, to notify the Federal Trade Commission and the Department of Justice of their intentions prior to the incorporation of the joint venture. Generally, the thresholds are $10 million of annual sales or $100 million in total assets. Venturers should be aware that these threshold tests include guarantees pledged to the credit of the new venture. The statute is inapplicable to the formation of joint-venture partnerships.

FOREIGN AND EXPORT JOINT VENTURES

U.S. antitrust law applies to the formation and activities of joint ventures operating overseas. In the landmark joint venture case of *Timkin Roller Bearing Co. v. United States,* 341 U.S. 593 (1951), the U.S. Supreme Court ruled that agreements to divide world markets have a direct and substantial effect on domestic commerce and, therefore, are subject to

U.S. antitrust laws. This means that the discussion of domestic joint ventures applies to offshore joint ventures of U.S. companies. There are, however, certain important exceptions.

The Justice Department will decline to intervene in practices that directly affect only foreign markets and that have no competitive impact upon U.S. markets or the import and export opportunities of U.S. firms. According to its 1988 proposed Guidelines for International Operations, the Department of Justice will not challenge a joint venture performing a foreign project that has no competitive effect on U.S. markets, even if the joint venture has engaged in conduct which would clearly be illegal if it affected markets in the United States. The Justice Department will exercise jurisdiction when the U.S. government bears 50 percent or more of the cost of the foreign project, since it is the U.S. taxpayer who suffers the harm in this instance.

Congress has reduced the impact of antitrust laws upon foreign conduct, absent substantial and foreseeable effects in the United States. In 1982, Congress enacted the Foreign Trade Antitrust Improvements Act, 15 U.S.C. Sec. 6a. This statute renders the Sherman Act inapplicable to conduct involving trade or commerce, other than imports, with foreign nations unless such conduct has a ''direct, substantial, and reasonably foreseeable effect'' upon domestic or import trade, or upon the export trade of a person engaged in export trade in the United States. This law was intended to help eliminate business thinking that the antitrust laws inhibited the formation of efficiency-enhancing joint-export activities.

Note that the Clayton Act was unaffected. However, the formation of a joint venture having no direct, substantial, and foreseeable effect upon domestic or import trade, or export trade of U.S. persons, would seem unlikely to substantially reduce in competition in any of those markets. In other words, a joint venture shielded from the Sherman Act by the 1982 legislation would seem unlikely to be susceptible to attack under §7 of the Clayton Act.

The commentators have concluded that export joint ventures can combine competitive as well as collaborative skills in export efforts which do not effect U.S. interstate or import commerce.

The federal courts of the United States have declined to exercise jurisdiction over antitrust matters when there has not been sufficient evidence that U.S. markets have been affected by the alleged conduct.

This is not to say that joint-venture activity outside the United States should be conducted without regard to exposure to U.S. antitrust laws.

Most international businesses have some dealings in U.S. markets. Standing to assert claims under the U.S. antitrust laws is not limited to U.S. citizens, and in fact such claims can be brought by foreign governments if the required link with domestic or foreign commerce of the United States can be established. The U.S. Supreme Court ruled in 1978 that foreign governments can sue under the U.S. antitrust laws. The Foreign Sovereign Antitrust Recoveries Act of 1982, 15 U.S.C. Sec. 15 (b) and 15 (c) restricted the right of foreign governments to recovery of actual damages, without trebling.

Moreover, U.S. companies are responsible for the actions of their foreign subsidiaries which have antitrust consequences affecting U.S. commerce. Although a decision of the U.S. Supreme Court in 1984 abolished the legal fiction that a U.S. company could conspire with its own wholly owned foreign subsidiary to violate the Sherman Act, activities of foreign subsidiaries in joint ventures affecting U.S. commerce remain within the reach of U.S. antitrust law.

CONCLUSION

The formation of joint ventures is subject to U.S. antitrust laws, and will be analyzed with the same criteria used to evaluate mergers. A central question for the antitrust review of a joint venture deals with the potential of its participants to enter the market directly in the absence of the venture. If it is reasonably probable that one of the participants would have entered the relevant market while another participant would have remained a significant potential competitor, the joint venture may fail in its antitrust review. The full analysis of a joint venture under the U.S. antitrust laws will include review of market-entry impact and possible collusion in other business lines.

These concerns apply to the domestic joint-venture activities of foreign companies. Joint venturing by U.S. companies and their foreign subsidiaries which affects U.S. domestic or import/export markets is subject to U.S. antitrust laws. Joint-venture activity which has no impact whatsoever on U.S. commerce, including the import and export markets, is generally beyond the reach of U.S. antitrust laws, except in the case of foreign projects funded by the U.S. government.

Index

A

Abbott, 414

Abegglen, James C., 365, 369

Abu Dhabi, 312, 313

Accountants, independent, 54–55, 142

Accounting, 41–55
  cash versus accrual method, 233
  and JE, 339–41
  pushdown, 421
  and taxes, 157

"Accounting for Contingencies," 53, 107

"Accounting for Income Taxes," 49

"Accounting for Investments in Real Estate Ventures," 44

Accounting Principles Board Opinion, 42, 107, 109

Accounting Research Bulletin, 48, 108

Accounting Series Release, 51

Accrual method, 233

Acquisitions, and mergers, 17

ADP. *See* Automated Data Processing (ADP)

Advances, and loans, 227–28

Adventures in Joint Ventures, 406, 408

AEG-Westinghouse, 404

Aeronautical radio, 132

Affirmative measures, 159

AFR. *See* Applicable federal rate (AFR)

Agency review, 178–79

Agreement on Government Procurement (GATT). *See* General Agreement on Tariffs and Trade (GATT)

Agreements, 76, 84, 390–92
  buy-out, 403
  consortium, 87
  contractual, 63, 64
  cooperative, 18–19
  co-tenancy, 275
  development, 275
  franchising/licensing, 18
  information-exchange, 389, 433–35
  integrated and nonintegrated, 87–90
  joint-venture, 153–56, 436–38
  management, 275
  and Middle East, 310–12
  and Soviet Union, 326
  supplier, 19
  and waste disposal industry, 201–5

Agro-Industrial Bank of the USSR, 332

AICPA. *See* American Institute of Certified Public Accountants (AICPA)

Superfund Amendment and
  Reauthorization Act, 200
Superintendency of Foreign
  Investment (SIEX), 351
Supplier agreements, 19
Supreme Court. *See* United States
  Supreme Court
Supreme Court of Judicature
  (England), 247
Surface transportation, 180–85
SWDA. *See* Solid Waste Disposal Act
  (SWDA)
Sweden, 14
Switzerland, 14
Syria, 303
System Boards of Adjustment, 193

T

Tactics, and Japan, 371
Tagamet, 9
Taiwan, 80, 405, 410, 424
Takeda, 414
Take-or-pay contracts, 53
Tangible property, 224-25, 229
TAP Pharmaceuticals, 414
Tariff barriers, 10–11
Taxes, 67
  and accounting, 157
  and cost sharing, 118–23
  direct foreign, 238
  and Europe, 252–53
  excise, 225–26
  foreign credit, 237–42
  and foreign joint ventures, 217–46
  and healthcare industry, 72
  income, 49
  indirect, 343
  indirect foreign, 239
  and Japan, 377–81
  local, 343
  and Middle East, 312–17
  PAYE. *See* Pay-As-You-Earn tax
    (PAYE tax)
  and real estate, 102–3
  separate versus unitary, 243

Taxes—*Cont.*
  and Soviet Union, 341–43
  state, 243–44
  and U.S. concepts, 231, 233–37
  U.S. with European companies,
    400–401
Taxpayer, defined, 121–22
Tax Reform Act (TRA), 103, 104,
  107, 119, 120, 232
TCI, 132
Teaming agreement, 76, 427
Technology, 7–8, 144–45
  and Japan, 361
  transfers of, 392
Technology industry, 112–31
Telecommunications industry,
  132–43
Telenet Communications,
  Corporation, 134
Telephone, and franchise, 138–39
Television, 132, 137
Termination, 155, 244–26, 392,
  402–3, 437–38
Teskey, R. H., 264
Texas Air, 187
Texas draw, 102, 403
Thailand, 80
Thelen, Marvin, Johnson, and
  Bridges, 303
Thin capitalization, 223–24
Third-party payment issues, 71
3-M Japan, 407
Thyssen Rheinstahl, 80
*Timkin Roller Bearing Co. v. United
  States*, 448
Tokyo, 77
Tonen, 407
Tort liability, 117
Toshiba, 414
Toshiba Westinghouse, 414
Townsend-Greenspan & Co., 13
Toxic Substances Control Act, 199
Toyota, 11, 38, 39, 144, 145, 147,
  148, 159, 368, 370, 414, 416
TRA. *See* Tax Reform Act (TRA)
Trademarks, 156